C000271780

Signs of the Time
Lier en Boog Studies Volume 6

Signs of the Time

Willem Elias

To Veronica
a pleasure to meet
" "
to read too,
I hope

[signature]

11-12-06

Rodopi

Amsterdam - Atlanta, GA 1997

Amsterdam- Atlanta, GA 1997
Lier en Boog studies
Editors: Annette W.Balkema, Hubert Dethier, Henk Slager

CIP
Signs

Signs of the Time / Willem Elias
Amsterdam: Rodopi
(Lier en Boog studies; Vol. 6)

Editing/Translation: Annette W. Balkema
Cover: Marcel Broodthaers, "Porte-moules" ou "Pupitre Moules", 1964
(Courtesy: Estate Marcel Broodthaers)
Design: Hein Eberson

ISBN: 90-420-0112-7

Keywords: Philosophy of Art/ Aesthetics

Copyright (c) Editions Rodopi B.V., Amsterdam/ Atlanta, GA, 1997
Printed in The Netherlands

This publication was also made possible by the Research and Development
Council Vrije Universiteit Brussel and The Institute of Fine Arts - Flanders

CONTENTS

INTRODUCTION

<u>Signs of the Time</u> is an investigation into contemporary art theory and the philosophy of art from 1945 till postmodernism. Five major movements are discussed, criticized and related to schools of contemporary art and to contemporary artists without accounting for chronology. On the contrary, these movements - Freudian, neo-Marxist, linguistic analytic or Anglo-Saxon, existential-phenomenological, and structuralist - are dealt with in a parallel manner.

The term movement has a broad meaning: various authors belong to various movements. For example, Marcuse is sometimes called a Freudian-Marxist, the existentialist Sartre had a Marxist period, and many (post)-structuralists had a profound phenomenological training. Moreover, Foucault did not consider himself a structuralist, the structuralist Barthes started as a Sartrian existentialist, and similar ambiguities characterize Lacan, Althusser and Derrida. These last three philosophers of structuralist persuasion conclude the chapters where Freud, Marx and Heidegger respectively function as precursors. In the chapter where Wittgenstein has this role, the Anglo-Saxon philosopher Goodman, related to structuralism, finishes out the chapter.

If one adds Mukarovsky to the four precursors already mentioned, these are the sole five authors treated on the basis of texts before 1945. Except for the five precursors - Freud, Marx, Heidegger, Wittgenstein, and Mukarovsky - only post World War II philosophers are under discussion. This post World War II period could be considered the true heyday of French philosophy. First, it was fashionable to be an existential-phenomenologist, and then, from the 1960s on, one had to be a so-called French structuralist. Philosophers such as Derrida, Baudrillard and Lyotard were responsible for this overwhelming influence of French thought. Obviously, structuralism wins over the other movements, or at least penetrates them.

However, it is not only the booming of Parisian thought that explains an extensive investigation of (post)-structuralism. Its related theoretical exploration of the work of art as a "text" offers very interesting positions, as compared to traditional aesthetic theories focusing on artworks signed by artists. The work of art as an autonomous sign seems exemplary for studying the signification process of our entire culture. Furthermore, Derrida's concepts of grammatology and deconstruction and related insights are considered very important. Another theme of structuralism is the position of the subject, i.e. the critique of subject centrism and related theoretical proposals of decentralization of the subject, which puts the situation of the spectator immediately in the picture. Therefore, the first two chapters form a diptych, and their construction differs from the other chapters.

In the first chapter, the problem of the Freudian unconscious is discussed. In addition, a number of aspects resulting from the psychology of art will be treated, specifically in relation to observation. Psychologists of art, such as Gombrich, contribute to the semiotic approach.

In the second chapter, the influence of (Marxist) ideology comes to the fore. Besides a number of views from the sociology of art, Frankfurter critical theory is emphasized together with Althusser's criticism of ideology. How Hadjinicolaou applies this criticism to art is stressed explicitly.

In the third chapter, the often essentialist answer to the question "What is art?" is criticized. Wittgenstein is the central philosopher in this chapter; Goodman is discussed because of his view on art as a symbolic system.

But Chapters Four and Five in particular are at the core of this study: the confrontation between two different perspectives such as phenomenology and structuralism and their respective relationship to hermeneutics and semiotics. This 1960s discussion has grown more and more complex, precisely because the realms are not clearly distinct but rather separate, divergent views. This discussion is even more emphasized in Chapter Six, where the postmodern debate takes place as a conclusion. Things become more complicated, because the post-structuralist and old-Marxist Lyotard enters into a discussion with Habermas, a neo-Marxist critic of ideology.

The philosophers' trains of thought are stated as precisely as possible - although slight interpretations by the author of the book seem hard to prevent. Therefore, quotations from original texts have been inserted frequently. The personal visions of the author are represented in a clear cut fashion. After all, the participants in a dialogue should be distinct. The author's commentary is dual: 1) resulting from internal criticism, i.e. focused on inconsistencies in argumentation and 2) resulting from external criticism, i.e. statements and opinions contrary to the author's personal insights and experience. This book has a practical-empirical dimension, due to the author's contacts in the art world and numerous discussions with visual artists. Its purpose is to represent the views under discussion as clear and distinct as possible, whereas the various argumentations and the practice of art are criticized and emphasized in the context of the different views.

1. Art and the Individual

1.1.*Movements in the psychology of art*

The branch of psychology concerned with art is often called "experimental aesthetics" as opposed to "philosophical aesthetics". It is characterized by an empirical approach inherent in science. As a branch of psychology, it is also directed towards the human being as the various movements within psychology want to know him in his relationship to art, that is, as producer or as spectator. This book will limit itself to the latter.

Fechner with his book Vorschule der Ästhetik (1876) is the founder of this experimental approach. The empirical method this experimental aesthetics employs, implies that it accepts solely the results of controlled repeatable observations and that it regards ideas and insights as hypotheses which have to be tested.

For a long time, experimental aesthetics has been seen as part of the psychology of observation. Up till now it is still closely related to it. Basic concepts as 'acculturation', 'leads', 'educational patterns' all refer to this original method of approach. Amongst its findings are, for example, that education plays an important improving role that cannot be disregarded and that classifies the subjects depending on whether or not they have been educated in the related branch of art. One finds that education does not consist of consolidating the elementary habits, but of improving and liberalizing the observational system, which brings about the acculturation without involving the person. This system of observational references is not eliminated by education, but enriched by new schemata admitting the assimilation of a greater part of new and complex elements. Thus, after a certain age (12 till 15 years), acculturation has brought about a complex whole of observational habits which can no longer be eliminated from the experiences, though they may be improved. Obviously, these kinds of facts are important. Francès claims, "Experimental aesthetics form a interdisciplinary domain where the co-operation between the experts of physiology, perception, language, social phenomena, and even of pathological phenomena is indispensable. One could blame its insufficiencies, its almost entire absence in certain domains, the inertia of its movement, sometimes even the obviousness and relative sparsity of its results. Should it still be repeated that scientific, that is objective and verifiable, knowledge is always laborious and slow, and that progress is guaranteed to the extent where one refuses a priori all proof in order to subject oneself to the trial of experience?" (Francès 1968, 43)

A set of four psychological approaches to art will be sketched, which all employ a more or less experimental method: psychoanalysis, Gestalt psychology, behaviorism and information theory. Not all research can be divided exactly into one of those four classes, as is often the case with such classifications; some fall outside of it and others combine insights found interesting in various approaches. Thus, these four directions are movements of thought rather than a strict classification.

1.1.1. *The psychoanalytical approach*

Psychoanalysis questions the sources of pleasure of the spectators of art. One assumes that each adult possesses drives and desires, due to fixation and regression, which have remained partially infantile or primitive. Their satisfaction is prevented by social rules as well as by the norms of the superego. The observation of works of art provides an indirect, illusory satisfaction for these unsatisfied desires in a sublimated, thus socially acceptable form. Mechanisms similar to those of the dream and the daydream enable this satisfaction. The latent content of the work (hidden by symbolism, metonymy, inversion and other dreamlike metaphors) activates the repressed desires and satisfies them in fantasy. The spectator can identify himself with this content and projects his unconscious drives on it with impunity. After all, he is protected against the superego by the socially accepted manifest content of the work of art. Freud compares the pleasure of the experience of art with that of a temporary narcotic, which gives a gratification different from the satisfaction of pleasure in real life. Still, he considers it a better alternative than no satisfaction at all. Moreover, a cathartic effect arises, a purification, in that the indirect gratification through art temporarily limits the efforts to reach a direct satisfaction in reality.

1.1.2. *The Gestalt psychological approach*

The main thesis of Gestalt psychology is that the whole is more than the sum of its parts or the relationships between the parts. A Gestalt is a whole with qualities which cannot be reduced to its component parts, nor can they be studied on the level of these parts. Applied to aesthetics, Gestalt oriented researchers, like Arnheim, have stressed the role played by observational organizational factors in determining the experience of art of the spectator, that is, what he will perceive exactly. Their main contribution has been to demonstrate how the various elements of a work of art are transformed into a united whole in the experience of the spectator; how the observation of a relatively bad Gestalt can evoke a tension; and how the mutual relationship between the various elements in a work of art can be understood very well by means of their role and place in the whole. The main achievement of Gestalt psychology as far as aesthetics is concerned lies in the unravelling of the effects of the formal aspects of works of art, for example lines, tones, forms. Its interest in the content of art has remained tied up closely with these formal elements. In its most important contribution in this field, Gestalt psychologists have tried to demonstrate that the observation of expression and of emotional meaning is an integral part of the process of observation, almost as direct and unmediated as the perception of line, color or the tone as such. This view is known under the name of "theory of expression" (Arnheim 1949, 156-71) or "physiognomic perception" (Gombrich 1978, 45-55).

Arnheim stresses the cognitive function of art. His book <u>Visual Thinking</u> (1969) is an attempt to emphasize the unity of visual observation and thought. Arnheim does so by bringing about a close integration of visual observation with cognitive processes. In his book, Arnheim arrives at this "visual thinking" by arguing that, on the one hand visual observation implies essential thinking, and on the other hand that thinking undeniably makes use of visual imagination.

Arnheim notes and regrets the general misunderstanding of art at all levels of the educational system. Nevertheless, according to him, from an educational approach one should consider art as a visual form which is the outstanding medium for thinking productively. After all, art teaching is not a matter of developing good taste. The central function of art within general education is the conviction that in each cognitive field, thinking productively is thinking perceptually. Therefore, the role of the artist is to organize complexity into visual patterns and to conceptualize problems in visual terms.

1.1.3. *The behaviorist approach*

The behaviorist approach examines experimentally the spectators' preferences for works of art and parts of them, and measures the physiological reactions that go with this. It is a rather restricted contribution to the understanding of art to limit the study of the experience of art to the statement that this experience is only a judgement of taste, which is expressed in a preferential enunciation, and that the degree of preference for the total work is the sum of the preferences for its different elements considered separately.

Within a behaviorist framework Berlyne made progress in experimental aesthetics. In his view, the most characteristic property of a work of art is that it provokes an increasing stimulus, and that the stimulus is reduced thereafter. The increase is due to what he calls "collative stimulus variables", that is, qualities such as newness, complexity, the heterogenous and surprising elements. In the spectator, these will produce a conflict between a variety of attentional reactions, alternative associations, or possible interpretations. In penetrating the work of art, the stimuli conflict is resolved and the uncertainty is limited, because of which the attentional stimulus decreases.

1.1.4. *The information theoretical approach*

In the information theoretical approach, the concepts of 'suspense' and 'information' are involved. Suspense is presented as an unstable situation, which is relatively unpleasant or even frustrating when the expectations of the spectator are not granted because of the ambiguity of the situation. Information is quantitatively determined in terms of eliminated alternatives or increased probability of some alternatives. Information will decrease the suspense and, therefore, is supposed to be a source of pleasure to the extent that it reduces tension. The degree of redundancy (superfluousness) plays a role. If redundancy is too high, boredom could occur. If it is too low then the spectator could be overwhelmed by the chaotic. For aesthetics, information theory is a vehicle for analysis and identification of styles of art in terms of redundancy and relationships of probability. It is also used for the explanation of correspondences in experiencing art. It offers the possibility of correlating aesthetic reactions and experiences with sequences and dynamic developments in a work of art. Vague descriptions of style and structure can be substituted by operational concepts and by new quantitative categorizing of the stimuli in terms of their information content or their value in terms of redundancy or of surprise. Considered from a broader theoretical perspective, this approach is based on the conviction that a work of art is a carrier for the communication of meaning, as the philosophers Cassimir, Langer and Morris stated. Information theory tries to measure that. It does so on the basis of aspects of the formal structure.

The information theorist Moles points out that each spectator will obtain different information from the message. "Everybody has his repertoire, where one recovers his redundancy and his particular originality, functions of his knowledge, mental behavior and education." (Moles 1973, 130) He also makes an important distinction between semantic information and aesthetic information. A work of art which is known through and through will give information with a redundancy tending towards 100%. However, that work of art can still be fascinating, hence the distinction. In Moles' view, the semantic information is structured according to a universal logical model, it can be expressed and translated into another language. The aesthetic information, on the contrary, is untranslatable and refers to the common contexts of the transmitter and receiver. "... the aesthetic information which is untranslatable refers to the transmitter and the receiver instead of to a common repertoire of knowledge and remains untranslatable in another 'language' or system of symbolic logic since this other language does not exist. One can relate it to the concept of personal information." (Ibid, 134)

Because of their form, works of art can lend themselves more or less for transmitting semantic and aesthetic information. Moles gives the example of Surrealism which increased the semantic information by breaking through the "normal" relationship as suggested to the spectator by the world. By decreasing the structure, the semantic originality increases, because the forms and their normal relationships are transformed or dissolved. The non-figurative movements, on the contrary, go on with increasing aesthetic information, because, among other things, they break through styles as well as through traditional color relationships. At any rate, an experimental aesthetics will have to determine the connections between aesthetic and semantic symbols.

1.1.5. *Psychologisms*

One could hardly claim that the theories within the psychology of art as sketched above have been developed especially to explain the experience of art. Rather, they are applications of general psychology to the realm of art, where applicability is used sometimes in support of the general theory. Furthermore, a theory often exists in putting forward an aspect of the experience of art which might have been somewhat neglected hitherto, frequently at the expense of other aspects.

In the psychology of art, the "homeostatic" model seems to have been applied often. This model is based on the supposition that there are optimal conditions for the existence and the survival of organisms. These conditions are defined by a certain balance between internal and external processes and between mutual internal processes. Organisms will strive to preserve and restore this equilibrium when it is out of balance. Every distinguishable stimulus which reaches the organism could disturb an equilibrium in the total system or in subsystems, and could activate mechanisms for repairing the equilibrium. This disturbance of the balance puts the organism in a situation of mobilizing active energy or tension. In a whole collection of processes, it will manifest itself physiologically as activation. If the tension has been organized for achieving a certain goal, then it will assume the form of a need. The tension is neutralized by a certain action which will cancel out the need and restore the equilibrium. The concept of "lust" is connected with the fluctuation of this tension. Lust would be at the core of the experience of art.

Such "psychologizing" of the experience of art seems productive for psychology using art as an interesting concentrate of stimuli in order to test reactions in spectators, rather than for the understanding of the phenomenon of art or even its effects. Often we cannot avoid the impression that psychology neglects the admittedly relative autonomy of the work of art and presupposes the structure of the need of the spectator to be a firm fact. The reactions of the spectators are only facts within a system where those reactions have economic repercussions, for example within a psychological study of buying behavior. The public structure of need seems more important to applied art, such as design, fashion etc., than for art. In applied art, an industrial production apparatus wants to anticipate the need of the public. However, the "production" of art does not happen in that way, except for commercial "art". By definition, art never conforms to the public pattern of taste. A work of art is always "right", an attainment resulting from the fact that the artist distances himself from it at the moment he determines that it is complete. From then on the work of art goes its own way, without corrections, no matter how "consumer unfriendly" it may be. The reactions of the spectator are not the problem of the work of art, nor even the artist's. Indeed, the spectator has the freedom to avert his gaze, to close his eyes. The work of art has more patience than the spectator has. The work of art is able to postpone the pleasure of being watched as long as it exists. However, if it does not become the object of pleasure in time, chances are great that it will perish.

1.2. Art and illusion (Gombrich)

1.2.1. Perception cannot separate reality and illusion

As stated before, there is a close relationship between experimental aesthetics and the psychology of perception. Therefore, we will go into a number of aspects of perception on the basis of a discussion of a standard work in this field: <u>Art and Illusion</u> by Ernst Gombrich. Many philosophers of art appeal to this study, which does not mean that Gombrich does not have any critics. Semioticians also often refer to him. On the basis of many examples, Gombrich explains that learning to perceive an image is connected with codes.

Summarizing, Gombrich claims the following. All representations will necessarily allow an infinite number of interpretations and the choice of a certain reading is part of the contribution of the spectator. What we see we can never clearly separate from what we know. It happens that we make mistakes while observing. When we know the mistake, we cannot see the objects as before. When we observe we are able to see the same sight in a thousand various ways, from which we will choose. It is this activity of the mind, a kind of longing for meaning, which has to prevent the world crumbling into total ambiguity. We will transform the spot on the canvas in correspondence with its meaning. These transformations will give an explanation of the paradox that the world will never be able to look completely like a painting, but that a painting is able to look like the world. However, it is not the "innocent eye" that brings this about, but solely the exploring mind that knows how to face the ambiguities of perception. The artist who wants to paint a real thing, or a thing existing only in imagination, cannot start with opening his eyes and looking around. He has to depart from the postulated choice and forms from which he builds up the intended representation. We often forget this, because, in many paintings from the past, each form and each color had to signify only one thing from nature; for example, brown strokes of the brush for the tree trunks, green spots for the leaves. In contemporary art, a form may indicate various things at the same time. Therefore, we become attentive to various possible meanings of each color and each form, just as a good pun may make us aware of the function of words and their meaning.

According to Gombrich, ultimately there is no indisputable distinction between observation and illusion. "It is in the logic of this situation, as Popper has shown, that confirmations of these 'hypotheses' can never be more than provisional while their refutation will be final. There is no rigid distinction, therefore, between perception and illusion. Perception employs all its resources to weed out harmful illusions, but it may sometimes fail to 'disprove' a false hypothesis for instance, when it has to deal with illusionist works of art." (Gombrich 1980, 24) The idea that a true to nature reproduction of reality is possible is refuted completely. To paint is always to translate. "It is a transposition, not a copy." (Ibid, 42) And basing himself on physics Gombrich concludes: "The truth of a landscape painting is relative and the more so the artist dares to accept the challenge of light." (Ibid, 43)

In order to explore this, the scientific researcher should be a creative artist himself. In Gombrich's view, the Impressionists, for example, have clearly demonstrated that the limitations of the medium can be overcome. All too often the conflict between artist and public, between tradition and renewal is treated without any attention being paid to this simple fact, "On the one side we are shown the purblind public, bred on falsehoods; on the other the artist, who sees the truth. History based on this fallacy can never be good history. And nothing may help us to overcome these limitations better than Constable's description of landscape painting as an inquiry into the laws of nature." (Ibid, 44)

Nevertheless, Gombrich wants to modify Constable's formulation on one point. What is explored by a painter is not the nature of the physical world, but his reaction to it. He does not engage himself with causes, but with the mechanism of certain effects. For the painter, the issue is the following psychological problem: to evoke a convincing image in spite of the fact that not one shade agrees with what we call "reality". "In order to understand this puzzle - as far as we can claim to understand it as yet - science had to explore the capacity of our minds to register relationships rather than individual elements." (Ibid, 46)

Thus, the relationships are more important than the individual elements. That problem presents itself for instance in restoration. Not only must scientists reckon with the chemical composition of the paint, but also with the psychology of perception. Not only must they restore the individual pigments to their fresh color, but also maintain the relationships, and that is much more delicate. Not only is the issue of the relationships of importance within each painting, but also between the paintings themselves, by the way they have been hung and can be observed. This is because our expectations play a huge role in deciphering the cryptograms of the artists. "We come to their works with our receivers already attuned. We expect to be presented with a certain notation, a certain sign situation, and make ready to cope with it." (Ibid, 53)

Gombrich attaches much importance to the function of expectations. For him, all of culture and all of communication is dependent on the exchange of expectations and perception, on the waves of fulfillment, disappointment, right guesses and wrong movements which make up our daily life. And so it is with art. "A style, like a culture or climate of opinion, sets up a horizon of expectation, a mental set, which registers deviations and modifications with exaggerated sensitivity. In noticing relationships the mind registers tendencies. The history of art is full of reactions that can only be understood in this way." (Ibid, 53)

1.2.2. Originality is connected with schemata

Gombrich also refutes the myth of pure originality. An artist cannot do without a certain degree of standard design. The material and skill play a role as well: "The artist clearly, can render only what his tool and his medium are capable of rendering. His technique restricts his freedom of choice. The features and relationships the pencil picks out will differ from those the brush can indicate."

(Ibid, 56)

What the artist notices when he wants to paint a landscape is not one image on the retina. When Cézanne observed the Mont Sainte-Victoire, an endless series of images fell on his retina, and these images sent a complicated mosaic of impulses to his brains. Neither the artist, nor the researcher are aware of this. "What we do know is that these artists went out into nature to look for material for a picture and their artistic wisdom led them to organize the elements of the landscape into works of art of marvelous complexity...". (Ibid, 58)

The artist who wants a painting to "resemble" passes through a process progressing in detail. How long this takes and how difficult this is depends on the basic form from which one departs. Thus, an artist does not start with his visual impression but with his concept. Psychological research on the process of copying proves that this is affected by the rhythm of schema and correction. "The schema is not the product of a process of 'abstraction', of a tendency to 'simplify'; it represents the first approximate, loose category which is gradually tightened to fit the form it is to reproduce." (Ibid, 64) The "will-to-form" rather proves to be a "will-to-conform", that is to assimilate each new form with the schemata and patterns an artist learned to handle. The study into the failures of copying proves that precisely this is not so easy. "Only a pathology of representation will give us some insight into the mechanisms which enabled the masters to handle this instrument with such assurance." (Ibid, 67) The artist feels attracted by motives he can reproduce in his idiom. When he looks out over a landscape, the details he is able to reproduce well with the schemata at his disposal press heavily on his attention. The style, as well as the medium, create an attitude which will make the artist look for certain aspects from his surroundings which he can represent. "Painting is an activity, and the artist will therefore tend to see what he paints rather than to paint what he sees." (Ibid, 73)

Their technical skill imposes a limit on artists, who will often start specializing because of this and will be forced to work in a stereotypical way to a certain extent. "Even Dutch genre paintings that appear to mirror life in all its bustle and variety will turn out to be created from a limited number of types and gestures, much as the apparent realism of the picaresque novel or of Restoration comedy still applies and modifies stock figures which can be traced back for centuries. There is no neutral naturalism. The artist, no less than the writer, needs a vocabulary before he can embark on a 'copy' of reality." (Ibid, 75)

Thus, in Gombrich's view, "the language of art" is not just a metaphor (Ibid, 135-148). In order to describe the visual world in images, one will need a well developed system of schemata. "All art originates in the human mind, in our reactions to the world rather than in the visible world itself, and it is precisely because all art is 'conceptual' that all representations are recognizable by their style." (Ibid, 76) Without starting schemata we will never be able to make our experiences crystallize. If we do not possess any categories, we will not be able to select impressions. What those initial categories are, is not so relevant. Gombrich argues that language does not so much give names to things and concepts already existing but rather articulates the world in which we live. The images of art intend to do the same. The differences in style do not mean that no correct descriptions will be possible. From various perspectives the same information could be provided after all. "The world may be approached from a different angle and the information given may yet be the same." (Ibid, 78) The facts coming from the visible world are so complex that no painting could ever comprise them all. Therefore, a correct portrait is the final point of a long road via schema and correction. "It is not a faithful record of a visual experience but the faithful construction of a relational model." (Ibid, 78)

On the basis of the discussion of Gombrich's work, a number of views on the "absoluteness" of the process of creations came to the fore. By putting that into perspective and by indicating some current prejudices, we will seek arguments to open the gaze of the average spectator for that which cannot be perceived: realism as a perfect copy of reality or originality, as if an artist were able to escape submitting to a certain tradition.

1.2.3. The "innocent eye" could be blamed

Gombrich points out that the artist in all styles of painting starts from a vocabulary of forms and that the knowledge of that vocabulary rather than the knowledge of perceived things will distinguish the experienced artist from the beginner. All representations could be classified in a gradation that goes from the schematic to the impressionistic. At the first stage making will dominate copying and it will become a conceptual art with rather "primitive" traits. At the second stage copying will beat making and an art will arise which has more to do with perception than with knowledge, as for instance with Turner: "There is some justification in the idea that he suppressed what he knew of the world and concentrated only on what he saw." (Ibid, 250) What actually "perception" is, is not that simple. The "innocent eye" Ruskin talked about is a myth. For perception is never merely registering. "It is the reaction of the whole organism to the patterns of light that stimulate the back of our eyes, in fact, the retina itself has recently been described by J.J. Gibson as an organ that does not react to individual stimuli of light, such as were postulated by Berkeley, but to their relationship, or gradients." (Ibid, 252)

Each observation has to do with expectations and, therefore, with comparisons. In illusionist art, the issue is not to forget what we know about the world already, but rather to think of comparisons that pertain to it, in other words to find the spot which can be considered a certain representation from a certain perspective. This is a difficult task, the more so because knowledge influences the manner of perception. "The stimulus patterns on the retina are not alone in determining our picture of the visual world. Its messages are modified by what we know about the "real" shape of objects." (Ibid, 255)

By "real" one has to understand the aspect of an object that reveals the greatest number of characteristic traits on the basis of which we classify things. The statement that our knowledge will influence our perception has to be defined more precisely as our desire for knowledge, our effort to achieve meaning. Or, in Gombrich's terms, expectations, guesses, hypotheses will influence our perception. "Perception, in other words, is a process in which the next phase of what will appear when we test our interpretation is all but anticipated." (Ibid, 256)

The painter interprets nature in terms of painting, thus in strokes of paint. The artist analyses the phenomenal forms as types of attributes, and then tries to copy those attributes, which he is able to reproduce in his medium. Thus, gradually he brings elements into line with each other. In this context, the complicated problems of form and color in particular will present themselves. Every representation is based on schemata which painters have learnt how to use. "The injunction to "copy appearances" is really meaningless unless the artist is first given something which is to be made like something else. Without making there can be no matching." (Ibid, 264)

The painter learnt how to look critically, how to see through his observations by testing other possibilities of interpretation. In that sense, he shows the abilities of the creative mind to dissolve old classifications and to call into being new ones. After all, categories are often intangible, among other things because of ambiguities connected with the stimuli configuration, which means that various readings will have to be tried out. Only from there could one trace back the ambiguity of perception. This is the reason why the art of representation has a history. "To read this artist's picture is to mobilize our memories and our experience of the visible world and to test his image through tentative projections." (Ibid, 264)

Gombrich arrives at the paradoxical result that only a painted image can explain an image that was perceived in nature. "We have come to the paradoxical result that only a picture painted can account for a picture seen in nature." (Ibid, 265) Obviously, this is only valid for the art of painting that intends to imitate nature; if this was not the case the first painting would not yet have been painted. However, the first painting did not want to be an imitation. "There are few civilizations that even made the change from making to matching, and only where the image has been developed to a high degree of articulation does that systematic process of comparison set in which results in illusionist art." (Ibid, 265)   But here also, the vocabulary of art appears to resists modification. This also appears from the stability of styles in art. In that sense, Gombrich agrees with Wölfflin: "All paintings, as Wölfflin said, owe more to other paintings than they owe to direct observation." (Ibid, 268) Only through experiment could one come out of an existing style. The artist cannot start from scratch, though he can criticize his predecessors.

Gombrich seems to apply Poppers's criticism to the scientific model of the 19th century. For Popper, each observation is the consequence of a question we present to nature and each question supposes an exploring hypothesis, that constantly has to be examined by way of refutation. "This inductivist ideal of pure observation has proved a mirage in science no less than in art." (Ibid, 271)

1.2.4. *The suggestive projection of the spectator*

In Gombrich's view, the ability to project plays an important role in decoding a painting. What we project in forms is dependent on our ability to recognize things or images which are hidden in our mind. (Ibid, 89-93) The imagination of the artist presupposes imagination in the spectator. Therefore, the presence of the power of imagination in the artist is more important than technique. "It is an art in which the painter's skill in suggesting must be matched by the public's skill in taking hints. The literal-minded Philistine is excluded from this closed circle." (Ibid, 165)

Thus the spectator has to learn how to use his imagination in order to be able to project. The loose brush stroke of what seems a "sloppy" work requires from the spectator a mental attitude of willing to recognize the images the painter wants to show him. Behind the lack of finishing touch hides a hidden skill and technique. Painting with unfinished and rather vague indications boils down to making schemata in which we can project the images from our memories. However, these projection screens remain empty if one has nothing to project. At the end of the 18th and the beginning of the 19th century this meant that one had to have experience of the represented world: "... they are screens onto which the sitter's relatives and friends could project a beloved image, but which remain blank to those who cannot contribute from their own experience." (Ibid, 168)

Since the Impressionists, the game of projection is no longer that simple. Impressionism demanded more than reading brush strokes. "It demanded, if one may so put it, a reading across brush strokes." (Ibid, 169) In Impressionist painting the direction of the brush strokes is no longer helpful in reading forms. "It is without any support from structure that the beholder must mobilize his memory of the visible world and project it into the mosaic of strokes and dabs on the canvas before him." (Ibid, 169)

The principle of guided projection here reaches its height. "The image, it might be said, has no firm anchorage left on the canvas, it is only 'conjured up' in our minds." (Ibid, 169) The willing spectator reacts to the suggestion of the painter, because he experiences pleasure in the transformation which takes place in front of him. Art acquires the new function of completing the work of art with the eye. "The artist gives the beholder increasingly 'more to do', he draws him into the magic circle of creation and allows him to experience something of the thrill of 'making' which had once been the privilege of the artist." (Ibid, 169)

From here the change starts which will lead to the visual puzzles of 20th century art, which provoke our ingenuity and make our mind search for the unexpressed and unarticulated. Actually, the Impressionists were not the first to discover and apply the magic and the challenge of the representation deliberately kept incomplete. However, in contrast to the old masters, who prepared the spectator for this artifice, the Impressionists just wanted him to enjoy the visual shock completely. In the background of old paintings, we find fragments which seem very daring in our eyes. Perhaps that which we call "guts" results from these fragmentations themselves, because of which these become separate from their context, and so separate of those gradual transitions which the older masters valued so much. Yet, in this we see an argument for abstraction as the pre-eminent aesthetic perception. It demonstrates how painters, in whatever situation, sympathize with the purely painterly. Next to the history of the emerging of the perfect reproduction, one could sketch a history of purely pictorial pleasure. In the first phase, this history would deal with perversities - the extra pleasures of the commission painters - and not until Impressionism would it acquire the right of existence and enjoy full freedom in abstract painting, which will take painting itself as its subject. Conversely, the medium of the artist is limited compared to the quantity of information reaching us from the outside world, so even the most convinced realist has to work in a suggestive way. "Even the most meticulous realist can accommodate only a limited number of marks on his panel, and though he may try to smooth out the transition between his dabs of paint beyond the threshold of visibility, in the end he will always have to rely on suggestion when it comes to representing the infinitely small." (Ibid, 182-184)

From Gombrich's perspective, that suggestion is advanced by what the spectator is expecting. "Where we can guess, we cannot disentangle seeing from knowing, or rather, from expecting. (Ibid, 187) It is the power of expectation, rather than the power of theoretical knowledge which shapes that which we "see", and this is not just valid in art. According to Gombrich, expectation or mental attitude boils down to the willingness to project, in other words "... to thrust out the tentacles of phantom colors and phantom images which always flicker around our perceptions." (Ibid, 190) the "reading" of an image is checking the representation for possibilities, trying out of what is fitting. Thus, the reading of representations is guided by anticipations.

"The pre-image, if one may coin this word for our anticipation of where the figure will be next, is confirmed by an anchorage for the after-image." (Ibid, 192) We have been trained in attributing a potential environment to each image to such a degree, that we do not have any trouble in adapting our reading to a configuration in which each figure is surrounded by its own context. We always see that happen when a group of figures is collected within a framework, without it being the intention for them to have a common environment. Here too we read such images by checking their relationship in double-quick time. Apart from that, it is obvious that projection cannot happen completely randomly, there must be a certain consequence in it.

"Without knowing it, we have carried out a rapid succession of tests for consistency settled on those readings which make sense. Without such a test, even the images of traditional art may yield as variegated and fantastic a result as the proverbial shapes of clouds and inkblots." (Ibid, 192-193) Thus, we must carry out tests for consistency in order to reject incorrect guesses. According to Gombrich, we are hardly aware of this process. It often happens by empathy or identification with the artist. "The idea of art, we have seen, has set up a context of action within our culture and has taught us to interpret the images of art as records and indications of the artist's intention. To react adequately to the sketch, we instinctively identify ourselves with the artist." (Ibid, 195)

Gombrich considers art essentially communicative. In order to increase communication, concessions may be made to the knowledge of the receiver. Gombrich expects for the spectator empathy of the artist: "The beholder's identification with the artist must find its counterpart in the artist's identification with the beholder." (Ibid, 196) Obviously, this can only be partially the case: "the artist creates his own élite, and the élite its own artists." (Ibid, 196)

We doubt that this communicative process still has that meaning in contemporary art. Today, art seems more like a puzzle that has to be solved, a labyrinth in which one has to feel one's way. In this process, concessions are not necessary. Communication is only in the background, but becomes more intense because of this. There is a slighter chance of superficial communication. Either there is no communication and even aversion, or, for those who are able to solve the puzzle or at least try to do so, it is more intense.

1.2.5. *The ambiguity of the image in modern art*

The above is not meant as a refutation of Gombrich, since he constantly emphasizes the multiplicity of interpretations. Though it is indeed important that he points out the impossibility of holding two inconsistent views at the same time. "We are not aware of the ambiguity as such, but only of the various interpretations. It is through the act of "switching" that we find out that different shapes can be projected into the same outline." (Ibid, 198) If one wants to free oneself of a certain projection, then one should switch from one to the other. Therefore, the "test of consistency" consists of "the possibility of classifying the whole of an image within a possible category of experience." (Ibid, 200)

Obviously, ambiguity also presents itself with the problems of perspective. In this respect, Gombrich claims that a number of modern movements, "Cubism, I believe, is the most radical attempt to stamp out ambiguity and to enforce one reading of the picture - that of man-made construction, a colored canvas." (Ibid, 238) Braque, for example, does not use perspective, texture and shadow effects for harmonization, but for conflict. By reversing the mutual relationships, Braque makes clear that for him an exercise in painting is at stake instead of evoking an illusion. Cubism resists illusionist interpretation by introducing conflicting indications, which refute the test of consistency. In Cubism, the coherent forms play hide and seek in the incomprehensible web of ambiguities. In abstract art, there is no test at all on the basis of which we could decide which reading we will adopt. Abstract art characterizes itself by an open ambiguity. Yet even non-figurative painting derives its meaning and effects partly from the habits and mental attitude which one has acquired in looking at pictures. After all, each three-dimensional form on canvas would be infinitely versatile without the knowledge of certain probabilities. Perhaps that could be prevented, if the painter can succeed in making us see his signs or strokes of paint as traces of movements and actions, as is the case in "action painting". That is why these painters want to avoid all resemblance with familiar objects or even with spatial organization. Yet, in Gombrich's view, the spectator has to follow the traditional path in order to be able to determine the absence of all meaning. "But few of them appear to realize that they can drive into the desired identification only those who know how to apply the various traditional tests and thereby discover the absence of any meaning except the highly ambiguous meaning of traces." (Ibid, 244)

One clearly feels that Gombrich's heart is not completely in these recent forms of art. The function he can attribute to it is secondary: "If this game has a function in our society, it may be that it helps to 'humanize' the intricate and ugly shapes with which industrial civilization surrounds us. We even learn to see twisted wires or complex machinery as the product of human action. We are trained in a new visual classification." (Ibid, 244) However, Gombrich goes a little too far in his (pre)conception of gestural forms of art. There is no reason to call industrial forms ugly a priori. Besides, there is no reason either to undermine the autonomy of certain movements of art by looking at them as a means of training, which has to adapt man to a new visual world, no matter how useful such a function of art might be. Gestural abstract art has as much right to an autonomous place as any other movement. There is no reason to classify a part of abstract art a priori in the category where it certainly does not want to end up, namely in the decorative category. Of course, this category is a tempting danger, because an experiment and the repetition of its results cannot always be separated that easily. It is not the art theorist's task to pass such a judgement. This could only be the case in an art criticism context, and even then, it is doubtful.

Two short but nonetheless fundamental criticisms can be made. First, Gombrich, with his theory of perception based on the test of consistency, attaches too much to the recognition of what can be seen. There is more to the perception of a painting than the problem of "does one see what there is to be seen". This neglects the ways in which things can be seen. The merit of abstract art is precisely that it demonstrates in an extreme way how something could be seen. Whether the colored spot is the nose in a portrait or just a spot does not matter from a painterly perspective. What is shown is the spot in relationship to other spots. Secondly, Gombrich neglects the art criticism aspects of perception.

1.3. *Aspects of Freudian aesthetics*

In spite of the view of most psychoanalysts for whom philosophy is nothing but one of many defense mechanisms - or a "travel guide for anxious people" to quote the words of the father himself - it is still possible to articulate Freud's philosophical dimension.

1.3.1. *Freud and art*

One can hardly maintain that Sigmund Freud was a lover of modern art. There-fore, in Freud's work, we do not immediately find a theory on art. Certainly, art means something else to Freud than that which we consider modern art. Lyotard expresses this very concisely: "However, we know how much the aesthetic cor-pus Freud based on was limited to Classicism and even to a narrow academism, in particular concerning non-literary art, and how this Viennist generated the entire music production of Schönberg's school and how this modernist with regard to psychopathology generated the entire modern art of painting of which he nonetheless was not a contemporary." (Ehrenzweig 1974, 12)

A number of Freud's statements in the first paragraphs of his article "Michelangelo's Moses" (Freud 1983, 129-163) upholster our objections to a strictly Freudian approach to art. Freud admits as a "non-connoisseur of art" to be more attracted to the content of a work of art than to its formal and technical properties. Though it is important that he also states that the artist values content in the first place. Yet, works of art have a powerful influence on him, provided that he can understand them. Moreover, Freud is the pre-eminent example of the view that the understanding of art corresponds with discovering the artist's inten-tion, that is, as far as he succeeds in expressing this intention in his work. However, even if intention is the issue, which we doubt, then the intention which the artist was unable to express in the work, is possibly more important, because it is an immediate indication of the failure of the ability of the artist. Furthermore, the concept of "intention" presupposes that there is an artist's intention, and a conscious one as well, which is, of course, a lack of assessment by the unconscious. Freud believes in the possibility of discovering the intention of the artist. For him the work of art is one of many possible ways of getting to know the psyche of the artist. Thus, what interests him is not so much the work of art itself, as the work of art as window to the psyche of the artist-neurotic. "But why would not it be possible to indicate and articulate the intention of the artist, just like any fact from the inner life?" (Freud 1983, 134)

Thus, the analysis of an object of art is nothing but a part of the analysis of human beings who produce such objects as a jointless extension of the psy-chic constellation. Important is that Freud assumes that the discovery of the meaning and content of what is expressed in a work of art, in other words the interpretation, will offer an explanation of "why I am overwhelmed by such a tremendous impression." Thus, Freud reckons with the spectator he is himself, but who might be anybody.

In Freud's view, great works of art are works through which one can see great human beings, that is human beings with extraordinary intentions and a special psyche. Freud is unaware that form plays a huge role in producing that image. In addition to this, he supposes that the work of art is the artist's heir in terms of content, as if this content present in the work, for example a moral content such as honesty, would be a guarantee of its presence in the producer. We do not agree with Freud's obsolete view on the understanding of classical art, but there are some interesting elements in his writings. After all, many authors have pursued Freud's thought on art.

1.3.2. *Correspondence with the dream*

In his book Psychoanalytic Theory of Art, Richard Kuhns provides a contribution to an art philosophical analysis on the basis of Freud's theory. In The Interpretations of Dreams, Freud considers dreams as special forms of thought. Possible correspondences between dreams and works of art are easily demonstrable. His distinction between manifest and latent content is also important in art. The manifest content of a dream is conscious, the latent one is unconscious, but the latter may become conscious through interpretation. Kuhns points out that the exposure to works of art can be surprising, because they can suddenly introduce thoughts unaware in consciousness. Art can play a role in the process of the transition from unconscious to conscious. "It is as if works of art have the power to transport certain thoughts from the unconscious to the preconscious through their having been, as it were, "aestheticized". The whole complex activity of art-making and art-using can be understood as a cultural loosening of the ordinarily rigid boundaries of the unconscious and the conscious." (Kuhns 1983, 18)

Putting this into perspective somewhat, Kuhns draws attention to the importance of the concept of "aestheticizing" in this process and he also gives an explanation for the concept of "iconography of the medium" (Kuhns 1983, 27). It widens the concept of iconography to include all the elements of the various media themselves in their pure aesthetic immediacy, on the basis of information on the oeuvre and on the artist. In dreams as well as in art the manifest content is solely the starting point of interpretation. In order to understand, one has to find the path from the manifest to the latent. This path leads through symbols which represent unconscious material. If one applies the psychoanalytic concept of "transference" to cultural objects such as art, then the problem of the degree of development of the spectator arises. A complicated "mirror"- relationship comes into being between the degree of consciousness of the artist himself, the extent to which that is visible in the object, and the degree of consciousness of the spectator who can enter into all these levels via a collection of conscious and unconscious associations. That supposes individual junctions in the unique experience of development, indicating correspondences, but no identities. Although psychoanalytical interpretation is a-historical - since it is based generally on the analysis of cultural objects without accounting for time and place - it still has something temporary to it. Psychoanalytical interpretation considers the response to art on the basis of the spectator's maturity and his increasing sensitivity to the latent content. According to Kuhn, the primary and secondary processes distinguished by Freud (on the one hand the laws valid for the Id, on the other hand those which manifest themselves in the Ego) are two concepts of primordial importance for the interpretation of art. However, he considers precisely the functions of art an aid to the discovery of the unconscious. That will work out best if artists succeed in representing thoughts from the primary process. Art produced under the pressure of the secondary process can also reveal primary process thinking, but in that case interpretation is much harder. "When artists do find ways of representing primary process thinking, their work opens up to us wide ranges of the unconscious that we, unaided, would never be able to encounter. On the other hand, art produced under rigid ego control - art produced under the domination of the secondary process - may also reveal primary process thought, but in forms that make interpretation more difficult." (Kuhns 1983, 34)

1.3.3. *Correspondence with the joke*

In his article "Freud's Aesthetics", Gombrich (Gombrich 1966, 30-40) changes Freud's explicit disregard of the form in a peculiar but interesting way. First of all he emphasizes the classical 19th century view, with its preference for the "spiritual content". Freud always remained an adherent (Wollheim 1983, 203-19) to this view, no matter how contradictorily his teachings dealt with this tradition. "It is an irony that Freud's teachings were largely instrumental in undermining and destroying this tradition." (Gombrich 1966, 30) The hostile attitude to modern movements of art which Freud expressed in his letters is connected with his conservative view. "The uncompromising hostility that is expressed here must indeed have surprised those who saw in Freud the champion of all contemporary trends." (Ibid, 33)

From Freud's perspective, Expressionists and Surrealists are lunatics. Even the latter movement cannot be appreciated by Freud, although they chose him as a patron saint. Not until a meeting with Dali (in London in 1938) did he compromise on the basis of Dali's undeniable technical mastery. We will not

linger over the value of a statement on the quality of the techniques of art by an
82 year old scientist, who hardly showed any interest in form during all of his
career. Fact is that Freud considered Expressionism and Surrealism as non-art.
Gombrich departs from Ernst Kris' important work <u>Psychoanalytic Explorations
in Art</u> (1970), where Kris presents Freud's book <u>The Joke and its Relationship to
the Unconscious</u> as the germinative model for each explanation of artistic creation along the Freudian line. The joke, in the sense of the very refined French
concept of "mot d"esprit", is, according to Freud's formula, a preconscious idea
which is exposed to the working of the unconscious for a moment. However, the
content of the joke is not indebted to the unconscious, but rather the form is. The
pun in particular draws from what Freud calls the primary process. Freud's
rejection of Expressionism and Surrealism has actually to do with his view that
artistic value cannot be contributed to the primary process as such. It is a mechanism that belongs to each mind. One could say that Freud considers modern art
too much as a "joke". Whether the model of the joke applies completely to
explain artistic creation is not the question. What is important, according to
Gombrich, is that it demonstrates the relevance of the medium as well as its
mastery.

The pun is dependent on the medium of a certain language. However, it is
not really produced but rather discovered in language. The structures of language, for example possibilities of rhyme, are a limiting reality. Not taking such
a reality into account is precisely what Freud considers to be the "lunatic" element of modern art. In his view, it is exactly in this fact of reality where the distinction between a dream and a work of art is to be found. "Far from looking in
the world of art only for its unconscious content of biological drives and childhood memories he insisted on that degree of adjustment to reality that alone
turns a dream into a work of art." (Ibid, 36)

On the basis of this interpretation, Gombrich points out that
Expressionism cannot be conceived as literally deduced from "ex-press": the
pressing out, by means of art, of an unconscious thought which occupies the
artist inwardly in order to touch the public afterwards. In that sense, the form
will hardly be a veiling of unconscious content, revealed by the consumer in
turn. According to this Freudian interpretation, one could state that it is often the
wrapping itself which determines the content. Only unconscious ideas, to be reconciled with the reality of formal structures, can be transmitted. Their value lies
at least as much in the formal structure as in the idea: "The code generates the
message." (Ibid, 36)

This formal structure is partly fixed. There is a constant interaction
between existing art and its further evolution. The artist will start joining a form

of art which already exists in order to subsequently introduce modifications. In that respect, Gombrich quotes Klee, who describes line, color and forms as the many elements the artist creates his order from. "Klee sees the artist as a builder of structures who lifts the element up into a new order." (Ibid, 37)

This is far from the psychoanalytic view of the centrifugal theory of artistic expression. However, Freud himself has a centripetal theory of the joke. In this theory, the aspect of play, the childlike pleasure of trying out combinations and rearrangements comes to the fore, which is similar to the way the artist feels attracted to play with forms. The artist who plays with visual forms will draw from the preconscious process Freud talks about, but then in centripetal direction, in other words, his art goes into the direction of his mind and not the other way around. "But it is his art that informs his mind, not his mind that breaks through in his art." (Ibid, 38)

Perhaps Gombrich goes a little too far in this interpretation of Freud, but that does not mean that it is not an interesting reflection on Freud's statements. Our recurrent conclusion that there is a discrepancy between the fascinating vision of a learned theoretician of philosophy of art and his vision in practice of the actual contemporary artistic event should not lead necessarily to rejecting his interesting theoretical vision, but indeed to the stating of the discrepancy between theory and practice, between thought and perception. Presumably, the reverse could be demonstrated as well, namely that the art critic often formulates obsolete traditional concepts by way of illustration of his view of actuality. It is also striking that some critics with an art historical education often employ an incorrect philosophical jargon. For their part, critics with a philosophical training sometimes particularly enjoy conjuring with technical terminology, as if they had mastered the skill themselves.

1.3.4. *The unconscious perception of the hidden order*

In his book The Hidden Order of Art, Anton Ehrenzweig provides an interesting contribution to the problem of the artist- work -spectator relationship. He does so from a psychoanalytic perspective, however, with a distinct appreciation and knowledge of modern art.

To speak of "hidden order" presupposes that modern art comes across as chaotic, which is the consequence of the "polyphonic" character of art. This has to be disentangled in order to bring the unconscious action of the creative form to the surface. To normal consciousness, this seems chaotic. However, Ehrenzweig rejects the assertion that we look at once for a schema while perceiving, since that would be too great a loss on the line of communication. "My main thesis will be of course that normal vision of reality is not based on the interpretation of pattern, but goes directly for the visual object with little interest in its abstract shape." (Ehrenzweig 1970, 29)

In another work, The Psychoanalysis of Artistic Vision and Hearing, An introduction to a Theory of Unconscious Perception (1953), Ehrenzweig tries to demonstrate that perception, in dreams as well as in a state of wakefulness, acquires its imaginative quality by means of its unconscious structure. The imaginative quality of perception, which enlivens reality, depends on the repression of the Gestalt rather than on accurate articulation. Consequently, the forms on the outside of the visual field will withdraw themselves from conscious attention. Depersonalized sight is inclined to a sharper peripheral field, but is paler and, to a certain extent, imaginary. The clarity of detail is attained at the expense of plastic reality. Ehrenzweig maintains as well that the imaginative quality of a pictorial space in a painting can be understood as a conscious signal of an extended unconscious substructure. Thus, it is important to learn to arrive at unconscious perception. "Learning to see involves forming such an unconscious substructure of vision; suppressing irrelevant details produces an awareness of intensely plastic objects without definite outline. This blurred plasticity is more important for the efficiency of vision than making out precise shapes and patterns." (Ibid, 30)

So each creative sensing implies a whole range of possible choices which can be regarded as an inner eye, and which surpass conscious understanding. In creating a work of art, the unconscious perception actually runs parallel to unconscious elements. A mere conscious control of the process of working is impossible and also undesirable. There is a planned coincidence, connected to the subjectivity of the artist, which still falls beyond the form intended by him. Because of this the notion of "intention" of the artist is indeed relativized. Ehrenzweig does not do so explicitly, because he assumes the unconscious to be a "hidden order", but nevertheless no less an order. The important role of the unconscious is an additional argument against the importance often attached to the discovery of the artist's intention by the spectator.

Yet in Ehrenzweig's work on the level of modern art, we discover an indication for the predomination of less obvious aspects of the work of art, such as representation and theme. In these aspects, he sees the key to our openness with respect to the non-Western or traditional art. "We do not really mind that we cannot reconstruct the conscious intentions of the Stone Age cave painters or of the old Mexicans, because we feel instinctively the relative unimportance of the artist's conscious message. It is perhaps due to the fact that our own modern art

34

is often content to work from low irrational levels of the mind alone, that our civilization has become so receptive to the art of other civilizations, prehistoric, historic, primitive and exotic. What alone seems to matter to us is the complex diffuse substructure of all art. It has its source in the unconscious and our own unconscious still reacts readily to it, preparing the way for ever new reinterpretations. The immortality of great art seems bound up with the inevitable loss of its original surface meaning and its rebirth in the spirit of every new age." (Ibid, 91) Ehrenzweig adds the dimension of the unconscious to aesthetic perception. Why we continue to be attracted to art from outside our culture and time can be explained from the assumption that we apparently merely sympathize with the diffuse subculture of all art: it is this which continues to fascinate the mind, released of its original superficial meaning. From a psychoanalytic perspective, an answer is formulated to the important question Marx asked himself in that respect.

Modern art, which provides us with that openness, characterizes itself by a dissociation between surface sensibility and depth sensibility, between intellect and intuition. It creates an experience of chaos and disruption. In this context Ehrenzweig thinks of action painting which in its initial phase confused the eye and meant an outburst of the unconscious subculture of art. Cubism too sent the eye wandering by breaking with the habit of focussing the eye sharply on a particular point; a point around which the rest of the composition is then organized. With this breach in focusing, a path was opened up for a free, all-over, broad view. The unconscious perception creates an openness through which the superficial impression of chaos and disruption can be surpassed. Thanks to this, an appreciation can come into being for the conclusive, repressed formal system, since the chaotic fragmentation can appear as a hidden order. "This hidden order redeems the near-schizoid character of the excessive fragmentation found in so much modern art." (Ibid, 82)

So far for Ehrenzweig's chaos or hidden order, as essence of the modern work of art. However, the question remains what the path is for the spectator to that hidden order. Or do the artist and the spectator play hide and seek with each other? The hidden structure of art is created on lower levels of awareness, but can only be observed on a higher level. "The hidden structure of art is created on lower levels of awareness that are nearer to the undifferentiated techniques of primary process. But once it is created it can only be observed on a higher level of awareness." (Ibid, 92)

The integration of the substructure of art is only observed via the conscious signal of that substructure, namely the pictorial space. "In this way we are forced to observe the unconscious structure of art with the gestalt techniques of

35

the (conscious or preconscious) secondary process which will automatically infuse a more solid and compact structure into it." (Ibid, 92) Therefore, the work of art remains unknowable or, to make the comparison with the dream: "Art is a dream dreamt by the artist which we, the wide awake spectators, can never see in its true structure; our waking faculties are bound to give us too precise an image produced by secondary revision." (Ibid, 93)

It is important that Ehrenzweig does not overrate spontaneity at the expense of intellectual control. He only wants a clear recognition of the limitations of such control. In that respect, the pictorial space is definitely situated outside conscious control.

There is still another reason why one cannot rely on the first impression, the entrance to the surface structure. Observation, in particular perception, stands for our grip on reality. Consequently, we are not easily inclined to accept that perception is unstable. Yet, it turns out to be that way: "Yet perception has a history; it changes during our life and even within a very short span of time; more important, perception has a different structure on different levels of mental life and varies according to the level which is stimulated at one particular time." (Ibid, 100) Exactly this is a difficulty in appreciating art. It may change very strongly over time, even though the same work of art is concerned. In that respect, the work is never complete. When the work of art has been finished by the artist, it is only an intermediate phase that has to be completed by the spectators. "We begin to suspect that even the final result, the work of art as it leaves the artist's hands, is an interim result, only an 'inner fabric' still to be outwardly clothed with plastic effects and to be animated by a mysterious presence which is partly in the eye of the beholder." (Ibid, 102)

Thus the process of completion does not stop with the artist. Of course, the continuation of the work of the artist does not happen on the basis of purely formal and technical aspects, but on what Ehrenzweig calls the "intimate content". This "intimate content" occurs in every profound aesthetical experience, where there is no division between form and content. "For once form and content are one and cannot be separated by any artifice." (Ibid, 107)

Ehrenzweig points out a general shift of approach in the spectator compared to the conscious intentions of the abstract artist. Being unable to discover a conscious intention in the abstract work of art, the spectator notices initially an ambiguity, which is part of the content of abstract art itself. In a second stage, it becomes a screen for self projection. "The spectators of today like to project any meaning they like into an abstract picture. They are quite happy with somewhat amorphous patterns that serve them as a neutral backcloth for projecting their private daydreams." (Ibid, 112) In their extreme positions, both stages lead to attitudes which prevent communication between artist and spectator.

No doubt, Ehrenzweig's work is an important contribution to the approach to art, especially because he introduced - because of his psychoanalytic interest - the unconscious into the world of modern art. However, a weak point is that many of his views on painting are only valid if one keeps in mind the American lyrical Abstractionists. In other words, his theory is based too strongly on one particular movement.

1.4. *Two contemporary psychoanalytic schools on art*

Before proceeding to Lacan - who will receive our attention because he is the most philosophical of the psychoanalysts - we will deal briefly with Szafran's study, as an example of an exponent of a current non-Lacanian tenor.

In Szafran's work, one will find the division into two main movements concerning the application of the technical rules in the various psychoanalytic schools. The Lacanian direction attaches great value to the unconscious, which is said to be structured as a language, in other words the unconscious as symbolic order. Lacan rejects the concepts of "knowledge" and "personality" as completely imaginary. The second movement, criticized by Lacan but defended by Szafran, departs from a completely different definition of the unconscious. Here it is the collection of repressed biological (and thus real) instincts. That real component within us is the origin of our maladjustment to the real component outside of us, which is expressed in "object relations".

1.4.1. *The study of object relations*

The approach of Willy Szafran is based on the concept of "object relations". "The object relation is a psychoanalytic term, which indicates the type and style of the relationship of the subject with the outside world, where the 'object' stands for 'the other'. The form of relationship to the outside world is the result of the way of organizing the more or less phantasmatic perceptions of those objects and the defense mechanisms employed by the subject." (Szafran 1974, 71) In the object relation, the subject tries generally to reach a compromise between his inner world and outer reality, so that the Id is satisfied and anxiety resulting from a conflict with the Superego is avoided. The Ego should realize this compromise between the Id and the Superego in harmony with outer reality.

Thus the method of psychobiography, such as Szafran employs, consists of a reading of works based on the analysis of object relations and at the same time on biographical reconstruction. For the latter, one uses the autobiographical facts of the author, details provided by third parties, the author's behavior in his environment and, finally, information on the societal, political and economic circumstances. Szafran points out various methodological difficulties: the work of objectification of the biography is not that easy. After all, one often has to balance inconsistent sources of information against each other and account for mistakes, improbabilities and distortions acquired from third parties on the basis of their own problems. The question of manipulability of facts by the analyzer presents itself with respect to works of art, where for example preference might play a more important role than in the therapeutic relationship between psychoanalyst and analysand. "Moreover - and this is an element not to be neglected - the researcher should always practice a certain self criticism in selecting and organizing material, because he can manipulate the biographical material on the basis of his own person and on a certain idea that he forms unconsciously about the author. He has to beware of prejudices, which can be even more dangerous if he does not know them himself, since in that way he handles all too easily a seeming objectivity. This is the problem of 'counter transference'." (Szafran 1987, 71)

A number of aspects which are related to the reception of art arise. The analyst of the relationship work - artist can be considered a particular kind of spectator, who accepts in principle scientific standards. With the "normal" spectator this is not the case. In that respect the question arises whether one should draw up a psychobiography of the spectator. Outside psychoanalysis, this means that perception is closely connected with the biographical facts of the spectator. Within psychoanalytic theory, this means that the perception of works of art can only be guaranteed if both the artist (whether or not via his work) and the spectator are analysand, and thus psychoanalytically screened to a great extent. The opinion of a number of authors that Freud's interpretation of Michelangelo's Moses would be inspired by the dissidence of a number of his former devotees points in that direction and then still on the level of the trained analyst. This psychoanalyzing of the psychoanalyst who interprets art does not refute the psychoanalytic approach, on the contrary, however it does limit the field. Szafran's research concerns literature. It becomes more difficult if the medium of the artist-analysand and the analyst, namely language, is no longer identical and the formation of images is involved. This is mostly not circumvented by analyzing the work of art, but rather by the artist's life. Two classic examples of analyzing paintings are by Abraham (1965) and Klein (1950). Szafran states in this connection: "The purpose strived for by these authors is similar to Freud's: to acquire a better knowledge of the unconscious, if necessary via the unconscious of the artist." (Ibid, 45) Szafran's remark on Klein's interpretation of the work of the painter Kjar (especially that she would paint to fill up her inner empty space, which is projected to the outside) is short but correct: "Here we have a fine example of 'application' of theoretical concepts and of the absence of interest for the aesthetic aspects of the work of art." (Ibid, 46)

1.4.2. Lacan

In the reports of Jacques Lacan's seminars, the function of painting is treated in a complex way. Lacan develops a dialectic between the gaze and the eye. It is of importance that the way he approaches a painting fits in with his criticism of the privileges Cartesian thought attributes to consciousness. Parallel to the purity of the function of the subject, Lacan develops a dimension of a way of perceiving, where the scale (l'optique géométrales) is important and the point by point correspondence of two units in space is essential. Thus, art and science are entangled. In Lacan's view, this scale perspective is not similar to perception, but an orientation in space, which could even be imagined by a blind person. However, the function of perception has to be explored further. The gaze has to be discovered in the painting, be present in it as a trap. In this context, the gaze has a drive, an exhibitionist function. Thus, with reference to Holbein's work *The French Ambassadors* Lacan argues: "This picture is simply what any picture is, a trap for the gaze. In any picture, it is precisely in seeking the gaze in each of its points that you will see it disappear." (Lacan 1979, 89)

Between the two characters in 'The French Ambassadors', a distorted figure, an anamorphosis is to be seen: a skull following us when we slowly move to the left and then back again to the right. Lacan's reading is that this enigmatic presence of the skull reflects our own futility. As a subject the painting calls us and includes us literally in it by luring us as spectator into a trap. For Lacan, this trap, this web, this labyrinth is a general characteristic of the visible. "In this matter of the visible, everything is a trap, and in a strange way 'entrelacs' (interlacing). There is not a single one of the divisions, a single one of the double side that the function of vision presents, that is not manifested to us as a labyrinth." (Ibid, 93)

Lacan breaks with the traditional philosophy of perception, which cautions against the so-called optical illusion, but still adheres to a geometrical approach to perception, that is perception situated in space, which is not the visual in its essence. For Lacan, the essence of the relationship between being and appearance is elsewhere. Not in a straight line, but in the shining point, source of reflecting flashing. "Light may travel in a straight line, but it is refract-ed, diffused, it floods, it fills, - the eye is a sort of bowl - it flows over, too, it necessitates, around the ocular bowl, a whole series of organs, mechanisms, defenses." (Ibid, 94)

The status of the subject in his relationship to light is not the geometrical point, as is defined in geometric optics, but all that is watching me is situated in the place of the shining point. Therefore, the following statement of Lacan can-not be understood metaphorically. "No doubt, in the depths of my eye, the pic-ture is painted. The picture, certainly, is in my eye. But I am not in the picture." (Ibid, 96) What is light is watching us. Because of that light in our inner eye, something paints itself there: not so much the constructed relationship - thus the object philosophers talk about - but an impression, which is a sparkling of a plane. However, the impression should not be situated in the perspectival dis-tance, within the geometrical relationship, but in the depth of field which can hardly be mastered by the ambiguity and variability connected to it. In Lacan's view, it is the depth of field which embraces the spectator. Between them there is an opaque screen which is of another nature than the geometrical space.

Lacan refers to Caillois in order to regard animal mimetism as analogous to what is presented as art among human beings. "A remark of Callois' should guide us. Callois assures us that the facts of mimicry are similar, at the animal level, to what, in the human being is manifested as art, or painting." (Ibid, 100) The study of mimesis with its three main dimensions of camouflage, disguise and intimidation shows the paths of perception followed by the subject when he inscribes himself into a painting. In Lacan's view, the relationship subject-paint-ing is more complex than simply emphasizing the obligation of the painter to manifest himself as a subject, as a gaze. However, Lacan considers it more com-plex as well than merely accentuating the object-side of the production of art. The gaze in a painting is not the gaze the characters cast at us, but indeed the gaze of the painter. Even in a painting without human figures there is a gaze, which one will perceive as a watermark. In other words, the specificity of each painter gives the feeling of the presence of the gaze. The function of the painting to whom the painter shows his work, is not that of an eye-catcher, but it gives food for the eye, in all tranquility. "The painter gives something to the person who must stand in front of his painting, in part, at least, of the painting, might by summed up thus - You want to see? Well, take a look at this! He gives something for the eye to feed on, but he invites the person to whom this picture is presented to lay down his gaze there as one lays down one's weapons. This is the pacify-ing, Apollonian effect of painting. Something is given not so much to the gaze as to the eye, something that involves the abandonment, the laying down, of the gaze." (Ibid, 101)

Expressionism presents a problem for Lacan and falls outside of his scope. In Expressionism, a kind of active satisfaction of a pulse takes place and, thus, one cannot speak of the same Apollonian effect. Lacan has obviously traditional art in mind, although he does not cling to the necessity of a realism. The following shows the importance he attaches to anamorphosis: "Anamorphosis shows us that it is not a question of a realistic reproduction of the things of space - a term about which one could have many reservations." (Ibid, 92)

With respect to the technique of painting, Lacan often talks about the successors of traditional art: the Surrealists, such as Dali. Yet, one could not claim that Lacan is not open to contemporary art in which the pictorial prevails as a testifying result of the painter's gesture, or as he formulates it: "the strokes pour from the brush of the painter, strokes about which Cézanne talks lovingly as 'those little blues, those little browns, those little whites'. The gesture of the painter - about which for example Matisse was stunned at seeing a movie in slow motion in which he sees himself working - is not the result of a choice, but the materialization of the cumulative residue of the testifying aversion of the gaze. Lacan uses again the metaphor of the analogy between art and mimesis, but now the other way around: "Should not the question be brought closer to what I called the rain of the brush? If a bird were to paint would it not be by letting fall its feathers, a snake by casting off its scales, a tree by letting fall its leaves? What it amounts to is the first act in the laying of the gaze."(Ibid, 114)

The stroke is the final point of the gestural movement, but at the same time the initial point of the moment of perception. Because of this, between artist and spectator, between gesture and impression a point of contact arises. "This terminal moment is that which enables us to distinguish between a gesture and an act. It is by means of the gesture that the brushstroke is applied to the canvas. And so true is it that the gesture is always present there that there can be no doubt that the picture is felt by us, as the terms 'impression' or 'impressionism' imply, as having more affinity with the gesture than with any other type of movement." (Ibid, 114-115)

In this respect, Lacan uses the term "scène de bataille" which one may also hear from the lips of the artist: "adventure, fight with the angel" etc. Important is that in the gesture, Lacan sees the explanation for the bottom or top of the painting, whether figurative or not, and likewise the left-right direction with diapositives in paintings. Although it is not always recognizable - the German painter Baselitz (1938), for example, paints his works upside down - Lacan still demonstrates with this a penetrating vision of the process of painting. As a psychoanalyst he is constantly involved in the artist behind the painting.

Still he has an eye for the materiality of the work by situating the meeting point of painter and spectator in the stroke itself, as evidence of the gesture. Unlike many theoreticians who put the intention and the psychobiography of the artist first in order to understand a work of art, Lacan does not jump through the work of art, like a lion in a circus. The spectator is as it were teleguided by the desire of the artist to make something visible to him. "Modifying the formula I have of desire as unconscious - man's desire is the desire of the Other - I would say that it is a question of a sort of desire on the part of the Other, at the end of which is the showing (le donner-à-voir)." (Ibid, 115)

That "making visible" satisfies the visual hunger of the spectator. The real function of the eye as organ is greed. Lacan calls that the evil eye, which is related to envy. Because of the fascinum, the dialogue between the producer and the spectator comes to a halt in an aesthetic contemplation before the work. "The evil eye is the fascinum and it is precisely one of the dimensions in which the power of the gaze is exercised directly." (Ibid, 118) The work of art approaches the fetish. In the "fascinum" the spectator becomes accessary to the phantasm of the painter and transgresses the limits of the perspective. Wrongly, one could avail oneself of this to criticize formalism. But let us not forget that, by situating the meeting point of artist and spectator in the stroke as deposition of the gesture of the painter, Lacan himself makes a link between a formalist and a psychoanalytic approach of art. One could wonder to what extent the psychoanalytic approach of art is relevant to the aesthetical and educational value of the work of art. Julien Quackelbeen, vociferous representative of the Lacanian movement, analyses the oeuvre of Holbein the Younger (Quackelbeen 1984, 109-127). He reaches the conclusion that this 16th century painter shows characteristics typical of obsessional neurosis. He cautions against interpreters, such as Pinder, who see in Holbein's work - especially in the series *Dance of Death* - a proof of his "social involvement", his sensitivity to the division rich-poor and powerful-repressed. Indeed, psychobiographical facts of the artist as supplement to the understanding of a work of art could be interesting. Yet we believe that this is an example of the danger of not limiting oneself to the formal characteristics of the work of art. Whether or not Holbein was driven by an anal obsession in depicting references critical of contemporary society does not seem relevant. On the basis of its formal characteristics, a work of art gives evidence or otherwise of meanings, regardless of any obsession which may lie at the base of its conception.

1.5. *Psychoanalysis and philosophy*

In his metaphilosophical article "Sign as theme. A confrontation of the classical philosophical sign and the structural sign" (1969), Herman Parret underlines the importance of the philosophical slant of Freud's move; in particular the so-called "epistemic" turn which brings about the end and thematizes at the same time the limit of a past that corresponds largely with the theoretical epoch of the Greco-Western tradition. He puts Freud on one line with Nietzsche and Heidegger by stating: "Thus, Nietzsche preaches the active forgetting of being and thus the end of philosophy; the Freudian revolution shows the illusion of conscious activity, undermines the complexity of knowing and power and decentralizes the autonomy of the subject; thinking the limit of metaphysics and the indication of onto-theo-teleology in Heidegger means at the same time criticizing humanism and the infinity of subjectivity; thus also Michel Foucault presumes 'the end of the human being' and the privileges of the inexhaustible creative consciousness." (Parret 1969, 232) To the four names mentioned, Parret also adds the name of Marx, as witness of this epistemic turn to a "post-theoretical time". This time starts at the moment thought becomes a thought of the margin which is not identical, but carries in itself the lie and the illusion. This is contrary to the classical philosophical figure of "theorein", where thought presents being as presence. Parret postulates that the whole of history of philosophy, from Plato to Husserl, has as its purpose (telos): the ontologizing of thought, the logocizing of grammar (speaking) and the phoneticizing of writing. Therefore, the onto-teo-teleology incarnates the fascination of the foundation or the origin, which is evidence or presence. Although Husserl turns against metaphysical speculation, still the "Wesenschau" (the viewing of essence) is paradigmatic for all metaphysics as "view", as the question of origin, and as movement within the ideality of presence.

In his article "Philosophy and Psychoanalysis" (1969), Samuel IJsseling agrees with this view. He points out that in the circles of Lacan, the Freudian discovery is seen as a "decentralizing". This means that Freud does not situate the real center of the human being in the same place as the humanistic tradition had assigned to it. The statement which became almost proverbial is concisely formulated: "... dass das Ich nicht Herr sei in seinem eigene Haus" (that the I is not master in his own house). (Mooy 1979, 98)

Man is neither the center of his own existence, nor the center of the world. In his speaking, he is not so much the subject of his words, but rather the subjected. He is not so much "producer" of his own life story, but rather "product" of a story told about him in which he tries to obtain a place as a character. Therefore the criticism of psychoanalysis on phenomenology (as philosophy which intends the immediate presenting of presence of man to himself and to the world) is that such an attitude is possible only in the imagination and finally proves to be untenable. Phenomenology, as philosophy of perception, might be an accurate description or phrasing of what presents itself to consciousness within perception or experience, but it forgets that perception and consciousness are perverted. However, the criticism of psychoanalysis on philosophy oriented towards phenomenology is also a philosophy in itself. IJsseling answers the question "What is philosophy?" with two contrary statements:

"1. Philosophy is a whole of well-founded confirmations and justified denials which whole shows a certain coherence, in other words a 'science'."

2. Philosophy is a whole of questions, which interrogates that which has been said (the whole of confirmations and denials) again and again, in other words a not-knowing." (IJsseling 1969, 273-274)

Greatly simplified he states that philosophy as science is the structure of philosophy from Plato through Hegel. Philosophy as not-knowing is the structure of philosophy inspired by Wittgensteinian as well as Heideggerian thought. Both thinkers, strongly differing from each other, agree that they let others speak and that they themselves only try to pose questions. Heidegger constantly questions the unthought in that which has been thought and the unsaid in that which has been said in order to keep open or to break open a real future. It is on this point that IJsseling leaps to psychoanalysis, more particularly to Lacan. From a Heideggerian point of view, the differences between Lacan's psychoanalysis and philosophy have become senseless, because, ultimately, Lacan's psychoanalysis and Heidegger's thought have a similar intention and they even approach factual philosophy in more or less the same way. IJsseling points out that, although there are great differences, still, on the basis of comparison of a number of concepts, the issues of Heidegger's unthought and unsaid and Lacan's issue of the unconscious at least overlap.

In the same spirit and also appealing to Lacan, Antoine Mooij emphasizes the anthropological dimension of psychoanalysis, which assumes a reflective attitude with respect to psychiatry: "Psychoanalysis does not apply to psychiatry, but questions it critically." (Mooij 1975, 361) Furthermore, Mooij emphasizes that psychoanalysis is a specific form of language analysis. Pure registration of facts is impossible, because the most elementary report contains an interpretation, merely by the choice of words. Every story is an interpretation and supposes the activity of explanation in which an articulation takes place. The speaking subject does not design language with its grammar and vocabulary, but he subjects himself to this language. This also assumes the existence of others. Therefore each notion of an independent subject is fundamentally wrong. Moreover, interpretation will never end. Again and again it might be resumed, be corrected or it might provoke further interpretation. That implies that a definitive justification is excluded. Each final point is arbitrary. At the same time, this means that man as a speaking subject can indeed be addressed, but he is ultimately not responsible for what he will say and do. For psychoanalytic theory in Lacan's spirit, there is no reality outside of the symbolic order within which symbolizing occurs, neither as subject, nor as object. In symbolizing, the immediacy of experiencing is transgressed by its symbolic indication. In saying everything, something remains unsaid, and the unsaid cannot be filled in, thus remains excluded. The unsaid has to do with what psychoanalysis calls the unconscious. However, that unconscious is the continuous consequence of our speaking, which denies an immediate access, even to ourselves. Psychoanalytic theory goes further and wonders if human relationships are possible. Not only does it investigate the history of a subject, but it also questions what precedes this history, the conditions which have to be satisfied so that the subject can function. In Mooij's terminology that is the anthropological dimension of psychoanalysis. How this takes shape boils down to the already cited conclusion of the fundamental passivity of the subject, not as a founding principle but as a constituting one. The subject is not sovereign, is neither lord nor master, nor origin, but holds a second-class position. That goes against classical philosophical thought about man.

This classical philosophical thought is represented in a exemplary way by Descartes. In his book on Lacan's theory of psychoanalysis, Mooij sketches that problem concisely. After a universal doubt experiment, Descartes reaches the indubitable conclusion "I think, therefore I am". Thus, consciousness becomes the pre-eminent source of indubitable truth. The philosophy building further on this is a philosophy of consciousness. For example, according to phenomenological philosophy the task of philosophy is to describe the experience of consciousness on the basis of the certainty of the cogito. This experience of consciousness, for example in perceiving a painting, should be described on the basis of its essential characteristics. The phenomenological attitude will free a field of phenomena of consciousness regarding the immediate perception. According to Mooij, the question one has to pose is "Am I as I think I am?" Which question psychoanalysis answers in the negative. Psychoanalysis demonstrates that consciousness is separated from its own meaning because of a margin consciousness does not control. Thus Mooij argues in a Lacanian way: "After all, I am systematically mistaken about myself and delude myself continuously. This error and this elusion have a meaning. Part of this meaning can be traced back to the analytic dialogue. However, in doing so one needs essentially the intervention of the Other, who by virtue of their being the other can break through the narcissistic blinding of self-thinking consciousness. The purpose of an analysis is to identify misunderstandings and to recognize their meaning. However, this purpose lies in infinity, because an ultimate and definitive meaning, an ultimate transparency, is not an attainable ideal: one can certainly shift the margin between conscious and unconscious, but one cannot cancel it." (Mooij 1979, 204)

Thus, statements about oneself are not adequate. There is a separation within the subject which cannot be canceled and which means that the subject does not correspond with itself. That theme is not new in philosophy. However, in Lacan's view, this separation cannot be canceled and it does not function as a moment that can be transgressed, precisely because he relates it to the linguistic existence of the subject. Therefore, an immediate "presence of the subject to the world" - such as phenomenologists sometimes assume - or to itself is impossible. "The access to objects and to ourselves is only possible through language, so direct access is impossible and also impossible as a final result: one cannot jump over language. Thus language is not only the condition for revelation, but also the medium to veil. Therefore no one single revelation is complete: to reveal is at the same time to veil. Thus, Lacan can state that the truth has never been said, it is only half-said: "la vérité est mi-dite." (Ibid, 205) Obviously this goes against the central role which consciousness plays in traditional philosophy. This theory conflicts with the subjectifying and anthropocentering of the philosophy of consciousness. It is also obvious that such a view has its repercussion on the perception of art. Not only does the question "What is there to be seen" apply in the relationship between art and the spectator of art, but also "Who sees?". Both questions are related to speaking and to the whole of the philosophy of language.

In this first chapter, we tried to demonstrate, on the basis of a number of views borrowed from psychology and psychoanalysis, that the perception of the perceiving subject is not an evidence without problems. Not only is visual perception related to the nature of the eye, at the same time it is culturally determined. Again and again, it turns out that facts are interpretations of facts. Each view is partial. This gives perspective to each claim of being absolute of a perceiving I, who likes to give itself a central place within the philosophy of consciousness. However, the margin between conscious and unconscious cannot be drawn unequivocally, which obscures the distinction between illusion and reality for the spectator. One should take account of these psychological facts in all respects, when one reflects on the possible functions of art. The complexity of the artistic facts tests the innocent spectator. Because of this, the problem of presentation, which presents itself for all visible things in our world, presents itself even more in the confrontation with art. Art tempts the eye or provokes it, but it seldom evokes "neutral" perception. It means that the psychology of art is indispensable for the study of the relationship between art and spectator. But also, the other way around, the study of aesthetic perception is certainly illuminating for psychology itself.

2. ART AND SOCIETY

Titles such as Art and Society sound rather ponderous but that is due to the increasing complexity of the problems since the 1980s. This chapter has a double purpose. On the one hand, it forms, together with Chapter 1, Art and Individual, the framework for two related fields: psychology and sociology, the "offspring" of philosophy so to speak. On the other hand, it is beginning the giving of a voice to the social philosophy of art.

Psychology as well as sociology criticize departure from determinisms or influences revealed by them. They can treat an identical theme with a different scientific methodology characteristic for each field. Social philosophy of art refers mainly to "Neo-marxism", one of the dominant philosophical movements of this century. Philosophers are not placed on a pedestal in the center of power structures. Their place is on the periphery or even in the margin. But now that Marx has been knocked off his pedestal in Eastern Europe, we can again be inspired by Marxist thought with an easy conscience.

2.1. *The social function of art as explored in a number of art sociological movements*

2.1.1. *Empiricism*

Empiricism starts from the outcome of intersubjective observation in order to obtain valid patterns or laws. In the view of empirical art sociology, theories which cannot be supported by empirical research are part of speculative philosophy or criticism. Empiricism arrives at knowledge of the whole by means of quantitatively researching the parts. The processes and structures which develop around the work of art, such as number and type of spectators, can indeed be explored quantitatively. However, the social content of the work of art is deduced from the conceptual universe of the "receiver", rather than from the characteristics of the artwork itself. Moreover, these characteristics are disputable. Concluding, one can state that it is not that interesting to determine empirically the sociological relevance of a work of art in terms of the number of persons involved.

2.1.2. *Structural functionalism.*

Structural functionalism analyzes the structure of society, to disentangle its constitutive parts, and to establish the function of those parts. Not surprisingly, art is considered a "social institution", which can be subdivided into analyzable substructures. Social institutions are structures which organize and stabilize human activities in the form of a system of roles and norms directed towards the satisfaction of a certain social need or function. For example: "What is the function of art?" or more specifically: "What social functions does art fulfil?" (Albrecht 1970, 2)

From the perspective of philosophy of art, a number of problems arise. The autonomy of the artwork will encounter difficulties when sociologists start researching how the art work should look in order to fulfil a certain function. It is unheard-of - and it should remain so - that art will comply "socially". The social function of art is precisely its temporarily "anti-social" meaning as a device to criticize the dominant socialization. With regard to this, structural - functionalist art sociology does not proceed interpretatively, but is explanatory in a genetic-causal manner. Thus, the issue is which external factors have played a role in how the artwork looks. Its interpretation, its meaning or its sense, once the artwork has been completed, is not at stake.

A quote from the interesting work by Helmut Gaus, modern historian, will clarify even more the distinction between the field of philosophy and structural-functionalism. Gaus is a defender of functional analysis as far as cultural phenomena are concerned. He once chose as a preface quotation, "There is an entire spectrum of sociological problems which we would hardly know how to treat today other than with functional analysis, no matter how vague and badly defined this method is." (Gaus 1979, 1)

In a paragraph on "The functional problem-position and the aestheticizing approaches", Gaus compares functionalism and Kagan's thought. This Russian aesthetician is said to have been representative for Marxist aesthetic thought in the former USSR. His Western counterparts are Wellek and Warren. They all published on the function of art.

Gaus agrees with Kagan's view that the history of aesthetic thought is the history of the various opinions on the social function of art. However, Gaus is less happy with Kagan's four functions of art mutually determining the social value of art. These four functions are: the communicative, the explanatory-instructive, the educational and the hedonistic.

The communicative function implies that art is a specific language which can pass on the spiritual activity of some who observe the world in a very sensitive way. Except for literature, art is a universal language, "... a 'language' which is accessible to all of humanity." (Kagan 1974, 515) The artistic language is able to create emotional and affective contents in the spectators.

The explanatory-instructive function assumes that "Art contains a certain way of knowing about life and, thus, functions for human beings as an important form of explanation and instruction." (Ibid, 516) Art has the potential to spread knowledge acquired through contact with reality.

Kagan's educational function means that knowledge cannot only be acquired, but be experienced through art as well. "In the end the emotional and the intellectual relationship of human beings to reality, their world view and their *Weltanschauung* will become involved in the activity of art where these will be actively and firmly educated." (Ibid, 521)

The hedonistic function is art's capability to evoke aesthetic pleasure. "This capacity is the 'magnet' which draws people into art; without it art will just appear to be senseless and independent of ideological and epistemological qualities." (Ibid, 526).

Rightly, Gaus criticizes Kagan's formulations of 'the' functions of art as too general and presuming the definite characteristics of the artwork itself. "If we inquire into the very function of art or literature in society, this implies an invariable function. But why should we accept this hypothesis instead of its inverse, notably that, in the different periods of its evolution, literature did not always fulfil the same function, through the fundamental difference in the social situations in which it occurred." (Gaus 1979, 36) We could go even further. The formulation of 'the' functions of 'the' art is not only senseless because functions will constantly modify themselves as the social situation evolves, but also because the type of art will change. And this is not limited to the obvious classification of art as music, literature, architecture, visual art, etc. Within a category of visual art such as painting, certain works can fulfil a particular function which will completely differ from that of other works. Not every painting has the same function; this is not even the case in an identical social situation. It would be interesting to explore the various autonomous 'worlds of art' within a certain geographic area.

Theme as well as form can give different functions to an artwork. In a way, one should study each artwork separately in order to examine its concrete function. Gaus particularly criticizes Kagan's study because it refers to Kagan as the sole authority to determine the arguments of the functions of an artwork. "The reader is left no other possibility but to use his own intuition, experience, and knowledge on the subject as criteria, because he gets no answer to the question: 'How does Kagan know that it is so and not otherwise?' As long as deductions cannot be made from more generally received data than the personal opinions of an author or a reader, it is rather difficult to speak of scientific findings." (Duvignaud 1972, 102)

This quotation explains a nuance. Clearly, Gaus looks for the *actual function* of art, whereas, from a philosophical perspective, one examines the *statements* on the possible functions of art. Contrary to Gaus, philosophers believe that the results of a structural-functionalist public survey on the actual functions of art are not a priori more important than the statements by professional philosophers of art on the possible functions of art.

2.1.3. *Sociology of knowledge*

Sociology of knowledge analyzes the various forms of knowledge as an expression of the social domain. Knowledge can be understood very broadly. Thus, art is a product of the human mind and related to society. Some paradigms in the sociology of knowledge run the risk of being narrowed down to a one-sided explanatory model which, for example, reduces art to a mere result of social causes. In a certain way, that kind of reductionism can be considered a specific version of the sociology of knowledge. Incidentally, some forms of Marxism are also being blamed for such reductionism. Sociology of knowledge as an explanatory method can be understood as a model structured by the notion of an affecting factor and a reality being affected, where the latter is explained by the former.

If one assumes that in explanation, the aspect of genesis is stressed, and in interpretation, the aspect of meaning, interpretation is still possible for the sociology of knowledge, albeit with some trouble because the genesis will continue to play a role. The sociologist Karl Mannheim attempts to instigate an interpretative sociology of knowledge. According to him, the self-sufficiency of the work is central rather than its genesis. Important in Mannheim's view is the concept of "modification of function", which implies modification of meaning: "... the mere modification of the function of a context of a sentence already means a modification of meaning - one of the most essential proofs for this is that history is a creative place of related meanings and not only a place of the realization of immanent related meanings which could be conceived as pre-existing." (Mannheim 1964, 383).

Mannheim distinguishes between an immanent and a sociological modification of function. The modification is immanent if a concept passes from one system of ideas to another. For example, the meaning of the concept of Romanticism will modify depending on the system in which it is used. In Mannheim's view, a sociological modification of function is a modification of meaning of a concept. This occurs if a concept is accepted by a group which lives in a different social environment, causing the essential meaning of a concept to be modified. "Thus, each 'signification' changes its meaning, as soon as it relates to another way of being." (Ibid, 384) So, the interaction between the modification of function and the modification of meaning is very interesting for the study of art.

Sociology of knowledge could lead to a sociology of the spectators. Then questions will arise such as "Why is somebody a lover of art?" "What does the spectator think about art?" "How does the spectator behave towards art?" It could furthermore provide insight into the influence of socially determined knowledge on the perception of art. Knowledge as the veiling or revealing of perception is an important aspect of the approach to art.

Naturally there are other sociological theories which can contribute to the investigation of the phenomenon of art. In the next section, two movements will be explored in greater depth: Neo-marxism - the critical theory of the Frankfurt School - and its structuralist reading: Althusser's ideology critique. Both schools of thought will be treated as philosophies no matter how difficult the distinction between sociological theory and social philosophy. When treating Marxism, those forms of Marxism will be accentuated which did not grow overly dogmatic as far as political ideology is concerned. The vast field of Marxist theory of art will provide a number of important aspects particularly interesting for the field of painting.

2.1.4. *The functions of art. Sociology of art versus the philosophy of art*

This study intends to be part of the philosophy of art. Its constitutive question is always, "What is art?" The answer to this question cannot be acquired through a study of the history of art. Neither does a system of possible characteristics of works of art described as objects provide the right tack. The most obvious question is the one that deals with the possible functions of art. Therefore, this detour will be used in order to arrive at the core question of "What is art?".

Thus, the exploration of the function of art does not mean the investigation of the needs of a possible audience. The functions art could fulfil in society or the functions certain societies would like to impose on art are not under consideration. The issue is the clarification of the concept of art and the reflection on the phenomenon of "art" as a contribution to the philosophy of art. Consequently, several questions will arise. What is the concept, the essence, the meaning of art? What are its characteristics (systematics)? How is analysis and interpretation possible (methodology)? Could one explore the value of the artwork (criticism)? What are other aspects of art (i.e. creation, distribution, reception) and what could one do with it (function)?

The question of utility is an instrumental one, an indirect way to clarify questions such as "What is art?" and "What are its characteristics?" Art results from an action; it is a product of human beings for whom it is somehow necessary to create that product. Between creator and spectator could - but not necessarily - exist an interaction. Since the spectator is the theoretical starting point, not surprisingly the focus is on the description of the work of art and the various effects it will have as a relative autonomous object, apart from the artist's intentions. Thus, "functions" imply the various "effects" a work of art can exert. Such a meaning might be close to the etymological meaning. A sociological definition will reveal a contradiction clearly demonstrating the distinction between art sociology and the philosophy of art: "In sociology, function (Lat. *functio* = performance, action, *fungi* = to perform, to achieve) is that part of a social system which contributes to the preservation of this system." (De Valk 1977) It is not obvious to consider art a "preservation" of the system. One relates art and social critique exactly because of the desire to interfere with existing systems. The function of contemporary art is its "absence of any function". Of course, one could maintain that an aesthetic protest against a certain system will contribute to its preservation. If one applies Merton's elaboration on the concept of "absence of function" to art, it seems as if social criteria have been created to distinguish "good" from "bad" art. "In particular, Merton refined the concept. Besides the function as described above (also called by him 'eufunction'), he distinguishes between the concepts of 'dysfunction'- or that which is harmful for the survival of the system - and 'latent function' - or a consequence of social action which is favorable to the social system although the actor did not intend so; this is in contrast with the 'manifest function', where the intended effect is consciously desired." (ibid)

One could formulate this paradox in the following way: art's dysfunction is its eufunction. Obviously, the sociology of the creator of art does not correspond with that of the "receiver". The manifest (possible) dysfunction of the artist's action resulting in a work of art is firstly the artistic value of that product. All other functions are latent and there could be many. However, as far as the "receiver" is concerned, the artwork can fulfil a great variety of manifest functions.

2.2. Marx and art

It is not that easy to discuss Karl Marx's aesthetics and philosophy of art. Neither Marx nor Engels wrote about art in a systematic way. One cannot speak of Marxist art theory. Therefore, Marxist aesthetics can be totally contradictory or, "... a luxuriant confusion of ideas and theories. There are Marxist positions which regard classic realism as the only basis for revolutionary art, condemning all modernism and avant-garde works as complicit with reaction, and there are others which propose the precise opposite. Some regard the arts as second only to the sciences in the validity of their insights into reality, while for others they are the site of constant ideological struggles." (Laing 1978, vii)

2.2.1. *The development of sensuousness will advance social emancipation*

According to Marx, human sensuousness can never be developed and emancipated enough. A human being is a totality. All organs of human individual existence, including the senses which are social by definition, refer through their orientation toward the object to its appropriation, i.e. the human world. Private property infatuates a human being due to his one-sided attitude that an object only belongs to him if he possesses it. Possession alienates the senses. Therefore, the transgression of private property will humanize sensory practice. "The transcendence of private property is therefore the complete emancipation of all human senses and attributes; but it is this emancipation precisely because these senses and attributes have become, subjectively and objectively, human. The eye has become a human eye, just as its object has become a social, human object - an object emanating from man for man. The senses have therefore become directly in their practice theoreticians. They relate themselves to the thing for the sake of thing, but the thing itself is an objective human relation itself and to man, and vice versa. Need or enjoyment have consequently lost their egotistical nature, and nature has lost its mere utility by use becoming human use." (Solomon 1975, 58-59)

In the object world, a human being is not only confirmed by his thought, but also by his senses. The importance of the plurality of the senses should be emphasized in this context. An object appears to the eye in a different way than to the ear. The particularity of each sense, as essential power, constitutes the specific way of objectification.

One can see the subjective aspect in a different way. Marx deducts from the statement that those who do not have a taste for art cannot even taste the most beautiful art and that the taste for art is evoked by art. The senses of those who have no eye for the social, are different from the senses of those who do have an eye for it. Then the humanizing task for the senses could be described as, "Only through the objectively unfolded richness of man's essential being is the richness of subjective human sensibility (a musical ear, an eye for beauty of form - in short, senses capable of human gratifications, senses conforming themselves as essential powers of man) either cultivated or brought into being. For not only the five senses but also the so-called mental senses - the practical sense (will, love, etc.) - in a word, human sense - the humanness of the senses - comes to be by virtue of its object, virtue of humanized nature. The forming of the five senses is a labor of the entire history of the world down to the present." (Ibid, 60)

Thus, it appears that Marx's interest in human improvement related to the sensory perception of art cannot be separated from the social environment. But also of importance is the emphasis on the particular nature of each sense - and through this on the specific improvement which each category of art can imply. The concept of 'the' art covers a much too indefinite category of objects or situations. Therefore, this study will limit itself to the art of painting, and even so one should distinguish within that field.

2.2.2. The aesthetic pleasure - transhistorical or not?

An interesting perspective on the concept of the "aesthetic" is one of Marx's questions discussed in almost all works dealing with his view of art. According to Marx, there is a solid relationship between art and the society producing it. Greek art could not have come into being in the era of steam engines and printing presses. Its basis was a mythological system: "It is a well-known fact that Greek mythology was not only the arsenal of Greek art, but also the very ground from which it sprang." (Ibid, 61) And this is contrary to the fact that Greek art is still a source of aesthetic pleasure, also in Marx's days. "But the difficulty is not in grasping the idea that Greek art and epos are bound up with certain forms of social development. It rather lies in understanding why they still constitute for us a source of aesthetic enjoyment and in certain respects prevail as the standard and model beyond attainment." (Ibid, 62)

Marx presented the problem, rather than resolved it. The discussions often appear to be contradictory to the historical materialist view and put themselves more in an idealistic perspective. Marx's statement on Greek culture as the childhood of humanity seems a rather romantic nostalgia for lost naïveté as well. "Why should the social childhood of mankind, where it has obtained its most beautiful development, not exert an eternal charm as an age that will never return? There are ill-bred children and precocious children. Many of the ancient nations belong to the latter class. The Greeks were normal children. The charm their art has for us does not conflict with the primitive character of the social order from which it had sprung." (Ibid, 62)

Later Marxists tried to formulate a positive answer to this so as not to be obliged to consider this as Marx's capitulation. Summarized, there are two versions: "...that Greek society possessed certain features inherently superior to the European class societies which succeeded it, and therefore its art retained certain essential human values missing from feudalism and capitalism where the commodity-form is dominant (e.g. Lifshitz), or that great art of any period inherently retains the ability to outlive its origins. The latter argument can take two forms, either insisting on the realism of a work's portrayal of the historical moment of its production (thus Marx and Engels on Lasalle), or on its possession of a harmonious perfection of form." (Laing 1978, 10)

Henry Lefebvre emphasizes the importance of art as a witness to the past. Each ideology presupposes certain illusions of people about themselves. The progress of knowledge will destroy these illusions. And within these illusions, works of art will be created. Even if these illusions have disappeared completely, certain works of art will continue to have an active influence. "While the ideological illusions destroy themselves in the course of progress, while knowledge makes progress step by step, art continues to be a sensible witness, lively and active on the surpassed moments. Thus, Greek art restores the health, freshness, vitality and charm of the beautiful flourishing years of one's youth ...". (Lefebvre 1953, 72-73)

Marx's explanation of the "childhood aspect" remains obscure. Perhaps one should turn to Hans Hess (Laing 1978, 10). In addition to the historical bond Marx observes between forms of social development and production of art, Hess maintains that that bond also exists while perceiving art. One should not try to find the later admiration of Greek art in some transhistorical essence of the works themselves, but in the aesthetic ideologies or philosophies which prevail in modern societies and their corresponding cultural institutions.

In posing the question why Greek art from Antiquity provides aesthetic pleasure now, it is important to verify whether that pleasure is aesthetic indeed. Of course, one could call each pleasure which arises while perceiving art "aesthetic pleasure". However, this term should be clarified. The admiration of the "beauty" of art from Antiquity might be merely the admiration of Antiquity, of the past, of the historical instead of art. In that respect, the issue is not so much "aesthetic" pleasure, as well as the attractiveness of all that belongs to history. Art also belongs to that domain. As Lefebvre maintains, "... art continues to be a sensible witness." Greek art as expression of the health, freshness and liveliness of childhood seems to belong to the ideology of a nostalgic Utopia. In that respect, Hess emphasizes the influence the social component has in the reception of art. Then, presently, the "aesthetic pleasure" of Greek art cannot be dissociated from the new mythology of, say, tourism. However, in this context, "aesthetic pleasure" in a philosophical and theoretical sense is not under discussion.

The pleasure of observing a historical residue is a version of the pleasure of recognizing and appreciating the theme as content. The aesthetic gaze, whether or not connected with pleasure, occurs when the form is abstracted from all but the form itself. This is not synonymous with absence of substance; it means that one has an "eye" for the formal structures of the work. Thus, a manner of perception which will not prevent content or even the historical past from coming to the fore in a second phase. In other words, perception will exclude the artwork's original social context, but not the ideology of the spectator. Therefore, the appreciation of classic Greek art can stem from an ideology of the right dimension, from the perfect model. For example, the 20th century appreciation of so-called primitive art is attached to an ideology of the power of the form of expression or the emphasis on certain parts of the form. Moreover, the experience of aesthetic pleasure in works of art from the past could stem from the aesthetic pleasure in contemporary art, because one can read a similar aesthetic ideology in these works from the past. The pleasure might even result from an interest in a more technological realm, e.g. an interest in how artists in former times dealt with pictorial problems. The admiration of old masters by contemporary painters is an example of this.

It is important that, in contemporary art, "aesthetic pleasure" be able to return to the past within a context. As stated previously, the issue is not the pleasure, but whether it is aesthetic pleasure. The "experience of beauty" is different from "aesthetic pleasure". The appreciation of contemporary art can result in appreciating so-called primitive art (Rubin 1984), which issue is far more important today than the example of Greek art Marx presented. There is a formal relationship between "primitive" art and a large part of contemporary art. Not surprisingly, both types of art are perceived in the same way. Naturally, in this case, the aesthetic gaze is an advanced abstraction of the work's original social context which, as goes without saying, is very strongly present in primitive art. Yet, the earlier ethnological function should remain separated from the contemporary aesthetic meaning.

This process of aesthetization is not an undermining of art; that would mean a misunderstanding of the autonomy of design. Each era has its particular design of themes that can be similar. This is obvious if one takes a look at the reinterpretation of works of art, for example in Picasso or Bacon. Therefore, a "dadaism" of perception should be possible. The aesthetic gaze means the liberty of perception. Perhaps that is exactly the aesthetic pleasure.

2.3. *A Marxist view on the priority of the function of the stimulation of creativity as compared to the other functions of art*

2.3.1. *The novelty of the aesthetic function*

From a Marxist perspective, Adolfo Sanchez Vazquez, the Mexican aesthetic, points out that the function of art has been modified. A critical approach to his article (Sanchez Vazquez 1977) will clarify a number of viewpoints on this issue. According to Sanchez Vazquez, the aesthetic function is a new function which presently plays a prominent role, where the work of art is not perceived as a means but as a purpose. "From a historical perspective, art fulfilled the most diverse functions. Each function was important and influential as a means (to education, propaganda, adoration etc.), instead of a purpose, in other words, as art itself. The condition of art will transgress from means to purpose since a new function is arising which imposes itself on the others. It is the aesthetic function. The aesthetic function implies:
1)separation from the historical-cultural world where it originates in order to allow the work of art to reveal itself;
2) abstraction from the other functions so that it can become the prominent one;
3) elimination of all considerations of its destined purpose in order to become purpose in itself;
4) domination of intense perception in the creator-spectator relationship;
5) ideological neutralization after having subordinated the ideological content to the form." (Ibid, 113)
These five aspects are an interesting contribution to the clarification of the concept of "aesthetic function". However, a number of critical remarks can be made on Sanchez Vazquez's view. According to him, the aesthetic function originated "from Europe with its so-called Western culture, in the beginning of Modern Times." (Ibid, 113). Before that, one speaks of "craft" rather than of art (point 1). If all other possible purposes of art have to be left aside, it does not make sense to abstract from other functions, as the aesthetic will have become the only function (points 2 and 3). The emphasis on intense perception in the creator-spectator relationship (point 4) is correct. This point should revise the two previous ones.

The predominance of the aesthetic function implies the highest possible freedom for the artist; in other words, the artist is hardly bound to commissions or directions concerning the form. This implies as well the full freedom of the spectator who, as an aesthetician, will perceive the design intensely and will only activate the possible other functions by means of the aesthetic one. Then these former functions are indeed secondary, since one can hardly speak of art if the primary aesthetic function has not been fulfilled. Though the secondary functions could refer to images for propaganda, didactics, cult actions and so on.

According to Sanchez Vazquez, the quality of a work of art is a basic requirement. But who will determine what this quality is? Furthermore, the generalization of the aesthetic function assumes that there are aestheticians, as a democracy assumes that its members are democrats. In introducing the aesthetic function, the spectator is provided with the freedom to take all sorts of objects as objects with an aesthetic function. Obviously, the generalization of the aesthetic function presupposes an aesthetic education.

Sanchez Vazquez formulates point 5 in an over-simplified way. The subordination of the ideological content to the form is no requirement for the realization of the aesthetic function. This is rather a condition for a work of art. The aesthetic function will serve particularly as an approval for the form to prevail. Because of this, the (ideological) content is expressed more powerfully, although it is not highly visible at first glance, and does not come across immediately as ideological content until the mediation of a powerful form. Ultimately, the form itself is ideological and the acceptance of the aesthetic function itself is founded in an ideological way.

Without a clear transition, Sanchez Vazquez's text takes a remarkable turn. His statements on aesthetic function suddenly appear to be made in the context of a bourgeois view of art, which evolved during the last four centuries - particularly during the last one. The concept of the aesthetic function is a historical one and can only be applied to art of the past retrospectively. "It is only because of this that a Negro mask has the right to be exhibited in a European museum or that a Mayan sculpture can enter a museum of modern art as a work of art. From the moment they enter a museum, they do so as works of art and they are appreciated because of their aesthetic function." (Ibid, 114)

We believe that these examples of non-Western art are not chosen very well. As demonstrated in the previous section, the relationship between non-Western - or so-called primitive art - and contemporary art is such that non-Western art can be considered part of the formal precursory movements of contemporary art. However, as far as the perception of art is concerned, contemporary art teaches us to perceive non-Western art according to an aesthetic category which renders all former categories superfluous, even as a source of interpretation.

According to Sanchez Vazquez, this bourgeois view is disturbing because it raises art to the level of the universal and neutral. "All this happens in modern times with the development of the capitalist way of production, and it is the bourgeoisie which raises art to universality and neutrality by means of its corresponding ideology." (Ibid, 114)

Much can be said about the bourgeois reduction of art by confining objects, which have in common universality and neutrality, to museological spaces. But once the concept of "bourgeois view on art" has been advanced, Sanchez Vazquez proceeds with views stated too generally. The following statement is at the very least over-simplified: "The bourgeois conception of art with its aesthetic function took art from the street, from the public forum and separated artistic creation from everyday life. Thus, it has contributed to the privilege of creation and to its removal from broad social fields by deepening the gap between creators and non-creators." (Ibid, 114) We believe that "its aesthetic function" leads to a pan-aesthetic perspective instead. If a possessive pronoun were to be used in relation to the "bourgeois" view on art, than this should be related to "its economic function". In our view, the aesthetic function continues to preserve a revolutionary power, if only by a different way of observation, a change in the habit of perception. Nevertheless, Sanchez Vazquez does not go into this economic aspect. However, the following statement is contrary to the previous one. "The bourgeoisie emphasizes the economic function and in that way, it is consistent with its interests, by acting in agreement with the nature of the system. In relation to the economic function, the artists stress the aesthetic function and in other cases (mainly when they feel committed) they emphasize the ideological-political function." (Ibid, 116) Now the artist does emphasize the aesthetic function, and the bourgeoisie the economic one. Sanchez Vazquez formulates three dilemmas resulting from the confrontation of the economic, aesthetic and ideological-political functions.

The first dilemma - art and revolution - presents the contrast between a revolution in art and the instigation of a social revolution with the aid of art. Revolutions in art are quickly recouped. History demonstrates that social revolutions often assume an aesthetically conservative attitude. Sanchez Vazquez more or less shifts in his definition of the problem. "Revolutionize socially with the aid of art" is quite different from the statement "... the social revolutions are ... conservative as far as aesthetics is concerned." (Ibid, 116)

If one could instigate a social revolution with art (which we seriously doubt), then artists will do so; in other words, the attitude of social revolutionaries has little to do with that. Yet, if the social revolutionary power of art does not succeed in convincing the militants, it will probably not be able to influence the rest of the people either. The concept of revolutionary only makes sense if one specifies its context. Fortunately, Sanchez Vazquez chooses art in a rather Utopian statement with a somewhat credulous undertone, "If the real socialist revolution arises to liberate the people of all forms of alienation and to develop their creative faculty, then the art corresponding to this cannot be a simplistic, pure ideological art, but an art which possesses an inherent value because of its creativity as an expression of that faculty that the revolution should develop in the whole of society." (Ibid, 116) Clearly, the author does not choose socialist realism. In spite of this, Sanchez Vasquez omits the danger that, in a society where all people are freed of all forms of alienation, art will no longer be produced. Moreover, at once the eroded concept of "creativity" comes up. The value inherent to art is by no means dependent on creativity.

In the second dilemma, the relationship between elitist art and art for the masses, Sanchez Vazquez view seems rather naive and unrealistic as well. Capitalism does not offer a solution, but "in a true socialist society the dichotomy of elitist art versus art for the masses should disappear." (Ibid, 116) It is hard to believe that this dichotomy will disappear because of the importance of mass culture. Individual human beings should be able to produce and to perceive art. In both activities, as many individuals as possible should partake. At that point, the reprehensible element of elitism will have been superseded, since belonging to a minority as a consequence of one's own efforts does not seem to be an objectionable elitism.

2.3.2. The function promoting creativity

The third dilemma contrasts ideological art with art without immediate ideological content. In this context, the author emphasizes a new function of art: art as expression of the creative capacity of a human being. This function will surpass the aesthetic function, because its essence refers to creation instead of contemplation. The function that art should fulfil in socialism is "the capacity to inspire others to participate in the process of creation or to socialize creativity." (Ibid, 117) Sanchez Vazquez is clearly inspired by the myth that creativity is present in everybody. Even if this is true, the question is still whether the art of so-called major artists will promote creativity in the general public. With the same argument one could maintain that major artists will inhibit minor artists. Moreover, it can hardly be the function of Picasso's *Guernica* (to mention an example of a painting where the aesthetic function and ideology are present in a very balanced way) to inspire the whole of Spain to start painting pictures. In thinking about art, one should continue to separate the category of creativity as the ability to produce art - or what resembles it - and the category of aesthetic perception as potential to observe in art its intrinsic qualities. The two areas are not necessarily related. Firstly, the gratuitous word "creativity" should only be employed in the context of art in the sense of a stimulus for the creativity of perception. And secondly, as a means to acquire a creative view on the "world" itself. Painting may improve the spectator and bring about, possibly, self- realization as a kind of education. Some may even be inspired to start painting themselves. However, that is not the main purpose of painting. Handbooks like How to paint like Van Gogh seem unnecessary.

The discussion of Sanchez Vazquez's view on the aesthetic function of art has not been prompted by any anti-Marxist feeling. The purpose has merely been to point out that one should be very careful in formulating the possible functions of art, especially because the concept of function is extremely prone to ideology.

2.4. *"Socialist realism" as political dogmatism in the educational function of art.*

2.4.1. *Morawski*

A discussion of "socialist realism" should be part of the exploration of Marxist philosophy of art in relation to the possible functions of contemporary art. After all, socialist realism failed as an art theory because of the primacy of the educational function of art based on politics. The two extreme attitudes to this problem explain very little. On the one hand, one may not really criticize socialist realism due to its status as official Soviet art. On the other hand, in the view of anti-Marxists, this artistic movement does not tell anything. The book Inquiries into the Fundamentals of Aesthetics by the Polish philosopher Stefan Morawski might shed some light on the issue. Morawski succeeds in combining the Marxist humanist tradition with a thorough insight into non-Marxist oriented contemporary aesthetics. In the chapter with the somewhat pedantic title, "The Vicissitudes of Socialist Realism: A Little Lesson in History Which Should Not Be Ignored", Morawski thoughtfully discusses the concept of "socialist realism". He opens it to a new application. Formulated compactly, his decision amounts to the following: the concept of "socialist realism" is beyond reproach so long as it remains in all freedom a matter of artists and art theorists who consider it a possible and sometimes even advisable movement. Both terms of the concept, namely "socialist" and "realism", should remain open to evolution.

Morawski departs from the view that each art theory contains aspects which are relative and dated. Artistic and aesthetic ideas constantly threaten to become dogmatic, and corruption is quick to arise when these ideas are dominated by a privileged social group. "Nevertheless, it remains true that the chronicles of artistic and aesthetic ideas ... lead us to the conclusion that all art theories gradually succumb to a tendency toward doctrinization, and that there has been corruption whenever there has appeared the more or less despotic domination of a privileged social group." (Morawski 1974, 253) If theory predominates and dictates the path art should follow, then new movements are condemned. What is called "academism" is an example of this. The theory often stems from artistic movements which have been surpassed. "Such theory - dogmatic by nature - serves as a brake on the development of art, offering the public false, limited, and obsolete criteria of appreciation." (Ibid, 252)

Morawski demonstrates that "socialist realism" as a movement did not intend to be a dogmatic doctrine, neither as a theory nor as a practice of art. One can only speak of dogmatizing from 1932-34 on. The theory itself came gradually into being in the previous years as a combination of a number of aspects of the artistic developments of Soviet art. "The theory of socialist realism - as the facts testify - was put together gradually, in combination with the irregular development of Soviet art during the first fifteen years of its existence." (Ibid, 259)

A weak point is that the theory was focused on literature because it was impossible to apply it to all branches of art. Not until 1945 did one arrive at a consistent system for visual art because of the codification of Zhdanov's (a defender of dogmatic socialist realism) propositions. In the first decades of Soviet art, masterpieces were created under the influence of "socialist realism". True, "realism" was not as fixed then as in the period '32-'34. Moreover, in the first place, "socialist" should be understood as art focused on a new public. Some wanted to bring novel visual art into the factory or popularize the sense of beauty in the street. Others remained faithful to the painter's easel and the sometimes lyric, sometimes epic means of expression. But all considered the masses as the new heroes and the new spectators. "Socialist realism was not an invention of the devil, tending to destroy artists who claimed their right to the most elementary independence. It was, rather, a product of life, a reflection of truth expressed in myriad ways, and often subject to exaggeration - there were as many manners as searchers (or groups of searchers), but their vision and form were always intended to satisfy the millions of people who were then opening their eyes to art." (Ibid, 257)

An artist's view as Beuys' fits in well with this. Until 1932, there were various artistic groups which formulated an interpretation of socialist realism, but none was fully supported by the party. From 1932 on, socialist realism became an artistic dogma where the party obtained full control of the artists. Before that, various names had been circulating such as "revolutionary realism", "proletarian realism" and "heroic realism".

The basic problems disputed for years were comprised of questions such as "What should art of our decade be?" and "Does existing art correspond with contemporary need?" Lenin devoted himself to the popularization of culture. He demanded an art understandable to the masses. However, contrary to the adherents of the Proletkult, he attached importance to the cultural inheritance of the past. Lunacharsky, who could be called his Secretary of Culture, was a connoisseur of the new artistic movements of his time. Because he defended the ideals of the avant-garde, Lunacharsky often conflicted with Lenin. Yet, ultimately they adhered to the same aesthetic principles, that is, the belief in the existence of a proletarian culture created by artists involved in the revolution and the construction of socialism. Their art was a culture of struggle which would also be followed by workers and farmers rather rapidly, so that they could express their experiences. For Lunacharsky, the source of aesthetic pleasure was comprised of total surroundings (streets, houses, utensils etc.). He dreamt of a world in which the brotherly couple, the artist-technician and the technician-artist, would create the conditions for a revolution in aesthetics. Yet Lunacharsky recognized the formal value of experimental art. However, the inaccessibility of these forms of art annoyed him. The aesthetic hunger of the new public required new food.

Important is that in Lunacharsky's view the two opponent groups could coexist. On the one hand were the experimental artists sympathetic towards the problems of form. On the other were the masses demanding comprehensible art. However, Lunacharsky assumed that, in his writings, he would be able to explain movements such as Expressionism, Cubism and Futurism to everyone. "Such were the opinions of a man who made war with Lenin to defend the rights of art and the right of formal experiment, the man who popularized expressionism, cubism, futurism, and purism in his writings, and demanded, in 1926, in a fine speech entitled 'Let Us be Careful Vis-à-Vis Art', that an appeal to the current aesthetic level of the masses should not be used as a basis for the rejection of difficult works of art which will at some point in the future be comprehensible by and easily accessible to everybody." (Ibid, 262)

Not everybody was as tolerant as Lunacharsky with respect to the complex art of the Avant-garde and its lack of aesthetic pleasure for a non-trained public. For example, Gorky considered West European contemporary art decadent in its desire for new ways of expression. And he was not alone. "In his articles, Gorky was expressing the aesthetic opinions of the majority of Soviet artists." (Ibid, 263) In 1934, in a number of reports, Gorky and Zhdanov arrived at the formulation of these views. According to Morawski, their statements can be summarized in three main hypotheses (Ibid 263-65):

1) Daily life in all its aspects will provide material for art. It is the role of the artist to take advantage of this. It is true that the artistic truths are personal and the consequence of syntheses of contemporary facts. But intuitively, socialism is anticipated by them. These artistic truths are not neutral. They are "tendentious because reality is tendentious."

2) Committed art or ideologically progressive art can be supported by the ways of expression which fit the artist best. The doctrine of realism only appreciates this specific way if, from the ideological point of view, the artistic form is desired and efficient. The form should provide a sort of perspective on ideas.

3) Such art has a positive moral consequence as well. Art can help to understand life in a better way and, what is more, help one live a better life.

One cannot but agree with these points of view. They are in line with a tradition stretching from Aristotle via the Renaissance and Enlightenment to a number of 19th century movements like Romanticism, Critical Realism and Naturalism. Therefore, the fault must lie somewhere else. Morawski states, "I will not deny that its main ideas are presented in generalities; it is that which gives them both their strength and their weakness. Today we know that it is the weakness which has taken over." (Ibid 265)

Shortly thereafter, the guidelines had been determined on the basis of theoretical simplifications. Art theory started to enforce norms instead of describing and synthesizing the state of affairs. Gradually, socialist realism started to become institutionalized as an ideological means of propaganda, wherein deviant views on art were seen as subversive activities. "Zhdanov spoke as a dictator in 1948. He used epithets instead of relying on arguments." (Ibid 267) The principles of socialist realism turned into its opposite. The theory of the moral influence on art was replaced by the theory of the subjection of artistic ideas to the political promotion of propaganda and agitation. No longer was the issue art, but politics, pursuing a cult of glorifying the social. What could be called "Zhdanovism" really amounted to an apology of one single epigonic style. The inventive was condemned as the activity of the bourgeoisie. "The theory of the diversity of genres, styles, and forms was changed into a theory that served as apologist for a single style. 'Epigonism' was openly cultivated. Art was conceived of in an academic and conservative manner. Experiments in new forms were looked upon as diabolical inventions because they were also being carried on by contemporary bourgeois artists, who were damned by definition." (Ibid 268)

This shows the danger of theory (of art) being subordinated to political

Art and Society

purposes imposed from the outside. Moreover, each theory (of art) verges on dogmatism from within itself. Morawski also points out that aesthetic institutions were based on the implicit priority of the educational function of art, which is another cause for the failure of socialist realism. This priority entailed that art had to fulfil ideological functions controlled by the party, whereas "educational" should be understood literally as the contents disseminated by art or the ideas adhered to. Therefore, art had to be communicative instead of "difficult". Rightly, Morawski states that the pedagogical function must never obtain priority. "The priority of the pedagogical function strikes me as deadly to any rational aesthetics." (Ibid 271) This seems certainly to be the case when the pedagogical function amounts to the dissemination of contents.

According to Morawski, the essence of the moral function of art is contained in the educative influence which is the consequence of the creative freedom of the artist and the efforts of the public in confrontation with the degree of difficulty. The "truth of life" should be represented in a variety of adequate aesthetic forms. "The educative influence of a work derives from its content values integrated with its structure and aesthetic values sensu stricto. Each artist has a personal way of discovering the world, of giving it proportion, form, and color; he judges, simulates, and obliges us to think and rethink certain aspects of things, whether it be by recalling them to us or by making us discover them; he charms us by his language and composition. Therein lies the essence of the moral function of art." (Ibid 272)

2.4.2. Berger

John Berger certainly cannot be suspected of conservative prejudices against socialist thought. Therefore, his work might shed light on the artistic failure of socialist realism. Berger praises the efforts of the Russian public to understand visual art. "The widespread public indifference to the fine arts as found in Britain, Germany or the United States would shock even the least privileged provincial in the Soviet Union." (Berger 1969, 58-59) Hence the intense spiritual energy of Russian art appreciation, even when the works concerned are poor, "a spiritual energy which is in marked contrast to the cynicism, hedonism and sensationalism of much art 'appreciation' in the West." (Ibid, 62)

However, according to Berger, the Russian public has an eye for the experience represented in the painting but is not really involved in what the artist actually creates. "When Russians talk about a visual work of art, they often speak with great feeling and sensitivity about the experience contained within it, the original experience of the subject, the experience which has been preserved by being painted. But when they talk about their experience of the work itself, about what the artist has done, they usually talk in banal cliches." (Ibid 62) Whereupon Berger concludes: "Official Soviet policy after 1930 not only re-imposed a sterile academicism on the practice of art, it also blocked the development of the very public which it created for art." (Ibid 63)

According to Berger, this blindness for the medium of painting itself is at the heart of the problems socialist realism has within the visual arts. He points out that the distinction between "naturalism" and "realism" - as for example Lukacs developed for literature - cannot be applied to the visual arts. One can talk analogously about "naturalism", but "realism" will have to remain undefined for the visual arts because "... up to now it has been treated as a stylistic category, descriptive of a certain kind of subject - vigorous and popular - and of a certain way of rendering the appearance of this subject as faithfully as possible without succumbing to the obvious detailed triviality of naturalism." (Ibid 51) Realism has never been considered a model for transmitting a totality. In Berger's view, this is what causes the relative failure of Marxist aesthetics with regard to the visual arts. "Thus we can see the absurdity of measuring realism by the degree of approximation to a current convention of appearances: convention because what we mean by appearances is anyway only a fraction of what is see-able." (Ibid 52) Berger maintains that this is exactly what the Soviet defenders of socialist realism did. For them, realism was a naturalism that would captivate the public. And the secret of this captivation was the choice of the subject matter. In treating a subject, the conscious ideological meaning which that subject implies would be emphasized. Before starting to paint, the manner of treating the subject should have been thought out completely. In that way, the possibilities of the medium itself were completely misunderstood. "It is a question of applying the right dogma to the subject. The act of painting consists of illustrating the "treated" subject in the most transparent way possible. The medium and the function of its limitations are totally ignored." (Ibid 53) Thus, the art of painting became mere illustration.

Berger refutes the statement that for the masses this kind of naturalism - called "realism" - is particularly accessible because it approximates seeing nature. And this statement is based on what we know about the process of perception itself. But even the assertion does not hold that this style will lend itself to agitating propaganda because of its simplicity. Socialist realism has not changed much since the '30s. If it had been truly educative, then at least it should have evolved together with the political consciousness of the masses. "If its effect had been truly educative, one would expect a development in the art corresponding to the development in the political consciousness of the people which the art had helped to bring about." (Ibid 54)

Art should be separated from propaganda. The influence of propaganda is short term and its form conforms to that temporary and urgent function. The purpose of art is to be effective for a long time, and, therefore, art is more complex and will include contradictions. "It is the existence of these contradictions which may allow them (works) to survive ... The new totality which reality represents is by its nature ambiguous. These ambiguities must be allowed in long-term art. The purpose of such art is not to iron out the ambiguities, but to contain and define the totality in which they exist." (Ibid 55) Berger maintains that the educative value of art is precisely to help increase self-consciousness. Painting and sculpture do not lend themselves to propaganda. They are not functional enough for this purpose.

2.5. *The critical theory of the Frankfurt School*

In the discussion of the relationship of art and society, one must deal with the opinions of Herbert Marcuse and Walter Benjamin, two exponents of the so-called Frankfurt School. In the <u>Institut für Sozialforschung</u>, one sometimes pursued an almost reductionist analysis where art was reduced to a reflection on social tendencies. The institute interpreted art as a sort of coded language for social processes, which had to be deciphered by means of critical analysis. However, the emphasis on critical theory and its concepts of dialectics and negation prevented that art analyses from becoming simple exercises in decoding art in reference to social classes. Contrary to the more orthodox Marxist views, the art sociology of the Frankfurt School refused to reduce cultural phenomena to an ideological reflection of class interests. Unlike the Leninist view, art was not only considered the expression of existing societal tendencies, but also the last retreat of the human desire to that society "to come". Horkheimer wrote that art had become autonomous since it took over the role of religion to preserve Utopia. In line with Nietzsche, Stendhal, who said that beauty is "a promise of happiness", was often quoted. Thus, the claims of culture to transcend society were false in one respect, but true in another. Not all of society is bourgeois, as some Marxist too simply maintain. Not all of art refers to a false consciousness or ideology. Adorno pointed out that a dialectic art criticism will respect the principle that ideology per se is not false. After all, that falseness is due to its pretense of corresponding to reality. In Adorno's view, classical art, as well as a more anarchist form of art, is always a means of protest of human beings against dominant institutions - religious as well as others - as well as a reflection of their objective reality.

2.5.1. *Marcuse*

Herbert Marcuse's work was referred to previously in the discussion on socialist realism. Although one can hardly suspect Marcuse of being an anti-Marxist, his hypothesis is clear: Soviet realism conforms to the demands of a repressive state. Realism can be an exaggerated form of critical and progressive art, and, in presenting reality "as it is" against ideological and idealized representations, it even can defend "truth" against falsification and masquerade. In that sense, realism protects transcendence which, in Marcuse's view, is the necessary condition for the existence of art. However, Soviet realism is a different kind of realism. It accepts the established social reality as the only framework for artistic content. It conforms to the existing order without representing the future antagonistically to the present. Since this form of realism freed itself from the domain of the sacred, the unbridgeable gap between essence and existence of human beings does not exist, and it is exactly this that makes up the essence of art. For Soviet aesthetics, the function and content of art is a reflection on reality in the form of artistic images. Because of this, art becomes superfluous: its "promise of happiness" coincides with reality itself instead of transcending it. "Soviet aesthetics ... insist on art while outlawing the transcendence of art. It wants art that is not art, and it gets what it asks for." (Marcuse 1969, 131)

Marcuse particularly dislikes that, in Soviet aesthetics, the social function of art results from the interest in the cognitive function of art. According to Soviet aesthetics, there is no fundamental opposition between art and science. Thus, art will express the "objective truth". However, Marcuse maintains that art is a very special representation of truth. It does not have anything in common with the scientific way of gathering information or with common day-to-day language. And the reason for this is that, "On its deepest level, art is a protest against that which is." (Ibid, 132) This is exactly the political power of art. Art is art to the extent that it produces liberating images which entirely dismiss the prevailing reality. Marcuse even gives a formula for this. "The more totalitarian these standards become, the more reality controls all language and all communication, the more irrealistic and surrealistic will art tend to be, the more will it be driven from the concrete to the abstract, from harmony to dissonance, from content to form." (Ibid, 133)

Marcuse concludes his thesis on Soviet Marxism by stating that "bourgeois" anti-realist artists and the "formalists" are more faithful to the idea of freedom than socialist realist artists are, since Soviet aesthetics rejects in a highly reactionary way those forms of art which precipitate shock, such as "formalism" and the entire structure of "abstract and dissonant" art. The harmonic forms lost their critical transcendence. No longer are they opposite to reality, but a decoration to this reality, an instrument of social coherence. They provide entertainment and embellishment disseminated as they are by the mass media.

In his book <u>One Dimensional Man</u>, Marcuse treats art as what he calls "repressive desublimation". In his view, art became one-dimensional because the antagonism of culture and social reality had been superseded. The oppositional and transcending elements in the higher culture had been destroyed so another dimension could emerge. This did not happen because of the denial of "cultural values", but because of their full incorporation into the established order through mass reproduction and display. The aspect of pleasure became the main characteristic of the products of culture. In line with Brecht, Marcuse maintains that alienation is an important aspect of art. Artistic alienation does not coincide with what is called "alienation" in Marxist terminology. On the contrary, artistic alienation tries to transcend this state of Marxist alienation. Breaking with daily social reality is needed: art should be experienced as a feast. The "other dimension" should not be incorporated. "Whether ritualized or not, art contains the rationality of negation. In its advanced positions, it is the Great Refusal - the protest against that which is." (Marcuse 1964, 63) Yet, incorporation does take place. "The artistic alienation has become as functional as the architecture of the new theaters and concert halls in which it is performed. And here too, the rational and the evil are inseparable. Unquestionably the new architecture is better, i.e. more beautiful and more practical than the monstrosities of the Victorian era. But it is also more 'integrated' - the cultural center is becoming a fitting part of the shopping center, or municipal center, or government center." (Ibid, 65) Rightly, Marcuse points out that oppression has a particular aesthetics. If democratic oppression is the issue, then one should speak of a particular democratic aesthetics. Marcuse attaches justifiable interest to form and its ideological connection. However, it seems that his example does not hold completely. There is no reason to use the concept of "monstrosity" in relation to architecture from the Victorian era and, besides, the general public loves old architecture but boycotts the "artistic alienation" of modern architecture. Mistakenly, Marcuse neglects the existence of a contemporary "higher" culture, which precisely fulfils the function he thinks so necessary. The "repressive desublimation" could ultimately be called the transformation of "the higher culture into a general culture". Time and again art arises which deviates from the "general culture", although the intervals become smaller and smaller, at least for the very specific kind. However, 20th century art will still provoke artistic alienation in the general public. Marcel Duchamp's *Fountain* even causes resentment and anger.

The thought of desublimation does hold for "older" art. "Its incorporation into the kitchen, the office, the shop; its commercial release for business and pleasure is, in a sense, desublimation - replacing mediated with immediate gratification." (Ibid, 72) Since a decrease in the general oppression of the authorities is not attached to this immediate gratification, Marcuse calls it "repressive desublimation".

In his book <u>Konterrevolution und Revolte</u>, Marcuse continues to deal with the ambiguity that art as expression of the ideology of the dominant classes can be conservative. But since there will always be a tension between art and reality, there will always be progressive art as well. Although art shows an imaginary world of dreams, there is a certain subversion connected to it. This is formulated clearly in the following statement: "Artistic alienation turns the artwork, art's universe into something fundamentally unreal - it creates a world which does not exist, a world of pretense, of appearance, of illusion. But in this transformation of reality into pretense, and only into that, the subversive truth of art appears." (Marcuse 1973, 116) A statement like this refers to the aspect of the content of art. But Marcuse extends it. He maintains that the subversive is contained in the form, a rather unusual statement for philosophers writing on the relationship between revolution and art. Moreover, Marcuse points out the importance of what one could call the "withdrawal" of perception. "In this exploration, each word, each color, each sound is 'novel', different - breaks with the familiar context of perception and understanding, sensory certainty and reason, in which man and nature are trapped. Transformed into components of the aesthetic form, words, sounds, outlines and colors are lifted from their normal function and freed for a new dimension of being. That is the capacity of the style a poem, fiction, a painting, or a composition is. The style, embodiment of aesthetic form, subjects reality to another order, where the 'law of beauty' reigns." (ibid 116-17)

There is much to say about the concept of "style", but even more about the concept of "aesthetic form", a term often used by Marcuse. A better term would be "artistic" form. After all, the concept of "artistic" refers to the creator of the form, whereas the concept of "aesthetic" alludes to the manner of perception. However, Marcuse is a political thinker, who does not care much about the terminology of aesthetics. To him, art, more than any other product of human culture, is presumably a phenomenon with the connotation of Utopia, of a new world. Marcuse is hardly interested in the "revolutions"' which take place within the evolution of art. Ultimately, in line with Adorno and Benjamin, he reflects on the function of art but does not analyze it.

In his book Eros and Civilization, Marcuse treats the aesthetic dimension departing from Kant and Schiller. He states that it is not easy to know what Kant exactly means by the "aesthetic" since Kant combines the original meaning of "referring to the senses" and the novel meaning in his time of "referring to beauty, especially in art". Marcuse points out that, in Kant's philosophy, the aesthetic dimension has a central place between sensuousness and rationality. Therefore, in the aesthetic dimension, there should be valid principles for both poles of human existence. In Kant's view, the aesthetic dimension is the medium where senses and rationality coincide and imagination as the "third" mental faculty, mediates. Moreover, the aesthetic dimension is that which constitutes nature and freedom. This twofold mediation is needed because of the omnipresent conflict between the lower and higher faculties of human beings. The conflict is produced by the progress of civilization stemming from the subjection of the sensory faculties to reason and the repressive use of these faculties for social needs. "Thus, the philosophical attempt to bridge sensuousness and reason is an attempt to reconcile both realms of human existence, since these are separated through a repressive reality principle. The mediating function is fulfilled by the aesthetic faculty, which is related to the senses." (Marcuse 1955, 164)

A very important function of the aesthetic component is its attempt to free sensuousness from the repressive oppression of reason. "If indeed on the basis of Kant's theory the aesthetic function becomes the central theme of the philosophy of culture, it is used to prove the principles of a non-repressive civilization, wherein reason is sensuous and sensuousness rational" (Ibid, 164) The development of sensuousness is indeed an important function of the aesthetic especially in its original meaning of "referring to the senses" where the cognitive function is included. Rightly, Marcuse remarks that the cognitive faculty of sensuousness fades more and more to the background because of the prevailing rationalism. In agreement with the repressive view on reason, knowledge became the last purpose of the "higher" non-sensory faculties of the mind. Aesthetics was appropriated by logic and metaphysics. Referring to Baumgarten and Schiller, Marcuse emphasizes the importance of an aesthetics as a science of sensuousness. In that context, the senses acquire an inherent degree of truth, so that an order of sensuousness will appear opposite to logic as the order of reason. In line with Schiller, Marcuse states that an aesthetic culture assumes a total revolution of perception and attitude. In this respect, he reserves a fascinating task for aesthetic education. "Freedom would have to be sought in the liberation of sensuousness rather than reason, and in the limitation of the 'higher' faculties in favor of the 'lower'.

In other words, the salvation of culture would involve abolition of the repressive controls that civilization has imposed on sensuousness. And this is indeed the idea behind the Aesthetic Education." (Ibid, 174). Whether this will bring "salvation" is something else. However, like Marcuse, we believe that aesthetic education need not be an education merely giving access to the Arts or Beauty. It is an exercise for the senses, which, in our world based on intellectual constructions, have almost become rudimentary with respect to their cognitive power.

The Aesthetic Dimension, the last work Marcuse devoted to the aesthetic problem, is particularly interesting. It formulates more explicitly a possible way out of the impasse - a work of art as both affirmative and negatory - where Marcuse's earlier work ended. In a somewhat early article, 'Über den affirmativen Charakter der Kultur', Marcuse states that the receptive aspect still assumes a conservative and affirmative character, because the work of art provides the receiver an illusion of immediate present satisfaction. This is contrary to the classical work of art, where the evoked representation uses the multi-faceted nature of human possibilities as a critical complaint to the contemporary repressive conditions of existence. To Marcuse, the "affirmative character of culture" refers to the characteristics of bourgeois culture. In other words, the culture whose development led to the disconnection of the spiritual-moral world as an independent value of civilization. In this culture, a world will appear which is generally obligatory and unconditionally affirmed. A world which will essentially differ from the factual world of the daily struggle for existence.

In Marcuse's work The Aesthetic Dimension, an honest critique is formulated at the orthodox Marxist view. Important in Marcuse's train of thought is that he attributes political power to the artistic form as such, instead of having it depend on the class it stems from or on the theme expressed in the artwork. This has been expressed in the preface. "But in contrast to orthodox Marxist aesthetics I see the political potential of art in art itself, in the aesthetic form as such. Furthermore, I argue that by virtue of its aesthetic form, art is largely autonomous vis à vis the given social relations." (Marcuse 1979, IX) As autonomous activity, art resists this social relationship, in order to transcend it at the same time. Furthermore, art does not only undermine prevailing consciousness, but common experience as well.

Marcuse becomes imprecise when he states his belief in a standard norm in order to determine bad art or good art. This norm is indeed tempting when reflecting on art from the past, but totally useless with respect to contemporary art. One wonders whether the following statement will even hold for art from the past: "I would say that throughout the long history of art, and in spite of changes in taste, there is a standard which remains constant. This standard ... allows us to distinguish ... between good and bad art ..."(Ibid, X). Perhaps it would be more correct to speak of a relative consensus among specialists.

According to Marcuse, a work of art can be revolutionary in various respects. In a narrow sense, when it represents a radical change in style and technique, for example in the real Avant-garde. However, Marcuse prefers another form of revolution in art. The following statement proves that Marcuse's emphasis on the formal aspect is ambiguous. In his view, the issue is not a defense or a free play of the form of art, but the evolution of a (intrinsic) play of forms as such. Therefore, he criticizes the initial indicated state of being of the revolutionary aspect in art. "But the merely 'technical' definition of revolutionary art says nothing about the quality of the work, nothing about its authenticity and truth." (Ibid, XI) Nevertheless, this century's art criticism judged the quality of contemporary art on the basis of this so-called 'nothing'. Art criticism does not concern itself with authenticity (the relationship author-artwork) nor with truth (the relationship artwork-world). Therefore, Marcuse prefers the view that a work of art is revolutionary if it represents, by means of the power of aesthetic transformation, the prevailing lack of freedom and rebellious powers in the exemplary fate of individuals. In that way, the work of art can crack the mystified and petrified social reality and open up a horizon of change, of liberation. Thus, each authentic work of art can be revolutionary; "subversive of perception and understanding, an indictment of the established reality, the appearance of the image of liberation." (Ibid XI). However, because of this view, a number of problems present themselves. The art critic will be reassured by the notion of "the power of aesthetic transformation." But how does one measure that power? And who will determine what an "authentic" work of art is? Perhaps the artwork is authentic when it is revolutionary! Because ultimately, the revolutionary is more visible than the authentic. The problem will be solved partly if one accepts that the aesthetician will only speak after the art critics do and, therefore, will only be confronted with relatively "good" works of art to reflect upon. Once the quality of the form is guaranteed, Marcuse's following statement makes sense: "revolutionary by virtue of the form given to the content. Indeed the content (the established reality) appears in these works only as estranged and mediated. The truth of art lies in this: that the world really is as it appears in the work of art." (Ibid, 6) The revolutionary component is contained in the distorting form of a given reality functioning as content. However, in this context, Marcuse neglects that the content will change if the form changes. The content does not correspond to a given. The thought that the truth of art is contained in how the world really appears in art is beautiful. How Power tries to represent reality, or even tries to manipulate it, is confronted with another reality which implies more truth. In this way, art acquires a cognitive function. Important as well is that, according to Marcuse, art represents one aspect of reality, which is different from the view that art represents mere fantasy. "The world formed by art is recognized as a reality which is suppressed and distorted in the given reality.' (Ibid, 7)

The inner logic of the work of art leads to another rationality and another sensuousness, which challenge the rationality and sensuousness contained in the dominant social institutions. Marcuse continues to point out the ambiguity of the work of art. On the one hand, the work of art provides an affirmative reconciling factor because a given reality is sublimated. On the other hand, the work remains the bearer of a critical, negating function. In Marcuse's previous work, desublimation was repressive. In The Aesthetic Dimension, he attributes to art a declinatory power in particular because of the process of perception. The transcendence of immediate reality will reveal a new dimension of experience: the resource of a rebellious subjectivity in the spectator. "Thus, on the basis of aesthetic sublimation, a desublimation takes place in the perception of individuals - in their feeling, judgements, thoughts; an invalidation of dominant norms, needs and values. With all its affirmative-ideological features, art remains a dissenting force." (Ibid 7) In Marcuse's view, the critical function lies in the aesthetic form and not in the content. "A work of art is authentic or true not by virtue of its content (i.e., the 'correct' representation of social conditions), not by its 'pure' form, but by the content having become form." (Ibid 8) In this context, Marcuse does not understand "form" as the artistic form, i.e. what an artist actually creates on the canvas with paint, but as content adopting the form "painting". However, he neglects the final phase in the process of art: once a certain content has obtained the "form painting", then this painting itself will produce new content or will at least interpret the content in a different way. Marcuse's criticism of orthodox Marxist aesthetics, where socialist realism is revolutionary by virtue of expressing the contents of the revolution, is too superficial. According to him, the revolutionary component is contained in the "aesthetic form" instead of in the content. This is a reflection on the social situation. The revolutionary quality is not that a socially determined content acquires the form of a work of art (for example paint on canvas), but how the design of the work of art is realized. A work of art is not revolutionary because it is a work of art. How the artist shaped "content" is revolutionary (this is what Marcuse calls the revolutionary in a narrow sense on the basis of "technique"). Yet, a form might be revolutionary because the content acquires a totally different meaning because of the new form. We believe that art can only claim a revolutionary dimension if this is expressed in what the artist does with the elements of form. A great deal of the forms of art Marcuse talks about (paintings, poems, etc.) are often very conservative.

In Marcuse's view, art has been forced to look at the world in such a way that it alienates the individual from his fundamental social existence and action. Thus, art liberates sensibility, imagination and reason in all realms of subjectivity and objectivity. The element of alienation obliges the spectator to develop a counter-consciousness as a negation of the real conformist state of mind. Then, art fulfils a cognitive function. It transmits knowledge in a manner not possible in another language, because of which "it (art) communicates truths not communicable in any other language; it contradicts." (Ibid 10) Art differs from the one-dimensional optimism of propaganda called art within socialist realism because of "the notion which sees art as performing an essentially dependent, affirmative-ideological function, that is to say, glorifying and absolving the existing society." (Ibid 11) Art has its own language and it is only through this language that it sheds light on reality. This dimension does not coincide with the social process of production. "Moreover, art has its own dimension of affirmation and negation, a dimension which cannot be coordinated with the social process of production." (Ibid 22)

Art's domain is wider than the realm of the political struggle for changed consciousness. A "new system of needs" is the goal, which assumes a liberation of the exploitation of sensuousness, imagination and reason. This system cannot coincide with a political, strategic use of language. "This emancipation, and the ways toward it, transcend the realm of propaganda. They are not adequately translatable into the language of political and economic strategy." (Ibid 37)

Marcuse briefly discusses art as a witness of the permanent search for identification by means of discovering the non-identification or the other. Art indeed always endeavors to capture "something" in a different way, and that "something" might be subjective or objective, but it is not sure. Those moments of uncertainty and indecisiveness are connected with the infinite adventure of the human effort to try to understand the self and the world. The "something" claims to be a transindividual view on something, but ultimately it proves only a personal view on that something. Or the other way around: something presents itself as an individual mythology, but it expresses the truth of the role mythology still plays for contemporary man. Art often seeks to grasp the ungraspable, comparable to a child's attempt to catch a soap bubble and the discovery that it is only wet foam, but continuing to grasp the next soap bubble from the air. The constant effort to capture the object with the limited possibilities of the subject is the purpose of the artist. He wants to understand the object but differently than other subjects would or have. After all, only the unicity of this object-capturing gives the artist's effort meaning in the collectivity of subjects. In that way, it acquires a place in the infinite series of random pictures of artists. Marcuse does not use many words for these ideas. He limits himself by stating, "In all its ideality art bears witness to the truth of dialectical materialism - the permanent non-identity between subject and object, individual and individual." (Ibid, 29) Perhaps the concept of "ideality" could be understood here as the infinite series of possibilities to understand reality in part.

"Art cannot change the world" is a thought in line with the thought on the revolutionary autonomy of art: "Art provides an aesthetic dimension which can only be acquired by means of art". An old dream, or better put, a fallacy will disappear. "The basic thesis that art must be a factor in changing the world can easily turn into its opposite if the tension between art and radical praxis is flattened out so that art loses its own dimension for change." (ibid, 35) We believe that art is very sensitive to contextual fluctuation and that it has a tendency to become non-art or no-longer-art or pseudo-art, for example, in the sense of art propaganda (too much content in relation to form) or artistic decoration (too much form in relation to content). Art does not accept a compromise.

A consequence of the autonomy of the revolutionary power of the aesthetic dimension is that the group of spectators has been limited or selected a fortiori, or better put, has selected itself. Marcuse relativizes the concepts of "the people" and "the elite". Like Brecht, he believes that "the people" could be a militant minority. And "the elite" stems from the use of a particular language. Therefore, in Marcuse's view, the task Nietzsche mentions in his <u>Zarathustra</u> can also apply to art, "For all and nobody" may apply as well to the truth of art." (Ibid 31) The design is specific in such a way that the public becomes specific as well. A variety of artists assumes a variety of spectators. The more languages there are, the more people there will be. Fortunately, art transgresses nations.

As stated before, the question of whether art can change society seems an incorrect problem. Of course, it cannot do that. But political revolutionaries do not need to reject art because of this. It would be a shame if such an idealist view would destroy at once the relationship of art to politics. The only consequence one can draw from this is that art should be removed from the socio-political domain in order to be transferred to a socio-cultural world. In other words, the question of whether art could change society should be replaced by the question of whether art could change human beings, or more precisely, whether art has educative value for the individual. If art has an educative function apart from the aesthetic one, then that is already sufficient as social value.

The above quoted thought, that art cannot change the world, is new in Marcuse's work and even causes surprise within his rather abstract utopian mode of thought. The thought is expressed most explicitly in the following statement: "Art cannot change the world, but it can contribute to changing the consciousness and drives of the men and women who could change the world." (Ibid 32)

Thus, art is not the driving force of change in the world, but a school for starry-eyed idealists. This statement seems important because, within Marcuse's mode of thought (whose main concern initially was the social process of change of which thinking about art is only a part), it transfers art's power of change from the political-economical field to the socio-cultural field that is involved in the education of the population. This is a huge shift in Marcuse's thought. "There is in art inevitably an element of hubris: art cannot translate its vision into reality. It remains a "fictitious" world, though as such it sees through and anticipates reality. Thus art corrects its ideality: the hope which it represents ought not to remain mere ideal. This is the hidden categorical imperative of art." (Ibid 57) One could go even further in this argumentation and relativize the objectives somewhat and reduce the potentiality of changing "the world" to "their" world. Departing from the educational ideal, that the more people change their world the more "the" world changes, one attains the same purpose.

As previously stated, it is unclear how Marcuse understands form; his writings on it do not show a thorough knowledge of the artists' concerns nor an insight into contemporary art. However, the following statement could refute this assertion somewhat. "The 'tyranny of form' - in an authentic work a necessity prevails which demands that no line, no sound could be replaced (in the optimal case, which does not exist). This inner necessity (the quality which distinguishes authentic from unauthentic work) is indeed tyranny in as much as it suppresses the immediacy of expression." (Ibid 42) This quote does express the concern of the artist: too many touches of paint on the canvas could make the painting "overdone" in the artist's opinion, so that he has to start all over again. Contrary to what Marcuse states, this does not necessarily have to be a repression of the "immediacy of expression". However, it is Marcuse's purpose to warn against the destruction of form which could arise when one attempts to achieve immediate expression. Such loss of form will result in banality, because of which, Marcuse fears, the opposition against the establishment will disappear. The autonomy of art constitutes itself as a contradictory autonomy. According to Marcuse, this autonomy must be preserved: "When art abandons this autonomy and with it the aesthetic form in which the autonomy is expressed, art succumbs to that reality which it seeks to grasp and indict." (Ibid 49) Therefore, according to Marcuse, the aesthetic sublimation must be preserved forever. That is why he rejects "anti-art", because this will mean self-destruction from the very beginning. "Anti-art" or "non-art" both assume that the present disintegration of reality will prevent a self-contained form or some attempt at meaning. In this context, Marcuse refers to collages, mixed media, or the rejection of each aesthetic mimesis. In Marcuse's view, this fragmented attack on aesthetic form is wrong. He believes that the catastrophe is not so much disintegration as full integration of that which is: the enforced authorized unification. The rejection of the aesthetic form cannot cancel out the difference between art and life. "The exhibition of a soup can communicates nothing about the life of the worker who produced it, nor of that of the consumer." (Ibid 51)

It is a pity to have to conclude this section on Marcuse with the statement that, based on the last quotations, this philosopher of art obviously does not have a good eye for art. Not only because of the last quotation, where the exhibition of a can of soup does not say anything about the life of the artist. (Which, moreover, is not so certain, because if the artist exhibits a can of soup of his favorite brand, we might know more about that artist than we learn about Cézanne when observing his painted apples). But particularly because this spiritual father of the student uprisings in the 1960s is obviously very conservative in his vision on art. What then remains the substance of his theory on the revolutionary element of art? It is an example of the danger which lurks in the division between the art critic, as the judge of concrete works of art, and the philosopher of art, who reflects on the concept of "art". The application of abstract theories becomes dangerous or at least useless if one does not know exactly what the philosopher speaks of.

Marcuse uses the concept of the autonomy of art as an independent "form", which can be the opposite of the prevailing reality precisely because of its independence. However, Marcuse neglects the relative autonomy of what one could call the development of form. He speaks of form as if there are forms independent of other forms, which is valid for existing forms, as well as for forms still developing. The contemporary artist will think more of the autonomous play of these developing forms than of the autonomous form independent of the "prevailing contents". We believe that artists will search for forms which are "anti-banal". However, in order to achieve this, in this century, they have also taken forms from banality. They have debanalized banality instead of having banalized art, as Marcuse feared. Anti-art is no less important as a form than the art it opposes. The most banal in art seems like the manual of how to paint like Van Gogh. Nevertheless, once this painting practice is mastered, one could apply Marcuse's theory to the result of this useful form of recreation.

Be this as it may, Marcuse refers to Benjamin's wonderful statement rightly considered by him a clear rejection of vulgar Marxist aesthetics. "The tendency of a literary work can be politically correct only if it is also correct by literary standards." (Ibid 53) Although Marcuse agrees with the principle, as far as visual arts go, he does not have knowledge of these standards no matter how relative they may be.

2.5.2. Benjamin: loss of aura because of reproducibility

Walter Benjamin was not as educated in philosophy as Adorno, and was less political-philosophically involved than Marcuse. But he was more of an artist, so that his philosophy of art comes across more genuine. In Benjamin's view, the concept of "criticism" means more than exposing the interests of the power structures. Criticism is to discover a hidden truth in a positive sense, and is directed toward revealing essential alternatives to what exists and what could exist as a positive utopia. To Benjamin, art and philosophy are fields where truth, imperceptible by the senses, can be represented in media, which are perceptible. The political-social component shows itself indirectly as well. Because of its technical reproducibility, the function of art changes: its ceremonial constitution gives way to a political one. Indeed, this is associated with what Benjamin calls a loss of aura. Physical shock effects result instead of experiences arising from contemplation. After such a shock, the experiences are reunited. The continuity of what we usually perceive is interrupted. Similarly to an emergency brake in a train, the activity of a shock while experiencing art could stop routine perception. For a moment, art can stop the world one observes, whereupon one moves on with reopened eyes but not necessarily into the direction of technological "progress".

In his article The work of art in the age of mechanical reproduction, Benjamin discusses a problem which fits within the scope of this book. Although we do not completely agree with the elaboration of his hypothesis on a couple of points, his main thought - if specified somewhat and made more topical - is very valuable. Benjamin formulates his central thesis as follows: The public's reaction is not dependent on the question of whether a work of art can be reproduced, but on how the work has been made or designed. The mass reproductions of Picasso's work did not make a conservative public more progressive. And the Chaplin movies make the public laugh because of malicious delight in "the little man" and not because they understand his social position. Benjamin is naive to think that one could "mobilize the masses" with film - the prominent example of non-aura art. Mistakenly, Benjamin sees in movies revolutionary possibilities because they do not require attentive concentration. Rightly, Benjamin does not consider "contemplation" as a means of solving the problems the masses cope with. However, his attitude with respect to "entertainment" as a political means of education is too positive.

It seems doubtful that film could mobilize the masses, although the masses could possibly be sensitized by it in an ethical-aesthetic way. From an educational-philosophical perspective, movies are presently the most important artistic medium, because of their very low threshold and general public's familiarity with audio-visual culture. If the cinema had not had any aesthetic educative influence, one could even state that each attempt at aesthetic education of the general public could be stopped. The problem with painting is that its act of perception is synonymous with "contemplation" and, therefore, assumes attention and duration. Often this is a huge intellectual effort requiring some practice.

In the article under discussion, Benjamin reassesses the concept of "entertainment", usually employed in a negative sense within philosophical discourse. Because of Benjamin's view on and context of "entertainment", he could be considered the precursor of the philosophy of animation. In the 1960s, this concept became popular in the terminology and methodology of social-cultural work.

Benjamin's concept of "aura art" refers to the function of art in a posthistorical period and its inescapable devaluation in the present. The loss of what Benjamin calls "aura" is the loss of authenticity, the totality of all that art originally passed on, from its material permanence up to its historical evidence. All this has been lost because of the reproducibility of art. Benjamin points out how perception depends on history. "During long periods of history, the mode of human sense perception changes with humanity's entire mode of existence. The manner in which human sense perception is organized, the medium in which it is accomplished, is determined not only by nature but by historical circumstances as well."(Benjamin 1973, 224) Presently, this modification of perception is characterized by the decline of aura. Benjamin illustrates this by attributing to the aura of natural objects the cryptic quality of "a once-only appearance at a distance, no matter how close it is". This becomes somewhat clearer when he ascribes the characteristic of permanent unicity to the artistic image. In a reproduction, fleetingness is connected with repetition. The statement: "The adjustment of reality to the masses and of the masses to reality is a process of unlimited scope, as much for thinking as for perception"(ibid 225) seems applicable to the nature of reproducibility of the mass media than to artistic images.

Even Van Dale (Dictionary of Contemporary Dutch) does not give much clarification by defining aura as "a radiation encompassing a human being"; therefore, we will try to explain a number of elements. Aura is either a characteristic of certain objects or a characteristic of a certain way of perception, or these characteristics together. In other words: an aura is a characteristic of a phantom. In the first case - aura is a characteristic of a certain object - the concept of aura could become useful in demonstrating whether a work of art satisfies objectively the best conditions, such as authenticity of color, appropriate veneer, no traces of "overdone painting". In short, a complete work, which satisfies the artist objectively. If the aura is a characteristic of a way of perception, then the so-called "subjective willingness" or the susceptibility of the spectator will play a role, and so will the total context at the same time: the space where the work is exhibited, the lighting, possible other works around it, etc. Combination will only increase the aura character of an experience. It goes without saying that these characteristics will be present sooner in a "real" work of art than in a reproduction.

In Benjamin's work, the concept of "reproduction" is vague as well. The next statement is disputable: "An ancient statue of Venus, for example, stood in a different traditional context with the Greeks, who made it an object of veneration, than with the clerics of the Middle Ages, who viewed it as an ominous idol. Both of them, however, where equally confronted with its uniqueness, that is, its aura."(ibid, 225) No doubt, medieval man might have seen a Roman copy and might even have noticed that the Greek sculpture was in bronze and the Roman one in stone. However, the concept of aura becomes somewhat clearer because Benjamin situates the work of art in its function as cult object. In that way, a "nearby distance" could be understood as the religious concept of "inapproachability". But it is wrong to state that cult sculptures will be unique, except in the meaning of "delightful". The concept of "unique" is connected with the issues of the Avant-garde and not with issues related to the creators of cult sculptures. The "unique" even plays a role in the economy of art, because uniqueness is one of the determinants for financial value.

Benjamin observes that the work of art can never detach itself completely from its ritual function. As a matter of fact, one can speak of a beauty cult as a profane form of secularized rituals. According to Benjamin, this is no longer possible if the work of art is the result of its technical reproducibility. In this context, he has film in mind.

Yet it is important to distinguish between the artwork and the reproduction, because Benjamin interchanges the reproduction and the artwork produced on the basis of a reproduction. Reproduction is not the same as multiplication - a concept related to Pop art but never used by Benjamin. A reproduction reproduces an original, thus, it is by definition imperfect (has a less objective possibility to possess an aura), or, in milder terms, is of a different quality than the original. There will always be an intermediate stage between original and reproduction, which engenders the modification of quality (and, objectively, a decline in aura). At the same time, the reproduction often has a different size than the original. Benjamin provides a short history of reproducibility. "In principle a work of art has always been reproducible. With the woodcut graphic art became mechanically reproducible for the first time. During the Middle Ages engraving and etching were added to the woodcut; at the beginning of the nineteenth century litography made its appearance." (Ibid 220-21)

Graphic techniques (woodcut, copper plate, etching and lithography) are not reproduction techniques because there is no original. The wood block, metal plate or stone are not originals. In contemporary art, these techniques are used for the particular "aura" which might result connected to the uniqueness of the material. In this context, one could speak of a copy. A successor of these 20th century techniques, the litho offset, offers both possibilities: reproduction by means of a photographic reflection of an original drawing or immediate drawing on a film instead on a stone. The litho offset technique can realize 7,000 copies per hour of the same quality (same aura?). The aesthetic eye does not see any difference in the results of the lithograph. However, the eye of the printer could trace technical differences. But perhaps these technical comments will cause loss of aura in the philosophy of art.

Even if copies do not demonstrate any decline in aura on the basis of their material qualities, this may still be the case if we consider the "aura" as a characteristic of the manner of perception. Uniqueness, not rarity is then a factor. If one encounters a reproduction of the same artwork in dozens of places, a heavy decline in aura will occur. In Benjamin's view, the Dadaists turned the work of art into a missile. Thus, they achieved "a relentness destruction of the aura of their creations, which they branded as reproductions with the very means of production."

The Dadaists made the artwork into the center of scandal. It should openly offend. Benjamin takes a rather conservative stand with respect to Dadaism. Dadaism can only offend a public which is in favor of the "Fine Arts" and the concurrent social values. To a public open to Dadaism, these works are exactly the proof that the aura can arise in the most banal objects, on the condition that the artist provides an environment where the object will thrive.

2.6. *The Althusserian criticism of ideology*

Louis Althusser is particularly known as a political philosopher. Nonetheless, he wrote a number of interesting texts on art. Moreover, his approach to the concept of ideology is applicable to the analysis of art and can even be considered a possible function of art. In particular Hadjinicolaou refers to Althusser in his attempt to formulate a new view on art and art history from a materialistic philosophy.

2.6.1. *Althusser*

In his <u>Lettre à André Daspre</u>, Althusser outlines concisely what the task of art is, "Art (I mean authentic art rather than the average or mediocre work) does not provide knowledge in a strict sense, thus it does not replace knowledge (in the modern sense: scientific knowledge), but what it offers does preserve, nevertheless, a certain specific relationship with knowledge. This relationship does not imply identity but difference. Let me explain. I believe that the distinct property of art is that it 'reveals something to us', 'makes us perceive something', 'makes us feel something' which alludes to reality." (Althusser 1980, 10) What art gives us in the form of "seeing", "observing" and "feeling" (not the form of knowledge) is the ideology from which it stems, from which it releases itself and to which it alludes. Art has a very special relationship with ideology. With respect to this, Althusser is not clear at all. This is particularly evident in statements such as, "I do not count real art among ideologies." (ibid, 9) In fact, he randomly situates art as an "allusion" to reality, between science as systematic knowledge and ideology as inevitable illusion. Althusser considers art a discourse of intertwined aesthetic and ideological elements.

He wrote different articles on the Italian painter Cremonini, including a text as a reaction to the statements of spectators and critics who classified Cremonini's work as "expressionism". However, Cremonini's work is certainly not expressionist. The term "surrealism" seems more appropriate. Cremonini creates works which refer to dream images where the figures expand vaguely and, thus, never can be grasped. That sort of dream expression (as a form, dreams do not have to be necessarily represented) is a post-war descendant of surrealism.

However, Althusser would not be satisfied with the classification of "surrealism" or "neo-surrealism", and neither does his writing say much about the form itself. He calls this type of art criticism a commentary on aesthetic consumption based on a judgement of taste. A different view is needed from the one which approves or disapproves "objects". Such a view will perceive Cremonini as the "painter of abstractions". He paints relationships which relate objects, places and times to each other. In Althusser's opinion, "abstractness" is not an imaginary non-existent form, but the "painting of relationships between objects and human beings". Cremonini paints similarities among rocks, plants, animals, people while indicating precisely their differences. His work is inspired by a certain ideology about the direct relationship between man and nature. The order he represents is an order of descent, implying the true relationship of man and nature; this order serves as an example for the relationship of the artisan to his tools and his product. If Cremonini's faces are transformed, this is not because they have an individual form, or a form of subjectivity in which "human beings" recognize immediately that man is the subject, the center, the author, the "creator" of his objects and his world. In that sense, Cremonini breaks with humanist ideology. Because of this anti-humanism we can, "We cannot recognize ourselves (ideologies) in his paintings. And since we cannot 'recognize' ourselves in them we are able to get to know ourselves in the specific form art - in this case painting - provides us." (ibid, 46). It is not immediately clear what the "specific form" is which art will offer in order to provide self-knowledge. Supposedly, this must be understood similarly to the role Brecht attributes to the effect of alienation.

Althusser gives an interesting reading of the oeuvre of a painter. However, a weak point is his considering that reading as absolute, instead of one of many possible interpretations. At the same time, he employs what he blames the critics for, namely, "an esoteric terminology only understandable to initiates." (ibid, 47) The meaning of the sentence, "The prolonged shriek of mute stalks, a flower unfolding sharply, expanding as a praying bird in the sky" escapes us. (ibid, 37) Moreover, the reading of Cremonini's paintings shows much affinity with the characteristics Althusser contributes to the notion of "ideology". An ideology is the expression of the imaginary relationship of human beings to their actual life conditions. Thus, an ideology expresses how human beings experience, see, feel and undergo reality. The imaginary relationship of human beings to their world does not originate in the individual but in social-institutional practices. Because of an ideology, the individual has the illusion of seeing himself as a subject. This illusion is inevitable. What Althusser describes as Cremonini's anti-humanism appears to be his own anti-humanism, in the sense of a rejection of the foundation of theoretical humanism, namely subjectivity as real "cause" of history. Althusser departs from Lacan in his view on the subject as the core of the theory of ideology. Thus, the individual is always a subject, because he has always been rooted in ideological practices. The subject is constituted by mirroring the rules of behavior. As a matter of fact, this reference to Lacan affirms the statement that for Cremonini, the term "surrealism" is better than "expressionism".

Althusser maintains that each work of art stems from a project which is aesthetic as well as ideological in nature. Like every other object, a work of art can turn into an element of ideology. In other words, it may become part of a system of relationships which make up the ideology. This ideology reflects the (imaginary) relationships which members of a social class maintain with the structural relationships constituting life conditions. This is how Althusser expresses it, "Perhaps even the following thesis can be advanced: if it is the specific function of the artwork to reveal the reality of the existent ideology (of one of its forms) by creating a distance regarding it, the effect of the artwork should be directly ideological; therefore, it has much closer relationships with ideology than any other object; and it is not possible to review only the specific aesthetic properties of the artwork without accounting for its special relationship to ideology, that is, without accounting for the artwork's direct and inevitable ideological effect." (ibid, 47)

Althusser suggests two ways of elaborating on an aesthetic theory. If art is an ideological practice, it will have a conservative function. In order to prevent this, one should try to discover how art can produce a subversive consciousness as a practical ideology. Furthermore, an aesthetics should be developed where the distinction between the relationship artwork - ideology is specified in such a way that a demystification of the falsehood of immediate consciousness will become possible by means of art. Hadjinicolaou elaborates on that second alternative.

2.6.2. Hadjinicolaou

The book <u>Histoire de l'art et lutte des classes</u> by Nicos Hadjinicolaou is an application of Althusser's philosophy to the history of art. At the end of the introduction, Hadjinicolaou writes explicitly that the subject of his study is not aesthetics but the theory and practice of art history (Hadjinicolaou 1977, 14). Nevertheless, his book is important for this study. It deals in particular with the role which art plays for a human being, and puts aside a number of prejudices concerning the perception of art.

Hadjinicolaou mentions three obstacles which prevent a definition of the object of the history of art. Although the problem of art history as a science is not the same as the problem of the possible ways of perception from the perspective of the function of art, it seems important to verify these obstacles.

The first obstacle concerns the artists' influence. According to Hadjinicolaou, it does not make sense to take the creators of images as a point of reference in explaining their works. The history of artists does not coincide with the history of the creation of images. A work of art cannot be explained by facts about artists. However, three perspectives on art history do so. Firstly, the psychological explanation: "Perhaps the analysis of the 'motives of artistic creation' might be an interesting object; it might even be the object of scientific research. But such an analysis is not able to substitute for the statement of a picture." (ibid, 32)"

The same can be said about the second perspective, the psychoanalytic explanation. "The psychoanalytic perspective can resolve satisfactorily some problems which occur with respect to art and artists; however, it fails to understand other problems completely." (ibid, 36) Psychology and psychoanalysis employ art as a document in order to research the creators of images.

The explanation by "environmental" components is a third form where the artist-creator is studied instead of the work of art. Although Hadjinicolaou overstates his view, he points out an important aspect of the history of art which has been neglected so far, that is, the ideological and class-related aspect of art. However, Hadjinicolaou considers his perspective the only true method, which is a weak point. One could criticize Taine's theory of environment, but one cannot reject it completely. Taine concentrates on three totalities to which, in his view, each image belongs:

1) the totality of works produced by the artist;
2) the school of artists or the artist family in the same country and time;
3) the general spiritual and moral climate.

Hadjinicolaou believes that Taine's view corresponds to the ideology of the liberal bourgeoisie. However, these totalities do not really exist; they are present in an ideological conception of society and production of images. We agree with Hadjinicolaou that these are not "totalities", but disagree that these three aspects would not have any influence on the production of a work of art. A similar ideology can be expressed in various forms. Each individual is influenced by his personal history, and there is not real continuity nor determined causal connection in the oeuvre of one artist. Conversely, in most oeuvres one can follow very precisely the development of form, even if the work evolves between being abstract and figurative. The concept of "evolution" is often on the lips of artists. The concept of "artist's school or artist's family" is somewhat obsolete, but ultimately an apprentice-artist will start in a certain school, with a certain professor, at a certain point in time. This is even the case for the artist-autodidact albeit in another system of education. Geographically, the "same country" has been replaced by "international" today. In the recent history of art, the influence of temporary (five years or so) movements has been demonstrated often. The movement of the "Neue Wilden" was a clear evidence of this and conceptual art as a movement made many a brush dry out. And these molds for form, so to speak, permit several ideologies.

The second obstacle Hadjinicolaou notices concerns the history of art as part of the history of civilization. The images are reduced to a totality called "spirit", "culture" or "society", which leads an absolutely autonomous life. In the domain of these theories, a relatively autonomous history of the production of images is inconceivable.

A third obstacle is the view of art history as a history of works of art. This view eliminates any way of perception wishing to transgress the framework of observation and the analysis of "works of art" understood as an autonomous series with its particular history. Attention is paid especially to the form (Wölfflin's school), the structure (Riegl and the structuralists), and the concrete work (the neopositivists).

We believe that Hadjinicolaou's three obstacles could be criticized beyond his reproach that they fail to account for the "class struggle". How Hadjinicolaou understands "ideology" and "pictorial ideology" is a more interesting exploration. Referring to Althusser, he departs from the point of view that, in an ideology, the real relationship of human beings to their real conditions of existence are inevitably colored by the imaginary relationship; a relationship expressing a will (conservative, conformist, reformist or revolutionary), or even an expectation or nostalgia rather than describing a reality. Moreover, each ideological representation is a "representation" of reality, which is indeed an allusion to reality but which will produce at the same time an illusion. Thus, ideology provides human beings with a certain "knowledge" of their world, or rather it allows them to "recognize" themselves in their world, while, in fact, they "misunderstand" that world.

Hadjinicolaou understands the "ideology of the artist" as "The relatively coherent overdetermined entity of regional ideologies (aesthetics, politics, morals etc.) which forms the artist's personal 'credo', his 'world view'." (ibid, 90). The "world view" or "personal ideology" of the artist is different from the ideology of his works. The artist has a particular ideological perception of his work. Therefore, the "consciousness" he has of his work belongs to the aesthetic ideology of the artist as part of his overall ideology. This is not the same as (scientific) knowledge about the work. From this it follows that the political-social ideology of an artist does not necessarily correspond with that of his works. An artist with progressive political opinions could be a producer of conservative works without knowing this and vice versa.

Inevitably, in Hadjinicolaou's work the concept of "style" arises. In his view, Antal is the first art historian to define the concept of style adequately and to demonstrate that each style is originally the style of a class or part of a class. He quotes him as follows, "If we understand each style as a specific combination of thematic and formal elements, then the thematic elements enable a direct transgression to the general worldview, to philosophy, from which the images involved derive... The formal elements, for their part, are ultimately likewise dependent on prevailing philosophies; however, their relationship is less direct and can only be clearly distinguished after the primary relationship has been understood... But the audience of a period is by no means unanimous as far as their view on life is concerned and it is exactly this diversity of opinions within the various layers that explains the coexistence of the various styles in one and the same period. In its turn, this diversity reaches back to the fact that what we call audience is not a homogeneous body but separated in various often antagonistic groups." (ibid, 101)

Hadjinicolaou remarks that the concepts of "outlook on life", "philosophy" and "philosophy of life" have to be understood as equivalents to the Marxist concept of "ideology". This could mean that Hadjinicolaou sometimes merely deals with concepts. In his terminology he defines style, "As a specific connection of formal and thematic picture elements, which is one of the particular forms of the entire ideology of a social class." (ibid, 103) Thus, according to Hadjinicolaou style is nothing but a "pictorial ideology" (idéologie imagée). That concept he understands as: "... a specific connection of formal and thematic picture elements through which human beings express how they relate to their conditions of existence: a connection which is one of the particular forms of the encompassing ideology of a class." (ibid, 105)

Obviously, the ideology of the dominant classes cannot coincide with the ideology of the dominated classes. And if one defines "image production" as on the ideological level, then it follows that what is valid for ideology in general is also valid for the pictorial ideology. As a consequence, different social classes also have different pictorial ideologies. Theoretically, each class or its part "should" have its typical pictorial ideology. In fact, these matters are somewhat more complicated, for "a) In history, classes existed without any 'particular' pictorial ideology, because they lacked a production of pictures entirely. The reason is that the need of a production of pictures in itself corresponds to a certain ideology and a certain social position. b) The pictorial ideology or ideologies of the prevailing classes pervade extremely powerfully the picture ideologies of the dominant classes, sometimes to such an extent that they denature these completely." (ibid, 110-11) In most cases, images are products in which the dominant classes in particular recognize themselves.

The question arises as to what pictorial ideologies contemporary art belongs. Hadjinicolaou does not say one word about modern art or avant-garde art. One thing seems obvious, namely that the pictorial ideology of avant-garde art is limited to a small part of a class. Reference should be made to what in France is called "the intellectual", who would as a rule adopt a leftist attitude (Erwald 1978, 52). In connection with our subject, one wonders whether or not modern art belongs to the dominant ideology, which is antagonistic to the pictorial ideology of the dominated classes. If that is the case, it would be unfounded to want to involve the general public by any means in this pictorial ideology. Then each attempt to aesthetic education is a hidden form of repression, an enforcing of a "must" which is not even needed in a theoretical sense.

Another possibility is that modern art as the collection of successive avant-garde movements does not belong to the pictorial ideology of the dominant classes. Then modern art is the protest rich in imagery, an iconoclastic fury so to speak against the pictorial ideology of the establishment. In that case, this pictorial ideology limited to few must be opened to a larger public on the basis of solidarity and protest against the dominant class. In this respect, we believe that kitsch, folk art, "bad taste", is closer to the avant-garde art of the "ugly" or the anti-taste than to the bourgeois taste of distinction, the collective enemy. There will then be a basis to have aesthetic education as a general educational goal. That the bourgeoisie appropriates the revolutionary pictorial ideologies is an economic matter. The continuous power of corruption of all that manifests itself as the other, as "anti" belongs to the ideology of the bourgeoisie as dominant class. The bourgeoisie will constantly capture the weapons of the enemy, i.e. critical images, as loot (a term used with regard to the acquisition of that rare work of art which has not proven overcostly) and will hang it as a trophy on the wall.

In the same spirit, Hadjinicolaou questions pictorial ideology as a form of knowledge. With this he does not mean the knowledge necessary to create a work of art, nor the normative view on the educational role art should fulfil. Obviously, as far as the latter is concerned, Hadjinicolaou believes that art plays a far more important role than the educational one. According to him, the function of art is to reveal the ideological view with its dual aspect of recognition-misunderstanding and illusion-allusion with regard to "reality". Thus, pictorial ideology and scientific knowledge do not coincide. The task of image production (a term he prefers to "art" which refers to the broad view on the nature of images, thus to the fact that he puts high art on a par with low art) is not to pass on scientific knowledge. However, pictorial ideology should do so. It should be understood as "the essential characteristic of objects and facts which belong to the realm of image production." In order to deepen the concept of pictorial ideology, Hadjinicolaou has to distinguish between positive and critical pictorial ideology. He understands this as follows, "We understand 'positive pictorial ide-

ology' as the pictorial ideology of a work which does not have a conflicting relationship with other types of ideology of which it contains certain elements. This
positive and non-conflicting relationship can go as far as glorifying other types
of ideology in the pictorial ideology (which is the case in all political, religious
allegories etc.) However, with 'critical pictorial ideology' we mean a work's pictorial ideology, which relates critically to other types of (non-pictorial) ideology
of which it contains certain elements. This criticism expresses itself in how the
subject of the work has been treated." (ibid, 184). Hadjinicolaou states that if the
passing of knowledge must be an issue in image production, one should speak of
"sensory" knowledge. This knowledge only becomes scientific knowledge
because of the mediation of an historian.

A fundamental problem Hadjinicolaou raises is that of the relationship
between discourse and object of discourse: the pictorial ideologies. In this connection, he refers to the semiologist Marin, who considers this relationship the
ontological foundation of art history as a science. First, because it is language
"of" something (pictorial ideology) which is not be a language itself or in any
event "is" in a different way. And secondly, because it is language "about" something which remains necessarily outside of language and which presents itself as
a challenge to language from the very beginning. An illustration of how
Hadjinicolaou understands "pictorial ideology" is his identification of this concept with Marin's concept of "manner of painting" (Marin 1979).

The art historian should do more than interpret a discourse; he should
explain it. In a work, he has to recognize the type of necessity which determines
it and which cannot be reduced to one meaning. Hadjinicolaou points out that
the necessity of a work is based on the multiplicity of its meanings. To explain a
work means to recognize and to discern the principle of such diversity. A work
is not a unity created by intention. It is created from very determined conditions.

So far, all statements by Hadjinicolaou steer toward the problem of the
object of art history. We dealt in particular with those aspects which are applicable to the question of the function of art and the possible aspects of the situation
of the spectator. Even more interesting is the chapter which Hadjinicolaou
devotes to an aesthetics or, to remain within his terminology, to an "aesthetic
ideology". He maintains explicitly that apart from the pictorial ideology of each
work there is no such thing as an aesthetic effect. "Each object, each human
product (entirely apart from the importance attributed to it) considered, heard or
felt, evokes reactions ranging from pleasure to disgust, depending on the relationship between the aesthetic ideology of the spectator and the pictorial ideology of the work." (Hadjinicolaou 1977, 213)

According to Hadjinicolaou, the aesthetic effect is nothing but the pleasure the spectator experiences when he recognizes himself in the pictorial ideology of the work. Obviously, the history of reception becomes of great importance in analyzing the pictorial ideology. Countering the idealistic question "What is beauty?", Hadjinicolaou poses the materialist question "When and why does what type of person experience this work of art as beautiful?"

We would like to add two objections to this enlightening theory. First, Hadjinicolaou suddenly attaches great importance to the judgement of the spectator. Initially, he argues colorfully that methods of research which give data about the artist are not valid because they do not inform one about the work of art but about the creator. Next, he comes up with the spectator as a deus ex machina who becomes indispensable in analyzing the pictorial ideology. In our time, something like that is possible with the research techniques of the social sciences. But what is the value of a history of reception? Such a history will usually be the history of commentary of specialists. This will imply more or less that masterpieces are discussed (he gives the *Mona Lisa* as an example). However, Hadjinicolaou emphasizes that his method refers to low as well as high art.

A second objection is that his theory - "taking pleasure in an image and recognizing oneself ideologically in the pictorial ideology of that work are one and the same" - only seems to concern the aspect "pleasure" in the sense of to like, be attracted to etc. His question "What is beauty" could be stated more succinctly as "What do I think beauty is?" In short, his theory holds for these kinds of statements but not for a definition of quality. The general public limits itself to the category of "to like". Specialists such as art critics, art historians etc. are also supposed to be able to determine the quality of works they do not like and in whose pictorial ideology they do not recognize themselves. Thus, Hadjinicolaou's theory is not completely applicable to these specialists.

Hadjinicolaou's insights are explicatory of the position of the spectator. After all, these insights explain the attitude of the general public, which will initially only appreciate art in which they recognize themselves ideologically. Moreover, art receives the important function of being conscious of ideologies by means of the reading of the pictorial ideology of the work. The transformation has to come about by means of a medium with an eye for this aspect of art. Johnson writes about Althusser's aesthetics: "The contention that art allows us to 'see' ideology as an effect does not go very far at all as an analysis of the enlightening capacity of the artwork. Althusser's 'us' can only refer to the scientific critic. Only a recipient able to interpret the work of art in the light of a knowledge of the real relations which govern the ideological instance can recognize the non-ideological character of the authentic work of art." However, we cannot agree with Johnson completely as she concludes: "Only an already enlightened recipient is able to suggest that the internal absences within the work reveal that ideology has a relation to something outside itself: the real condition of social existence. Art, on this viewpoint, teaches us nothing we don't already know." (Johnson 1984, 126)

Although we are convinced that the wealth of interpretation depends to a great extent on the wealth of the interpreter, we believe that art can teach us something we did not know before. Even if that were limited to the insight that what we knew already is stated clearer or in a different manner through the specificity of the form of the artwork. Hadjinicolaou is very determined about that. On the one hand, because he continuously emphasizes that form and content cannot be separated. On the other hand, because he specifies clearly that the concept of pictorial ideology cannot be compared to the concept of ideology in general. A pictorial ideology is irreducible. "If one equates it (the pictorial ideology) or reduces it to ideology then one makes the fundamental mistake of ignoring the specific character of the pictorial ideology." (Hadjinicolaou 1977, 212)

That specific character gives art the exact function of revealing ideology in an extraordinary way, or better put, in an indirect way. Because of this, the mediator can discuss ideology in a critical non-dogmatic way. The spectator may experience heightened awareness of his particular ideology and other ideologies. The mediator can direct the confrontation between the pictorial ideology and the ideology of the spectator. The purpose of this is to make the work comprehensible, to discuss the personal ideology of the spectator critically, or to just exchange thoughts about the multitude of ideological perspectives.

3. ANALYTIC PHILOSOPHY

After the psychologically and sociologically colored theory of art in the previous chapter, we will turn to "pure" philosophy of art in the next three chapters. We will start with analytic philosophy, not because of chronology or some personal preference, but because the introduction to this field will give us a chance to discern a number of descriptions of concepts. There are two fields, analytic philosophy of language and structuralism, where language is central of interest to study - among other things - art in a philosophical way. In the chapter on structuralism the phenomenon of art will be analyzed as a linguistic phenomenon, and linguistic methods will be explored in order to develop a grammar of the various forms of art. Conversely, the field of analytic philosophy of language intends to increase the insight into art based on analysis of how one speaks of art. The problem of value judgements is at its center, but qualifying statements also play a role, such as "this is a work of art", and the old problem of the essence of art is fully exposed. This field rejects the essentialist descriptions of philosophers labeled as idealists. An "idealist" like Croce is often targeted.

Analytic philosophy of language provides the opportunity to explore the thorny question of "What is art?". However, Van Haecht (Van Haecht 1978, 92-93) is probably right in stating that such an approach seems scientific but does not achieve anything. In spite of the quest for accuracy, it is striking that there are many unfounded statements in the writings of analytic philosophers. Although empiricism belongs to their tradition, there are often signs of a lack of empirical experience. For example, Walter de Pater states, "As Eric Torres formulated, the art critic should be a lover of art. He does not merely record; he is a fan. Perhaps outside of art one can evaluate without pleasure or disgust but in art this is impossible. Even the judgement that something is aesthetically mediocre implies an emotional reaction." (De Pater 1970, 141) Without claiming that a judging person is beyond any emotional effect - that is a psychological issue - there is equally no reason to assume that art criticism should be based on an emotional component. Moreover, it is conceivable that an art critic could hate art. This is neither a contradiction nor an impossibility.

The next statement is no doubt often on the lips of art dealers. However, for an analytic linguistic philosopher it is a peculiar method to determine what a "real work of art" is. "If someone decides to buy a painting the right thing to do is not to buy at first sight. The buyer should return several times and if the painting still fascinates him after about five times, then there is an indication that he is on to a real work of art. The basis for this test is that preference or disgust (I like blue) will dominate in the beginning, then will loose its power after a certain extent of contact, while one never will get enough of the real aesthetic. Only the real work of art will never grow tiring." (Ibid, 144-145) That sustained and repeated seeing is the test to control the quality of a work of art is difficult to prove. In art as in love, first sight is delicate. This durability test needs an expert's eye, a trained eye, a coded gaze. Otherwise the solution to a large part of our problem has already been given: a real work of art will never grow tiring. And aesthetic education can be limited to seeing a painting about five times.

Pater's view on the role of culture in determining the value of art deserves comment. This is especially true when he speaks of the possibility of mutual appreciation of the Zulu culture and the Inuit culture with regard to works of art as "artistic" products. He links the role of "art" in both cultures immediately to our Western vision of art: "But why would this be strange? There are Europeans who have a taste for both. The amazement arises from the (perhaps unconscious) assumption that Inuits do not know enough about the Zulu lifestyle. But once they would know enough about it, I am sure that they will be able to enjoy Zulu works (of art), just like we find satisfaction in Etruscan works. The only thing necessary is a certain degree of education." (Ibid, 161) Obviously, De Pater does not understand that "education" could mean "westernization" in this context, and that Western appreciation of art from other cultures is a form of intellectual colonialism. Moreover, to have a (European) taste for art is in fact a Western concept. Neither the Zulu nor the Inuit would call his products "art" as Europeans do; they see such objects in their religious or social context.

With these three examples of "nonsense" within an analytic linguistic oriented text, we do not want to denigrate this approach to art. De Pater also makes moving statements about the importance of education for experiencing art. Rightly he points out the importance of repeated seeing as the only sound method. "One could always invite the other to look again and again, hoping he will have the experience which we call epiphany but it will not always happen to everybody." (Ibid,167)

We wish to draw attention to the over-simplified use of concepts while speaking about art. Art is one of the many products of human beings, nothing more, but nothing less. If analytic philosophy of language could make any attribution, then it is that appeal for austerity.

3.1. *What is art?*

3.1.1. *Not all art is identical. (Gallie)*

In his text The Function of Philosophical Aesthetics, William Gallie understands "philosophical aesthetics" as analytic linguistic criticism of what he calls traditional or "idealist aesthetics". He formulates the task of this philosophical aesthetics as follows: "It might be suggested that the job of philosophical aesthetics is to examine the main kinds of comparison and analogy found useful in criticism, with a view to determining as exactly as possible the points at which they cease to be illuminating and in fact give rise to contradictions or confusions." (Elton 1954, 29) Thus research is directed towards the main kinds of comparison and analogy insofar as they are useful to criticism. The emphasis is on determining as exactly as possible which parts no longer appear to clarify as a consequence of the comparison, but cause contradiction and confusion instead. In all respects, this is a useful though somewhat abstract formula to fight the babble of tongues in the realm of art.

According to Gallie, the idealist view that the true work of art is an internal image shaped in the mind of the creator or the spectator results from the confusion between "the value and the existence of a work of art". The true work of art is what one starts from in order to enrich his mind. Gallie's statement includes more than a mere refutation of the idealist view. The question of what a work of art is or is not is too often mistaken for the problem of evaluating the quality of a good work of art, in other words, of what is worthy of being called art. To decide what is art is one of many questions about being. Something is or is not art. In this respect, the artistic realm may exist as a transgression, but it is certainly the task of a philosophical reflection on art to formulate a theory about this. In contemporary art, the quality of what is described as art is determined by art critics. Ancient or non-European art is judged by art historians or other experts.

In the view of essentialists, an analytic linguistic approach is at the very least appropriate. Essentialists are in the bad habit of stigmatizing art as good, real and true - or in the opposite case as bad and untrue - if art does not fulfil the alleged essential characteristics. Most philosophers of art who advance the division real-unreal as a value judgement are not particularly open to the avant-garde. Thus, their statement "this is art" does not say much about the quality of the object.

Because of revolutionary interventions, the classification of what is an object of art or an artwork changes constantly. Therefore, Gallie wonders how it is possible that idealist aesthetics relate the notion of art to only one object in spite of the ongoing movements in the artworld. An analytic linguistic approach could undo many misunderstandings by simply analyzing the concept of "art". Perhaps then, for example, unrelated forms of art such as constructivism (Neo-geo), post-expressionism and conceptual art could no longer be compared to each other within contemporary art. After all, only within a certain movement is such a comparison possible.

3.1.2. Objects interpretable by the public. (Sharpe)

Robert Sharpe is another example of an analytic philosopher who tries to answer the question "What is art". He does not want to go into the criticism of Wittgenstein's adherents who consider each determination of the nature of art a false essentialism. At the same time, in his view, the Wittgensteinian concept of "family resemblance" for indicating the relationship within the various forms of art difficult to comprehend is only a temporary solution. Sharpe wants to remain faithful to the basic principles of analytic linguistics, but move on beyond the analysis of the conceptual apparatus. Therefore, he attempts to define the artwork from the spectator's perspective, i.e. art as the creation of objects interpretable by the public: ".... I think of art as the creation of objects which the public can interpret." (Sharpe 1983, 183)

Refuting this statement, Sharpe immediately raises two objections - a touch of self-criticism always honors the philosopher. Firstly, a lot of objects can be interpreted by the public. However, the objects of art distinguish themselves in this respect by allowing several interpretations, none of them necessarily the only true one. Secondly, in less complicated works of art, the interpretation will be minimal. Thus, Sharpe falls into the same trap as the criticized essentialists: while speaking of "high art", he wants to justify the view that art is a mixture of sensory attraction with intellectual demand.

There is nothing wrong with Sharpe's quoted statement as a product of common sense, but it will not lead to the essence of art. Interpretability, even if multiple, is not art's exclusive domain. - This will be addressed particularly in the next chapters when dealing with the hermeneutic and semiotic perspective. In profound interpersonal communication, each sign has multiple interpretations. Sharpe's statement does not become more meaningful by expanding the concept of interpretation. Each work requires a thorough study. Only a small part of the general public will be able to interpret a work of art fundamentally; not even all critics or art historians can do so.

With respect to Sharpe's second objection, one could remark that it is not always the case that "high" art should be interpreted maximally and "low" art minimally. That would be a deterioration of the view on the world and a denial of "high" art. Conversely, it is characteristic of art that it can be interpreted on various levels at which the lowest level is the level of non-interpretation; that is, nothing but the awareness of presence or reading of name plates next to the work. However, one does not have to be Freud either in order to be able to see Michelangelo's Moses. In general, there is hardly any interpretative activity involved in viewing an exhibition. The conclusion is that it does not seem very effective to define what art is on the basis of the faculty of interpretation of the public.

3.1.3. *The use of the term "art". (Aldrich)*

Virgil Aldrich's work Philosophy of Art contributes in an interesting way to the analytic linguistic perspective on art. In this book, the author tests the possibilities provided by Wittgenstein. In the chapter "The logic of talk about art", Aldrich points out shifts within philosophy of art. The question of the essence of art and its real definition became replaced by the question of how the term "art" is used. Aldrich classifies three logic modi in discussing art: description, interpretation and appreciation. In his view, "art" as a descriptive term is an essentialist fallacy. In line with Weitz, he classifies "art" in terms with an "open texture". This concept means that most empirical terms are characterized by an open structure as a result of the essential incompleteness of empirical concepts. Thus, the incompleteness is calculated in from the very start.

The vagueness of the term "art" can also be understood by means of Stevenson's concept of "persuasive definition", meaning that there are terms loaded with emotive meaning. Most definitions of art praise some characteristics of art, presented, however, under the guise of a general definition. Another concept that can purify the term "art" is Austin's "performative meaning" of statements, that is, a term often has a recommendatory meaning. "To say that "art essentially is Y" - form or emotion for example - is thus to commend works of art in which Y is present." (Aldrich 1963, 83)

Aldrich is aware that his rectifications of the use of the term "art" are insufficient in solving all problems of talking about art. Ultimately, art is still is a matter of good perception. "The important point emerging out of this consideration is that even the bedrock data of art are accessible only to one who can look at things, including works of art, in the relevant way. I have called this way "prehension", distinguishing it from "observation". (Ibid, 85)

Describing art is done as well by means of expressive use of words. However, verbal impressions cannot be researched objectively. The logic of the reproduction of objects differs from the reproduction of the impression of objects. And talking about art is part of talking about impressions of objects, thus, talking according to the logic of expressive observation. In Aldrich's view, the basic terms of art philosophy in aesthetic perception, which have to bring about looking and talking at the same time, are: medium, content and form. Looking remains a first condition for employing them: "You must see what grounds the expressive portrayals in which they occur before you can even begin a line of significant talk about art or understand another's utterances in that mode of expression. This is the bedrock of descriptive art talk."(Ibid, 87)

In Aldrich's view, the liberating function of the analytic linguistic perspective on art is that the criteria implied in certain definitions lose ground. This is liberating in a theoretical way indeed, though in practice few artists, except for conceptual artists, will concern themselves with definitions. The latter are in a certain way closely connected with analytic philosophy and explore as well the "essentialist" consequences of the use of the word "being". Remarkably enough, Aldrich links a limiting formula to a rather broad definition. He writes, "A work of art is a material thing produced for prehension as an aesthetic object. This by itself is a rather empty notion, which however gets some substance in connection with the previous treatment of the materials, medium, content, form, and subject matter of a work of art, together with what has been said about prehension as the aesthetically relevant mode of perception of things. As one or more of these items is subtracted or minimized in a particular work, the application of 'work of art' becomes more questionable." (Ibid, 99) This statement is rather general, and, therefore, perhaps superfluous. One cannot comment much on the definition of a work of art as a material thing produced in order to be understood as an aesthetic object. Unless it shifts the problem to "What is aesthetic?" Besides, it remains an open question why the term "work of art" will suffer if one of the factors - material, medium, content, form and subject matter - is lacking or is present in a minimal way. A large part of contemporary art, such as material art, fundamental painting, conceptual art and minimalism is based on minimizing one factor and maximizing another.

3.1.4. *Typology of art theory. (Stolnitz)*

As demonstrated by the authors previously quoted, analytic philosophy mainly criticizes that one aspect of the aesthetic experience considered essential becomes an absolute term. Jerome Stolnitz considers aesthetics a form of meta-critique. In his book <u>Aesthetics and Philosophy of Art Criticism</u> (1960), we will find three types of aesthetic theories with various definitions of art which evolved over the ages together with the development and multiplicity of art-forms. Stolniz distinguishes mimetic ("imitation"), formalist and expressive ("emotionalist") theories. The mimetic theories relate in particular the term "beauty" to the mimetic nature of the work of art. According to these theories, the essence of a work of art is that it represents reality or what could be considered essential in it. The better a work of art portrays reality, the more beautiful it is. In formalist theories, the organization of elements within the work of art is understood as the essence of the artwork. In these movements, beauty is related to formal criteria such as balance, rhythm and the degree of harmony. In expressive theories, the work of art is understood as a means of expression of human emotions. In these theories, the intensity and the authenticity of expression are the criteria for the quality of the work of art.

As an analytic philosopher, Stolniz opposes this by saying these various types of theories make an absolute of one single aspect of the aesthetic experience. Aesthetic experiences are fed by mimetic and expressive as well as formal characteristics of aesthetic objects. A work of art can be understood as a combination of these three aspects. Furthermore, an attribute of a successful work of art is that has an "open" character. It does not allow a unanimous interpretation of one of the three previously mentioned theories. This openness of the work of art will enable it to evoke an aesthetic experience outside its specific cultural context.

3.1.5. *The art world as institutional framework. (Dickie)*

The definitions of art by analytic philosophers remain very broad. They are characterized by vagueness, or better, by scrupulous fear of expressing themselves. They continue to be something accompanied by human intervention and something where a public is involved. In the work The New Institutional Theory of Art, George Dickie maintains this as well. The work is an adjustment of his book Art and the Aesthetic. Dickie's "institutional perspective" means that artworks are art because of the place they occupy within an institutional framework or context. His theory of art intends to classify, in other words, the enunciation "art" does not necessarily imply that it is "good" art, but that it entails the broad class of objects where masterpieces as well as minor works find their place. From a traditional perspective, such as in mimetic and expressive theories, art is viewed in an overly restricted way. The institutional theory intends to situate the work of art in a network of greater complexity, which thought constitutes this theory. Dickie formulates his definition as follows: "A work of art is an artifact of a kind created to be presented to an artworld public." (Haller 1984, 63) He joins in the traditional theories by assuming that works of art are artifacts in the sense of a common dictionary definition: "an object made by man, especially with a view to subsequent use." This includes non-physical objects. Dickie refers to a poem as an example of a non-physical object, although the empty space as a conceptual work of art would have been a better example.

With respect to being artifactual as characteristic, Dickie rebuts his two colleagues Ziff and Weitz. In a novel view, they state that the members of a class of artworks do not have one single theoretically meaningful characteristic in common, even not artifactuality. An object becomes a work of art if it sufficiently resembles a previously established work of art. Dickie can refute that easily by pointing out that there will never be a first work of art if sufficient resemblance is the precondition. It means, more or less, that there will be no art. In Ziff and Weitz's theory, an entirely novel movement also be impossible. Another problem is the question of who is able to recognize those resemblances, since pseudo-art and decorative art indeed have demonstrated "sufficient resemblance" with respect to art.

So Dickie sticks to the opinion that art is something that is made: "Artifactual art is generated by the human activity of making." (Ibid, 58) But what about Duchamp's ready-mades? To the statement that this is art because ready-mades are not artifacts, Dickey objects that ready-mades are artifacts within an art world. In Duchamp's Fountain, the pissoir is used as an artistic medium in the same way as paint or stone in more conventional works. However, another term from his definition has been introduced, i.e. "art world". This term allows an object to become art because of the position it acquires in an established course of events. One can discover this when comparing two identical objects, for example a pissoir and Duchamp's Fountain or a painting and a randomly colored surface. The pissoir and the surface are not works of art because they are not included in the context of an art world. We could add to this that both identical objects could be just as "beautiful", but one is a work of art and the other is not. This "becoming" a work of art by means of artistic context presents another problem though: does the artifact continue to be a work of art once it is outside that context? Not really. Duchamp's Fountain is not a work of art but a relic of a work of art. Duchamp's real work of art was his act to represent that artifact as art at a certain moment and in a certain space. In doing this, he broke with traditional art and its classic materials, and at the same time he put the sovereign right to determine what art is into the hands of the artist. If one adds to this that many "originals" have been lost and were replaced not by one, but by a series of copies, then the problem of true and false has been solved right away. Perhaps the real Dadaist message is the paradox of the enforced admiration of copies of relics, a pleasure we will grant the Duchamp post festum.

In his definition, Dickie includes as well the "public" factor which plays a role in determining what is art. And that in a somewhat reversed way. The fact that some artists refuse to show their work, because they think it is inferior, is proof for Dickie that it has been made for a public, or else there would be no reason to conceal it. The public of an art world is not just a public; it has the necessary knowledge which corresponds in many ways to that of the artist. "The members of an artworld public are such because they know how to fulfill a role which requires knowledge and understanding similar in many respects to that required of an artist." (Ibid, 61)

Such a statement should be examined. We believe that knowledge of art from the perspective of the creator could differ strongly from the knowledge of art from the perspective of the spectator. The former cannot or barely see without the creative process in mind, the latter can hardly assess the creative process. Moreover, the problem of snobbery, of pseudo knowledge did not arise either.

Dickie points out that indeed there is as much variety in public as in works of art, and that the knowledge required will correspond to this. A variety of roles can be fulfilled within the art world. The minimum framework consists of the artist and the public. The role of the artist has two core aspects: on the one hand the awareness that what has been created as representation is art and, on the other hand, the skill to use one or more of the possible techniques which yield the reproduction of a certain kind of art. With regard to the latter aspect, Dickie adheres to an obsolete view. Artists who maintain they know no art technique are accepted as artist by the art world. Taken to the extreme, one could even consider the construction of ideas as an old craft.

The role of the public has two core aspects as well: the awareness that what is represented as art is art and, the skill and the sensitivity to perceive and understand the art one is confronted with. In addition to these two main roles of artist and public, there are others such, as "critics, art teacher, director, curator, conductor, and many more." For visual art, the following series seems relevant as well: critic, curator, organizer, mediator, gallerist, researcher, art dealer, cultural employee. The art world entails the totality of such roles. "Described in a somewhat more structured way, the artworld consists of a set of individual artworld systems, each of which contains its own specific artist and public roles plus other roles. For example, painting is one artworld system, theater is another, and so on." (Ibid, 63)

We would like to carry this even further. Painting as an artworld system consists of more than one autonomous artworld system. Those who know the artworld know that every branch of art consists of more than one artworld within which, in each case, a complete set of rules will function. Be this as it may, we agree how Dickie defines art departing from the concept of artworld. Yet, a number of problems arise. The concept of artworld as a defining framework is an evaluation in itself. It is conceivable that somebody will produce works which will not be recognized as art by any artworld for a long time. This danger lurks even larger because Dickie attributes a major role the to public within the artworld, because of which the equalization of art with established art is advanced. His concept of "established practice" is not enough to refute our criticism.

However, Dickie's institutional theory goes completely awry in the following statement: "a work of art is a artifact of a kind, created to be presented to an artworld public." This statement is meant to be a refutation of the remark that his definition is valid also for other artifacts. However, an art magazine is "an artifact of a kind created to be presented to an artworld public" as well. So are some design mirrors, certain fashionable clothes etc. Dickie's answer to this remark he anticipated himself is weak. His definition shows refutable elements. "To forestall an objection to the definition, let me acknowledge that there are artifacts which are created for presentation to the artworld publics which are not works of art: for example, playbills. Such things are, however, parasitic or secondary to works of art. Works of art are artifacts of a primary kind in this domain, and playbills and the like which are dependent on works of art are artifacts of a secondary kind within this domain. The word 'artifacts' in the definition should be understood to be referring to artifacts of primary kind." (Ibid, 63) By introducing the classification of "primary and secondary" and a term as "parasitic", Dickie undermines his definition, because who is going to determine to which category a certain artifact belongs?

3.1.6. A deitic definition of art

Making critical remarks concerning this matter is easier than formulating a proposal. Yet, we will try to answer the question of "What is art?" along the lines of analytic philosophy. We believe that such a definition cannot be made merely on the basis of perception of alleged essences. On the contrary, the definition should lead the perception. With each definition departing from the thought that certain people in certain circumstances can determine what art is on the basis of their perceptive faculty of recognition, one will come across the question: "According to what criteria?" This results in the issue becoming a definition of a certain kind of art, since evolutions of form will constantly escape definition.

We agree with analytic philosophers that so-called traditional art theories often lapse into essentialism in making one or more characteristics absolute as generally valid irrefutable essences. However, we disagree with analytic philosophers that this is a reason for rejecting these theories as nonsense. It is sufficient to read these theories as contributions to the approach of the phenomena of art, where the represented essential characteristics are not made absolute, but considered as characteristics alongside proposals. It is necessary to have as many different art movements as possible speak in turn. This is the result of a postmodern view of science. The variety of artistic products requires a variety of theories, on two levels. First, a certain theory is only relevant for a certain kind of art. Secondly, each kind of art should be open to several theories.

We also agree with analytic philosophers that "art" is too broad a concept in comparison with concepts like "happiness" or - somewhat more concrete - "food". Therefore, we believe that so-called traditional theories are too eager to define art, too eager to determine what art is and should be. Conversely, analytic philosophers emphasize two other elements of the triad "artist - work of art - spectator", which seems a rather interesting view. However, they are mainly interested in the spectator.

"Reception aesthetics" extends this approach even further. In this view, the role of the artist is limited to creation. Within this theory, it sometimes seems that the absence of a public, more so than the presence of an artist, will determine what art is or is not. In our view, however, the artist will first determine what art is. This is similar to scientists who determine by means of research what science is, in spite of humanities students or their professors, no matter how interesting the remarks of philosopher of science afterwards.

Therefore, we propose a "deitic" (demonstrative adjunct) definition: art is what an artist calls art, and what he has possibly made himself. In this way, the problem has been shifted to the question of "What is an artist?" An artist is someone who calls himself an artist. In line with Dickie's institutional theory, we want to add that the self-confirming and identifying statement - whether or not explicitly formulated - "I am an artist" can be endorsed in a quantitative sense by the number of spectators (role of the public) and in a qualitative sense by professionals, depending on how and why they agree with them (role of critics, etc.). At a certain moment, after the death of the artist, the statement "this is art" should be taken up by one or more art historians. What else is an art historical monograph but a fundamental testimony - indeed a sort of testament - where, on the basis of biographical and other documents, the final word is given on which objects the artist terms as art? But strictly speaking, for a living artist the statement "I am an artist" in combination with the indication "That is my work" is sufficient to turn something into art.

How should one distinguish somebody who makes such an identifying statement from somebody who claims to be Napoleon? The concept of "continuity" (though without excluding certain developmental flaws) will provide the distinction. One should verify whether the person who calls himself an artist continuously produces objects which he calls "artworks". This could be done by means of exhibitions, but also via the studio and storage room. From the perspective of the artwork, it might be possible that there is an artist who only made one work of art. From the perspective of the art world this cannot be the case. In this world, being an artist means that somebody is continuously - of course relatively seen - involved in realizing products that will be called "art".

As a matter of fact, one work of art will obtain its meaning because of another; a shift in meaning will occur by producing the next work. But this will also occur retroactively. The latter work contributes to the former and, in the other way around, the former obtains its meaning because of the production of the latter. In an extreme approach, it means that the meaning of an artist's first work will only be completed - at least with respect to the artist's contribution to the process of production of meaning - after the last work has been made. This interrelationship is the profound meaning of the term "oeuvre".

So far, so good. However, a merely individual definition limited to one oeuvre is too weak. For example, how does one distinguish the products of the "professional" artist from the products of the amateur? In this phase of definition, one should refer to perceptive recognition: not to recognize quality - except for that aspect of quality relating to originality - nor to investigate whether or not art is at stake on the basis of some essentialism. That is already the case because the two previous conditions have been fulfilled. The identifying self-confirmation of the acting person is fundamental as the first condition. The second condition is existential, in the sense that the self-image is extended in space and time under control of the continuity of action. However, this latter behavior is still too similar for too many categories of action; not only artists produce objects in a studio and exhibit them. In order to specify this action, a third category is necessary to verify the acting person (first condition) and the action (second condition) within a social context, in order to arrive at a clear differentiation non-hierarchical in nature, but merely pertaining to coordination. This verification stems from the study of the code of how to determine previous and existing relationships.

However, we should not fall into the trap of redefining the definition of art in terms of a value judgement on "good" art. As stated previously, perceptive recognition will lead to a circular argument and to the question of how to translate the criteria of the image into those of the word. This translation proved to be impossible. Thus, with respect to the third condition, we must trust (and keep to it consistently) the assertion of the artist that he is oriented towards historicity and the criticism of the context. This orientation is no imitation, because it is the difference which must stand out. As a third rule of thumb for determining what art is, we claim that the one who calls himself an artist must place himself within a as recent as possible art historical tradition. The dynamics of the evolution of art enables anti-tradition to also fall within the "tradition", namely within a continuous "renewing" tradition. The artist contributes to this tradition by employing novel or other forms, which may differ from the tradition or even transform it, but are never a copy of what came before. Each new invention is welcome. Of course, that cannot result from the handbook "How to paint like Van Gogh". The criteria can be stated by art critics (situated within contemporary art) and art historians (situated within art history). Thus, perceptive (re)cognition only comes to the fore by way of testing.

At the same time, art critics can base their criticism on this third principle. The artist situates himself within the existing artistic context by exhibiting his works. The relationship with what exists is what the art critic should reveal. However, if this cannot be revealed, in our view, there is no reason why people outside of art should have the right to criticize work some people freely make in their leisure time. In other words, one cannot criticize amateur art, or at least there is no ground for it. If this form of criticism exists, than it is itself amateur criticism, that is, connected to different codes. Such criticism will employ other criteria as well.

In the possible distinction between "amateurish practice of art" and "professional creation of art", the words "amateurish" and "professional" seem superfluous. The distinction between "practice" and "creation" is telling enough. To the "practitioner of art", the process within the person as a pleasant creative form of development is more important than the resulting product. To the art-creator, this is exactly the reverse: even if he kills himself, it is the result that counts. Of course, we do not intend to completely separate the inner process of creation from the product.

Obviously, the nature of the product and the appreciation of the public contribute to the development of the creative possibilities of the amateur as part of his personality. Similarly, even the factor of destruction of non-artistic aspects in the life of the artist can reinforce the artistic aspects of his personality. If one evaluates the art-practitioner, one will try to explore the inner process of development. For the creator of art, one only reviews the product.

This attempt at explication does not mean to make any statements on the quality of the work, certainly not with respect to the first two rules of thumb. The same holds for the third principle. Someone is not a minor artist when he fails in his purpose to contribute to the problem of form of his culture within the existing framework of art. He may be a minor artist, but still he is an artist.

Perhaps the deitic definition is too nominalist and too pragmatic. However, it may be operational and, of course, it is open to criticism. One could draw the comparison with the definition of a sportsman, although it does not entirely apply. A sportsman is somebody who sees himself as a sportsman and who regularly practices a sport. Furthermore, he is someone who strives for ranking against existent times and achievements. Somebody who finishes last in a bike race is no lesser sportsman than the one who finishes first. However, a great difference with the art world is that the one who drives the Tour de France in opposite direction will no doubt be declassified as a sportsman immediately, whereas among artists he would probably be the winner.

Perhaps one could compare the term "art" with the term "nature", where one person thinks of the sea and somebody else of the mountains. Nature-lovers who only use the term "nature" in exchanging experiences will discover afterwards that they did not talk about the same thing. A similar disillusionment will befall the lovers of art, if they must decide after a dialogue (or rather two monologues) on art that their possible unanimity cannot be based on their view on concrete works of art.

3.2. *Wittgenstein*

The role which Ludwig Wittgenstein contributed to art cannot be formulated in an easy way. Although his statements are often phrased in very simple language, few statements can be understood univocally. Even a book such as Lectures and Conversations on Aesthetics (1966) deals with many additional philosophical problems. Yet, it is important to include his work and not only because he was an art connoisseur.

Yet, we can be brief regarding his thought on art, because many of his views have been treated when discussing philosophers of art he inspired. The task of philosophers, as Wittgenstein sees it, already implies an aesthetic attitude. According to Wittgenstein, the task of the true philosopher is merely descriptive: he does not explain anything nor does he pretend to reform the use of language (the work of art) in any respect.

To act counter to prejudices, to open one's mind to versatility, the term "spectator" and the absence of definite methods are all elements which can refer to the mediator who tries to construct a bridge to the work of art. Wittgenstein's preference for colloquial language is conspicuous as well. One could wonder whether the description of the effect caused by the confrontation with art would require anything but colloquial language. In addition to the rather large visual inhibiting effect, the art historical jargon is basically another verbal obstacle. Therefore, being aware that the problem should be dealt with at this level, a philosophical foundation for the use of that colloquial language is very appropriate. Initially, the philosopher's task as a mediator of art is to remove sources of misunderstanding on that level.

3.2.1. *Ethics and aesthetics are one*

The texts which will provide an impression of Wittgenstein's view on art did not appear until WW II. However, his work Tractatus Logico-Philosophicus contains a sentence, the somewhat oracular statement 6.421, which will be our leitmotif: "It is clear that ethics cannot be put into words. Ethics is transcendental. (Ethics and aesthetics are one)."

Besides ethics and aesthetics being one, the problem of the unspeakable is also presented in this statement. Another statement proves that Wittgenstein is convinced there are things which cannot be expressed but, conversely, reveal themselves. He considers them the mystical. Morality, or better said ethics, discourse on morality, and art, or aesthetics all belong to this domain of the mystical or the ineffable.

"6.522. There is indeed the inexpressible. This shows itself; it is the mystical." Also in that line is the famous final sentence of the Tractatus, "7. Whereof one cannot speak, thereof one must be silent."

In this context, it is important that the ineffable and the silent do not prevent the mystical from revealing itself. The mystical shows itself. For art, this means a confirmation of autonomy. The impossibility of the word is compensated by visibility. Of course we will break the silence. Wittgenstein's statement is no ban on speech, but rather the rejection of the ground on which the ability to speak in a meaningful way is founded. Ultimately, art merely "shows" itself, and all words fail. No matter how many statements one makes about art, again and again one must return to the source which shows itself.

We understand the unity of ethics and aesthetics as the ability to reveal the power to reveal. Aesthetics will reveal what can be revealed, i.e. ethics. In L'art pour l'art aesthetics reveals itself, again as ethics. In that sense, both are inseparable, almost as connected as form and content are. Ethics is always a demonstration, an example, a theater, a didactic picture not about how it is, but how it should be, must be, or should not be.

In our view, Janik's and Toulmin's presentation is too simplistic. They claim that the issue is merely the poetic faculty of language. "Wittgenstein is trying to set the ethical off from the sphere of rational discourse, because he believes that it is more properly located in the sphere of the poetic: 'Ethics and aesthetics are one and the same'." (Janik&Toulmin 1973, 193) The domain of the "mystical" to which ethics and aesthetics belong is ambiguous. Firstly, the mystical relates to what the world has in common with its image, its mirror, namely language. Secondly, it points out the poetic capacity of language to reveal the "meaning of life". Language can pass on experience, but it can also give sense, meaning to that experience. The former will become possible because factual statements are models with a logical structure; the latter is poetry. The Tractatus wants to keep these two components separate. On the basis of correspondence, Janik and Toulmin demonstrate that Wittgenstein considers his Tractatus both a philosophical and a literary work, but in particular an ethical one. Through his texts, Wittgenstein believes he has drawn boundaries around the ethical, what he did not write. In his view, this demarcation from within is the most important component.

Barett also addressed the statement "Ethics and Aesthetics are one" as well (Haller 1984, 17-22). He points out that one can find some clarification in Wittgenstein's Notebooks. In this work, the relationship between both concepts is considered as sub specie aeternitatis. Ethics considers the world sub specie aeternitatis, whereas aesthetics considers the objects as such, with the whole world as a backdrop. In the same Notebooks, one will find two other relationships: the mystical, as mentioned previously, and happiness. Wittgenstein perceives art with a joyous eye. Art creates happiness. Ethics is engaged in the happy life. Barett poses the somewhat rhetorical problem of aesthetics engaged in observing things and ethics in observing life and action. "To repeat, aesthetics has to do with looking at things; ethics has to do with living and acting." (Ibid, 20) We believe that Barett confuses the terms ethics and morality. Morality has to do with (rules of) life and action. Ethics, on the contrary, has to do with examining life and action. In that sense, the connection is clear. Barett arrives at a similar answer by pointing out that aesthetics is a "form of life" and by indicating the ancient relationship between the beautiful and the good already determined by the Greeks.

So far, this gives an outline of what one single Wittgensteinian statement can cause. His other writings on aesthetics are not much more clarifying and are meager, so much so that Bouveresse states, "Speaking of Wittgenstein's ethics and aesthetics, for example, is almost merely speaking of his unwritten work and in addition of his biography or his personality."(Bouveresse 1973, 15)

3.2.2. *Wittgenstein as aesthetician*

On the basis of his biography, we know that Wittgenstein was a great connoisseur of art. Music, for example, was to him what it was to Schopenhauer: "The
true universal language which one understands everywhere and which expresses
the world in its manner and resolves all enigmas". (Ibid, 13) However, as stated
previously, at the same time, one of his fundamental philosophical convictions
was that what expresses itself in this artistic language cannot be restated or
explained in verbal language. Jacques Bouveresse considers writing a book
mainly devoted to ethics and aesthetics in Wittgenstein's philosophy as a completely senseless undertaking. Yet, he dedicates a chapter to this subject in his
book La rime. Bouveresse claims that Wittgenstein is not a philosopher of language or logic, but primarily of ethics and aesthetics. A claim we by and large
agree with for further discussion of Wittgenstein's work.

According to Bouveresse, the Wittgensteinian view on aesthetics and
ethics is fundamentally eudaemonistic. Products of art should have an essentially positive effect. They should offer a solution rather than a problem. No matter
how unexpectedly, Wittgenstein seems to have a passion for more popular genres, like detective, comedy and adventure films. In other words, entertainment
plays a role in his life. He is convinced that art somehow should intensively help
one live. Therefore, Wittgenstein prefers the popular, rejects "art for art's sake"
and demand some morality in the artistic product. He emphasizes implicitly or
explicitly the compensating, comforting and educational function of art; indeed,
even the edifying function in Tolstoy's meaning. This overly positive interpretation has often led to the negation of the artistic component. Yet, the justification
of art has to be explored. After all, in this century, art seldom offers a solution,
but rather presents a problem for art criticism and philosophy.

The connection between ethics and aesthetics Wittgenstein proposes in
the Tractatus is exactly the justification of the object of art. This relationship is
the authorization of acquiring meaning, contrary to the factual world of contingency. Art, as well as morality, is an attempt to signify the world. In
Wittgenstein's view, then, the word "beauty" has little sense within aesthetic
reflection. In this respect, he refers to two points. Firstly, "beauty" is used in
numerous ways. Moreover, the meaning of this word changes considerably
depending on the context. In addition, "beauty" and related words play an
absolutely minor role in the practice of aesthetic judgements. Viewed grammatically, they are adjectives and they are used as interjections. Wittgenstein cautions that we pay too much attention to the (word)forms and not enough to their
usage. Words are used naïvely by those unable to express a true aesthetic judge-

ment. Connoisseurs prefer terms such as "right" and "correct". Actually, aesthetic adjectives hardly play a role. However, an insider could point out how something should be read or seen. The more one knows about art, the more one starts reading or observing in a different and more intense way. Suddenly, the work of art has meaning; it appeals. "A man says it ought to be read this way and reads it for you. You say: 'Oh yes. Now it makes sense.'.. But the important thing was that I read the poems entirely differently, more intensely, and said to others: 'Look! This is how they should be read.' Aesthetic adjectives played hardly any role." (Wittgenstein 1966, I,4-5)

Concerning the "sudden understanding" of art, Bouveresse remarks that, in Wittgenstein's thought, the discovery of the author's intentions or reasons does not mean we will succeed in formulating a satisfying hypothesis on the process that takes place in the person's mind while composing the work. Even if someone wants to explain something to us by all means, it is possible that we are unable to see what could be seen or what someone would like us to see.

Wittgenstein repeatedly points out the importance of the spacial and cultural context of aesthetic appreciation, exactly excluding the description of such an appreciation. "It is not only difficult to describe what appreciation consists of, but impossible. To describe what it consists of we would have to describe the whole environment." (Ibid, I, 7) And on the cultural ties of expressions of an aesthetic judgement, he writes: "The words we call expressions of aesthetic judgement play a very complicated role, but a very definite role, in what we call a culture of a period. To describe their use or to describe what you mean by a cultural taste, you have to describe a culture." Which includes being bound to time: "What we now call a cultured taste perhaps didn't exist in the Middle Ages. An entirely different game is played in different times." (Ibid, II, 8) Thus, a language game belongs to an entire culture. A statement such as "this is a fine crown gown" could be said now as well as in the days of Edward II, but with a different meaning. In emphasizing this cultural context and the relativity of taste, Wittgenstein seeks to demonstrate that if one wants to understand, one should most of all watch the language game which factually occurs in certain objects and in certain circumstances, with respect to verbal aspects as well as non-verbal ones. As long as one fails to do that, the problem traditional philosophy was engaged in - i.e. how is it theoretically possible that an aesthetic difference of opinion prevails - is futile.

We would like to add the distinction - which Wittgenstein omits - between the words "to think" and "to be" where the statement "I think it is beautiful" is not by any means contradictory to "I don't think it is beautiful", because the problem does not present itself. In using the verb "to be" in line with

Wittgenstein, one should appeal then to the role the language game plays.

Wittgenstein cautions against the usual confusion between "beautiful" and "pleasant", since the relationship between aesthetics and psychology is an issue. In Wittgenstein's view, it is utter nonsense that aesthetics would be a branch of psychology and that, in the future, "all the mysteries of art" could be understood by means of psychological experiments. Aesthetics gives possible reasons why one element in a painting is better than another. What an artist has to say cannot be compared with the "effect" he has in mind. In this context, Wittgenstein draws a parallel with understanding language: "Cf. the mistake of thinking that the meaning or thought is just an accompaniment of the word, and the word doesn't matter. 'The sense of a proposition' is very similar to the business of 'an appreciation of art'. The idea that a sentence has a relation to an object, such that, whatever has this effect is the sense of the sentence." (Ibid, IV, 29)

What words try to say is not their effect, since they could have a specific meaning without a specific effect. If two works have the same effect on the spectator, will both then be interchangeable, Wittgenstein wonders? The answer appears to be negative. It is clear that the meaning of a work of art does not correspond with all that is able to produce the same effect. The work of art is no means of attaining a certain effect. It has a purpose in and of itself. What counts in a painting is not our experience but the painting itself. Its effect is important, but not the most important. "What a painting evokes in us, what it reminds us of etc. is undeniably something important but it is not 'the most important'. (Bouveresse 1973, 177)

Wittgenstein points out that associations have significance. One may have similar associations with different paintings; however, it is a particular painting that matters. And he adds something which could have been said by a painter: " 'That means the chief impression is the visual impression'. Yes, it's the picture which seems to matter most. Associations may vary, attitudes may vary, but change the picture ever so slightly, and you won't want to look at it any more." (Wittgenstein 1966, IV, 36) Obviously, Wittgenstein defends the priority of the work of art as a material object, and he forces the psychological view - in particular that effects on the spectator can change the meaning of the work of art - to the background. For Bouveresse, such a psychologism is a rude way to present the function of art. "However, this will lead to a very crude conception of the function of the artwork, namely the idea that we will observe a painting particularly to have a certain psychological experience."(Bouveresse 1973, 178)

Without mentioning the concept, Wittgenstein posits against this an explicit form of formalism. At the same time, he opens a door to an abstract way of seeing. He claims that the two schools of 1) emphasis on color planes and lines and of 2) emphasis on facial expression are not contradictory. However, the former does not specify that different color planes are of differing importance and that different changes may have various, even opposite, effects. Therefore, Wittgenstein dares to state: "A picture must be good even if you look at it upside down. Then the smile may not be noticeable." (Wittgenstein 1966, IV, 35) Wittgenstein expresses very well the formal priority of the painting. Whether a painting is good does not depend on the recognition of a smile, but on the formal structure. The latter may be just as visible when the painting is upside- down. By applying this abstract way of seeing, one can eliminate a prejudice against non-figurative art. If the upside down position is rejected as abstract, then the potentially negative attitude could disappear when the "smile" becomes visible in the regular position.

3.2.3. *Seeing and seeing as*

In his Philosophical Investigations (1953), Wittgenstein devotes attention to aesthetic problems in discussing phenomena such as "seeing and seeing as" and the "sudden flash of one aspect." He departs from the familiar psychological example of studying the perception of ambiguous figures: the graphically presented H-D head, which can evoke the image of a hare as well as that of a duck. Wittgenstein points out that the shift in aspect, i.e. hare or duck, expresses in fact a new perception while the first one is still present. "The expression of a change of aspect is the expression of a new perception and at the same time of the perception's being unchanged."(Wittgenstein 1953, 196) In this context, Wittgenstein states that one should not detach the impression of the face from the drawing although this impression of the face does not coincide with the drawing either. The drawing is not in one's inner image, yet, this inner image is no indication either of "this here". If one were to draw the inner image, one should have to return to the original drawing. Wittgenstein writes: "'seeing as...' is not part of perception. And for that reason it is like seeing and again not like."(Ibid, 197) In "seeing as", one always articulates what one sees; seeing is completed with the description of the perception, and thought is connected with perception. Wittgenstein calls this "blending". "Hence the flashing of an aspect on us seems half visual experience, half thought." (Ibid, 197) Wittgenstein question seeing in a dual way. On the one hand, we are too certain about what we see, as a result of which some parts of seeing appear enigmatic to us. On the other hand, we should question those certainties more often. In aesthetic perception this problem is even more distinct. "We find certain things about seeing puzzling, because we do not find the whole business of seeing puzzling enough."(Ibid, 212)

Wittgenstein clearly stresses the idea that there are no descriptions of what we see which should deserve priority and overshadow other descriptions. "The concept of 'seeing' makes a tangled impression. Well, it is tangled. (...) There is not one genuine proper case of such description."(Ibid, 200)

Wittgenstein continually emphasizes that although the aesthetic experience cannot be called objective in a strict scientific sense of the word, it is not subjective in a pejorative sense either. Contrary to traditional philosophical aesthetics, he rejects the myth of the inner private experience which cannot be shared. It is impossible to make an exact distinction between "seeing" and "interpreting", between "seeing" and "knowing", and between "seeing" and "thinking". One will see a painting the way one interprets it. To experience something assumes that one is able to experience, that one has learned how to control it. "The substratum of this experience is the mastery of a technique (..). It is only if someone can do, has learnt, is master of, such-and-such, that it makes sense to say he has had this experience."(Ibid, 208-209)

Thus, there is no such thing as a pure condition of seeing. Seeing is always connected with interpretation, which is a form of thinking and acting. We may see an object first as one thing and than as another. We will interpret it and see it as we interpret it. Thus "seeing" becomes "seeing as". By using it, one will learn the meaning. Therefore, experiencing is rather testing, not in the sense of undergoing as much as that of producing. Or, as Bouveresse claims, "This is not only aesthetic perception, but perception in general as well, and all perception which is exploratory, attentive, anticipatory, projection, transformation, etc."(Bouverese, 1973, 202)

3.3. Goodman

3.3.1. Conventionality of art as a system of symbols

In his book Languages of Art (1976), Nelson Goodman employs art as the starting point for a general theory of symbols. Goodman aims to understand the world but also desires to "create" it by means of studying systems of symbols and their function in our perception and action, in art as well as in science. Similar to Gombrich, Goodman belongs to the theorists who spread the view that artistic activity is guided by cultural conventions. In his book, Goodman deals with a number of aspects of art and the experience of art which are strongly related to the issue of meaning in contemporary art. Goodman's statement that a painting be considered as a pictorial symbol will be the starting point for delving into the problem of realism, expression, authenticity and the relationship between the emotive and the cognitive component.

Goodman discards the so-called mimetic theory which defines art as an attempt to approach reality as exact as possible. In his article "The Way the World Is" (1960), Goodman states that "what the world is" amounts to the many ways it can be truly viewed, described, represented and so on. Thus, there is no such thing as "the way the world is". If one copies reality, one chooses one of the many possibilities of reproduction. In line with Gombrich, Goodman rejects the possibility of the innocent eye. "The eye comes always ancient to its work, obsessed by its own past and by old and new insinuations of the ear, nose, tongue, fingers, heart, and brain. It functions not as an instrument self-powered and alone, but as a dutiful member of a complex and capricious organism. Not only how but what it sees is regulated by need and prejudice." (Goodman 1976, 7)

Nothing is seen in a simple way. Goodman breaks with the view that there could be something like a perfect copy. We believe indeed that art's most important role is to represent certain ways of seeing by means of a certain medium, because of which something can emerge from the dullness of the everyday habitual gaze. Fascinating art is often the result of a fascinating eye which is not innocent, neither on the level of the artist nor on the level of the viewer. By pointing out the mythical character of the innocent eye, Goodman arrives at his assertion that absorbing information cannot be separated from interpretation. The most ascetic vision, for example a sober portrait, or the most exaggerated vision, for example a caricature do not differ on the basis of how much is interpreted, but merely of how it is done.

"But reception and interpretation are not separable operations; they are thoroughly interdependent." (Ibid, 8) Therefore, mimetic theory on the art of representation becomes unsettled. An image does not represent something with or without its characteristics, it represents something "as", in its quality of. Thus, again and again a part of the whole is described. This assumes a choice. The rule of preference within this choice is a form of classifying objects and characteristics. It is not a matter of transferring a passion. Indication of new elements or groups and their relationships by novel means of identification (labels) or new combinations of old means of identifications can provide new insight. Art can contribute to knowledge, or to put it in the words of one of Goodman's favorite thoughts: art can make and remake the world. "If his picture is recognized as almost but not quite referring to the commonplace furniture of the everyday world, or if it calls for and yet resists assignment to a usual kind of picture, it may bring out neglected likeness and differences, force unaccustomed associations, and in some measure remake our world. And if the point of the picture is not only successfully made but is also well-taken, if the realignments it directly and indirectly effects are interesting and important, the picture - like a crucial experiment - makes a genuine contribution to knowledge." (Ibid, 33) Art goes against the cliché of the everyday look. That requires imagination. Effective representation is a creative act. Goodman even dares to say that nature is a product of art. "In sum, effective representation and description require invention. They are creative. They inform each other: and they form, relate, and distinguish objects. That nature imitates art is too timid a dictum. Nature is a product of art and discourse." (Ibid, 33)

In Goodman's view, it is understandable that we assume similarity as the measure of realism. After all, the habits of representing realism are inclined to call forth similarity. That an image resembles nature often only means that it resembles the way nature is painted in general. Thus, in a certain way similarity is the product of representation rather than its criterium. The criterium for determining whether a representation is realistic depends on its level of transparency. And this depends on how stereotypical the manner of representation is, on how the labels and their use have become a cliché. This standard is highly relative and related to culture, person and time. "Realism is relative, determined by the system of representation standard for a given culture or person at a given time." (Ibid, 37) Because of this it is necessary to learn how to read a realistic image. "Realism" is often the name for a particular style or a system of representation, because we tend to omit the specification of our own frame of reference. Thus "realism" often stands for a traditional European way of representation. It the standard which determines what realism is. "But how literal or realistic the picture is depends upon how standard the system is. If representation is a matter of choice and correctness a matter of information, realism is a matter of habit."(Ibid, 38)

Goodman classifies representation and description as denotation. In that way, he wants to free representation from the idea that an idiosyncratic physical process, like the mirror, is in question. He considers representation a symbolic relationship which is relative and variable. Important as well is that the symbolic value is related to the pictorial characteristics of the symbol. "To represent, a picture must function as a pictorial symbol; that is, function in a system such that what is denoted depends solely upon the pictorial properties of the symbol."(Ibid, 41-42)

Goodman also puts a number of prejudices about the concept of "expression" behind him. From the popular conviction that the first function of art is to arouse emotions, the false conclusion follows that an artist himself should have the feelings he expresses in his work. Sometimes also another erroneous view results from this, that is, that the artist expresses feelings which will be the same as those aroused in the spectator. An artist can take feeling as a theme, and obviously the expression of a certain feeling can arouse other feelings in the viewer, such as sorrow when seeing pain. Moreover, Goodman indicates that expression, even facial expression, is connected with habits and culture. Thus, the same holds true for expression as for representation: "With representation and expression alike, certain relationships become firmly fixed for certain people by habit; but in neither case are these relationships absolute, universal or immutable." (Ibid, 50)

Representation as well as expression are forms of denotation, where the former refers to something concrete and the latter to something abstract. Goodman thoroughly analyses the concept of expression. It is interesting to find out what consequences his analysis has for the understanding of art, since in this context, he tries to clarify the aesthetic problem departing from a comparison with the scientific domain.

3.3.2. The trained eye is imperfect: the false work of art

One of the relevant problems Goodman poses is the difference in aesthetic impact of a real work of art or a false one, and whether such impact could occur by merely looking. Initially, he remarks that merely looking is not only dependent on inherent visual abilities, but also on practice and exercise. In this context, Goodman gives the somewhat peculiar example of twins who are only recognized by persons familiar with them. Apart from the fact that this is not a difference between real and false, the choice of the example indicates that neither is a difference of aesthetic experience involved. At most, research into the differences in factual data is concerned, which could be the basis for another aesthetic experience. This research could be conducted with instruments such as a magnifying glass or a microscope if necessary. Then the question of the limit of aesthetic perception should be raised. However, we believe that such a scientific form of perception does not coincide with an aesthetic experience. Goodman's opinion is that once one knows which work is false and which work is real, one will have a different view, even if one regards the same work, since one's view will be more critical. Moreover, this should be the start of the learning process of being able to make a distinction. "Thus the pictures differ aesthetically for me now even if no one will ever be able to tell them apart merely by looking at them." (Ibid, 106)

We believe that there is no reason why Goodman does not pursue his relativism. He could, for example, admit that there is no corresponding difference in aesthetic experience when one does not recognize the real-false difference. Unless, of course, one should accept this difference at an unconscious level. In this context, unlike Wittgenstein, Goodman emphasizes insufficiently the relativism related to the enormous differences between the faculty of perception of the various spectators. This regards both the inherent visual ability and the trained visual ability of the various spectators. The training of visual perception cannot be compared with a simple educational activity like learning the alphabet. It is not sufficient to utter the word "training" and to conclude from this that this activity will lead to a similar result in everyone. The next statement seems very probable: "Thus pictures that look just alike to the newsboy come to look quite unlike to him by the time he has become a museum director." (Ibid, 103) But not all newsboys will see the same object despite looking at the same object, and neither will this be the case when they are museum directors. Goodman cites the example of Rembrandt's Lucretia. A special committee of investigation reversed the authenticity of several works by this master, clearly demonstrating that even trained eyes perceive in different ways. In that sense, Goodman is right: the moment one knows that a work is not a Rembrandt, it becomes less fascinating. This factual relativism of the public indicates the weakness of pure seeing and raises the question of what exactly aesthetic experience is. Be that as it may, we adhere to an extremely theoretical relativism which says: if falseness is not visible, it will not play a role in the aesthetic experience and merely be an art historical problem or rather an economic one.

Fortunately, Goodman does not lapse into the pedantic prejudice that, by definition, the real work will be of better aesthetic quality. On the contrary: "All I have attempted to show, of course, is that the two pictures can differ aesthetically, not that the original is better than the forgery." (Ibid, 109) Because of this, he ultimately remains dedicated to his relativism. Goodman states that the aesthetic difference is accompanied by a difference in perception, which may result from the knowledge of what is real. By means of the example false-real, he intends to show that not merely the perceived aesthetic qualities are at stake, but also the qualities which determine how one should look. ".... (I) have simply argued that since the exercise, training, and development of our powers of discriminating among works of art are plainly aesthetic activities, the aesthetic properties of a picture include not only those found by looking at it but also those that determine how it is to be looked at." (Ibid, 81)

As a footnote to the statement that if the real work is not better a priori, one could point out the socially denied role of the forger in contrast with the accepted role of copier. One can see the forger as another form of human genius. Even in his function as anti-social protester, the artist remains a socially accepted institution of human exception which will be recognized sooner or later. The forger does not have that image, although he is often more gifted than many an artist. This is a theoretical construction and, if you will, a philosophical one. Marijnissen points out that in actual practice, however, there are not many gifted forgers or copiers. Of course the philosopher could respond that the gifted forger will not be exposed.

3.3.3 The cognitive function of art

At the end of his book, Goodman arrives at the comparison of the aesthetic and scientific attitudes breaking with a number of prevailing misconceptions in both fields. Thus, he opposes the view that the aesthetic attitude is a passive contemplation of the immediate given, the direct understanding of what is represented, not affected by any definition, isolated from all echoes of the past and the threats or promises of the future. The painting should be read. And this is not a static, but a dynamic aesthetic experience. The aesthetic attitude is more an action than an attitude: it is creation and recreation. "It involves making delicate discriminations and discerning subtle relationships, identifying symbol systems and characters within these systems and what these characters denote and exemplify, interpreting works and reorganizing the world in terms of works and works in terms of the world. Much of our experience and many of our skills are brought to bear and may be transformed by the encounter. The aesthetic "attitude" is restless, searching, testing - is less attitude than action: creation and re-creation." (Ibid, 241-242)

The distinction between aesthetic and scientific research cannot be explained by the assertion that the former does not pursue a practical goal. Technology does so indeed. But the strict scientific attitude is just as disinterested as the aesthetic one, for it verifies knowledge for its degree of truth and not for its ability to conduct behavior.

Goodman rejects the idea that the degree of intensity of pleasure could be a criterium of the aesthetic. A scientific experiment could provide as much pleasure. The view that the aesthetic experience distinguishes itself by a special aesthetic emotion, or that a type of "objectified" pleasure could exist as a characteristic of the object itself, or that the use of the term "satisfaction" would do any good, find no favor in Goodman's eyes. After all, according to Goodman, it is wrong to present pairs of concepts such as knowing and feeling, the cognitive and the emotive, as dichotomies. The scientific domain is not purely cognitive and the aesthetic one does not necessarily have to evoke emotions in order to be aesthetic. Therefore, Goodman opposes the mimetic theory of representation, as if art would be a poor substitute of reality. At the same time, he disagrees with the cathartic function of art. According to that function we will be purged of negative emotions. But art does not belong to the field of health care, and Goodman comments ironically: "Art becomes not only palliative but therapeutic, providing both a substitute for good reality and a safeguard against bad reality. Theaters and museums function as adjuncts to Departments of Public Health." (Ibid, 246)

The representation of two clearly defined fields as a dichotomy, i.e. the cognitive versus the emotive, prevents us from seeing the close relationship between them, in particular how emotions act in a cognitive way in the aesthetic experience. We agree with Goodman's statement that "... in aesthetic experience the emotions function cognitively." (Ibid, 248) In an extreme way, one could even state that we can feel how a painting looks and how it feels. The spectator often notices the sensation of movement rather than its structure, provided both can be discerned. In Goodman's view, emotion in the aesthetic experience is a means to observe what characteristics a work has and expresses. This does not mean that one should not feel emotions, but rather that they should be present in the first place. The cognitive action involves emotions and sensory perceptions - let us call them feeling and touch - that are different from each other and are associated with each other. The purpose of this is to evaluate and to understand the painting and to integrate it into the rest of our experiences, into the full totality of the world. Emotions function cognitively; not as separate components, but in connection with each other. Moreover, they interact with other faculties such as perception and recognition. "Perception, recognition, and feeling intermingle and interact; and an alloy often resists analysis into emotive and non-emotive components." (Ibid, 249)

Goodman emphasizes that emotion is a form of knowledge, no matter how it is judged: positively or negatively. If it concerns the aesthetic experience then both judgements are a way of being susceptible to the work.

By revealing the role of emotion in the aesthetic experience, Goodman does succeed in distinguishing it from all other experiences. Rather than searching for a criterium, he chooses to recognize the aesthetic domain by means of symptoms. Goodman arrives at four symptoms of the aesthetic, to which he later adds in a different book a fifth symptom: 1) "syntactic density", where in a certain respect the finest differences form a difference between symbols; 2) "semantic density" where symbols cause things to be distinguished by the finest differences in certain respects; 3) "relative repleteness", where relatively many aspects of a symbol are meaningful; 4) "exemplification", where a symbol, whether or not referring; functions as a language for the qualities it has literally or metaphorically; 5) "multiple and complex reference", where a symbol fulfills several integrated and interactive referential functions, either immediately or by mediation of other symbols.

Goodman's main point is that an experience does not have to exhibit all of these symptoms in order to be aesthetic. In his opinion, one is sufficient. Rather than classifying an entity as aesthetic or not-aesthetic, it is important to identify aspects which are either aesthetic or non-aesthetic. A component of an aesthetic event could be very unaesthetic, for example a rehearsal. On the other hand, an aspect of an unaesthetic matter could be aesthetic, for example the test of a scientific hypothesis; reason to stress again the possibility of affiliation between art and science: "Art and science are not altogether alien." (Ibid, 255)

It seems important that the distinction between aesthetic and non-aesthetic is detached from each opinion of the value of the aesthetic. A "good" work of art belongs just as much to the aesthetic as a "bad" one. To determine the value is not simple. Concepts as "beauty, truth, satisfaction" are not sufficient criteria for evaluation.

Goodman considers works of art symbolizations, and believes one should question what purposes such symbolizations could have. He rejects three functions often mentioned: the practical, the playful or the passionate, and the communicative function. The "practical function" corresponds with what one usually calls the educational function, or art as a means to develop abilities with an eye toward future situations. Goodman rejects this function with a masterly example of irony: "Aesthetic experience becomes a gymnasium workout, pictures and symphonies, the barbells and punching bags we use in strengthening our intellectual muscles. Art equips us for survival, conquest, and gain. And it channels surplus energy away from destructive outlets. It makes the scientist more acute, the merchant more astute and clears the streets of juvenile delinquents. Art, long derided as the idle amusement of the guilty leisure class, is acclaimed as a universal servant of mankind." (Ibid, 256-257)

Goodman also dismantles the second, so-called hedonistic function, as well as the communicative one, albeit with less ardor. In his view, they are secondary compared to the main cognitive function. Art as symbolization should be judged based on how it serves the cognitive purpose. "Symbolization, then, is to be judged fundamentally by how well it serves the cognitive purpose: by the delicacy of its discriminations and the aptness of its allusions; by the way it works in grasping, exploring, and informing the world; by how it analyzes, sorts,

orders and organizes; by how it participates in the making, manipulation, retention, and transformation of knowledge. Considerations of simplicity and subtle-
ty, power and precision, scope and selectivity, familiarity and freshness, are all
relevant and often contend with one another; their weighing is relative to our
interests, our information, and our inquiry." (Ibid, 258) This is a statement which
glorifies symbolization in the broadest sense of the word, instead of solely in the
aesthetic sense. General excellence becomes aesthetic when it is expressed by
aesthetic objects, in other words, independent of the particular constellation of
characteristics qualified as aesthetic. The subordination of aesthetic excellence
to the cognitive function does not exclude the sensory component or the emotive
one. What we know by means of art is also felt physically. Therefore, interpretation of symbols is not only a matter of the mind. What we can learn from a symbol varies depending on what we contribute to it. As our experience becomes
richer, our understanding of symbols will increase. The confrontation with
works of art will change our view of the world. In short, the aesthetic experience
is not an isolated experience.

Nevertheless, Goodman starts circumventing the problem of criteria for
the appreciation of art by pointing to the dynamic character of taste. "A work
may be successively offensive, fascinating, comfortable, and boring. These are
the vicissitudes of the vehicles and instruments of knowledge." (Ibid, 259) To
him as a logician, it is probably hard to accept that such a criterium cannot be
formulated or may not even exist. Yet, we believe that the absence of criteria
cannot lead to the denial of the importance of the aesthetic quality. Goodman
does so, stating, "To say that a work of art is good or even to'say how good it is
does not after all provide much information, does not tell us whether the work is
evocative, robust, vibrant, or exquisitely designed, and still less what are its
salient specific qualities of color, shape, or sound." And further: "Estimates of
excellence are among the minor aids to insight. Judging the excellence of works
of art or the goodness of people is not the best way of understanding them."
(Ibid, 261-262)

Goodman makes the aesthetic function disappear entirely into the cognitive function of art. However, in our view, the aesthetic function prevails: the symbol, to use Goodman's term, should be art in the first place and the best art possible in the second place; by all means the symbol should be perceived as art. The
better the quality of art, the better the cognitive value of that symbol. In rejecting
the aesthetic value, Goodman demotes or, more neutrally, classifies art as a symbol among symbols. In his view, art is only measurable on the basis of pure cognitive value. Then art is no longer art, but a symbol loaded with cognitive value
equal to other images from visual culture, where the form is indeed important as a

bearer of content, but in itself fails to provide a special cognitive meaning. Although Goodman is known as an art lover, in our view, such a contradictory argument follows from Goodman's lack of practical familiarity with art.

We believe that the aesthetic function should prevail whereupon, as Goodman claims, the cognitive function will dominate all other functions. As a matter of fact, in our view, the educative function results from the synthesis of the aesthetic and the cognitive function, where the former is a necessary condition of the latter. The educative is contained in the specific transference of knowledge provided by the aesthetic function. Goodman's misunderstanding of the criterion of quality does not prevent him from confirming the aesthetic function particularly where he closely connects art and science. Among other things, he points out that "truth" is not of great importance in the sciences. According to Goodman, the difference between the aesthetic and the scientific is situated in the differing prevalence of certain specific characteristics of symbols. "The difference between art and science is not that between feeling and fact, intuition and inference, delight and deliberation, synthesis and analysis, sensation and cerebration, concreteness and abstraction, passion and action, mediacy and immediacy, or truth and beauty, but rather a difference in domination of certain specific characteristics of symbols." (Ibid, 264) Goodman hopes that once one understands - contrary to what is the case now - that there are points of difference and of correspondence between art and science based on the specific nature of systems of symbols, changes in educative technology may result.

3.3.4. *When is art?*

In Goodman's book Ways of Worldmaking, he proposes replacing the classical question "What is art?" with "When is art?". The argument is based on the symbolic character of all art. Indeed, symbolic art is not the only type that belongs to a system of symbols. So-called "symbolic art" earned that name because symbols comprised the subject matter of this type of art.

Goodman argues against what he calls the "purist" view of formalism. This view concentrates on the intrinsic component rather than on the extrinsic one, and insists that an artwork is "what it is" rather than "what it symbolizes". The ultimate conclusion is that pure art is separated from each external reference. Goodman demonstrates that the line between internal and external is hard to draw. With the sample sheet of a tailor as an example, he points out that a sample will never have all properties which it exemplifies as a sample. The properties of the sample will vary largely depending on context and circumstances. "In sum, the point is that a sample is a sample of - or exemplifies - only some of its properties, and that the properties to which it bears this relationship of exemplification vary with circumstances and can only be distinguished as those properties that it serves, under the given circumstances, as a sample of." (Goodman 1981, 64-65)

Thus, the important properties in a purist painting are not so much the intrinsic properties as well as the properties which serve as an example, as a sample. Goodman calls this "exemplification". From this it follows that the purist painting made by the formalist will produce symbols as well: the form, the color, the texture. "Art without representation or expression or exemplification - yes: art without all three - no." (Ibid, 66)

In arguing in this way, Goodman does not want to enter into debate about certain styles of painting. He is in search of a starting point to pose the problem of when is or when is not a work of art. Apart from some nuances, Goodman's approach seems very similar to our "deitic" perspective. However, he is not convinced that there is a work of art if the artist indicates as such. Considering the symbolic character of the work of art, he rather believes that an object can be both: an object can be a symbol at a certain moment and in certain specific circumstances, and an object can also be a work of art at a certain specific moment. "Indeed, just by virtue of functioning as a symbol in a certain way does an object become, while so functioning, a work of art." (Ibid, 67)

Of course, Goodman is aware that functioning as a symbol is not the same as functioning as a work of art; certain characteristics are involved. In this context, he refers to the five symptoms mentioned before. He also knows that symptoms do not yield a definition, and that the presence of symptoms is no proof of the presence of the illness and vice versa. Nonetheless, Goodman considers an object a work of art if it functions in that way. He does not claim that by telling what something does, one tells what it is. However, in order to determine when something is art, he does not see any other solution but to substitute the question of "What is?" with the description of how it functions.

Obviously, Goodman poses here the problem of the "ready-made", a consumer object outside the art world and an artwork within it. Duchamp introduced this phenomenon into the art world with his bicycle wheel, fountain, etc. Goodman's theory cannot oppose the comedian or fool who maintains that a certain object should function as a work of art. Therefore, "ready-made" art is a good example of how the decision of what is art depends on the statement of the artist who will label the relevant object as art. Goodman's examples of objects which function as works of art are situated within the museum or gallery. In his view, the stone one comes across in nature may obtain a symbolic function in the museum and, as a result, become a work of art. Goodman goes too far with this example. The functioning of an object as a work of art within a gallery or within a museum is no answer to the question "When is art?". It is a reply to the question "When is a work of art recognized or established as art?" Answer: "If it functions within a museum or a gallery or a collection." The question of "When" should be posed in an earlier phase. After all, it does not make sense that a philosophical contemplation on what art is, reasons from two social institutions instead of the total social context. Furthermore, if one knows the gallery world's economic power of "defining" what should be sold as art and for what price; if one knows the museum world's ways of manipulation, then, obviously, a philosopher is only credulous when building these two components into his defi-nition. The gallery and the museum are only two, albeit very powerful, elements of the art world in deciding what is art. In our view, philosophy of art should react against the economic impact on the essence of art by revealing the struc-tures of manipulation. We believe that critical theory did a good job on that score. In this context, relativism, often a consequence of philosophical reflec-tion, will be able to oppose commercial "absolutism". However, Goodman's proposal to substitute the metaphysical question of "What is art?" by "When is art" is very valuable, if only to substitute the somewhat essentialist atmosphere with a more contextual one.

4. EXISTENTIAL PHENOMENOLOGY AND HERMENEUTICS

Phenomenology is an interesting perspective on art, as the emphasis on the concept of "perception" is very stimulating in approaching the phenomena created for visual experience. However, the question will arise of how "present" the perceivable is and what guarantees this presentation, thus, the act of perception itself, will offer. For those who wish to reflect on art, it is tempting to search for the "logos" (or the defining code) of the phenomena of art in an adequate description - outside of pure argumentation - of that which presents itself to consciousness. This description departs from the desire to become fully aware of what can be perceived. The assumption of the openness of the work of art and the thought that such an adequate description will never be completed is also important with respect to the application of the phenomenological reduction. Thus, the work of art becomes a source of infinite adequate descriptions. The description itself is the necessary condition for an increase in consciousness; however, the object is reduced to the meaning it offers to consciousness. In the phenomenological reduction, the difference with other phenomena will be emphasized, but what an object "is" and what it "means" will be equalized by "putting the world between parentheses". Thus, "what is" corresponds to what is experienced. This intentional presentation of consciousness can result in an aesthetic gaze. The Greek word "epochè" means: deferment of judgement, awaiting attitude, distancing oneself from all prejudices concerning oneself and the world. "Epochè" as "putting the world between parentheses" will increase the act of consciousness by reducing it to the (aesthetic) "fact", without burdening it with former interpretations or constructions of ideas.

The act of presentation may assume various forms, such as anticipating expectation or imagination not as factual presence. This can be very interesting for art. However, Husserl considers this presence always in the present tense and thus follows traditional metaphysics. Being or reality are compared with presence (for consciousness). Statements refer to a sign or are a sign of present reality. Conversely, Heidegger is more future-oriented. He emphasizes the sensitivity for a possible presence. Rather than being a sign (Zeichen), speaking reveals (zeigen) unconcealment (Unverborgenheit). According to Levinas and Derrida, presence withdraws continuously. It escapes the discourse while the discourse itself presses on as true reality.

Presence, as that which will become present, continuously escapes from painterly activity. Thus presence continuously withdraws. Yet, the result of this painterly activity gives the passing impression of presence as true reality. This intangible, this withdrawing character, might explain partly why painters, and in particular pictorially involved persons, reproduce the same themes over and over as if evoking presence in an almost magic ritual. However, the "Being of being" continues to be absent, since it has to be presented in a signifying way.

On the one hand, this short sketch of phenomenological problems aims to situate the value of this method for the approach to art. On the other hand, it intends to study the problem in depth from the perspective of a number of philosophers who pursued Husserl's phenomenology. In Heidegger's and Gadamer's thought, this phenomenology merges together with philosophical hermeneutics. The existential dimension is elaborated on, inspired by Merleau-Ponty and Sartre and by means of Dufrenne's problems of aesthetic experience. All these philosophers have one point in common as far as art is concerned: to emphasize the function of art in order to reveal truth. As a "supplement", we will deal with Derrida. His theory of deconstruction would certainly fit as well into the last chapter on postmodern thought. In this chapter, phenomenology and its view of "truth" is examined from the perspective of (neo-) structuralism.

4.1. *Heidegger*

4.1.1. *Ontology versus pictorial passion*

An ontology of art should treat Martin Heidegger. His line of thought is particularly interesting for the question of the sense of art. Some of our additional objections stem mainly from the fact that Heidegger's philosophy of art is only part of his metaphysics. It is an element in his search for truth and his attempt to reveal what he calls the "Being of beings".

Heidegger's text The Origin of the Work of Art (1935) is particularly fascinating with respect to painting; especially when he applies his ideas to a Van Gogh painting. It is not coincidental that Heidegger turns to Van Gogh's Peasant Shoes. Heidegger's preference for country life is well-known. His view of this painting is influenced in a rather deceitful and abusive way, because the aesthetic element becomes subordinated to ontology. In The Origin of the Work of Art, the farmer's craft as labor, which remains rooted in the natural environment, is of enormous importance. Heidegger's reading of the Van Gogh painting is also determined by this element. In the article Why do we stay in the country?, Heidegger's account of why not to teach in Berlin, he relates philosophy to the labor of farmers: "Philosophical labor does not proceed as a remote activity of an eccentric person. It belongs amidst the labor of farmers (...). The city dweller is mainly "inspired" by a stay in the country. However, my whole work has been

constituted and guided by the world of these mountains and these farmers."
(Philippot 1974, 41-42)

Heidegger's love for his rural home has overly influenced his view of the
Van Gogh painting. He did not look at it with an "aesthetic" eye and, therefore,
from a limited point of view. It is conceivable that a country cabin is the ideal
place to read poetry. However, visual art should be observed frequently in order
to train one's gaze. That is difficult in cabins.

In The Origin of the Work of Art, Heidegger points out the correspondence between works of art and everyday objects. An aesthetic approach is necessary to "understand" art. Yet, one should not lose sight of the thing-ness of art.
Besides the allegorical or symbolic level, the material element is of importance.
The essence of daily objects is their utility ("being-useful-for"). Conversely, the
work of art is self-satisfied, but the authenticity of tools is disclosed by a work
of art. Therefore, Van Gogh's painting tells us what the essence of shoes is.

Heidegger disregards how important it is to reveal the artwork's material
being. Instead of showing the peasant shoes as being-a-tool, a pictorial passion
makes Van Gogh reveal the quality of paint. Heidegger's approach to the canvas
is too rational. The painting only interests him as a means to arrive at "the Being
of beings". In fact, he is dealing with the farmer's Being as a human being who
employs his tools in harmony with nature. Art's Being is merely a mediator to
arrive at the being of the countryman. Not surprisingly, in Heidegger's view, the
function of mediation is the essence of art. Art fascinates him as far as its connection with Being is concerned. Heidegger reflects on art and the artwork from
the perspective of Being, which implies that the essence of art and the artwork
are determined by the activity of Being. In Heidegger's terminology, this means
that Being as unconcealment enables the true essence of art and the being of the
artwork in founding truth as a struggle between world and earth.

Heidegger approaches painting from the perspective of the spectator, who
must have the possibility of perceiving Being as unconcealment. Heidegger is
interested in the artwork as a final product, as a result. The creative process as a
method, as a road to be followed in order to arrive at Being as unconcealment
does not interest him. Heidegger - a layman in the visual process of creation -
poses the question "what" of the work of art instead of "how". If philosophical
labor can be compared with the farmer's craft, then the same counts for the
artist's work. However, it would be a mistake to maintain that Heidegger did not
think at all of the process of creation. Artistic craft is discussed when he treats
the Greek concept of "technè".

Indeed, the essence of art could be termed "to reveal the Being of being".
In this chapter, the path of aesthetics will be followed. Therefore, an opinion on

the "Being of being" will not be expressed, since that is the task of metaphysics. However, unlike Heidegger we believe that truth, the unconcealment of the work of art, is dependent on the form. The truth of art is its prevalence of "how" over "what". In other words, it does not matter what is painted but how this is done. Because of this "how", truth can reveal itself. This "how" will be expressed in plasticity and pictorality with their (unwritten) laws, which can be partly autonomous as a self-legislation of the artist.

In observing Van Gogh's Shoes, one will see an artist who has a passion for the pictorial. Color interests him, no matter how little it is varied. It is even possible to consider a magnified part of the Shoes as an autonomous abstract painting. Like many painters, Van Gogh was fascinated by the "magic" of the combination of little colored stripes and dots. His themes are for the most part unimportant. But this does not hold for his painterly reproduction of aspects of reality nor for his visual-pictorial legislation.

4.1.2. Experience and testing

In The Origin of the Work of Art one will find an interesting ontology of art. The question of Being is an important part of philosophical reflection. However, instead of a historical search for its untraceable origin, we would like, in line with Heidegger, to pose the question of the essence of art. "The question concerning the origin of the work of art asks about its essential source." (Heidegger 1978, 149)

Although one could imagine that an artist creating an artwork constitutes the origin of art, Heidegger maintains that it is the other way around. "The origin of the work of art is art." (ibid, 187) Thus, art as revealing "Being of being" is the origin of both the artwork and the artist. An artist will create works of art because he wants to reveal the "Being of being". This Heideggerian terminology conveys concisely what artists try to say they do, but generally fail to find a language for. Even in a nominalist way, Heidegger's statement is interesting. It is because of the word "art" that it is possible to speak of "artist" and "work of art". One could designate other names to producers of certain objects and these objects themselves.

Heidegger's terminology of "Being of being" and unconcealment could also be called "empirical", as he values everyday life and the immediate environment immensely. In this context, "empirical" should not be understood as quantitative or scientific, but as a type of real sensory experience - an experience one acquires by testing how to reveal unconcealment. With respect to painting, the term unconcealment is in itself a rather "empirical" term. After all, a painting slowly reveals its essence, stripe after stripe, dot after dot. In an art philosophical context, the term unconcealment could be valuable; it is much clearer than the term "truth" with its ethical burden from epistemology.

The Origin of the Work of Art is the first text in the book Holzwege. The perspectives on artworks, the trail the artist must follow in his process of creation as well as many other trails which the spectator has to go: they are all 'woodland trails', trails which will never be finished. The preface in Holzwege could refer to painting: in the woods (painting) are roads (perspectives) mostly blocked by bushes (parts which are not understood), and they will suddenly stop. Therefore, they are called woodland trails. One will follow one's own trail, although together with others in the same wood. However, this only appears to be so. Lumberjacks, trappers and foresters (art connoisseurs) know these trails by experience. They know what it means to be on a woodland trail, on a road to nowhere. Heidegger's empiricism can easily be deducted form his trust in lumberjacks and foresters. To pursue the comparison further: art connoisseurs wander about in the artwork but do not go astray; they can read the signs in the woods, they know what to do when the trail comes to an end. With their trained senses, art connoisseurs are in immediate harmony with the environment.

This touches on a delicate problem: the question of the efficiency of the senses in perceiving art. The forester can only survive by being in complete harmony with the wood, by being fully familiar with it, by being able to read all its signs. Likewise, the art connoisseur should posses these necessary traits. The concept of "beauty" is entirely superfluous in this context. In Heidegger's view, the mere possibility of revealing unconcealment is at stake. How does this come about pictorially? The "what" of the artwork is related to the "how" of the work. It is of no importance that this is related to beauty. (The forester does not see the beauty of the wood.) It is the power of expression (how) of unconcealment (what) that counts, because the "what" will only emerge in the function of a shape, the form of the "how". As an ontologist, Heidegger is not interested in this issue. However, we believe that from the perspective of aesthetics, it is fascinating to consider aesthetics as the theory of the sensory readability of the artistic fact, instead of aesthetics as the theory of beauty or the theory of art. A relativist theory of sensory perception will still entail a sensory experience based on training "seeing through" as a way of perception. This is valid for the other senses as well. This reflection is related to the extent of being rooted in an environment, which is an artificial one in the case of aesthetics. The efficiency of artistic experience is of the same order as that of the farmer who predicts the weather or tests the quality (fertility) of the earth, of the forester who knows all trails and is the best poacher, of the tracker who notices signs of life, of the tailor feeling the quality of the fabric and so on. A rather long but continually decreasing series because of technological development. Obviously, non-sensory knowledge is assumed as well, although of various natures and dependent on various types of training processes.

In emphasizing the empirical consequences of Heidegger's thought, it is interesting to go into three definitions Lalande gives for the "empirical". "That word is nearly always used as an antithesis to another term; one can distinguish three pairs of antitheses that intend to express this. First in contrast with systematic. That is a direct result of experience and cannot be deducted from any other law or known characteristic: 'an empirical procedure, an empirical medication'. Is used as well for persons when their knowledge and methodology are empirical in the sense just defined: 'an empiricist'. This meaning seems to be the oldest one." (Lalande 1980, 280). The empiricist's knowledge and perspective is determined by the result of the immediate experience. The systematic analysis can be very useful and necessary in certain forms of research. In the immediate aesthetic experience it creates a distance, a set of instruments which prevents penetrating the matter itself. This analysis might be too scientific to be philosophical, too distant to speak of familiarity. Systematizing offers a "review" of things rather than an insight into things.

Heidegger attaches great importance to proximity, as an immediate three-dimensional familiarity with the environment, which is understood as an artistic environment for our investigation. Only because of this growing familiarity - considered as penetration and not as numbing - will the aesthetic experience be useful and transgress the subjective seduction of beauty. Consequently, the artistic space is stripped of its non-committal character. It is not a cool background, but an eye-catcher, a proximity far from neutral. According to Heidegger, because of this familiarity, space is not observed in a neutral way. "When space is discovered non-circumspectively by just looking at it, the environmental regions get neutralized to pure dimensions. Places - and indeed the whole circumspectively oriented totality of places belonging to equipment ready-to-hand get reduced to a multiplicity of positions for random things." (Heidegger 1980, 147) Then the decorative will substitute for art.

We will conclude this paragraph on the "empirical" with a quotation from Lalande's Sur Empirique, "In German, since Kant, one distinguishes between 'Empiriker' (pre-science or non-sciences) and 'Empirist' (sciences)." The first term is relevant is this context: art in its function as information source in a pre- or non-scientific way.

4.1.3. *The proximity of the surrounding*

One of the important questions Heidegger poses is: does man still know his surroundings, a "home", an essential proximity of human beings and things, or is his ultimate fate to be thrown into an uncertain world? Manual work is the only kind of labor which connects man with his natural surrounding. In this kind of labor, Heidegger also includes thinking and writing poetry as interactive contact with one's personal approved language. It is interesting to verify this thought in relation to the functions of art. However, thinking and writing as possibilities for staying in the essential proximity of one's surroundings wither away. In the meantime, Heidegger's authentic "surroundings", a cabin in the mountains, belongs to one of the favorite programs of the tourist industry. Manual labor has become folklore in light of an expansive industry. The robot is no longer science fiction, but an operational instrument which reduces the number of workers in a "factory" from hundred to ten. Manual labor has been reduced to operating switches on the digital computer.

With respect to visual art, it is remarkable how it compensates for the loss of manual labor in various ways. For example, in replacing utilitarian manual labor (servitude) with an artificial revaluation of craft. There is no longer craft "in order to" realize, but craft for craft's sake. In a certain way, a form of perversion. However, the question is whether such proximity to one's surroundings is a state of alienation. Besides, in contemporary art, one finds the tendency to represent "traditional methods" in a pseudo-ritualistic way. Craft as ritual is part of the religion of art, of art celebrating its ultimate source. Art as a consecration of craft, as a perversion of pure functional servitude. At the same time, art can be considered alienation, since its religion is practiced by high priests represented as brilliant artists. If everybody had a personal religion and form of worship, certainly religion would not be alienating. Contrary to authentic religions, the religion of art does offer this option. Choosing one's own gods, one's objects of worship, the production and ways of worshipping these objects, even the possible negation of worship: all this is an essential part of the atheist religion of art.

Heidegger compares philosophy with craft and he emphasizes the close relationship of philosophy and writing poetry. Since poetry is not under discussion in this context, the poetic function of visual art as constructing a world will be emphasized. The experience of visual art as a search for objects of worship creates an artistic world (in the sense of an "imaginary museum"), which could be understood as a "home". Through contemporary art, the Being of new beings will be revealed. The proximity to this art will result in a new "home". It creates the possibility of "preserving" (Heidegger 1978, 183), of maintaining, in other words, of longing to be home in the openness of the work.

Contemporary art does not reflect a "rural" proximity. It is a combination of decay on the one hand, the disintegration of an old world with its old values, and, on the other hand, a new world which does not pretend by any means to be a better one, but indeed to be a world which is more "true", less false, less caught up in appearances.

The "novelty" of this proximity is not the only important element. The educational importance of this closeness to an artistic space results as well from the sensory necessity to become familiar with objects of art. Such sensory efficiency is essential in a process of de-alienation. An artistic training of the senses will turn the spectator into the forester admired so much by Heidegger in Holzwege: somebody who will find his way around, also on dead-end paths. Finding the way along the path of contemporary art means being familiar with a wide range of human possibilities. Access to the object of art assumes proximity, being close, being familiar. In that sense, Heidegger's philosophy of art is fundamental for the relationship of the spectator and the work of art. To be familiar with art is important in one's search for a life path.

4.2. Gadamer

4.2.1. Hermeneutics

Hans-Georg Gadamer considers Heidegger's philosophy a hermeneutic phenomenology. Even more than Heidegger, Gadamer emphasizes the importance of the hermeneutic tradition in understanding the work of art. Moreover, this thought is accompanied with a view of what art is.

According to Gadamer, hermeneutics and philosophy cannot be separated. Both concepts should be related in order to clarify each other. Gadamer views hermeneutics in a very broad way (Hirsch 1971, 245-64). Traditionally, hermeneutics is considered the explanatory perspective on texts. With respect to art, Gadamer expands the field of application in two phases. Firstly, he claims that besides the literary text, each work of art demands a hermeneutic approach. Secondly, he maintains that art is only one example - albeit rich in content - of the human power to express experiences. Hermeneutics views art as one of the many forms of expression connected with human life. Hermeneutics is a form of philosophy in the sense that it reflects on human life as a totality. Under discussion is the explanation of how human beings live and how they relate to truth. In this respect, art plays an important role. And aesthetics as a reflection on art should be resolved into hermeneutics. "Aesthetics has to be absorbed into hermeneutics."(Gadamer 1975, 146).

Hermeneutics as understood by Gadamer offers a very interesting perspective on art. Instead of questioning art in a scientific way, numerous general rules can be applied to the particularity of the interpretation of art, certainly with the experience of the spectator in mind. Gadamer conceives of hermeneutics as a conversation based on understanding. In line with Heidegger (Heidegger 1980, 182-88), Gadamer views a human being as a being capable of understanding. To a human being, this understanding is not a property among others. It is man's fundamental way of being, which characterizes all human acts and expressions in a particular and profound way. "Understanding is the original character of the being of human life itself."(Gadamer 1975, 230)

According to Gadamer, a strong commitment is demanded in the phenomenon of understanding. In the first place, understanding is understanding each other. It requires harmony. "Our starting-point is the proposition that to understand means primarily for two people to understand one another. Understanding is primarily agreement." (ibid, 158)

Obviously, in this context, the issue is not an exact scientific or logical conception of "understanding". To understand does not make the matter completely transparent. The finiteness of human knowledge is presupposed. The human mind does not know in an absolute way; it needs experience in order to comprehend reality. The finiteness of human capacity can be traced back to the impossibility of deciding which perspective on traditional thought is right. Others after us might understand the same thing in repeatedly different ways. According to Gadamer, experience will never be completed in conclusive knowledge. This also implies its openness. "The truth of experience always contains an orientation towards new experience. That is why a person who is called 'experienced' has become such not only through experiences, but is also open to new experiences."(ibid, 319)

Tradition should be understood as the continuity of remembering where one has to rely on new appropriation and explanation again and again. The perspective of tradition cannot be petrified as an outdated reality. Contemporary and current problems should be included. Understanding assumes more than a horizon which may in time become blurred at the edges. Scientific knowledge of the past, including the near past, consists of constructing the historical horizon and of superseding it at the same time precisely through such blurring. Gadamer assumes that we are not locked within our own horizon, though we can never recover the historical horizon as it was per se. The blurring of the horizon has the character of a conversation. To interpret is to have a hermeneutic conversation with the text in order to reach understanding. Because of the conversation, something is revealed which was not present in an articulated way before.

4.2.2. Art and truth.

In the introduction to Truth and Method, Gadamer has formulated the role of art in a fascinating way. He claims that, in the presence of an artwork, we gain an experience of a truth inaccessible by another path. Thus, he equates art and philosophy as a path to truth which cannot be attained by means of another, that is, scientific path. Art and philosophy force scientific consciousness to recognize its limits.

In Gadamer's view, truth is art's way of being. Art is the elevation of reality to its truth. He rejects concepts such as imitation, appearance, unreal, illusion, dream, which are all often employed in the context of art. In the work of art, the essential emerges. "And 'les beaux arts', as long as they are seen in this framework, are a perfection of reality and not an external masking, veiling or transfiguration of it." (ibid, 74) Gadamer does not maintain that we can comprehend the truth of the artwork. In his introductory text to Heidegger's The Origin of the Work of Art, he explains this using an illustrative metaphor. We should not see the knowing of truth as the act of a robber who reveals something that was concealed. Similar to Heidegger, Gadamer considers truth as a play of veiling and revealing, a tension between concealing and opening.

Amid the tension of revealing and concealing, Being reveals itself in the work of art. That action has several dimensions. Reality obtains its completion because it is portrayed. "What a picture is remains, despite all aesthetic differentiation, a manifestation of what it represents, even if it makes it manifest through its autonomous expressive power. This is obvious the case of the religious picture; but the difference between the sacred and the secular is relative in a work of art. Even an individual portrait, if it is a work of art, shares in the mysterious radiation of being that flaws from the level of being of that which is represented." (ibid, 132)

Gadamer points out the particular way of involvement in the work of art. He refers to Kierkegaard's concept of "simultaneity", giving this concept a special theological dimension. In this context, the sense of involvement is real participation in the Birth of Christ itself. According to Gadamer, the experience of art is fundamentally similar: its communication, its mediation should be conceived of as an entity. The justification of the gaze on the essence of the artwork cannot occur on the basis of the being-for-itself of the artist, for example his biography, nor of the performer or the spectator.

The spectator will keep his distance: the aesthetic distance necessary to participate truly in what reveals itself. Gadamer compares the religious moment to "parousie", the glorious appearance, the absolute moment where the spectator will forget himself (Selbstvergessenheit) in a work of art and simultaneously mediate himself. "That which detaches him from everything also gives him back the whole of his being." (ibid, 113-14) The spectator is an essential moment in the play which Gadamer calls aesthetic.

A second phase in the self-manifestation of the artwork is that the artwork itself justifies its existence. The play - and according to Gadamer, art belongs to the play - has the manifestation of itself as a way of being. "Play is really limited to representing itself. Thus its mode of being is self-representation." (ibid, 97) Thus, the play and the artwork represent themselves. There is no other purpose. Yet, the spectator is important because he will complete the play or the artwork. "Rather, openness towards the spectator is part of the closedness of the play. The audience only completes what the play as such is." (ibid, 98)

Gadamer understands the artwork's presentation of itself as the universal structure of Being itself. Therefore, he points out the etymological development of the concept of "beauty" and its relationship to and its difference with the concept of "good". In so doing, he refers to Plato. Gadamer particularly stresses that art should stay out of the domain of utility. In linking the element of "Beauty" to the element of "Art", Gadamer indicates the contrast with technology, the "mechanical" arts which bring about the utilitarian. What the Greeks understood as "Paideia" (the educative ideal) is called "kalon" (beauty). Beautiful things are convincing because of their very value. Thus, one cannot ask what their use is. Although there is ample connection with the "good", one should keep the distinction in mind. The beautiful is what can be observed, the observable. Via the connotation of "nobility", one arrives easily at the category of "good". However, beauty distinguishes itself from the absolutely intangible good, because it is easier to grasp. It is part of the essence of beauty to be apparent. The most important ontological function of beauty is to mediate between idea and appearance. "Obviously it is the distinguishing mark of the beautiful over against the good that of itself it presents itself, that it makes itself immediately apparent in its being. This means that it has the most important ontological function: that of mediating between idea and appearance." (ibid, 438)

In that sense, one should understand "méthexis" - the Platonic concept of participation - as the relationship between appearance and idea. "Presence" is a convincing part of the being of beauty itself. Even if one will experience beauty as the reflection of something higher, it is still present in the visible.

That beauty enlightens itself can be understood as a third aspect of the manifestation of the work of art. The sharp line between beauty and what does not participate in it is an acquired phenomenological insight. In this respect, Gadamer refers to Aristotle, who states that one cannot add anything to or remove anything from extraordinary works. Symmetry is not merely meant but rather "Vorschein", what comes to light. Thus, in this regard, light plays a fundamental role. "Beauty is not simply symmetry, but the appearance itself. It is related to the idea of 'shining'. 'To shine' means to shine on something and so to make that on which the light falls appear. Beauty has the mode of being of light." (ibid, 439) Gadamer constantly mentions the role of the spectator. This can be understood as a fourth aspect: the artwork reveals being. The artwork is appealing. It is more than the elation of the moment. "Whereas that which presents itself to the spectator as the play of art does not simply exhaust itself in the ecstatic emotion of the moment, but has a claim to permanence and the permanence of a claim." (ibid, 112) Thus, the spectator does not observe merely out of curiosity. The work of art appeals to the spectator and, therefore, it is not a non-committal incident.

To participate, to belong has, as a subjective way of being of human behavior, the nature of being-outside-of-oneself ("Aussersichsein"). This should not be understood as a form of lunacy but as a form of obliterating oneself in order to come closer to the work of art. If one is curious, one is still involved in oneself. "In fact, being outside oneself is the positive possibility of being wholly with something else. This kind of being present is a self-forgetfulness, and it is the nature of the spectator to give himself in self-forgetfulness to what he is watching." (ibid, 111)

4.2.3. *To interpret is to exist*

A recurrent thought in Gadamer's work is that interpretation means ensuring the long life of art. In order to continue to exist, the work of art should be interpreted on the level of the producer, the curator, as part of a collection and on the level of the spectator. "The work of art cannot be simply isolated from the 'contingency' of the chance conditions in which it appears, and where there is this kind of isolation, the result is an abstraction which reduces the actual being of the work." (ibid, 104)

Gadamer resists the view that, in art, form and content can be distinguished and that form will be responsible for aesthetic pleasure. Because of that, art would lose its function and the artist his position in society. On the basis of his experience with great works of art, Gadamer points out that such encounters open up a world. If we do not consider art as an object of pleasure but as a world instead, or better put, if we see a world because of it, then, according to

Gadamer, we will realize that art is a cognitive experience instead of a sensory one. Thus, we will see the world in a different light. Gadamer answers the question of what is a great work of art by the concept of the "classical". What is classical is independent of the passage of time, or the changeability of taste, and is immediately accessible. "What we call 'classical' is something retrieved from the vicissitudes of changing time and its changing taste. It can be approached directly." (ibid, 256)

In our view, there is no reason to place artworks outside of time and, moreover, their immediate accessibility is doubtful. Gadamer falls victim to a danger which threatens each lover of art, namely, that a favorite work must be a good piece or a classical masterpiece, and what one understands oneself will also be understood by others. This stems from the division between philosophy of art and art criticism. This relativity does not detract from Gadamer's view that part of the essence of art is that it should be actualized again and again in a continuous interpretation. "We started from the position that the work of art is a play, i.e. that its actual being cannot be detached from its representation and that in the representation the unity and identity of a structure emerge. To be dependent on self-representation is part of its nature." (ibid, 109)

Every era should understand a work of art in a different way. To an interpreter, the real meaning of a work is not related to the coincidental circumstances which held for the creator and the original public. The meaning of an artwork goes beyond the intention of the creator. "Not occasionally only, but always, the meaning of a text goes beyond its author." (ibid, 264) Therefore, understanding is not a mere act of reproduction, it is at the same time an act of production. This productive component is not bound to a better understanding but to a different one. "It is enough to say that we understand in a different way, if we understand at all." (ibid, 264) The work of art comes closer to itself the more it is interpreted in different ways. Gadamer makes the comparison with a feast. Periodical feasts are repeated. Each feast is always a "celebration" ("Begehung"), another presence. In interpreting, one participates in art in a similar way. As a spectator one can participate authentically. "To be present means to share. If someone was present at something, he knows all about how it really was." (ibid, 110)

4.3. *Merleau-Ponty*

Phenomenology as a philosophical method has characteristics which can be applied directly to painting as an inter-phenomenon, as a reality which has been interpreted. What else is a painting but a bracket of a world? However, there is as well the visual observation of the immediately observable. In the experience of art, where observation itself is so important, one should of course always return to perception and this is precisely what phenomenology does. In the work of the French existential phenomenologist Maurice Merleau-Ponty, painting plays an important role. He did not develop a particular theory of aesthetics, but considered painting as explanatory for his philosophical problems. Perception is at the core of his thought.

4.3.1. *Visibility by means of the spiritual eye*

In his work L'Oeuil et l'Esprit, Merleau-Ponty discusses the relationship between perception and painting. In the first pages, he emphasizes the enormous freedom painting enjoys as compared to the practice of language. Consensus, imposed on speakers of the same language, will create obligations because there is a theoretical code of intelligibility. The painter is only responsible for his personal code rather than for codes preceding him. "Of the writer, the philosopher, one asks their advice and opinion, one does not accept that they keep the world in a state of suspense, one wants them to take a position; they cannot decline the responsibility of speaking human beings. The painter is the only one who has the right to observe all kinds of things without the obligation of judgement. One could say that in his presence, words of knowledge and action lose their virtue." (Merleau-Ponty 1964, 13-14)

Not surprisingly, Merleau-Ponty has no interest in painting as a reproduction of reality. In his view, painting is a second-degree visibility. This means that it is not a reduced duplication, an optical illusion, or something with an additional meaning. A painting itself is not perceived as a thing within the actual space of the frame, the canvas, the wall or its surroundings. The painting shows a space which does not exist anywhere else. Conceptual artists also emphasize this second-degree visibility of the painting in exhibiting, for example, the back of the canvas. Some hyperrealists stress this second-degree visibility by trying to divest visibility of its metaphysics, because in Merleau-Ponty's view, this is how Being is perceived, "my gaze wanders in it (the painting) as in haloes of Being; I see according to it and with it rather then observing it." (ibid, 23) In a highly authentic way, a painting shows new visibilities instead of images which are, ultimately, only substitutions for reality. "The pictorial word has a bad reputation because one hastily thought that the drawing was a transformed image, a copy or something secondary, and that the mental image was a similar drawing from our private bric-à-brac. The painting and the facial expression of the actor are not additional matters I could derive from the real world in order to aim at prosaic matters by means of them in their absence." (ibid, 23-24)

Thus, the painted landscape and the portrait are not surrogates for nature or the person concerned. The imaginary presence does not coincide with a real absence, but provides a different and richer perception of the absent reality. In Merleau-Ponty's view, in painting the artist practices a magic theory of perception. Actually, the artist himself is involved in the magic of the eye, "to see is to possess from a distance." (ibid, 27) In painting, what strikes the eye is made visible again by the traces of the hand. Painting is pure visibility, "No matter from what civilization it springs, from what belief, motives, thoughts or surrounding ceremonies, from Lascaux till the present, be it pure or impure, figurative or non-figurative, painting will never celebrate any other enigma than that of visibility." (ibid, 26)

Thus, in the world of painting, there is nothing but the visible. Therefore, it is fractional. But, in being fractional, it is still complete, because everything has been drawn into this atmosphere. According to Merleau-Ponty, one cannot speak of a "memory of tactile values." At the same time, what the profane gaze considers invisible is given a visible existence.

In visual art, it is obvious that the experience will happen by means of the eye, by its very definition. Yet, we believe that in the structure of the work other senses could be addressed. In the first place, there is the tactile component. A good example of this is material painting. Perhaps, fortunately for the blind, this form of painting could be enjoyed in a tactile way. Some paintings are structured such as to arouse a synthetic feeling: smell, sound, touch, taste. Naturally, this synthesizing feeling is experienced by means of the eye because the composition evokes this poly-sensory atmosphere. However, in material painting, this feeling could occur more directly, because the experience could take place with closed eyes.

The "completeness" of painting only holds if one assumes that "all aspects of Being" are visible, which could also be the case in a partial aspect. The infinity of these partial aspects of painting, as fragile manifestations, refers to the infinity of being as the unknowable or perhaps even as the impossible.

Additionally, Merleau-Ponty treats the educative aspect of painting. With sheer visual means, the painter succeeds in visualizing what escapes common perception. Because of this, he will disorder our familiar categories. He will oblige us to see the world in a different way, according to unusual norms and habits of seeing. Then painting will become more than mere beauty; it will determine variety, the polymorphous way of seeing things. Freed of the rigid gaze, one will acquire a broader and richer view on the other. "Essence or existence, imaginary or real, visible or invisible, painting disrupts all our categories by revealing its dream universe of sensuous essences, of striking similarities and silent meanings." (ibid, 35)

4.3.2. *I think, therefore I do not perceive*

Merleau-Ponty disagrees with Descartes' view on painting. Though in his Discourse, Descartes does not pay much attention to this matter, what little he does is meaningful enough. To this 17th century philosopher painting is not a central act which will contribute to the description of our access to being. Painting is a way of being or a variation of thought, determined canonically by intellectual knowledge and evidence. Descartes emphasizes drawing, which preserves the form of objects. In his view, color is mere decoration. To Descartes it is evident that one can only paint things that exist. Painting is the substitution for absent things. Merleau-Ponty resists such an intellectual approach to painting, because it is inconsistent with his sensory-physical attitude. "There is no perception without thought. But it does not suffice to think in order to perceive: perception is conditional thought; it springs from what comes across the body 'on occasion', it is 'evoked' by physical thought. Thus, the situation is as follows: all one says and thinks about perception turns it into a thought." (ibid, 51-52)

Then why this discussion? Obviously, because the relationship between thought and perception is one of the largest obstacles in the perception of art. On the one hand, pure observation does not exist. Supposedly, one would not even see a thing. On the other hand, thought - which starts with "recognizing" a painting - actually prevents a specific aesthetical perception. Initially, recognition is not at stake in a work of art, but the form and the artistic quality of that form are. It is only afterwards that recognition or discovery of the representation will obtain any meaning, sometimes aided by titles of the works.

Merleau-Ponty concludes his handling of Descartes by stating that the connection between thought and form should be considered a texture, where profundity is important instead of an obvious layer of recognition. Space should be observed from the perspective of the individual as the ground zero of spaciousness. "I do not watch it according to its exterior presence, I watch it from within, I am surrounded by it." (ibid, 59) Basically, perception reveals more than itself. Therefore, one needs imagination. An inkblot could look like a forest or storms. This transcendental phenomenon is not a neutral act separated from each corporeality, where the spirit of the reader will only decipher the stimuli of light on his brain. "At stake is no longer to speak about space and light, but to have the present light and space speak." (ibid, 59)

That is the observation of the artist as well. He puts the texture of thought and perception with a gesture on the canvas; not to demonstrate his opinions of the world, but to give his painterly view. "Now, that philosophy which can still be thought inspires the painter; not when he expresses worldviews, but rather at the moment where his perception becomes action, when he 'thinks in the form of painting' as Cézanne would say." (ibid, 60)

4.3.3. *The multiplication of systems of equivalence*

According to Merleau-Ponty, the undermining of common categories does not come about because of a type of art which merely strives for the representation of the real world. It is striking how Merleau-Ponty attaches great value to the role of abstract art, contrary to somebody like Lévi-Strauss. The circle which connects nature with the expression on canvas by means of the eye and the hand does not allow an interruption. It is the way silence manifests its sense. The problem of the figurative and non-figurative presents itself differently: "This is the reason why the dilemma of figuration and non-figuration is posed wrongly. That precedent of what is to what we see and what we make to see; of what we see and make to see to what is, is perception itself. And in order to give the ontological formula of painting, one hardly has to violate the words of the painter, since Klee wrote the words 'I am unassailable in the immanence' which one has inscribed on his tombstone." (ibid, 87)

Merleau-Ponty assigns a metaphysical meaning to the history of modern art, with its attempt to free itself from illusionism and to acquire a specific dimension. However, this sense allows too many interpretations and, therefore, is hardly demonstrable. Merleau-Ponty states that the world no longer presents itself to the painter. Both are interrelated in such a way that the painting is "auto-figurative" in the first place. The colors should not be the colors of nature. "It has to do with the dimension of color, which creates out of itself identities for itself, differences, texture, materiality, a 'something'" (ibid, 67)

The freeing of the "auto-figurative" makes the artistic process infinite, both individually and historically, or as finite as humanity itself. It refutes the end of painting and even the end of the avant-garde. The reason for this is that the avant-garde, considered from a broader perspective, is a temporary historical phenomenon and is in itself less important than painting. It is the avant-garde which is finite in lieu off painting. This is not Merleau-Ponty's point of view, although he paved the way by pointing out the cyclical, indefinite component in painting. "The language of painting has not been established 'by nature': it has to be made and remade all the time. The perspective of the Renaissance is not an infallible 'trick': it is a particular case, a date, a moment in the poetic information about the world which will continue after it." (ibid, 51)

The avant-garde is not an inevitable device. It is merely an aspect of the continuous movement in art and of the non-existence of definite solutions, "Four centuries after the 'solution' of the Renaissance and three centuries after Descartes, depth is still novel and it demands that one searches it, not 'once in one's life' but throughout one's life'." (ibid, 64) The statement that the effort of modern art consists particularly of multiplying systems of equivalence is important. This relates to what is the main task of the artist: to mold ever new artistic forms from certain cultural concepts, motives, themes or content. It does not influence how or with what kind of material the artist will do this. "The effort of modern art did not exist so much in making a choice between line and color, or even between figuration of things and creations of signs, but rather in increasing the systems of equivalence, in breaking their devotion to the appearance of things; this could have demanded the creation of new materials or new means of expression, but sometimes it occurs as a new investigation and a reinvestment of what existed before." (ibid, 71-72)

Merleau-Ponty gives more depth to this thought by pointing out that it is impossible to speak of progress and divide civilization into hierarchies. In a certain way, the entire human history is stationary, a continuous procession where being will never be completely found. Yet, the search of the painter is always complete, even if it seems fractional, because all problems are related to each other, and each solution will foster different questions. Thus, there will never be a definite answer which will generally hold true. "Since depth, color, form, line, movement, outline and physiognomy are the branches of Being and since each of them could reduce the whole, there are, in painting, no separate "problems", nor real opposite roads, nor partial "solutions", nor progress by accumulation, nor irrevocable choices. One is never protected against these irrevocabilities." (ibid, 88-89) There are no real achievements. Each solution will open new ways to unknown realms. Each discovery will precipitate a new search. It is senseless to consider painting a generally understandable and communicable system. That is the task of language itself, although even this has its communicative problems in spite of being better equipped. Absurdist theater demonstrates this. Yet, painting should continue to be an unfinished product. "The idea of a universal painting, of a totalization of painting, or of an entirely realized painting, is deprived of sense. Even if it would last millions of years, the world, if there is anything left, will still be painted by painters, and it will end without being completed." (ibid, 90) One should not see in all of this a fate that prevents progress, "Rather, in a certain way, the first painting points to the distant future." (ibid, 92) In this statement, Merleau-Ponty formulates "avant la lettre", the movement in contemporary art which relates to primitive cultures and the exotic domain.

From these words of praise concerning perception can be concluded that "seeing" is not natural, but must be learned. Perception is a potentiality that will demand development. Not everybody will reach the same level. The study of art can become as empirical as the work of any research expert. At the same time, it is important that Merleau-Ponty considers the reality of the painting two contrasting realms. On the one hand, the real world which is represented in the painting. And on the other hand, the world of pure subjective impressions as a result of which - for the sake of arbitrariness - the painting will lose each claim to generalization or intersubjectivity. Between them, there is a world of continually new views on reality.

4.4. *Sartre*

Unlike Merleau-Ponty, Jean-Paul Sartre hardly attaches any value to art, with the exception of literature. He is a philosopher who employs painting as a screen for his political philosophy. According to Merleau-Ponty, painting is almost the materialization of philosophy, a sort of visible proof of philosophical thought; a coordinating activity so to speak. In Sartre's view, painting is subordinated to philosophy. Statements which deal only with painterly problems are rare in his work. Occasionally, he writes an introduction to the work of a painter friend, such as Giacometti, Masson, Wols, Lapoujade or Rebeyrolle.

Like many philosophers, Sartre has little eye for the pictorial aspect of painting. He reflects on the subject or the expression of the figures represented. Yet, Sartre is an important author within the core theme of this book, because he goes beyond the purely aesthetic approach and, therefore, reveals the relationship between the aesthetic function and other possible functions of art.

4.4.1. *Aesthetics of committed art*

Sartre feels pressed between the content and the form of artworks which, nonetheless, always present themselves in a manner of social commitment. Human terror should not be represented too figuratively, but neither should it be veiled. "In fact, the dilemma remains: if people and their terror are the issue, we can neither accept the representation of the cruelty nor its disappearance into beauty." (Sartre 1964, 369)

Sartre has to admit that there are exceptions to this basic political criticism of the aesthetic. For example, within the non-artistic theory of former resistance fighters, Picasso's Guernica became the symbol of the unity of political struggle and beauty. In this context, beauty is pinned down dogmatically to a work with a political motive. If the aesthetic-political meaning of Picasso's work would be limited to this, its meaning is of no importance. Sartre was in all respects moved by it. "Therefore, the canvas unites qualities which are irreconcilable. Without any trouble. Unforgettable uprising, commemoration of a massacre; at the same time, the painting seems to have only searched for Beauty and found it after all. The sharp complaint remains, but without disturbing the calm beauty of the forms. And, conversely, this beauty does not betray: it will help." (ibid, 368) Thus, beauty can indeed express a moral commitment, even in an abstract form. "Watch Guernica: it is a moral commitment. Nothing is ponderous; this beautiful classical and mythological painting evokes events but does not teach us anything. It transforms cruelty into abstract figures." (Sartre 1972, 322)

In Sartre's view, Rebeyrolle is the example of committed art, because he does not make literary art. Apparently, Sartre believes that painting has to elaborate on its authenticity and develop a technique which is not narrative and separate from the code of the narrativity of signs. After all, the narrativity of signs is still close to colloquial language. It continues to function according to familiar codes. Committed art often lapses into the pure narrative, into the literary, as some surrealists, and often social realism, will demonstrate. It is remarkable that a philosopher as Sartre, who attaches great value to literature, indicates the non-literary component as an important pictorial characteristic. Lévi-Strauss, conversely, disagreed in this respect. To Sartre, who prefers the non-figurative, a canvas hardly speaks. "A canvas does not speak - or very little. If it speaks then the painter is into literature." (ibid, 316) According to Sartre, committed art should fulfil two conditions. First, the technique should be convincingly progressive. "There is no commitment in visual art insofar as there is not a technique which claims it, by itself, as the only means of self-surpassing." (ibid, 316) Secondly, the political purpose should be at the root of the attempt to become a painter. If not, the technique does not surpass the commitment. Sartre believes that Rebeyrolle has succeeded in this and Picasso has not, but one could take issue with this. Sartre questions the effectiveness of the commitment of a painting (for example Guernica): "does one believe that it won one single soul for the Spanish cause?" (Sartre 1948, 63)

We believe that the commitment of art does not lie in recruiting "hearts" for the right cause, as Sartre maintains. That is the domain of political propaganda with its political slogans. Art's commitment is in the power of the form, which may express a political thought for human orientation. The revolutionary aspect of art is its wealth, resulting from each variation of form. After all, because of this, the depth of a (political) thought is enhanced. This is indeed contrary to the influence of slogans.

Yet, Sartre admits that painters may ask difficult questions. Moreover, painters recount things which are never fully comprehensible and which can only be expressed roughly in an infinite number of words.

We believe that an important function is hidden in the synthetic nature of painting in particular; in other words, an entire novel or tract can be expressed in one canvas. As a consequence, the trained eye can be confronted with a large variety of syntheses of world views in a limited time. Therefore, visual art seems to be the artistic medium which is very direct, and very time- and rhythm-oriented. The spectator can avert his eyes after one glance. But he can continue to look as well. Once the image is in one's mind, it can linger in one's memory. The history of painting can be traversed in one hour. At the same time, one can observe one detail of a canvas for an hour.

As far as commitment in painting is concerned, Sartre stresses that committed art is different from biased art. Painting is not literature but neither is it a pictorial slogan in the service of a party. "The painter who wants to create a communist painting is a bad painter; however, a painter who creates a committed painting, in other words, about what people do or should do and then that painting is claimed by a certain party because of its political meaning; then this meaning is given by the party, the painter accepts it, but what he needed to do in this painting, that which belongs to him, is not politics."(Sicard 1978, 20)

Thus, Sartre stresses the individual authenticity of the artist's painterly courage. At the core of his aesthetics is human freedom, which is the only possibility to paint or to write. "If one paints or writes with his freedom, then there is something particular and special in the work of art: the artwork is never a copy of nature (or of a natural object), but a product produced in spite of itself." (ibid, 16)

Sartre's unwritten aesthetics is related to beauty. Beauty does not necessarily have to be visionary. It can be found in ugly violence, since beauty and ugliness are not opposed to each other within the aesthetic domain. They are concepts with an ethical connotation, which still appears as such in colloquial language: an ugly or a beautiful act. In art, it is not the expression of a beautiful or ugly theme which determines whether a work of art is or is not "beautiful". The canvas can be treated with rough materials, dirty paints or bloody mud. In his terminology, Sartre formulates a possible approach to beauty. One can argue about terms, but Sartre is on the right track as far as situating, indicating and conditions are concerned. He formulates beauty as a certain relationship of elements within a whole. "Beauty is not necessarily Raphael's, it can be a tortured body! One should explain what Beauty is; on the level of unity it would be understood best as a unification, not as a total thing, but as a totalization of a whole." (ibid, 16) However, Sartre adds an element to his concept of beauty; something often heard from artists. Sartre states that artists often introduce purposely disturbing elements within a composition to prevent it from being perfect. An escape from perfection, so to speak, a negation of the opposite, a reference to another world as safeguard to one-sidedness. Affirmation and denial are connected dialectical. Between the lines of every "yes" a "no" is floating and the other way around. This also stems from the ambiguity of the subject or the author of the book. Or, in Sartre's words, "A canvas represents a subject (rather than an object) which is constructing as well escaping itself. For example, we can see a constructed painting with a form; but at the same time it is an escape; these are not the clear and simple forms of a Corot. On the contrary, it is something where the outlines are denied as well as posed at the same time. Beauty is a totalizing unification which offers by means of this totalization the specter of a totality which will never be attained; and in the relationship between totalization and totality I will find the idea of Beauty." (ibid, 16)

In Sartrian aesthetics, one can distinguish chronologically four periods (ibid, 139-145) The first one is closely connected with Sartre's literary work. It is characterized by a special interest in the sultry, the banal, where nausea and fascination play hide and seek, as we can read in <u>La Nauseé</u> and <u>Le Mur</u>. The second period comprises discussions of what almost could be called Sartrian artists: characters such as Wols and Giacometti (Sartre 1972, 291-346). They are Sartre's "figureheads" of the most authentic freedom: born artists, not too many neuroses and neither dadaists, obsessed by art at the risk of their very downfall. They want to develop their creations to the absolute totality. In a third phase, the critical experience of a kind of art is emphasized which reveals society's shortcomings. In this phase, a dialectical moment occurs between the self and the world, between the individual and the universal. In Sartre's view, Tintoretto is the prototype of the subversive inventor. His work is a compact texture of meanings which should be read as a praxis and a message. A fourth and last aesthetic period stresses political art, where an attempt is made to point out the material reality of the social domain. The symbolism of the material is at once a whole in an organic totality. This is the case in, for example, Rebeyrolle's work. The intersubjective component is very important is this phase, what we see in the following sketched profile of this existential artist.

It would wrong Sartre - selective as he was in the choice of the artists he wrote about - to maintain that he had no eye for existential content. There is room in his aesthetics for a theory of form. It consists mainly in pointing out the loss of meaning in the cliché. The form should free itself continuously and violently of the old design which grew into banality under pressure of the course of history. "Thus is the course of art history: each revived structure has been made to be undermined. As in history, one moves from form to form, there are no or little moments of degeneration, there are only deceptive appearances of modifications of structures. Each form is the phase of a transformation. And the transformation of a phase." (Sicard 1978, 143).

Each form is a passing state. We believe that this evolution is not that historic, not an evolution in the sense of human progress. Though it seems continually necessary to maintain the status quo, the momentous role of form meaningful. Therefore, it is possible to refer to old forms of design. However, this reference is not a simple adoption, but a resituation, a reintegration, an appropriate quote. Although the ideological recuperation of the authorities is not the only form of obsolescence, it is a major one. Social symbolism is always connected with an aesthetic theory. "The aesthetic theory cannot be divided from a social symbolism where something political filters through and deposits itself while creating itself as an antithesis in order to better recognize oneself. The artwork is a language outside every formalism (linguistic so to speak), because of the very fact that it functions as a distance and a transcription, not as an absolute but as a transmissor of traditional values or, conversely, of a revolutionary message."(ibid, 148)

Thus, according to Sartre, art continues to be a commitment. The visual domain refers to the social one. It seems important that Sartre attributes to the work of art linguistic possibilities not to be found in verbal language, much more rigid in its formalism. In a utilitarian sense, verbal language can be employed much easier because of the large consensus which prevails. In a symbolic sense, the visual language is richer because of its ability to combine a number of forces to communicate the message. This does not come about by means of long explanations, but because of the contextual construction of material and the cognitive and affective chains of meaning evoked by it. The artist can respond in an anti-ideological way by means of his material.

Sartre attaches great value to the role of the material component in painting. He even formulates an ontology of material. Painting does not speak and, therefore, it has to evoke meaning by means of the signification of its material. Thus, Sartre prefers material artists such as Giacometti and Wols rather than surrealists. In fact, surrealists create literature by painting surrealist narratives in the technique of classical painting. Therefore, the meaning of surrealist work can be read rather effortlessly. In material art, the meaning is less obvious. The material is a fact an artist cannot escape. Figuration arises out of the whirl of dots and marks of paint. Particularly in the 20th century, the autonomy of the material component gains importance. "In the 20th century, the awareness of the material, which had been forgotten completely in classical painting, revives together with the awareness of the frame, the way of painting, and the spectator. Thus, the total energetic process of the artwork is revived. One understands that the mere socialization of the finished product is no longer at stake. What counts is the exploration and decomposition of the actual materials so that they can reveal themselves freed from all external principles of functionality; the liberated material, thwarted by affects, loaded with coincidences, will reveal itself for the first time and will explode." (ibid, 153)

It is the intrinsic potentiality of the material which can be signified. In material painting, the theme of God's death, the theme of the unfounded order or the fundamental chaos is shown in a profound way. The layers of paint can refer to the decay of the old worldview. In an affirmative way, they can function as a search for a new, anticipated worldview. Sartre states that 20th century art has forgotten classical painting. Be this as it may, recently it has been commemorated: postmodern painting quotes classical painting.

4.4.2. The message of the existential artist

The existential artist draws, paints or creates sculpture in order to mark out a human essence within a space different from the space perceived. Giacometti creates figures, for example, full of elegant vulnerability and delicate inner decay; reflections of affected worldviews in confrontation with individual pride. Stylish decline, a sophisticated underworld, examples of precursors of a relatively new set of values decried by old bourgeois morals. The new human being, deserted by God and his believers. Characters who reveal an inner authenticity and its experience, carved out in their skin. They are not citizens who act as "puppets of a social convention". On the contrary, they are actors of the antisocial and unconventional domain, who, in the negation, discover the freedom to put anticipated different values on the canvas by way of experimentation. Obviously, existential art has a hint of the Kierkegardian aesthetic category, where the individual experiences himself as an exception and observes the world from a distance. However, in Sartre, this aesthetic attitude is atheist, and in an ethical sense, immoral instead of moral. The existential artists express their atheist attitude in works which are cries and testimonies where being collapses and adventure does not go beyond the imperfect. "One will die without having found salvation because art tries for the first time to leave the domain of religion. Atheist or cursed, one will laugh in an old monk's cowl, burning with the joy of living even as a cad: a cheerfulness will master the body as if all of this is of no importance and can even be swept aside; as if this were all of the highest necessity, the entropy of the irretrievable and of separation." (ibid, 141)

Painterly streaks will sometimes represent a metaphysical void. There is no ontological criteria because of which the existential artist is in constant uncertainty, a seeming characteristic of a large part of the art of this century. The artist will strive incessantly for perfection, but this striving is infinite. Art will continually question what heightens this uncertainty. Time and again, ideality and materiality are confronted with each other in different relationships. This infinite delay of the definitive will turn the artist into a lunatic, imprisoned in a loneliness resulting from the differences in perspective between author and spectator. "But there is in particular a difference of position between him and us. He knows what he wanted to do and we don't; but we know what he did and he does not." (ibid, 143)

4.4.3. The existential eye

The large autonomy of the critical spectator results from the aforementioned message of the existential artist. The work of art will only exist because it can be perceived. Conversely, the spectator is on his own because the artist's verbalization is not that relevant to the work he created, because he is too close to the process of creation and the development of his work. Ultimately, the spectator has to rely on himself. Sicard provides a synthesis of what Sartre understands as aesthetic perception. Sartre wants to put the viewer in contact with the work as directly as possible, without the intervention of a professional explanation, though the work should be situated within a context. "Contrary to certain decoders, epistemologists or art historians, with some contextual clarifications, Sartre places us directly in front of the painting: we are situated as public, the artwork reveals its nakedness - this is its violence. If the canvas is not a sign then there is no need of professional constructions. To be sure, each painting is a palimpsest and it is up to us to reveal the layer of shock out of the stratifications. Before enforcing its effect of retardation, the painting is a natural effect, a primitive and global affect." (ibid, 144) According to Sartre, it is sufficient to observe the canvas that hits the spectator in all its overwhelming compactness. Existential art will often scandalize in representing the figures in a distorted and violent situation, as in Giacometti's work.

In Sartre's view, perception is primordial to knowledge. What does Sartre mean by "perception"? After all, knowledge is often a consequence of perception. Perception must be an event where the eye perpetually rearranges while discovering different aspects. Against the scientific eye, Sartre poses an active eye directed toward experiencing life. "Thus, these works have been created in the first place to be perceived, in other words, the role played by the retina in its extreme efficaciousness in redividing perception. In general, the art critics, the scientific historians or the psychoanalysts aim to read: then the works of art turn into objects of knowledge." (ibid, 144) In raising perception to an event, being reveals itself by means of the masks of appearance. Through this phenomenological gaze, the work is approached continuously by degree while renewed descriptions are evoked constantly. Thus, the work is a mold, a network of descriptions and narratives. What is the value of such a narrative approach? "If one questions the art of affect, the critical discourse is a seismographic machine increasing the power of the artwork by pushing it beyond the limits of its capacity of emotion, understanding and rhythm." (ibid, 144)

The two ways of perception encompass a limitation which will render a discourse senseless and will neglect the specificity of art and above all its form. The scientist will project his expertise in the representation by overanalyzing the work. In that way, one glance can refer to the entire history of art, psychoanalysis, sociology of art and techniques of art, certainly when one starts discussing the work from an alien perspective. On the other hand, there is the existential gaze, which will start a mechanism projecting a personal experience of life as well as the evils of the world into the representation. In both cases, one will not necessarily account for the problems of artistic form; in other words, for the formal value of the work as an autonomous aesthetic whole.

We believe that this aesthetic criterion prevails because it constitutes the conception that the eye as processor of information is important in observing the formal qualities. Because of this, it becomes meaningful to create a message through an artistic medium instead of merely distributing it. The scientist as well as the existentialist are inclined to overlook this by stressing different aspects. Of course, it does not mean that one way of looking takes precedence over the other. Scientific knowledge can contribute much to better "perceiving" a work. On the other hand, nobody can claim to observe separate from existential involvement. Yet, it is important to abandon direct access to the work or recognition of the subject matter, to put on one's aesthetic glasses, so to speak, and take an indirect, difficult approach.

4.5. Dufrenne

The French art philosopher Mikel Dufrenne is one of the important defenders of the phenomenological approach to the aesthetic experience. No doubt, his work Phénoménologie de l'expérience esthétique can be considered a reference book on this subject. Dufrenne is known as the intellectual fighter of the 1960s. He stood up for existential phenomenology and its related humanism against the so-called anti-humanism of the structuralists, whose representatives are his contemporaries. Besides a number of aspects of the aesthetic experience, such as the relationship between beauty and truth, taste and public, we will go into the propaedeutic and political function Dufrenne ascribes to art.

4.5.1. The aesthetic object as beautiful and true

Dufrenne reinforces the notion of beauty in the aesthetic domain by assuming the aspect of truth as a condition. In that way, he hopes to arrive at an aesthetics which does not by any means decline the aesthetic appreciation but is neither subjected to it. Although one should be able to recognize beauty, in Dufrenne's view, one should not theorize about it. What are aesthetic objects? According to Dufrenne, they are "beautiful, the moment they correspond to truth." (Dufrenne 1967, 23)

Dufrenne is aware of the problem of employing the concept of beauty in a meaningful way. In aesthetics, one could have a preference for beauty rather than for truth, because the former tells more about the way one attains truth. "The difference between the two terms - which directs beauty to its aesthetic use and which justifies the preference sometimes claimed by aesthetics - is that beauty demonstrates the truth of the object when this truth is sensible and recognized immediately when the object announces authoritatively the ontological perfection it enjoys; beauty is the truth to which the eye is sensible; for reflection it enforces what is happiness." (ibid, 20)

Against beauty, Dufrenne does not place ugliness, but on the one hand the object as failure pretending to be aesthetic, and on the other hand the object indifferent to aesthetic quality. The question of what a failure is takes us back to criteria which cannot be recovered. The indifference is of importance. After all, the problem of complete aesthetization is posed. Rightly, Dufrenne departs from the relativity essential in judging. The failure of a work of art only reveals itself in the relationship of what it pretends to be and what it is or is not; "it should be judged from what it intends to be, that it will judge itself." (ibid, 21) Of course, this assumes the authenticity of the object as well as the authenticity of the artist. One cannot blame an object for not being "aesthetic" if there is no artist who intends to be as "aesthetic" as possible. Thus, the intention to create an "aesthetic" object is normative. Not until this norm is present can one judge whether or not the "aesthetic" aspect succeeds. Therefore, the norm is intrinsic to the work and cannot be imposed on the object from the outside. One can only explore to what extent the self-imposed norm has been realized in a certain object. In Dufrenne's view, the means not playing a role but, "the purpose that it (the artwork) poses itself to be a masterwork is at the same time the completeness of being sensible and the completeness of the meaning immanent to sensibility. However, the artwork is not meaningful in the way that it can be until the artist is authentic; it only speaks if there is something to say, only if the artist really has something to say." (ibid, 22)

   This sentence indicates immediately that Dufrenne selects very distinctly. He attempts to construct a formulation of the authentic work of art without collapsing into the Manichaean terms of good and bad, which indeed happens among art connoisseurs who do not have to justify themselves scientifically. He rejects each work of art that is not created by an artist who wants his work to be proof of what he is himself. Art is not a hobby, and neither a profession, but a life task. Of course, Dufrenne's terminology remains vague and can be evaded, because as a formulation it cannot be verified. Dufrenne is aware of the poverty of his formulation, "In fact we do not decide what beauty is; it is the object which decides for itself by manifesting itself. The aesthetic judgement comes about in the object rather than in us. One does not define beauty, one determines what the object is." (ibid, 22) Beauty does not provide a criteria for the aesthetic object, but rather a recommendation;, in particular where one can most likely see the criteria objectified.

4.5.2. The aesthetic perception and experience: taste and public

In the last paragraph, the norm appears to result from the absolute will to become an aesthetic object. To the extent that this norm is attained, it is valid as well for aesthetic perception. After all, perception has been assigned the task of approaching the object without any prejudice and with the greatest openness. In that way, the object has been brought into a situation where it can demonstrate its nature.

   Dufrenne transforms his phenomenology into an implicit deontology. He claims that the task of aesthetic perception is to observe faithfully. If perception is inadequate, it will pass over the aesthetic property. In this context, the word "faithful" seems very important, because contemporary art is still the victim of the public's bad faith. There is the snob's blind faith, but there is bad faith as well of a public which feels that their norms and values are being attacked. They only know how to defend themselves by considering the work of art as an object outside of an aesthetic context, and then to reject it with standard clichés. Those who are not prepared to explore the artwork's aesthetic qualities in a "faithful" way better keep their eyes shut. Because the aesthetic is indeed comprised in the manner of perception. Dufrenne maintains rightly that an artwork is aesthetic to the extent that it is perceived as aesthetic. "Conversely, the aesthetic object is the object perceived, in other words, perceived aesthetically." (ibid, 9)

There are other ways of experiencing art besides perception by unfaithful eyes. Therefore, eyes do not have to be exclusively aesthetic; for example, in cases where one wants to understand the work or situate it and justify its aesthetic quality with arguments. This is often the case with art criticism. Dufrenne considers art criticism an impure aesthetic activity. Art criticism is an act of judgement, founded on rules which are either chosen or imposed. Strictly spoken, it should not even be part of aesthetic perception. It might be rationally deductive, but verbal constructions can be deceitful if separated from a trained eye. However, art criticism can be purely theoretical and that is what happens in practice. Such a reading is not aesthetic, that is, not based on sensory qualities, but immediately directed towards the intellect, towards the understanding of argumentation. Conversely, aesthetic perception requires an extraordinary reading, "A reading different from the normal reading, where the eye as the immediate organ of intelligence seems necessary." (ibid, 116) The art critic does not necessarily have to introduce someone to aesthetic perception. A mediator trained to go beyond normal observation and who is averse to immediate rational input is at least as good. Dufrenne believes that the task of an art critic consists in judging the artwork's way of being, to verify whether the artwork is what it claims to be. "Yet we require that critics judge and we know that their function cannot be neglected. However, we rather expect judgements on existence than on taste from them; they should tell what the work is, how it is made, what it tells to the extent this can be translated, what kind of novelty it reports." (ibid, 100)

Dufrenne stresses continually that the artwork cannot exist without the spectator. It is completed by the public. This completion is in essence infinite: "the work tries to multiply its presence." (ibid, 81) However, Dufrenne maintains that the work of art will develop someone's taste at the same time and the particular component especially will obtain a more general nature due to the attention required to enter into the world of the artwork. As a consequence, there will be more understanding. Although previous training might help, ultimately, in Dufrenne's view, the important thing is to communicate with the work beyond each knowledge or technique. That will determine the concept of taste to which a non-expert may refer as well. "The artwork is a training in attentiveness. And to the extent that the ability to open oneself up is trained, the competence to understand will be developed; to understand what should be understood. In other words, the faculty to penetrate the world which the artworks open. Presumably we will say that understanding can be helped by previous reflection or training. But ultimately the communication with a work is at stake beyond each knowledge and each technique: which precisely determines the taste the amateur can claim on the same basis as the expert." (ibid, 101)

Dufrenne distinguishes between two conceptions about taste. There is the common meaning of subjective preference, as the adage "de gustibus ... non disputandum", where the subject surpasses the object he speaks of. In addition, there is taste as a faculty of judgement, superior to biases and prejudiced points of view. "To have taste is having competence to judge beyond prejudices and biases." (ibid, 99) Thus, Dufrenne believes in the possibility of a pure gaze. The problem seems to be highly complex. Subjectivism which appeals to taste as an individual criterion will cast a cloud on the perception of a work of art. Knowledge too will influence the manner of perception, in the sense that observation can be charged with data which are unseen or will even obscure perception. Conversely, a process of learning could imply a purification of an arbitrarily determined taste, unless training in perception has to purify the art of looking. However, Dufrenne does not say so. Or perhaps he means that by stating, "the artwork will determine what taste is because of its very presence." (ibid, 100)

Still, this remains confusing. On the one hand, Dufrenne disjoins art criticism from the judgement of taste, which in particular has to bring about the communication with the work. On the other hand, he assigns a task to taste which we should rather ascribe to art criticism: the faculty to judge a work which one may not experience oneself, but is able to notice its qualities anyhow. "Taste can steer preferences, but may as well oppose them: 'I do not like this work, but I can appreciate it, I recognize the work'." (ibid, 99) Such an art critical attitude allows the critic to judge and situate a work of art separate from his personal taste.

The confrontation between work and public will result in a multiple interpretability. But who is able to interpret? Experts, a certain segment of the public or everybody? Dufrenne opts for the second possibility. He does not say so directly, yet indicates that, as far as contemporary art is concerned, experts or professionals should be involved. Then who will become a mediator and what is

his task? Dufrenne leaves that matter aside. The art public will grow over time.
The relativity of the number of possible interpretations does not refute the basic multiplicity of interpretation. " since the meaning of the artwork is inexhaustible, the aesthetic object gains interpretative multiplicity. The reading of the meaning is never completed and the public should recommence the interpretation again and again." (ibid, 102) The aesthetic object will become increasingly richer as an ever-growing public contributes more meanings to the object. Although Dufrenne does not say so, the consolidation of the public where a growing number of persons attribute the same meaning to an object is not under discussion. The work of art in that case would become cliché, indeed not because of its construction, but because of its one-sided interpretation. In that sense, one could say that works such as the Mona Lisa and the Guernica became clichés. After all, it is entirely the many-sided meanings which constitute the richness of the work.

In Dufrenne's view, the aesthetic object will incite a team spirit. "The aesthetic object enables the public to form a group, since it presents itself as a higher objectivity which unites all individuals and forces them to forget their individual differences." (ibid, 104) The public is a specific group united around the objectivity of the work. As at a party, the spectators become mutually equal. Attentive observation is the rule of the game. Dufrenne does not speak of the ideological effect of the work. Or, more generally: he does not comment on the cause of the relationship of solidarity. Of course, this can be merely of an aesthetic nature based on a mutual interest in art. However, many causes are possible.

How does a public react to innovations in art? Dufrenne does not seem to be concerned about that. "It is inevitable that the public is very limited when the work is recent and has not had time yet to become known, or if it continues to have an esoteric character and seems to desire to preserve its secret." (ibid, 105) Rightly, Dufrenne points out the hermetic nature of some works of art. Since this vagueness belongs to the characteristic of the work itself, the obscurity does not need to be clarified necessarily as in a language game. The obscure element is an important motive in art. As far as the reserve for contemporary art is concerned, Dufrenne offers reassurance that, as a work ages, its public will increase in a vertical as well as in a horizontal way. Vertically, because more and more generations will become interested in the work. And horizontally, because the work will gain influence over the course of time. Of course, the degree of publicity will play a role.

However, the work will lose its innovative character at a certain moment. In his enthusiasm, Dufrenne forgets this aspect. One can say of some artworks, often masterpieces, that they withstand the test of time and continue to be novel. Yet, something will be lost. A work of art is novel in the same context as its first public. One could even say that later, one deals with a different work of art. The power of the artwork has been lost because the object will not draw a large public until it gains the stature of cultural heritage, next to the other curiosities of human history and obsolete artifacts. Dufrenne comforts himself with the thought that the reserve of the general public will produce the solidarity of the defenders. "A new work is greeted with indifference, sometimes disgust or anger: all so many signs of misunderstanding which enable its defenders to act and to unite." (ibid, 106) Whatever the differences of opinion, Dufrenne maintains that each increasing public will refer to the entire human race. "What is important is that as the public grows it will tend to stop being a public and start corresponding to humanity, where resemblances are discovered which will transgress particularity." (ibid, 106)

Unfortunately, the lofty thought of multiplicity of interpretations is thus overshadowed by a bourgeois humanism. There is no reason to assume that the work of art could bridge the gaps between people or groups of people. Unless its specific design could make these differences more understandable across linguistic barriers. But even this is not sure, because the relative tolerance towards art could even be founded on the lack of understanding of those differences. Dufrenne views the relationship between art and masses quite simply. He never means the masses when speaking of the public, even if the latter refers to humankind. In that case, the artwork should be obliged to defend mass values, which certainly is not the case presently. "Until recently, all art has been art for the masses, since in fact, as we stated previously, art has only just become self-conscious. 'Art for art's sake' is a very recent concept. Until then the artist has always served spontaneously his world view (Weltanschauung) similar to that of his community and his beliefs similar to the beliefs of his century. The artwork does not have a public but a mass of supporters recognizing themselves in the work and finding their beliefs confirmed in it." (ibid, 108)

We believe Dufrenne deals with the concept of mass art very peculiarly. This concept seems more suitable for some phenomena of this century. A type of art which serves religion and which glorifies the authorities still does not imply that its products are products of mass art. And some views such as "art will serve the prevailing worldview" or "art will often express a philosophy of life which will go against the prevailing mode of thought" seem even more interesting proof for the independence of the individual. Although Dufrenne does not want to reduce the relationship between work and public to the present taste in art, he does narrow that relationship to a message for a limited public which did not exist before. "It (the artwork) communicates another message to it (the public), but the agreement between the work and the public has not been presupposed and art creates a community which did not exist before art. In addition, the beliefs and values which connect this community are not necessary those which the aesthetic object expresses in its own way: they hardly reach the masses, they create a public." (ibid, 109) The task of the mediator is obvious in this respect.

4.5.3. *The propaedeutic function*

Dufrenne concludes his phenomenology of the aesthetic experience with the formulation of an ontology of art. We will deal only with art's function. Destruction as a principle of consciousness implies a move backwards. Thus, a distance has been created filled with purposes which relate consciousness to its object, but state at the same time that consciousness is not the object. This distance will enable perception. Before expression can be received from the domain of the real, the expression is read by the subject who initially is this expression. This expression is the truth of the real, or the world given as sense to the object. According to Dufrenne, the function of art is to create this truth. This function can be understood empirically. The aesthetic object is the model; it reveals a view on the world. Common perception does not notice expression, but perceives the object in a utilitarian way within a world of practical possibilities. Conversely, aesthetic perception does not know what haste is, does not look at a world outside the object. It explores the object in order to discover an inner world with this sensibility. This other world can testify for the real by revealing a view on what will be offered. This is entirely what Dufrenne calls the propaedeutic function of art: to practice the reading of the expression of the work of art as an exemplary object, where the whole of reality comes down to "being sensible" and will let us take part in an absolute experience of the affective domain. The aesthetic object, as surreal or pre-real object, as the unseen, will teach us the reading of the expression of the real. "In inventing new ways of representation, art will teach us how to see. By means of art, perception will rediscover its freshness and persuasiveness; art takes us back to the beginning." (ibid, 661)

4.5.4. *The political function*

In <u>Art et politique</u>, Dufrenne deals with the function of art in less metaphysical language but in a rather social-philosophical way instead. As the title indicates, he departs from the relationship, the difference and the similarity concerning politics and art. Obviously, the book is the product of the revolutionary days of May 1968 and often has a sloganesque undercurrent. Unfortunately, the category "Art" comprises a variety of works of art instead of art in a narrow sense. Dufrenne discusses masterpieces from the past, a smattering of the classical names of this century, adds to this the formal characteristics of the phenomenon of the feast and in addition decorative art, folk art, amateurish art and children's drawings, to mention a few of the less extreme examples. Moreover, he unsystematically discusses all subsectors of art. In short, the work is rather general and, therefore, rather superficial and reads as a well-considered manifesto rather than as an exploration into the possible relationships between art and politics.

What Dufrenne formulates concerning the truth of art corresponds by and large with what has been mentioned previously. Dufrenne states that the truth of art is the faculty to reveal what knowing cannot master, namely a certain view of a uncalculated world "where imagination celebrates its reunion with the real" (Dufrenne 1974, 9). This lyric sentence derived from Adorno indicates the spirit of this thought. Dufrenne rejects the artist as imitative of the scientist as demonstrated systematically in conceptual art. He prefers to see the work of art as "the product of a happy practice". Moreover, he regrets that, in addition to conceptual art, art falls victim to conceptualizing by theories which treat art as an object of investigation. In that context, the only pleasure is a lonely understanding, without connection to imagination and sensibility, which in fact should guarantee aesthetic pleasure.

Apart from the question of whether conceptual art falls outside the realm of imagination and sensibility, Dufrenne forces an open door. The reconciliation between a scientific analysis of art and the immediate pleasure of aesthetic experience is by definition contradictory. Most probably, he departs from his renowned criticism of semiology and the impersonal approach of structuralism. We indeed object to the somewhat euphoric idea of the experience of art as a feast. Nonetheless, one should distinguish between the analysis of cultural products and knowingly employing them.

Dufrenne goes into the problem of the relationship between art and religion as ideological state machinery in the Althusserian sense: an institution which serves the same interests as the state. In Dufrenne's view, it is inexpedient that religion as an institution, thus the Church, should control culture. In a Utopian twist, he wonders whether a new kind of art could take the place of religion in order to restore the experience of meaning and to reconnect the real with the imaginary. As a Utopia this is a very valuable idea. Of course, the characteristic of religion as an institution is that it intends to continue to be an institution. The characteristic of new art is that it is not allowed to become an institution, certainly not a pseudo-religious one. Apart from that, it seems that art indeed has a function as a substitution for religion. Throughout history, art has been a modality of something else. Time and again, art has had a different main function, such as religious experience and political glorification. Not until recently in art history has art's main function become "being art" and has its autonomy been claimed.

The concept of "aesthetic perception" and its object, particularly art, is extremely theoretical within the philosophy of art, since one will depart from a sort of ideal spectator. Of course, that stems directly from a non-empirical approach, as Dufrenne points out when he speaks of what he calls the perversion of the appropriation of art. The collector has a determining influence on the value of art, but also on artistic taste. Within a gallery or a museum, the spectator cannot observe the work of art freely either, because here the aesthetic value has been determined by experts. The mode of perception and the nature of accepted pleasure is determined by perceptive codes. "Here one has the right to appeal to perceptive codes: perception is guided completely by rules which determine the distance, relocation, and discretion of a tradition which will impose what can be seen and how. Don't touch the work! Don't play with the work! Don't indulge in fantasies! Don't show shameless pleasure! Good taste will castrate and the work will be castrated if perception becomes normative in such a way, if beauty which is not really sensuous is showered with Platonic honor; since the senses evoke another sensuousness." (ibid, 104)

The codes of perception disarm the often explosive power of the work of art. These codes enforce admiration and neutralize depth. The obliged respect keeps at a distance and suppresses the intimate contact which in fact gives pleasure. Information is provided, but one does not learn how to play with sensuousness and how to enjoy the shapes and colors. Desire is repressed and wild perception is forbidden. The message of the artwork is recuperated, its subversive quality is unrealized.

All of this does not mean the denial of the existence of the "committed" artist. He is often excluded from the institution of art. Dufrenne assigns two functions to political art: a critical and a militant one. Both functions are quoted in the discussion of critical theory. The critical function contrasts the imaginary and the real world. In line with Adorno, Dufrenne maintains that art is anti-social, because, due to its mere existence, it criticizes society and opens up another world. The militant function is even more complicated, because it assumes that art associates itself with the militant demands of a political strug-

Signs of the Time

gle. Dufrenne illustrates this with social realism and formulates its problem tersely. "It imposes an aesthetics of content to an art which is demanded to be apologetic." (ibid, 155) Within a political commitment, both functions will become part of the same struggle. If they both want to survive, they have to fight together. The critical function will only be fulfilled in a "different" art. "Because the critical function can only be fulfilled in the production of another art, which might be called non-art or anti-art, but which is still and perhaps even more art." (ibid, 156)

The militant function demands of art that it become a didactic discourse, or that art becomes something which is not art. But in being didactic, art is ineffective. The incompatibility of the two functions also reawakens the discussion of social-realism versus formalism or the form-content problem. Rightly, Dufrenne does not want to divide them, "like the material is inseparable from the form, the form is inseparable from the content". (ibid, 159) Without making this explicit, Dufrenne observes an actual synthesis of the critical and militant function in the Utopian function of art. "Utopian thought is neither learned thought, nor wise thought; it is, however, thought that will enrich the commitment and man's future in the world." (ibid, 173)

According to Dufrenne, Utopia is to think the possible, which announces itself in the real. As an exercise in innovation, Utopia will introduce the freedom of spirit. Dufrenne attributes to Utopia a pedagogic interest. According to him, Utopia is a stimulus to innovation without accounting for prejudices or even knowledge, and intends to liberate intelligence. "Utopia does not theorize, it animates." (ibid, 183)

On no account does Dufrenne want to introduce a patronizing element into his view on education. He maintains that education is mainly self-education, even in the case of the masses. "From a political perspective, the masses will only be educated if one gives them the freedom to educate themselves in their own surrounding." (ibid, 223) However, the moment Dufrenne expresses his thoughts on concrete educational problems he is wide off the mark. He rejects the "multiple" as a multiplicable artwork; he rejects that something can be production instead of reproduction. A reproduction is said to increase knowledge, and a production, pleasure. But pleasure is connected to possession. That is an aspect of a fake democracy and one should not be misled by this. Therefore, Dufrenne recommends the reproduction. "Here the reproductions are much more effective and their educational importance cannot be denied." (ibid, 247)

Dufrenne denies the value of sensuousness by means of this quote. After all, a reproduction can never provide the same sensuous sensibility as the original work. In Dufrenne's view, the educational aspect is the level of recognizing artworks and discussing their form and content. Because of this, he denies the material aspects of the work - texture of the material, the right size, the real color - which constitute the sensuous sensibility of the work.

4.6 Derrida (supplement)

4.6.1. Phenomenology and Structuralism

A paragraph on Jacques Derrida is added to this chapter, because Derrida's views are very close to the phenomenological and hermeneutic perspective. In his work Of Grammatology, Derrida points out that the concept of the supplement contains two meanings which are alien as well as necessary. The supplement will add, complete, and substitute at the same time. "The supplement adds itself, it is a surplus, a plenitude enriching another plenitude, the fullest measure of presence. It cumulates and accumulates presence. But the supplement supplements. It adds only to replace. It intervenes or insinuates itself in-the-place-of; if it fills, it is as if one fills a void." (Derrida 1967, 208)

Different from the complement, the supplement is called an external addition (see Robert). The paragraph on Derrida as a supplement to this chapter adds something, but as a supplement it refers at the same time to that what is absent in the next chapter. After all, Derrida does not fit into a chapter on semiotics and (post)-structuralism either. Derrida is always out of place, and that is where he prefers to be. The relationships between phenomenology-hermeneutics and structuralism-semiotics is not complementary as internal supplements of each other. They are mutually supplementary. The discussions of the 1960s - and between Habermas and Lyotard - do not testify to a mutually inspiring supplement, but of a mutually inspiring indispensability as a necessary supplement. Both movements have coexisted so long that cross-fertilization is inevitable.

In 1957, Derrida conceives the plan to write a study, led by Hyppolite, on ideality and the literary object. Inspired by Husserl's phenomenology, he intends to explore the act of writing. What makes a literary text a literary text? Derrida does not find the answer, but acquires a special interest in textuality. This is new in French thought where, at that moment, Sartre and Merleau-Ponty placed experience and perception at the center of attention.

The interest in textuality reveals immediately that a never completely comprehensible network of allusions and references is at work in every text. Derrida does not criticize texts, nor does he indicate the text's inaccuracies.

Neither does he interpret them in the traditional sense of the word. Derrida's perspective is not hermeneutic. From a hermeneutic perspective, one searches for the hidden or other sense; one tries to formulate in a better or at least different way what is actually there, and tries to explain each part (word, sentence, fragment, text) from the whole and the whole from the parts. However, Derrida does not explore the meaning, but rather the sentence's development or its constitution in and through the text. He intends by no means to say differently what is put into words by philosophers or poets, but keeps as strictly as possible to the letter. According to Derrida, the whole is never a fact and, therefore, it cannot serve as an ultimate explanation. "The" whole does not exist; at the most one can speak of "a" whole where the boundaries can be shifted again and again which will enable various interpretations. Therefore, Derrida's textual activity cannot be connected directly with hermeneutics.

Derrida's method is referred to as the now-fashionable concept of "deconstruction". It departs from the view that each text is a construction and part of a texture - to use an image from another domain. Similar to a constructed work, a text is a structure made of words, sentences, passages, fragments, themes and constructed according to previously given schemes and rules with respect to genre, style, design and so forth. Texts always refer to other texts, which refer to other texts, ad infinitum. If a text were not interwoven into the texture of other texts, it could not come into being nor could it be understood. That has far-reaching consequences, not only for the author but also for the reader. No author is ever completely lord of his own text, nor is a reader ever able to completely understand a text. The same holds for visual art if one considers it as a text, the painter as an author and the spectator as a reader.

Deconstruction is the attempt to reveal the joints of this system of texture, of this network of references. At the same time, the method reveals the many decisions made or rejected by the author while constructing a text. It refers to the many texts which are excluded and confronted with a triple absence - the reader, the author and what is described. Derrida's method of deconstruction makes the various defense mechanisms and strategies of conquest - which function in the margin of the text - step into the limelight. Derrida wants to show the construction of the text as construction by means of a never-ending analysis, which focuses on that what is in the text and on what has been excluded or forgotten.

Thus, Derrida does not search for the "essence" of objects because the objects are "absent". Yet, his texts are permeated with phenomenology in particular from Husserl's oeuvre. His writings show a Heideggerian influence as well; some even maintain that Derrida radicalizes Heidegger. In line with Heidegger,

Derrida reflects in discussion with philosophy, albeit to announce the death of metaphysics and to herald a new turn of thought. The concept of "grammatology" as explained in Derrida's book Of Grammatology is neither structuralism nor non-structuralism, although it is often considered post-structuralism. However, with respect to the discussion between existential phenomenology and structuralism, we do not believe that substituting concepts as perception, consciousness, subject, presence and so on with more recent and often trendy terms as lecture, reading, text, texture, context, discourse, sign and so on will solve all problems. Nonetheless, structuralism is fascinating in its avoidance of searching for Being and Truth (ontology). The same is true for Derrida's quest to follow up on Heidegger's "task of a destruction of the history of ontology".

4.6.2. Deconstruction of old metaphysics, the concepts of trace and play

Derrida's grammatology provides an interesting contribution to relate the philosophy of painting and the search for truth. The latter is not the search for theology, as this would mean finding truth. Derrida does not speak of painting, but of a specific form of ethnocentrism which he calls "logocentrism", or the metaphysics of phonetic writing. The history of metaphysics has always situated the origin of general truth in the logos.

We believe that contemporary painting has the possibility to run counter to this logocentrism, among other things because its language and meta-language are of a different order. After all, in the history of metaphysics, it is precisely this "being of the same order" that leads to logocentrism as the history of truth about truth. However, in Of Grammatology, Derrida speaks of linguistics instead of painting, although he refers indirectly to painting by excerpting Rousseau on the frontispiece to the book. "These three ways of writing correspond almost exactly to three different stages according to which one can consider men gather into a nation. The depicting of objects is appropriate to a savage people; signs of words and of propositions, to a barbaric people; and the alphabet to a civilized people." (Derrida 1974, 3)

The graphic sign is thought as proceeding from the trace, which refers to a presence which is absent. The trace represents a presence; it substitutes for it. The inscribed trace can be followed, but it will never reach being or the object itself. With this, Derrida differs from traditional metaphysics, which does believe in attaining the object itself. Thus, being is conceivable in principle, however, the object and the signified cannot be reversed. A sign represents beings, but it does not substitute for them. "The reassuring evidence within which western tradition had to organize itself and must continue to live would, therefore, be as follows: the order of the signified is never contemporary, is at best the subtly discrepant inverse or parallel - discrepant by time of a breath - from the order of the signifier. And the sign must be the unity of a heterogeneity, since the signified (sense or thing, noeme or reality) is not in itself a signifier, a trace: in any case is not constituted in its sense by its relationship with a possible trace. The formal essence of the signified is presence, and the privilege of its proximity to the logos as phonè is the privilege of presence. This is the inevitable response as soon as one asks: 'What is the sign?'; that is to say, when one submits the sign to the question of essence, to the 'ti esti'." (ibid, 18)

According to Derrida, Heidegger remains within the domain of meta-physics because his theme is constituted by presence in spite of his "destruction" of the history of ontology. "To the extent that such a logocentrism is not totally absent from Heidegger's thought, perhaps it still holds that thought within the epoch of onto-theology, within the philosophy of presence, that is to say within philosophy itself. This would perhaps mean that one does not leave the epoch whose closure one can outline." (ibid, 12)

We could even refer to a "metaphysics" of painterly perception. The painter acts as if he ultimately wants to present the objects themselves. Making art is an approach to the world which consists of making "images" proceeding from the construction of a "signifier". However, this is often understood as if the act of painting will be able to represent the objects or rather the essence of these objects.

It is fascinating to employ the concept of "trace" in the context of art. In Derrida's view, a presence will only come into being as a result of a trace. The sign is no longer thought proceeding from the affirmation of the original presence of being. "The instituted trace cannot be thought without thinking the retention of difference within a structure of reference where difference appears as such and thus permits a certain liberty of variations among the full terms. The absence of another here-and-now, of another transcendental present, of another origin of the world appearing as such, presenting itself as irreducible absence within the presence of the trace, is not a metaphysical formula substituted for a scientific concept of writing. This formula, beside the fact that it is the question-ing of metaphysics itself, describes the structure implied by the 'arbitrariness of the sign', from the moment that one thinks of its possibility short of the derived opposition between nature and convention, symbol and sign, etc. These opposi-tions have meaning only after the possibility of the trace." (ibid, 46-47) Thus, the trace must be conceived before being.

However, the trace is "inscribed" at the same time; it constitutes a sign. There is only meaning as long as the trace is fixed in the materiality of the inscription and, thus, has become an institution. According to Derrida, each sign will refer to another sign. Therefore, the trace is ineradicable. An element is determined by the place it has in relationship to all other elements of the system. Because it is part of a system, each element constitutes itself on the basis of the traces the system contains. An element is only signified in relationship to what it is not, as an imprint of what it is not. This texture is the "text". It exists as a thread of elements constituted by the traces of other elements in the system.

Derrida has a very interesting view on the concept of "play". "One could call play the absence of the transcendental signified as limitedness of play, that is to say as the destruction of onto-theology and the metaphysics of presence." (ibid, 50) Thus, meaning is no longer limited to the margin of the "transcendental signified", since such a transcendental signified would imply the possibility of indicating a being true in itself apart from the system of terms in which it is signified. According to Derrida, there is no "signified" apart from a "signifier". Each element refers to another element. Each "signified" is always in the position of a signifier. Therefore, each sign signifies another sign and is a sign of a sign.

The "gramma" as a continuous play of the signified becoming signifier appears to be an interesting concept from the perspective of a painting understood as a text, because only art will be able to play this play to its utmost extreme. The non-utilitarian nature of art preempts the need for one meaning. Thus, the play of the "gamma" can be expressed to its full extent. However, in order to understand the objects of art one has to know how to play. In art, the play has as a metaphysical background which is metaphysical destruction or - in line with Derrida - deconstruction. In a Nietzschian sense, the play in art is a derivation of the play of the world. "It is, therefore, the game of the world that must be first thought; before attempting to understand all the forms of play in the world." (ibid, 50)

Thus, painting can be understood as a texture of elements referring to each other in absence of the other, inside as well as outside the work. The dynamic nature of this process should be emphasized. It is not a position but a process without a predetermined direction. According to Derrida, "The immotivation of the trace ought now be understood as an operation and not as a state, as an active movement, a demotivation, and not as a given structure." (ibid, 51)

In painting, this play becomes clear as well because of the oeuvre of the artist. This oeuvre consists of the whole of the separate works, which are, in fact, not so separate. The oeuvre is a kind of whole, a chain or system where one work refers to the other. One cannot imagine an oeuvre merely consisting of isolated works. Each work is a trace to another piece. Many works refer to a similar signified. In a way, it is even conceivable that an entire oeuvre has one signified. A signified which is not static, but time and again becomes a signifier because of the play of signifiers, and refers to something else time and again. The artist, of course, is the only person who is able to play this play fully. He is the one who is allowed to refer to what is absent. In metaphysics and theology, absence is unbearable, but art succeeds in making this absence imaginable.

Thus, similar to myth, art situates itself in a remote corner of the world. The central thought of construction has been proven an illusion. Capital letters disappear. Entities either crumble or appear mere panoramas of ruins. Generality is the absolute expression of the particular, but not logically. Unity is replaced by fixed indeterminacies. Art can be understood as a play, as a series of substitutions which can neither be totalized nor defined. To create art as the substitution for absence is the undefined task of the artist. In the context of this task, one could think that the artist views himself in the center of his art world and, hence, in the center of the world. But this is not true. As a play, his task of substitutions is non-centric, even if he fulfils his work departing from a sense of nostalgia for the foundation and its soothing certainty.

Derrida deconstructs "the" metaphysics into a metaphysics where the "transcendental signified" is approached as a textual trace. Western culture is the text of Western metaphysics. One cannot live outside of this textuality. However, a deconstruction will be possible as a sort of inner dislocation of the metaphysical text proceeding from the textures. "The movements of deconstruction do not destroy structures from the outside. They are not possible and effective, nor can they take accurate aim, except by inhabiting those structures. Inhabiting them in a certain way, because one always inhabits, and all the more when one does not suspect it." (ibid, 24)

Contemporary art seems to be the outstanding textuality. On the one hand, as an indication of the metaphysical occupation of structures and, on the other hand, as a relocation of metaphysics within a factual textuality. After all, contemporary art employs a system of signs different from spoken and written language. Because of this, confusion will be somewhat avoided. The metaphysical void has been suggested illustratively by avant-garde art.

Art understood as textuality - within which signification occurs without absolute origin but as a determination in a referring system of signs - is a relocation of metaphysical truth, based on the absolute origin of signification in general. Derrida attaches great value to this being without origin. If a play of differences will work, then each difference should be inscribed into another one. The play is connected to the trace, but each trace only exists because of another trace; there is no such thing as a first original trace. "The trace is in fact the absolute origin of sense in general, which amounts to saying once again that there is no absolute origin of sense in general. The trace is the differance which opens appearance and signification." (ibid, 65)

Derrida's writings demonstrate that art can fulfil a function in the relocation of Western metaphysics. Art can go against logocentrism. Moreover, the possibility of relocating old metaphysics and onto-theology as a form of anti-dogmatism seems an important task for avant-garde art.

4.6.3. *Truth as well*

In his book La Vérité en Peinture, Derrida deals explicitly with art and its hidden meaning. The book can hardly be summarized, because deliberately there is no center which can be synthesized. Therefore, the book can only be commented on.

The title of the book has been derived from a statement by Cézanne. "I owe the truth in painting and I will tell it to you." (Derrida 1987, 2) This statement inspires Derrida to write four chapters on, or better, around art. "Four times, then around painting, to turn merely around it, in the neighboring regions which one authorizes oneself to enter, that's the whole story, to recognize and contain, like the surrounds of the work of art, or at most its outskirts: frame, title, signature, museum, archive, reproduction, discourse, market, in short: everywhere where one legislates on the right to painting by marking the limit, with a slash marking an opposition which one would like to be indivisible." (ibid, 11)

In La Vérité en peinture, painting is only a point of departure, a context. From there, Derrida explores the margin, the possibility of a definition and the transgression of philosophical knowledge, which intends to be universal knowledge. Furthermore, he questions the power and powerlessness of a philosophical discourse; what is within philosophical knowledge, what escapes it and what the margin between the inside and the outside is.

In this context, Derrida poses anew the fundamental aesthetic question "What is art?". But he does not answer this question, and even claims that one should not pose it, since it does not explore the essence of art. The question "What is art?" cannot be posed outside of metaphysics and, therefore, the essence cannot be determined nor indicated. Similar to the foundation of being, it will withdraw as soon as it reveals itself. Thus, one should develop a form of thought which will reach metaphysics or beyond. Does the question of the origin of the artwork and the truth of art differ from the margin which divides and connects both of them? However, that margin will also shift.

One will find a good example of "deconstruction" in Derrida's unravelling of the discussion between Schapiro and Heidegger on Van Gogh's Peasant Shoes. In the beginning of this chapter, Heidegger's interpretation of this work was discussed. The art historian Schapiro wrote a short article (Simmel 1968, 203-209) where he scientifically demonstrates that the painting concerned represents Van Gogh's shoes instead of a peasant's shoes. Since Van Gogh was a city dweller at that time, these shoes can hardly express the Being of a peasant shoe and its relationship to nature and labor (ibid, 205).

Schapiro's criticism on Heidegger is that the latter projected his imagination into the painting. In Heidegger's fanciful description, Schapiro does not find anything one could not have discovered in looking at a real pair of peasant shoes. Schapiro's interpretation is that one should have an eye for the personal and physiognomic aspects of those shoes. The shoes are in fact part of a self-portrait by Van Gogh. They refer to the difficult trip to the Borinage where Van Gogh was a pastor for awhile.

Derrida deconstructs the difference of opinion which actually sparked an exchange between Schapiro and Heidegger. Derrida deconstructs Schapiro's statements as well as those of Heidegger but is not as strict with Heidegger, supposedly because he considers The Origin of Art one of the last great texts on art. After the deconstruction, there is not much left except for the conviction that each interpretation tends to acquire an essential character and can be founded on speculative data. One should escape from essences. Thus Derrida states that Schapiro is: "The other one, not agreeing at all, says after mature reflection, 33 years later, exhibiting the juridical exhibits (but without asking himself any questions beyond this and without asking any other questions): no, there's been an error and a projection if not deception and perjury, ca revient, this pair from the city." (Derrida 1987, 259)

Derrida questions how one could know the two shoes are a pair. In addition to this kind of questions, he broadens the discussion with texts by Marx, Nietzsche and Freud. He points out that Schapiro neglects the first function of the pictorial reference. Schapiro underestimates Heidegger by stating that the latter's view on art as "setting-truth-into-work" could have referred to art describing a reality. Therefore, he equates the shoes in the painting with real shoes. From another perspective, Derrida demonstrates the danger of external arguments. Why should a painter who lives in the city not be able to paint or wear peasant shoes? "At other times the expert appeals to an external argument, the date, and when he wants to have us believe that once in Paris Van Gogh could no longer paint peasant shoes or any shoes other than his own, or the shoes of nobody." (ibid, 362) The art historian almost turns into a policeman who wants to know which shoes are the issue.

This deconstruction proves how "unfounded" an interpretation can be, not in the sense of senselessness but in the sense of being fragmentary and, thus, partly founded. Schapiro's approach is worthwhile and an interesting result of factual research, albeit with some less factual data. Certainly, Schapiro's interpretation is not refuted by Heidegger, because the latter does not really interpret Van Gogh's painting. He merely employs the painting he vaguely had in mind as a confirmation of his philosophical view on the unconcealment of Being. Derrida claims, "But separation is in itself already, in the word, in the letter, in the pair, the opening of the secret. Its name indicates this. So one would have to render this secret already, legible, like a remainder of a useless cipher. You don't have to render anything. Just bet on the trap as others swear on a Bible. There will have been something to bet. It gives to be rendered. To be put back on/put off." (ibid, 382)

5. STRUCTURALISM AND SEMIOTICS

In Broekman's publication of a discussion on the theme Structuralism: for or against (1974), a comparison is made between two fundamental philosophical attitudes. This comparison could illuminate the difference in approach between the previous chapter - with the exclusion of Derrida - and this one. Broekman points out how a hermeneutics constituted by consciousness shifts to a textual hermeneutics. Contrary to ontological philosophy, structuralist philosophy is a philosophy which departs from structures. Indeed, a philosophy oriented towards ontology is based on structure, but it achieves but one structure for the most part, whereas in structuralism the problem of structure is the very object of philosophy. With respect to art, one will find a similar attitude on structure in formalism. "In this case, the essence of art is described with aid of the concept of structure, the purpose of art is compared with the purpose of each structural-izing action, even the nature of the aesthetic effect itself is experienced as struc-turalizing." (Broekman 1974, 14)

The transgression of a philosophical idealist hermeneutics into a textual hermeneutics is characterized by the structure of a many-layered textuality; the meaning of a text does not refer to an essence of concepts or a coherence of words, but results from a linguistic act, from how a linguistic pattern and subjec-tivity - understood as the instance of signification - are inscribed into a text. Thus, the unity of a discourse can no longer be assumed but must be articulated time and again. From a philosophical perspective, such post-ontological thought is based on an anti-idealist, non-essentialist and non-subjectivist epistemology. Within such textual hermeneutics the specificity of the text is not connected with the author or the interpreter, but with the organizing structure of the text itself.

Such a relativism cannot but refer to itself. Not surprisingly, structuralism considers itself a disappearing view on the world. Moreover, structuralism is not a movement which broke with phenomenology and existential philosophy on the basis of shared views. Many designated structuralists do not want to be labeled as such. However, there is a relationship with other movements, even with phe-nomenology. Structuralism's break with thoughts on human beings, community and language should not be overestimated. "Thus, with a certain distance one can say that structuralism is not so much the Parisian movement which came to the attention in the 1960s, but a continuous element in thought on man and com-munity." (Parret 1974, 109))

Yet, the polemic of the 1960s was productive. Firstly, because the humanities became aware of the necessity of a methodological component in their science. Secondly, because it lead to a formulation of the complex relationship between science, philosophy and ideology. On the basis of this trichotomy, one arrives at a relativist and formal definition of "structuralism". Structural methodology becomes a methodology which imposes on science to construct its object in its systematics - in the term the system is presupposed - and in its linguistics. In this methodology, each human phenomenon occurs as a linguistic system. Thus, linguistics is at its core. Language is the paradigm of the entire human reality. Ideological structuralism, which is related to this, focuses on problems such as determinism versus freedom, and subject as function versus subject as origin, where the scientific unverifiable choice falls time and again on the first term of the polarity. Thirdly, because structural philosophy can be produced in the sense of an epistemology. The stature of such a structural epistemology will depend on how the overall relationship between scientific methodology and epistemology is formulated. First and foremost, structuralism is a reflection on the humanities, which has its place next to other classifications and paradigms.

In the first part of this chapter, we will discuss the view of a number of semioticians - from Mukarovsky to Eco - with respect to visual art. Then we will go into a few major representatives of this so-called structuralism, excluding the philosophers which were treated at the end of the previous chapter.

5.1. *Mukarovsky*

Jan Mukarovsky made a first attempt to systematize a semiotics of art within the history of aesthetics. In Prague, in 1934, during the 8th international congress of philosophy, he gave a lecture entitled L'art comme fait sémiologique. In this text, he limits himself to a basic statement of a program. This precursor of semiotics is not very well-known. In Prague, he was silenced by the regime.

Mukarovsky's structuralist thought has three phases, spread over twenty years (1928 - 1948). In the first phase, he emphasizes the object itself or the inner structure of the work of art. From 1934 on, he explores the series of norms occurring in each work of art which are valid for a particular collection. He calls this "collective consciousness". Around the beginning of the Second World War, his attention focuses on the role the subject plays in the aesthetic process. No longer is the subject understood as a mainly passive bearer of supra-individual structures, but rather as an active force which makes structures change in the course of a process of interaction.

Mukarovsky's interest in the aesthetic object is understandable because, in his first phase, he is an admirer of Russian formalism. In that period, he attaches great value to the material aspect of the work. In his view, aesthetics is the epistemology of art. "If aesthetics cannot be the logic of art, judging its correctness and incorrectness, it can nevertheless be something else: the epistemology of art. That is to say, every art has certain basic possibilities provided by the character of its material and the way in which the given art masters it." (Mukarovsky 1978, 179) In fact, the employed material limits the possibilities of art. On a theoretical reflective level, this knowledge belongs to the aesthetic domain. Since, in that context, aesthetics explores the most general rules dominating the material of art, the structural analysis will determine how these rules structure the material of a particular work of art.

Mukarovsky does not halt at a somewhat one-sided focus on the material basis of art. After all, not every work can be reduced to the level of sensory perception. However, Mukarovsky seems to become entangled in the abstraction of the concept of art, which becomes particularly meaningless if the material is the source of investigation. Yet, such an analysis of contemporary painting can be very productive, while important aspects of some movements - and even the essence of the movement itself - define themselves on the basis of the nature and possibilities of the material layer. Take for example fundamental painting, action painting and land art.

According to Mukarovsky, the description of the structure of the material aspect of art as a sign is no longer a purpose in itself. Therefore, the meaning of that structure becomes prominent in his second phase. The transgression is caused by Mukarovsky's reaction to the confusion between the psychology of the artwork and the psychology of the creating artist, a theme which often arises in theoretical reflections on art. Once the work has been finished, it becomes a sign which can be considered a social fact <u>sui generis</u>, which will serve as supra-individual communication, apart from the subjective psychology of the author. After all, the subjective nature prevents that information from the psychology of the creative process will correspond to the meaning of the work. No matter the intention of the artist, the result is a "sign" which is prone to interpretation by a (subjective) spectator. ("The spectator will always understand more than the artist intended, and the artist will always have intended more than any single spectator understands - to put it paradoxically." (Wollheim 1978, 135)) The communicative power of that sign does not change through knowledge of how it came about.

Thus, Mukarovsky's attention shifts from the study of the structure of individual works to the study of the aesthetic code upon which those works are based. In Saussure's terms, one could call this the transgression of the study of "speech" to the study of "language". Mukarovsky considers culture a complex

network of codes: art, science, religion, and so on. He views the phenomenological reality as a series of functions which structure the atomized empirical reality.
The code will differ on the basis of a correspondence to its dominant function,
which is to classify objects - or the atomized empirical reality. By emphasizing
the essential poly-functionality of all human actions and products, Mukarovsky
fuses the world of art and the world of non-art. No longer is the aesthetic function an exclusive feature of art, it is art which distinguishes itself from the rest
because of the dominance of the aesthetic function.

This approach to art clears up many problems with respect to classifications, margins, definitions and the inevitable question of "When is art?"
Secondly, the discussion between relating domains becomes easier. One can
speak of the religious function of art, or the aesthetic function of religion, without the need to determine whether it is art or whether it is religion. Thirdly, it is
possible to discuss with an open mind who is or is not an artist.

Mukarovsky certainly does not intend to consider art a daily practice.
However, that danger is implicitly present. Mukarovsky sees the need for an
exchange of three domains, illustrated in his description of structuralist aesthetics. "For structuralist aesthetics, everything within the work of art and in its relations to the external context appears as a sign and meaning. In this respect it
might be considered a part of the general science of sign, semiotics ... Its (structuralist aesthetics) essence and destiny are to elaborate the system and method of
the comparative semiotics of art. However, we must add that the comparative
orientation of structuralist aesthetics is not exhausted by art alone, for the aesthetic is potentially present in every human act and potentially contained in
every human product. This means that structuralist aesthetics pays attention to
the constant interplay of three phenomenal atmospheres: the artistic, the aesthetic, and the extra-artistic and extra-aesthetic, and to the tension among them
which affects the development of each." (Mukarovsky 1978, XVIII)

5.1.1. Art as a semiotic fact

Obviously, in this second phase, Mukarovsky is fully submerged in semiotics. In
his work L'art comme fait sémiologique, he presents five theses which contain
his main views on the subject.

His most interesting view is that, unlike the beliefs of psychological aesthetics, one cannot reduce the work of art to the mentality of the artist nor to the
mood it evokes in the spectator. Each subjective mood has a trace of individuality and transitoriness. Therefore, it is intangible and uncommunicable as a
whole, whereas the artwork has as a function to mediate between its creator and

the collective. The work of art as an "object" in the sensory world continues to exist and is accessible in an unrestricted way to perception. However, the work of art cannot be reduced to the material object. After all, the outer appearance and the inner structure of the material artwork will change completely if situated in another time and space. Mukarovsky distinguishes between subjective states of consciousness - with a meaning constituted by a collectivity - and additional subjective psychic elements. The meaning in the collective consciousness is determined by what the subjective states of consciousness - evoked in the members of a certain group by the materiality of the work - have in common. The subjective elements outside this common core can be compared with what Fechner understands as "associative factors" of aesthetic perception. These subjective elements of the perceiving subject can acquire objective semiotic characteristics, comparable with the connotation of words. This happens indirectly, via the center which belongs to social consciousness. Important is that each hedonistic aesthetic theory is rejected by refusing to identify the artwork with a subjective psychic state. Mukarovsky considers the pleasure an artwork provides to be an additional meaning, which at the most can be objectified indirectly.

Another important view in Mukarovsky's text deals with the idea that art - more than any other social phenomenon - is able to characterize and present a certain era, since the work of art refers to the entire context of social phenomena such as philosophy, politics, religion, economics etc. This reference results from the autonomy which Mukarovsky ascribes to the sign each work of art is. Contrary to non-autonomous signs, the work of art does not refer to a certain reality. It is merely characterized by its mediating role between members of the same collective. This implies that the artwork should be understood similarly by both the person who creates it and the person who perceives it. However, sometimes the social context will lag behind the stage which is expressed. Moreover, the artwork should not be employed as a historical or sociological document before the documentary value, that is the quality of the relationship to the factual social context, has been interpreted.

The work of art has a double semiotic meaning. In addition to the function of autonomous sign, it has the function of communicative sign. For example, it can express a psychic state as well as a thought or sensation. This function can be perceived in works of art where a certain theme is treated and where, initially, the semantic content seems to function as a communicative meaning. Mukarovsky even writes, "In reality, each component of the artwork - even the most 'formal' one - possesses a typical communicative value apart from the subject. Thus, the colors and lines of a painting mean 'something' even in the absence of any subject - cf. Kandinksy's 'absolute' painting or the oeuvre of certain surrealist painters. The communicative power lies in the virtual semiological character of the formal components vaguely called art by us without subject. Thus, in order to be exact, one should maintain that it is again the entire structure which, even communicatively, functions as the meaning of the artwork. The subject of the artwork simply plays the role of axis of crystallization with regard to this meaning, which would continue to be vague without it." (Mukarovsky 1936, 1068).

In the development of art with semantic content, there seems to be a dialectic antinomy between the function of the autonomous sign and the communicative one. This will grow highly problematic if one questions the relationship between art and the signified object from the perspective of communication. Different from art as an autonomous sign, art as a communicative sign directs itself towards a certain reality, for example a clear-cut event or a person. Contrary to pure communicative signs, the relationship between the artwork and the signified object has no existential value when judging the artwork. This does not mean that modifications in the relationship to the signified object will be without any meaning for the artwork. They function as a factor of the structure. "It is very important for the structure of a given work to know whether it treats its subject as 'real' (sometimes even as documentary), as 'fictive' or as oscillating between these two poles." (ibid, 1069).

There are works based on the balance between these two relationships to reality. The portrait, for example, tells something about the person represented and is at the same time a work of art without existential value.

This play between both relationships to reality can be considered a key to Ceci n'est pas une pipe - Magritte's famous surrealist work (Kaulingfreks 1984) - as well as a basic principle for certain aspects of conceptual art. The pipe painted in a rather realistic way gives the confusing impression to refer to a real pipe, which is true in a communicative sense. However, in an existential sense, this painting does not have the value of being a "pipe". The written statement under the painted pipe would normally accentuate the communicative character. But at the same time it falsely implies that there is no reference to a real pipe ("est" une pipe). In that respect, the work refers no doubt to "illustrative" education of extremely classical educational theory. However, the statement ignores the existential relationship, resulting in a confusion of the communicative function.

Mukarovsky attaches great value to the importance of the semiotic character of adequately exploring the structure of the artwork. Not only does he reject pure formalism, he also objects to each form of reflective theory, either psychological or sociological. "Without semiological orientation, the art historian will continue to be inclined to consider the artwork as a purely formal construction or even as the direct reflection of either psychic moods, and even the author's physiological moods, or of the distinguished reality expressed by the work and the ideological, economic, social or cultural situations of a given environment." (ibid, 1070)

From a semiological perspective, the theorist can acquire insight into the development of art as an immanent movement, having a continuous dialectical relationship with the development of the other cultural domains.

5.1.2. The aesthetic function

The second phase in Mukarovsky's thought is characterized by the development of an aesthetic axiology around three concepts: function, norm and value. There is an interaction between these concepts. Mukarovsky understands the concept of function as the active relationship between an object and its purpose. The concept of value is the purposive utility of this object. The concept of norm is the rule or series of rules which organizes the domain of a particular kind of category of values.

A technological relationship is not always functional. Repetitive use is a necessary condition of a function, and there should be social consensus about the purpose of the object. "A particular mode of using a given object must be spontaneously comprehensible to every member of a given collective." (Mukarovsky 1978, 236). Contrary to the "practical" functions, an object where the aesthetic function is dominant has a function in the object itself. The aesthetic function is, so to speak, the necessary dialectical negation of the function in general. In art, where the aesthetic function naturally dominates, the norm is subordinate to the value. This is very different from the domains outside art, where satisfaction of the norm corresponds to value. In art, the boundaries of norm are constantly transgressed. Therefore, the aesthetic norm can hardly be codified and is very unstable. In art, the system of norms cannot claim a monopoly position. In Mukarovsky's view, the aesthetic norm is a regulatory system which is continually violated. "... every norm, even the legal norm, makes felt its activity and hence its existence precisely at the moment when its violation occurs." (ibid, 54)

The history of art seems to be a permanent revolution against the norm. Art is not allowed to linger in areas previously explored. Art finds its dynamic in the norm by reacting against the norm. As a matter of fact, art differs from non-art to the extent it subordinates non-aesthetic functions to the aesthetic function. According to Mukarovsky, an object dominated by the aesthetic functions has a "zero utility". Because of this, it is removed from the day-to-day context and becomes art. Although "zero utility" is an important characteristic of art, this is certainly not sufficient ground: one can think of a great many zero-utilities which are not art. Moreover, Mukarovsky does not definitely distinguish between the artwork and design.

An important aspect of Mukarovsky's second phase of structuralism is that he includes art entirely into a greater whole of human culture. Furthermore, he elaborates on a semiotic frame of reference, enabling him to represent a complex network of signs bringing about the possibility of communication between individuals belonging to that culture.

In his third phase, Mukarovsky adjusts two weak aspects of his theory stemming from the second stage of his structuralist theory. These aspects are: 1) a relativism resulting from over-emphasis on social codes and undermining the epistemological basis of his aesthetics; and 2) a dependence on the social domain, implying a determinism of the historical changeability and causing the aesthetic element to lose its common ground. Therefore, Mukarovsky postulates supra-social invariants. (ibid, 57-69)

Mukarovsky's view on the subject as a member of a particular collectivity is rather limited, because the frame of the collectivity's consciousness is composed of contents of social consciousness. In this definition, the subject is a peripheral part of aesthetic interaction. As an artist, the subject merely communicates impersonal impulses from the previous tradition and the extra-artistic context. As a spectator, he merely supplements the social core of the meaning of a work with his subjective - and thus irrelevant to the community - private associations. In his last phase of structuralism, Mukarovsky emphasizes the subject again as the last source of all aesthetic interaction. This does not imply a subjectivism, which, as a matter of fact, would be inconsistent with the universalist tendencies of this last period.

5.1.3. *The autonomy of the perceiving subject*

In the third stage of his thought, Mukarovsky emphasizes the contribution of the subject as a spectator. In 1934, he defines the frame of reference of the aesthetic sign still rather vaguely as "the entire context of social phenomena". (Mukarovsky 1936, 1067) Whether this context refers to the author or to every spectator of the theme is not even indicated. In this third phase, Mukarovsky ascribes a pure potential character to all references which contain the aesthetic sign. In order to actualize this, one does not only need the mediation of a spectator, but also a re-orientation by means of the many aspects of the spectator's consciousness. The only reality the aesthetic sign refers to is the reality of the spectator. (Mukarovsky 1978, 89-128)

Mukarovsky values the relationship between art and spectator. He distinguishes three kinds of phenomena which reveal three kinds of attitudes of the subject. Firstly, there is the realm of natural events and objects. Since they are not designed by anyone, we can give them meaning corresponding directly to our immediate existential experience. The second group of phenomena is manmade; they are conceived beforehand and intentional in nature. Both characteristics are of importance in perceiving them. This domain can be divided into practical and artistic phenomena. In perceiving the former, their external context is accounted for. We contribute a meaning to them corresponding to either the creator's intention or their purpose. Artworks, however, are separated from the practical context. Their intentionality cannot be derived from what is outside them, but only from their internal structure. In art, intentionality is semantic energy which connects all heterogeneous elements of the work in a semantic unity, a sign. A special attitude from the spectator is demanded. As long as the spectator has this aesthetic attitude, he desires to discover a structure in the work which enables him to perceive it as an entity. Thus, the meaning of the work of art is derived from its very internal organization. "As an autonomous sign a work of art does not enter into a binding relation to reality, which it represents (communicates) by means of its theme, through its separate parts, but only as a whole can it establish a relation to any one of the perceiver's experiences or to a set of his experiences in his subconscious. (A work of art "means", then, the perceiver's existential experience, his mental world). This must be emphasized especially contrary to communicative signs (e.g., a communicative verbal utterance) in which each part, each partial semantic unit, can be verified in the reality to which it refers (cf. a scientific proof). Thus semantic unity is a very relevant condition in a work of art, and intentionality is the force which binds together the individual parts and components of a work into the unity that gives the work its meaning. As soon as the perceiver adopts an attitude toward a certain object, which is usual during the perception of a work of art, he immediately makes an effort to find in the organization of the work traces of an arrangement that will permit the work to be conceived as a semantic whole." (ibid, 96)

Each activity of perception demands two moments. One is directed toward the semiotic value in a work, the other aims at the immediate experience of the work as reality. The spectator fluctuates between a feeling of intentionality and unintentionality during the activity of perception. Or, better put, the work is at the same time a sign - a self-referential sign without a clear relationship to reality - and a thing. "By calling the work a thing, we wish to indicate that,

185

because of what is unintentional, semantically disunified in it, the work appears to the viewer as similar to a natural fact, that is, a fact which in its organization does not answer the question "What for?" but leaves the decision about its functional use to man." (ibid, 106)

Thus, the work of art as a semantic unstructured thing has the possibility to evoke personal experiences, images and feelings from the conscious as well as the unconscious of any spectator. "Hence the work of art has such a powerful effect upon man not because it gives him - as the common formula goes - an impression of the author's personality, his experiences, and so forth, but because it influences the perceiver's personality, his experiences, and so forth." (ibid, 107) The work of art as a thing can move the spectator on the basis of his strictly personal relationship to reality, because there is always an element of unintentionality present in the artwork. As a sign, a work of art can never be merely intentional. In that way, Mukarovsky arrives at a double-layered view of the spectator.

5.1.4. The aesthetic function among other functions

Mukarovsky's modified view on the subject leads to a different definition of his concept of "function". In his article "The Place of the Aesthetic Function among the other Functions" (1942), he elaborates on this. Mukarovsky argues that art is an oasis within the aesthetic realm, only a part within it. The question is not whether the beautiful will exist independent of man, but whether the aesthetic will exist within the context of human action. This has as a consequence that "the notion of function replaces the notion of beauty as the basic methodological premise". (ibid, 33)

Rather than natural phenomena, human creation and its results become the focus of attention. Mukarovsky considers nature and art as independent and unrelated, contrary to the view that art is subordinate to nature - art imitates nature and, thus, is not as perfect, or, conversely, nature is subordinate to art - nature becomes more perfect by means of art.

The functionalist approach precipitates an interaction between the aesthetic within art and the aesthetic outside of art. It views the transgressions and relationships between both. Because of this, the problem of the aesthetic moves to a more general anthropological level. Since there is no human activity where the aesthetic does not play a role, one can indeed consider the aesthetic the element of each human action and design. Obviously, in art, where the aesthetic functions dominate in principle, extra-aesthetic functions will play a role as well. Thus, art is no exception to the rule that human action is characterized by many functions and, at the same time, by omnipresence of the aesthetic function. "As a rule, several functions are not only potentially but actually present in an act or creation, and among them there may be some which the agent or creator did not think of or did not even desire. No sphere of human action or human creation is limited to a single function. There is always a greater number of functions, and there are tensions, variances, and balancing among them. The functions of a permanent creation can change in the course of time. We began, then, with a consideration of the aesthetic function outside of art, and we have quickly reached a conclusion pertaining to functions in general. It can be formulated as the basic polyfunctionality of human activity and the basic omnipresence of functions." (ibid, 37)

This structuralist functionalism differs from previous functionalisms. The latter were directed towards the object and always reduced to a clear-cut function. An example is the functionalism in architecture, where the function of a building was determined a priori. But a building has more than one function, just as all human design is polyvalent and polyfunctional. Thus, the functions cannot be projected onto the object unequivocally, but should be situated in the subject itself. By considering the function from the perspective of the subject, Mukarovsky arrives at a new definition of a function. "A function is the mode of a subject's self-realization vis-à-vis the external world." (ibid, 40)

This demonstrates that each human activity related to reality will strive for various purposes. Mukarovsky appeals to the phenomenological analysis to explore the specificity of the aesthetic function. There are two ways of realizing oneself in reality: immediately or by means of another reality. The first way can be brought about with the aid of a tool. In the second case, the mediating reality is a sign. "... the basic articulation of functions divides them into immediate and semiotic functions." (ibid, 40)

As self-realization departs from a subject and directs itself toward an object, a division in the dichotomy object-subject is required. The "immediate" function can be described as either a practical or a theoretical function. In the practical function the object is first. In fact, the transformation of the object is under consideration. In the theoretical function the subject is first. The purpose is to project a reality onto the consciousness of the subject. In principle, reality remains untouched.

The semiotic functions can be divided into two groups as well. In the symbolic function, the object is first. Attention is focused on the effectiveness of the relationship between the symbolized thing and the symbolic sign. In the aesthetic function, the subject is first. This function changes everything it encounters into a sign. The connection of the aesthetic sign to the subject does not direct itself toward particular realities as the symbolic function does. It reflects on reality as a whole. The aesthetic function resembles the theoretical one, but the theoretical function strives for a total and unifying image of reality. Conversely, the aesthetic function tries to construct a unifying attitude against reality. Within this typology of functions, there are correlations still to be explored. Be that as it may, the relationship is not hierarchical. Indeed, structuralism supposes that each hierarchy should be considered a dynamic process, which will continuously rearrange itself.

The question is whether Mukarovsky's unlimited transformation of the artwork's aesthetic function to all human activities will damage the specificity he assigns to the work of art. The artwork itself has various functions which are difficult to define precisely. Mukarovsky believes, however, that the aesthetic function is the most specific one, the conditio sine qua non. But he goes too far when he makes this function dissolve into non-artistic fields. "The functions of art are many and varied; because of their capacity for combination, it is not easy to present their full enumeration and classification. Among them, however, there is one which is specific for art and without which the work of art would cease to be a work of art. This is the aesthetic function. Yet it is clear that the aesthetic function is by no means limited to art but penetrates all the works of man and all the activities of his life." (ibid, 12) The vagueness, the indefiniteness or even the indeterminability seems to broaden the concept of the aesthetic to such an extent, that each theorist can classify his judgement or bias on the specificity of the aesthetic in this concept, whether or not referring to existing examples. Mukarovsky equates the concept of the aesthetic to concepts of the decorative, the pleasant and the charming. "Not even the most ordinary colloquial speech is in principle devoid of the aesthetic function. And so it is with all other human activities. Let us take crafts, for example. It is obvious that the aesthetic function is more visible in the goldsmith's craft than in the baker's or butcher's crafts; the goldsmith's craft is even mentioned in the history of art. But can we therefore say that the other two crafts are essentially devoid of the aesthetic function? That would mean forgetting about the shapes of a baker's products. Even their color and smell add aesthetic elements, and the same holds true, albeit to a somewhat different extent, for the butcher's craft. In brief, we shall find no sphere in which the aesthetic function is essentially absent; potentially it is always present, it can arise at any time." (ibid, 35)

These examples clearly demonstrate that Mukarovsky puts art at the same level as craft products, as cake design or fine butchery. As a learned citizen, Mukarovsky believes that the aesthetic function of the labor of the goldsmith is more visible than the baker's labor. To prove this, he refers to the presence of the goldsmith's craft in museums. However, aside from the perishable aspect, there is no reason why cakes could not be presented in the museum next to the goldsmith's craft. The cake is a worthy part of folklore. However, that many works of art do not even attain aesthetically the qualitative level of cake is not the reason a categorical equation could occur. The over glorification or sacralization of art is not the issue. One is allowed to subordinate art to cake, but one cannot equate them because that is of a different order. The view that the aesthetic function is always latently present seems a defensible position. But then art cannot be placed on the same level as the rest. Mukarovsky remains within the domain where the criteria of beauty reigns. Nevertheless, his theory on an autonomous sign and thing offers enough possibilities to stress the distinction. A cake is not an autonomous sign but refers to the taste buds of the one who eats it. Also the goldsmith's work does not refer to itself, unless he is an executor of pieces of art. According to a new semantic structure, the goldsmith's work is an ornament without any particular meaning.

Mukarovsky has been guided so much by his view on aesthetics - as a general philosophy on the aesthetic - that he neglects art as an object of study. He equates art with other human activities which can be considered aesthetically. However, his view on the four basic attitudes toward reality are interesting. He distinguishes between the practical, the theoretical-cognitive, the magic-religious and the aesthetic. The practical and theoretical attitudes direct themselves towards reality. The former wants to change reality immediately. The latter prepares the effectiveness of a possible intervention by contributing to our knowledge of it. The magic-religious and aesthetic attitudes transform the essence of reality into a sign. They are often difficult to distinguish. These three attitudes and their functions are related to tools in order to attain a purpose, and are only valuable to the extent these purposes are attained. Only the aesthetic function has a function in itself based on the way it has been created or organized. Nevertheless, "Art is not, however, the only vehicle of the aesthetic function. Any phenomenon, any action, any product of human activity can become an aesthetic sign for an individual or even for a whole society." (ibid, 21)

In his four-attitude theory, Mukarovsky does not pay enough attention to the relationship between the practical and the aesthetic attitude. The magic-religious and the aesthetic attitude can often hardly be distinguished, which is not the case with the aesthetic attitude and the practical one. The magic-religious attitude often finds the realization of its purpose in an intensification of aesthetic value. And, conversely, an aesthetic attitude can grow so extreme that it may coincide with a, possibly atheist, magic-religious attitude. Since the practical attitude should really change reality, its relationship with the aesthetic is different. It is not a priori impossible to make art out of dough - that has happened, for example à la Spoerri - but a cake is made primarily because of its edibility. The elements "taste" and "smell" contribute to the function of edibility rather than having an aesthetic intention. A real artistic cake should be inedible or at least be made with the intention of being inedible. A traditional decorative object has to be usable in a practical way, which is incompatible with the distinct "zero utility" of the aesthetic function. This uselessness only occurs purely in art. Only in art is the aesthetic sufficient in itself, which, in combination with the sign character of the artwork, gives rise to a semantic unity. This unity is "useless" since it refers to an indefinite reality, rather than to an immediate definite one.

Mukarovsky's view on physical education is another example of his oversimplified way of judging the unity of two functions. "Insofar as physical exercise is conceived in its practical function (strengthening of the body, training in dexterity, etc.), the action that the body performs is considered only with regard to these results, as a means to their attainment. Let us suppose, however, that an aesthetic consideration becomes concomitant or even predominant. Immediately the action performed in the exercise will acquire value in itself, and attention will be directed to all the stages and details of its course and continuation." (ibid, 20)

Physical exercises have practical functions such as strengthening the body and training dexterity. The practical function predominates over the aesthetic one within a similar activity. Only after the practical function has been fulfilled - a strong and limber body - can an aesthetic function be dominant in physical exercises. The aesthetic can start playing a role the moment one observes what a strong and limber body is able to do. Therefore, this is a false example. In the same sense, learning technique in art education can be considered a practical function. However, this does not coincide with the aesthetic: it is its precursor.

Mukarovsky does not neglect art theoretically. However, his examples show that he views the aesthetic in a somewhat classical way, as decoration, as beauty. Obviously, he does not distinguish between art and daily life. He considers the constant tension a continuous excitement in life. "Art constitutes a group in itself. Here we are no longer dealing with phenomena which acquire an aesthetic function only as a concomitant to the main function, and which sometimes acquire it accidentally, but with products created with the intention that aesthetic effect be their main task. It would, however, be wrong to believe that art therefore does not belong in this chapter on the aesthetic and life, that art is something like a quiet oasis of aesthetic contemplation beside the real events of life." (ibid, 24)

Moreover, Mukarovsky's article "The Essence of the Visual Arts" reflects a certain ambiguity caused by the equation of art with everything which could become an aesthetic object. Nevertheless, in this article he tries to reveal a number of interesting differences between a natural object and a visual work of art. The difference between both is not that the artwork has a creator, but that it has been created in a special way and, therefore, has been organized according to a specific unified intention. In the natural object, any intention is lacking and its organization is accidental. However, in every human creation one can discover intentionality. One can divide the products of human activity which bear traces of intentionality into two large groups: products which serve a definite purpose (tools) and products which are a purpose in themselves (artworks). "One of them serves some aim, whereas the objects of the second group are designated, if we may say so, as aims in themselves. The objects of the first group can be called implements in the broad sense of the word, the objects of the second, works of art. Each of these two groups is distinguished by a certain manner of intentional organization. An implement suggests that it is designed to serve some purpose; a work of art compels man to adopt the attitude of a mere perceiver." (ibid, 225)

Thus, according to Mukarovsky, an artwork is an object which is observed as a purpose in itself, with an eye for the "specific unified intention". If not, the natural objects are included as well. However, this is not the same as the argument that each artwork should be observed as a purpose in itself. The same object can be evaluated as a tool and as a work of art. That simply is the ambiguity of the organization. "It is not difficult to find such objects, for almost any practical instrument - at least at the moment when we examine it without using it - can be conceived in itself and for itself, regardless of the aim which it usually serves." (ibid, 225) In this context, Mukarovsky equates art and a "new" instrument, a bourgeois error between "novel" and "beautiful". He thinks of furniture and all products of artisan industry, such as "engraved glass cups" and "plastically embellished faïence bowls". By using the word "embellished", he reveals that "decoration" is under consideration rather than art. However, when the issue is art in a narrow sense, the spectator no longer has the freedom to ambiguously observe the artwork from its practical side. Then, the attention for internal organization becomes a necessity. "If works of art in the proper sense of the word, such as paintings or statues, are concerned, it is quite evident that the attitude toward the object is not left to the viewer's whim but that the work itself in its organization directly induces the viewer to focus his attention on itself, on the set of its properties and on the internal organization of this set, and not to look beyond the work for some external aim which it could serve." (ibid, 225)

There is no reason why one should not view a painting as a perfect secret door to a safe or as a present. Why shouldn't children be able to play on

Tinguely's machines? However - and this seems more fundamental - it is not obvious that a spectator with or without attention should have an eye for the properties of the work and its internal organization; or that the spectator has not been distracted by other aspects which mislead perception and have nothing to do with the work itself.

There is an interesting exception to our criticism of Mukarovsky's possible equation of artwork and implement, namely the application of the implement within dadaism - the ready-made - and the art of assemblage. The implement is not artistic because of its decorative form alongside a utilitarian one, but because of a new meaning it will acquire - either as an element or as a whole - within a new context. The decorative element will seldom play a role as a criticism to the frivolity of kitsch apart from a negative sense.

As stated previously, the equation between artwork and artistic object is so much the stranger - although an obvious consequence of Mukarovsky's theory of the aesthetic attitude - when one reads Mukarovsky's clarifying description of the artwork and its meaning. The artwork is a sign which is supposed to be a mediator for certain ultra-personal meanings. Meanings cannot be comprehended in words - the pre-eminent sign instruments for communication - but are immediately evoked in the spectator. "The work does not, however, communicate this attitude - hence the intrinsic artistic 'content' of the work is also inexpressible in words - but evokes it directly in the perceiver. We call this attitude the 'meaning' of the work only because it is rendered in the work objectively by its organization and is thereby accessible to everyone and always repeatable." (ibid, 228)

Mukarovsky's example is the color plane of a painting which is as an element - and in its relationship to other planes - bearer of a meaning and of a signifying factor independent of what it represents. Not only do the planes differ optically, but also semantically. However, "the semantic nuances which arise in this way cannot, of course, be expressed in words but can only be felt." (ibid, 230) Not as a communicative sign, but as a semantic sign does a painting have a complex semantic structure. All separate elements of the canvas obtain independent meanings which influence the meaning of the painting as a whole. This meaning of the whole is able to immediately evoke a certain attitude in the spectators which can be applied to each reality they encounter. "Thus it is not only by means of its theme but precisely by means of its artistic, verbally non-communicable meaning that a work of art influences the way in which a perceiver who has really experienced it thereafter views reality and behaves toward reality." (ibid, 231) According to Mukarovsky, this "influence on the attitude of a human being with regard to reality" is the most essential function of visual art.

In his view, the material of visual art determining its essence is the most effective means to realize the basic task of art.

5.2. The semiotic problems of visual art

5.2.1. The logic of the image. (Peters)

Although Jan Marie Peters' study <u>Semiotics of the Image</u>, deals with semiotics of film, one will find clarifying facts on the terminology of semiotics with references to painting in the first chapter. Peters understands semiotics of the image as a logic of the image exploring the relationship between image and thought. Because of its condensed formulation, the image is able to present thought more powerful than colloquial language generally does. For example, a news item seldom attains the power of Picasso's <u>Guernica</u>. A literary or philosophical protest against the acts of war could do so, but differently. However, a painting has to be read as well. Semiotics can be a useful instrument for this.

Peters initiates a semiotic approach to painting. Moreover, he makes a number of categorical statements illuminating the nature of painting; for example, on the "form" of the image. The form of the image is constituted by the difference between the way we perceive the object-in-image and the way the real object appears to us. "One could say that the form of the image consists of the way the image 'irrealizes' reality, or better the portrayed, representation; and that the extent to which reality has been irrealized, determines the awareness of form of the spectator." (Peters 1979, 14)

An artefact can be understood as an object, an image or a representation of something else and as a form. In other words, as the way a physical shape has been "transformed". This transformation will vary between two extremes: on the one hand, a creation of an illusion that it is not a representation but the model itself; and on the other hand, a transformation into an extreme abstraction turning the form into a means of making us see the model in a particular way. The idea that the form makes one "see" seems essential. However, it is unclear why, in an extreme abstraction, one should speak of a model. From a semiotic perspective, the following statement seems refutable: "Certain manipulations with the image as an object do not induce any modifications in the image as a form." (ibid, 15)

From this it follows that Peters does not consider the spatial context as an element of form. Thus, he excludes object art (for example, the ready-made). The statement "... thus, the form of the image remains unchanged as the original painting is reproduced on a smaller format .." (ibid, 15) proves that Peters does not consider the format of the proportion an element of the form, and neither the material qualities of the paint. This is because he equates the original and the reproduction as a form. One can hardly speak of the same form with regard to a Barnett Newman in pocket format, and a reproduction of Bogart's material art is different from the original in form. Peters points out that the spectator is compelled to share the creator's "way of looking", literally as well as metaphorically. "If perceiving is judging - and Gestalt psychology has demonstrated this clearly enough - in choosing the perspective, the painter or graphic designer or photographer will express his mental point of view regarding the represented object." (ibid, 17)

That is true in a metaphorical sense. Literally, this is not always so, because the spectator is not always in the same optical-spatial relationship as the creator. An action painting does not have to be perceived while the canvas is on the floor. In etching, one works in a mirror image.

Important for semiotic analysis is Peters' remark that images representing a "view" on an object consist of two levels: the object (denotatum) and how it is viewed. From this it follows that all signs which the denotatum comprises or of which it consists are represented as well and, thus, presented iconically. In a painting, persons and objects can be represented as symbolizing something else. This has consequences for the role of iconography. "Therefore, one should state that iconography, which is involved after all in the meaning of the objects represented rather than in the form factors of a painting, does not concern a semiotics of the image itself but a semiotics of representation. However, all these signs represented are represented at the same time." (ibid, 22)

Thus, Peters arrives at a clarification of the concept of form. The form of the image has mimetic and expressive functions. The former will constitute the resemblance with the object represented. The latter will interpret. However, if one divides an image into factors, these do not automatically disintegrate into two groups. A painting does not consist of an object and a form, but represents an object in a certain form. All factors one is able to isolate are form factors. Object-mimesis and expressive design cannot be separated. Sometimes the form tends towards the mimetic (recognition), sometimes towards the expressive (information). "Thus, there is a certain tension between the mimetic application of the form factors and the expressive one. On the one hand, the artist should try to apply line, color, plane, perspective, etc. in such a way that the spectator can recognize in the image the object represented; on the other hand, similar form factors should cause a difference with common perception, should the image be expressive at all. This difference and the tension between mimesis and expression can be minimal or maximal: the image can almost be a double of reality or, conversely, as in an abstract painting, almost merely expression." (ibid, 24)

Although Peters' explicitly uses painting as an example, one senses that his view of the image is influenced strongly by his expertise in the field of film. He strongly emphasizes mimesis and how the object is viewed, and the communicative value of these two functions in the form of the image. This emphasis supposes that he aims at an image not referring to itself but to the other images with which it forms a syntagmatic series within a film. Each image has both a meaning in itself and one as a part of a series, without which there will be no film. It is true, in painting each painting refers to another - i.e. as a work within an oeuvre and as an oeuvre within art history - but not as dominantly as in a film. In contemporary art, an image usually refers to itself. Therefore, the mimetic function is secondary. This is obvious even in hyperrealism, which seems explicitly mimetic at first glance. However, if one considers its relationship with some forms of abstract art, then hyperrealism seems less mimetic. Both forms appear to fade into one another. Some works of certain hyperrealists are mimetic in such a way that they make an abstraction out of the object, which is, moreover, often partially represented. At a certain level, abstract works can be very "hyperrealist". In painting, the object might be the object which is not visible immediately, for example a surrounding atmosphere, as is the case in (post-) impressionist painting. In post-impressionism, many works start with an object, which then disappears in the surrounding spatial synaesthetic atmosphere. Thus, Peters' fundamental question of "how can I 'say' as much as possible while keeping the objects recognizable?" (ibid, 25) and his concept of "recognition" retreat into the background.

In search of how the semantic content of a pictorial expression will be signified, Peters explains how an analysis of a pictorial expression takes place. "In the images of visual art, this occurs because of articulation of one or more form factors, and articulation means that a selection will take place out of one or more form possibilities. Thus, the painter can place his object on the left side or the right sight of the image plane, in the center or nearer to the frame of the image; he can turn one object into figure and another into ground, he can choose between light and dark, between volume and flat, between large and small, between foreground and background, between high or low perspective, between vertical and horizontal lines, between the static and the dynamic, between white and black, between line and color, etc. ... as far as these mentioned opposites are pairs, the choice of one means at the same time the omission of the other and thus a certain articulation of a form factor. Then each form factor is a signifier which is related to its antithesis and syntagmatically to the other form factors which are applied in the same painting as well. Since, in each painting a number of signifiers play together which will in turn work together with the signs represented in the painting." (ibid 30-33)

Peters emphasizes repeatedly the two levels of the image. In painting, the iconographic signs can be categorized under mimetic codes, but they can be used in an expressive sense as well, in particular when they are applied to say something about that object.

5.2.2. The artistic value of the iconic sign. (Wallis)

The Polish author Mieczyslaw Wallis is one of the pioneers in studying the relationship between art and the theory of signs. His articles show the degree of complexity in determining such a relationship. This might be the reason why the research in this field has not been much advanced. In Wallis' article "On Iconic Signs", he limits himself to the statement that the informative value of the iconic signs in artworks is difficult. After all the iconic sign in a work of art is never a complete and accurate reproduction of the real object but always a certain transformation: a selection, a simplification or a translation. Apart from the examples in modern art where sign and object coincide, Wallis remarks that "the chief aim of iconic signs in works of art is not to provide information about their representata, but to evoke in the receiver definite emotions by means of appropriate images and notions and judgements connected with them, and these emotions may be evoked both by an approximation to the reality and by a deliberate transformation of it in a work of art." (Wallis 1975, 12)

In actual practice, the question of information is entirely a secondary problem. For example, the information that, in reconstructing Warsaw, the architects employed Bellotto-Canaletto's work (which is considered unimportant in an artistic sense) does not have anything to do with art per se. Wallis points out that there is no narrow relationship between the informative value of an iconic sign and its artistic value. He considers their value the suggestive power which lies in their function as substitute for what they represent. In his examples, Wallis refers to the world of media and magic. The problem of art is disregarded. In another article, he remarks that "the history of painting and sculpture from the semiological point of view is still to be written." (ibid, 32)

In this article, Wallis provides a rather interesting set of concepts for categorizing artworks according to their semantic structure. However, he does not succeed in surpassing the phase of a terminological proposal. One does not need semiology in order to pass the following judgement on modern art: "The process which follows in the last quarter of the nineteenth and in the first two decades of the twentieth century, at least in one of the main currents in Western art, can in a most general way be described as the desemantization of painting and sculpture, a transition from concrete to abstract and from abstract to non-objective art. This process had, as it were, two aspects: the exaltation of the stimulative factors - colors, lines, shapes - and the progressive degradations of the representative factors and led first to the suppression or reduction of the representative factors in late Impressionism, Fauvism and Cubism and subsequently, in the years 1910-20, to their total elimination in non-objective paintings and sculpture - in the works of Kandinsky, Delaunay, Kupka, Malevitch, Mondrian, Arp and others." (ibid, 34)

Yet, in the conclusion of his article "The World of Arts and the World of Signs", Wallis gives an indication of the importance of observing art from the theory of the sign. Although we no longer ascribe a magical power to word and resemblance as the ancients did, signs continue to be something miraculous. They enable us to turn the absent and the past into a presence, and are essential in communication. "We live and move in the realm of signs, we are enveloped by a 'semiosphere'. Without signs there would be no culture, no human world, no Man." (ibid, 102)

Wallis formulates the sign character of a culture. In the series of definitions of human beings, he puts man as a sign-maker first and he relates the creation of art to this aspect. "Man is not only a sign-maker, but also an art-maker. The arts have made human life richer and deeper. It is an attractive task both for the semiotician and for the theorist of art to explore the manifold connections between these two great realms of human creativeness - the world of arts and the world of signs." (ibid, 102)

From the relationship between art and semiology, one could draw a different conclusion than does Wallis. The importance of art and the perception of art lies in the exploration of its particular sign character. Searching for signs in a, by very definition, richly varied source of signs as the artwork, the spectator will practice disentangling the sign character of culture.

5.2.3. Semiotics and iconography. (Damisch)

Hubert Damisch poses the problem of the distinction between a semiology of language and a semiology of painting. In so doing, he quotes two seemingly contradictory statements by Matisse. "To indicate the distance between the semiology of language and the semiology of painting we like to quote Matisse's statement: 'Each artwork is a whole of signs invented during its realization according to what the piece needs. In extracting them from the composition they had been created for, they no longer have any function.' Painting which presents itself as the dream of communication without system (without institutions): a dream, the right word, from the moment the oneiric activity does not seem to obey any postulated grammar. But this is exactly what another less frequently quoted text of the same Matisse seems to contradict: 'I have to find signs related to the quality of my invention. They will be new plastic signs which in turn will penetrate common language. The importance of an artist measures up to the quantity of new signs he will have introduced into the plastic language'." (Compagnon 1978, 403)

 This seeming contrast between Matisse's former and latter statement is resolved if, in the first statement, one understands signs as the smallest components of a painting: points, lines, planes, etc. In the second statement, the concept of "new signs" should be understood as a larger measure of unity; an artist will create new image-signs which consist of components. In the first case, colors and the nature of touch is under discussion; in the second case, the entire painting. A touch of paint is important on the exact spot it has been placed, and not on another spot within or outside of the painting. Thus, this kind of sign will, of course, lose its power on another spot. However, Matisse correctly states that the importance of an artist is determined by the number of new image-signs he will introduce. But in this context, the issue is a whole of signification of smaller elements which together create a form. This form as a new sign belongs to the artist's authenticity. It derives its importance from the whole of the work and the oeuvre because of its novelty with respect to existent signs and sign systems.

 In his article on the relationship between iconography and semiotics, Damisch points out a number of relevant problems which distinguish the semiotic approach from the older iconographic method. The latter is very logocentric and cannot evolve any further without referring to separate texts. After a phase with great names such as Riegl, Dvorak and Wölfflin, it did not succeed in renewing itself.

 The transition of iconography to semiotics implies the idea that an image should not only be perceived and observed, but read and interpreted as well, with reasonable effort. Iconography provides facts on the representation of the images, whereas semiotics focuses on dismantling the mechanisms of signification. "Whereas iconography attempts essentially to state what the images represent, to 'declare' their meaning (if we accept Wittgenstein's assertion of the equivalence between the meaning of an image and what it represents), semiotics, on the contrary, is intent on stripping down the mechanism of signifying, on bringing to light the mainsprings of the signifying process, of which the work of art is, at the same time, the locus and the possible outcome." (Sebeok 1975, 29)

The relationship between art and sign is not that simple. However, semiotics theoretically offers the possibility of a clarifying contribution to contemporary art. In this respect, Damisch refers to the concepts of "hypoicon" and "icon". Peirce also distinguished between these two concepts in his last writings. "Icon" is not necessarily a sign, and does not necessarily follow the triadic order of a representation. The images from visual art might be mainly "hypoicons". With this term, Damisch means images neither figures and nor signs, but images which border on a figure or a sign or even run counter to them. "The images of art might primarily be hypoicons: an idea which is hard to grasp, just as it is hard to see not only the visual products of alien cultures, but also those of the very few artists of our time who, from Cézanne to Mondrian, from Matisse to Rothko and Barnett Newman, seem to carry out their work on the near side of the figure if not against it, on the near side of the sign, if not against it." (ibid, 35)

The Impressionists forced the spectator to observe art from the articulation of color rather than from figurative denotation. The modern image imposes various concepts of meaning which cause various views on "taste", unable to be reduced to the norms of communication. According to Damisch, a semiotics of art should move in that direction. "This, rather than the logocentric starting point which a humanist history of Art refuses to give up, is the area in which a semiotics of art, whose very existence depends on its being comparative, might have a chance to develop." (ibid, 36)

In passing, Damisch cites non-Western art as an example of other concepts of meaning. In contemporary art, the influence of non-Western signs on the renewal of form and on the fundamental modification of the signifying concept will be further explored. We believe that some movements in contemporary art are to be considered a formal continuation of non-Western art, albeit loaded with other possibilities of signification.

In his book <u>Théorie du nuage</u>, Damisch investigates the "cloud" as an element of pictorial semiotics, as a junction of the meaning of a representation, or "graphe" as he calls it, where functions change depending on the phase. He understands "graphe" as: "... an intermediary between the various levels or institutions of the signifying process which will function in the capacity of a constructive element and as an inductive scheme of a thematic development at the same time." (Damisch 1972, 34)

Damisch's book attempts to contribute to the history of art. However, because of its semiotic approach, there are a number of passages relevant to the reflection on art's changing role. Damisch points out that there is no reason to think that the whole of material characteristics - listed under the categories of outline, color etc. - will be articulated systematically with a view to the production of a meaning. Perhaps they are merely effective or, even less, they might merely serve the iconic signs. Even if one should be prepared - let us assume - to recognize the elements of a signifying order in iconic signs, it is not obvious that these elements will be subjected a priori to a finite list. There is no valid reason either to purposefully reproduce its system, like linguists tend to do for elements (phonemes and types to be discerned) corresponding to the lower levels of linguistic analysis.

Damisch claims that a possible semiology of art should occur on the non-hierarchic higher level of real pictorial elements. The denotative iconic signs have their material texture. This texture operates as a signifier for a second meaning, a connotative message. And this message assembles the denotative message based on mimesis as in the relationship between signifier and signified. "However, if the project of a semiology of art has been founded, a description on the level of the pure pictorial elements cannot be limited to a search for an indefinite number of conventional representations, studio instructions or some characteristics; it has to relate to an analysis which is effective on a 'higher' level, which corresponds to a purely meaningful articulation (and one could easily demonstrate that each 'effect' is ultimately symbolic in nature). In the context of representative art in a strict sense, the pictorial process is on no account doomed to mere figuration, mere denotation of beings and objects by means of color and/or shape. From the moment there is painting, the iconic signs have their texture, a texture which is often deliberately part of 'taste' and even goes as far as imposing the idea that a style will partly derive its status from it. Thus, as far as it is relevant, the from now on classical opposition between 'literary' and 'pictorial' refers to the material basis of the pictorial process, of which one wonders whether it only has a decorative function. Will the 'treatment' of the image not rather be the signifier of a second meaning, of a connotated message which corresponds to the 'style' of the representation and which, in a certain sense, is beyond the denoted message which is founded on mimesis, on an analogy between signifier and signified which will not take the position of a code?" (ibid, 24-26)

Damisch pleads for the necessity of giving the authenticity of the pictorial order a chance in interpretation. The allegorical as well as the thematic interpretation are limited because they depart from a logic alien to the pictorial order. The allegorical interpretation of a logic serves a humanist rhetoric. Conversely, the thematic interpretation is psychological in nature. Although the pictorial order derives elements from both realms, it still has its authenticity: "But even if the pictorial order would derive something from the phantasmagory and the status of the discourse, could we claim that it does not have an authentic necessity, efficiency and legality?" (ibid, 40)

Signs and figures are determined in their sensory presence by the functions they fulfil on various levels and by the relationships they have with unities appropriate to connect with or to oppose. In other words, they are determined by all functions and relationships which could mean a revealing development to art theory.

Damisch provides a clarifying understanding of what could be called a "pictorial system". In his view, such a system has no reality - even not a theoretical one - outside of strictly employed categories in specific products, i.e. masterworks. "To resume and correct De Saussure's metaphor, the 'treasure' which artists draw from is not so much that of language which they cherish in practice, but that of 'masterworks', artworks which are of importance because of their completeness and authority. In this context, 'language' is rather understood as opposition to 'taste' (senses/organ) than as 'utterance'. One will benefit from pronouncing the question of systems, on the level of very rare realizations which acquire the value and power of models, where not only a quality of invention or a concern about style will emerge (as we will verify in a very prestigious example), but also a linguistic ambition unparalleled in the series of oeuvres (as they are dictated by the order of taste) and which will provide an initial characteristic to such investigation or detailed renewal which it will not obtain where this ambition fails in more inferior works or molded products." (ibid, 121-122)

Thus, in Damisch's view, the pictorial system obtains form out of real history, or better, historicity. Besides works which arise out of taste and which are meaningless cliches because of this, there are masterworks with a relatively continuous value, created out of a desire to achieve language (langue).

In a discussion of what Damisch calls scriptural space, he clearly distinguishes between phonetic and pictorial writing. Phonetic writing as a system finds its rationale outside itself: it can be deciphered in referring to a linguistic order. The history of such writing evolves to a simplification, particularly with a view to efficiency, "the phonetic model has ultimately no other privilege than this efficiency, and a transparency close to effacement." (ibid, 142) Conversely, pictorial writing is not necessarily directed towards simplicity, let alone towards "effacement". It is also less efficient. Different from the many possibilities of language, pictorial writing only disposes of visual means to express concepts and relationships. Although the word, the discourse, can make the image more explicit, there is still no duplicate or adornment. The pictorial narrative has its particular principles. But the grammar - which organizes the figurative elements within the two-dimensional plane - does not derive anything from the linguistic mechanism with which the translator attempts to describe the image. A code has to be established.

The problem is comparable to the explanation of dreams. Step by step, one tries to decipher a grammar of dreams without hope of arriving at a system which could explain them. However, the dream analyst can refer to a "script" stemming from the non-historical order of unconsciousness. Thus he can fall back on a syntaxis. Conversely, pictorial writing has a history. According to Damisch, theory should not yield to the tyranny of a humanism that only wishes to know the products of art in their individuality. Theory should certainly not refrain from the investigation of invariants and historical or transhistorical variants, from where visual reality can be determined in its generality, its fundamental structure. In Damisch's view, this is a condition to achieve a scientific or non-scientific theory and serious history of art.

5.2.4. *The non-mimetic element of the image-sign. (Schapiro)*

Several authors agree that Meyer Schapiro's research is unique. Schapiro's essay "Field and Vehicle in Image-signs" is an example of how semiotics can contribute to a new reading by the spectator of even traditional artworks. Such lectures teach aspects which, in the icon, deviate from the order of the sign in a strict sense of the word. Thus, aspects of articulation different from figurative denotation are highlighted.

In the essay mentioned, Schapiro discusses a number of non-mimetic elements of the image-sign and their role in the construction of the sign. For example, he deals with the meaning of the smoothly prepared canvas plane - which enters history rather late - as opposed to the rough stone surface of the cave paintings. The sense of the whole is dependent on varying habits of perception. Owners of Chinese paintings often put a stamp and written comments in the unpainted background of a landscape. Another aspect is to leave the preparations and initial sketches visible, which are then integrated in the image as signs of the author's action while creating the work. The palimpsest is a version of this phenomenon. In contemporary art, many of these aspects are employed deliberately in order to achieve a certain meaning. Besides treating the canvas plane, the framing or unframing of the canvas plays a role in the realization of meaning in the painting. In contemporary art, the absence of the frame often refers to the partial, the fragmentary and the contingent nature of the image. Open unpainted planes also contribute to expressive effects. "The space around it is inevitably seen not only as ground in the sense of Gestalt psychology, but also as belonging to the body and contributing to its qualities. For the aesthetic eye the body, and indeed any object, seems to incorporate the empty space around it as a field of existence. The participation of the surrounding void in the image-sign of the body is still more evident where several figures are presented; then the intervals between them produce a rhythm of body and void and determine effects of intimacy, encroachment and isolation, like the intervals of space in an actual human group." (Schapiro 1970, 492)

Remarkable in this passage is the capacity Schapiro contributes to the "aesthetic eye". This eye does not only perceive the object, but also the field of existence as empty space around it which is embodied by the object and, therefore, no longer seems to be empty. This is an important aesthetic function, where the fixation of the eye on the object and its denotative meaning has been breached by incorporating it, within the connotative of the closest spatial context, rather than in a denotative field of existence.

Schapiro points out other expressive factors connected with the place figures obtain within the field. The composition is non-communicative. Movement is possible along various axes, but there is a huge difference between horizontal and vertical axes. Certain conditions of the field necessitate a certain reading: from left-to-right or from right-to-left, or from top-to-bottom, etc. Within the field of a work, one should account for the meaning connected with "left" and "right". "Pertinent to semiotics is the fact that left and right are already distinguished sharply in the signified objects themselves. Everyone is aware of the vital importance of left and right in ritual and magic, which has influenced the meaning of these two words, their metaphorical extensions in everyday speech as terms for good and evil, correct and awkward, proper and deviant." (ibid, 495)

The same is true for large and small in relationship to the format of the field, in other words the form, the relationships and the dominant axes, as well as the sizes. Connotations such as grandiose or intimate, massive or sophisticated soon arise. However, the size can be determined as well in the function of visibility.

Within the context of meaning, artists provide this with respect to the right sign, in the right place, in the right relationships, Schapiro gives an example of an exception with definite theoretical consequences. He claims: "Nevertheless, in judging their work, artists often invert the painting in order to see the relationships of forms or colors, their balance and harmony, without reference to the objects represented. But this is only an experimental abstraction of one aspect; the unity is finally judged in a scrutiny of the work in its proper mimetic (or non-mimetic) orientation. However, abstract painters today discover new possibilities through that inversion, even a preferred form." (ibid, 492-3)

This experimental abstraction of one aspect can determine the meaning of the work at a certain moment. Take for example Baselitz' work. One could extend this view: from the perspective of the spectator, this experimental abstraction is the method to view aesthetically, turning the mimetic (or non-mimetic) orientation into an abstraction. The inversion of a work provides the possibility to free the aesthetic qualities of the work. Schapiro gives a number of clarifying insights concerning the non-mimetic elements of the image. One could call this the sign-bearing material, the image-substance of lines and dots with ink and paint. These elements have characteristics which differ from the objects they represent. "From the aesthetic point of view the line is an artificial mark with properties of its own. The artist and the sensitive viewer of the work of art are characterized by their ability to shift attention freely from one aspect to the other, but above all to discriminate and judge the qualities of the picture substance in itself." (ibid, 499)

The last statement is once more a confirmation of the interpretation that the aesthetic view (of the trained spectator) consists of the possibility to distinguish from an abstracted representation - this is "criticism" in its etymological meaning - and to judge the qualities - this is "criticism" in its current meaning - of the image-substance itself. Schapiro gives an indirect description of the artistic form. In the portrait, the same face can be represented in many different ways and with very varied schemes of lines and dots referring to characteristics. Thus, one should distinguish between the image-sign and the dissemination of the semantic function, which runs parallel to the arbitrariness of the qualities of the image-substance. The image-sign seems thoroughly mimetic, but the material parts of the image do not have a mimetic meaning in themselves. They do not obtain a value as distinct signs until they relate to each other in a certain way, and their qualities as marks contribute something to the appearance of the represented objects. The marks - for example lines and dots - represent something because of the context and the adjoining marks. "According to the context of adjoining or neighboring marks, the dot may be a nail-head, a button, or the pupil of an eye; and a semi-circle may be a hill, a cap, an eyebrow, the handle of a pot, or an arch." (ibid, 499)

One could reverse this remark. In that case, one should add that from the artist's perspective or that of the aesthetically sensitive spectator, it is ultimately unimportant whether a mark, for example a color dot, is a nose or merely a dot chosen in relationship to adjoining dots. Be this as it may, Schapiro views the artistry in the variation of the possibilities of form, the "how" as opposed to the "what", the mimetic representation. Schapiro's objections should be considered a reaction of an art historian to colleagues for whom the iconography of the representation is the only object of investigation. In Schapiro's view, one should also include the material-technical components. "These variations of the 'medium' constitute the poetry of the image, its musical rather than mimetic aspect." (ibid, 500) Important is that Schapiro underlines the narrow relationship between mimetic and non-mimetic art, albeit in a somewhat awkward way. He opposes those who consider abstract art a form of decoration and continues to emphasize that the aesthetic should be viewed on the level of the bearer, provided it will be understood as formal structure and expression rather than merely as color plane. "If the elements of the vehicle and their properties are roots of the aesthetic of the work, its intimate formal structure and expression, they owe their development and variety in great part to their service in representation. In abstract painting the system of marks, strokes and spots and certain ways of combining and distributing them on the field have become available for arbitrary use without the requirement of correspondence as signs. The forms that result are not simplified abstracted forms of objects; yet the elements applied in a non-mimetic, uninterpreted whole retain many of the qualities and formal relationship of the preceding mimetic art. This important connection is overlooked by those who regard abstract painting as a kind of ornament or as a regression to a primitive state of art." (ibid, 501)

What interests Schapiro greatly as a semiotician in abstract painting is that it clearly manifests itself as an image-field that corresponds in its totality with a segment of the space from a larger whole. "The conception of the picture-field as corresponding in its entirety to a segment of space excerpted from a larger whole is preserved in abstract painting." (ibid, 502) One could formulate this somewhat more concretely by pointing out that abstract art mostly breaches the view that an object should be represented mimetically. Conversely, abstract art often attempts to reproduce the spatial area, the atmosphere of the object as well as a segment of the texture of objects, whether or not enlarged. In many cases, one could state that abstract art is the "representation" of the "abstraction", of the "inconceivable", visual (chaos, movement, absence etc.), conceptual (emotions, desires, thoughts, memory), as well as synaesthetic (smells, tastes, tangibility, sound).

5.2.5. Pictorial semiology as metalanguage. (Marin)

In his article "Eléments pour une sémiologie picturale", Louis Marin raises immediately the crucial problem of the relationship between the visual image, which is visible and colloquial language, which is readable. The task of a pictorial semiology is to make the visible readable as well. But the pictorial is not just a language. "A pictorial semiotics is in the same situation .." (i.e. the task to fathom a world) .. "and its claim to be scientific poses immediately its existence and the nature of its foundations; its existence to the extent that it is language of something - painting - which might not be linguistic or, to be sure, of another kind; to the extent also that it is language of what should necessarily stay out of the domain of language and which will appear as a challenge to language from the start." (Marin 1971, 17) This impossibility of the correspondence of image and word, of the pictorial and written language comprises the challenge of a semiology of painting. Therefore, a possible pictorial semiology should be understood as a meta-language, since even extra-linguistic semiological systems need the mediation of language. Because of this, a painting becomes a figurative text where the visible and readable are interconnected. A reading can disentangle this interconnection by articulating the painting by means of language. Then "reading" means "scrutinizing a graphic whole and deciphering a text." (ibid, 19) Let us divide the two movements of this action. A painting is primarily a scrutiny of the field of the gaze, a unity of visual representation or a unity of perception of the painting. Marin points out that, within that unity, the painting reveals itself as a utopian space of festivity. "It is always the experienced space which cancels itself out in the existential space of the painting; it is the experienced space which becomes utopian festivity; it is the spectator who perceives the center of the painting and what the painting observes." (ibid, 20) Within the plane of the painting, the course of the gaze on the visual surface is an arbitrary path; in other words, never necessary. "The relative freedom of the course implies that doubt, return and differences indeed never induce the gaze to an irreversible linear movement. Because of this, the time of reading will increase, will spread out or circle around strategic points of the painting. It will turn into a dynamic and qualitative space, in the nuances and correspondences of values and colors. Thus, the open number of possibly realized or virtual courses will form a system." (ibid, 21)

The relative freedom implies that the painting is a matrix of directions followed by the gaze. Because of this, the particular aspects of the painting each determine a certain reading. Moreover, the painting as a system of readings comprises several degrees of compulsive forces within the arbitrary freedom of the courses of the gaze. Between the elements there is a compulsive force of internal coherence which still allows the free play of the gaze. Naturally, the nature of this force differs depending on the painting.

The second movement of the act of reading - deciphering the interpretation - can only be distinguished in an abstract way from the first one, in particular the course followed by the gaze. Reading and deciphering are immediately connected with the senses. However, some questions should be answered in order to be able to refer to the linguistic model with respect to a non-linguistic object such as painting. Is there in painting something similar to the principle of the double articulation (word, sound or phoneme)? Is it possible to retrieve the Saussurian distinction between "language" and "speech"? Marin deals again with the question whether a painterly or pictorial language is possible apart from a the domain of metaphors. Although some authors, such as Dufrenne (Dufrenne 1969), have strongly rejected this, the question should be posed again in order to determine the status of a semiology of painting. The fundamental condition of each pictorial semiology is the inseparability of the visual and the nameable as source of meaning. The "figures" or pictorial syntagmatic unities articulated by the signifiers of the narrative constitute the signifying units of the painting. Yet, a painting only refers to itself: "... the referent of the painting is nothing but the painting itself." (Marin 1971, 34)

Marin is rather explicit with respect to the linguistic distinction of language-speech. He claims that the opposite within the pictorial realm does not exist. "It is impossible - as in the Saussurian model - to set a "pictorial language" against a "pictorial speech" because pictorial language only exists in speech." (ibid, 34-35) The terms of the code can only be determined by referring to the "message" of a determined painting. Therefore, a painting does not refer to an object in the world, but to itself as a pictorial instance.

The painting as a connotative system actualizes internally the arising of the paradigmatic series. Therefore, the entire culture and entire painting are adopted within the painting. In reading a painting, one has to refer to the whole of painting. In that sense, autonomy becomes even more absolute. "In other words, one cannot read a painting until one observes all paintings, the whole of painting, but all these paintings do not acquire any meaning until this reading." (ibid, 35)

One might state that the authenticity of a painting is the paradigmatic absence of other pictorial solutions. Referring to Freud's explanation of dreams, Marin emphasizes the many readings of a painting. The relative arbitrariness of the paths the gaze will follow do not result in unreadability but in a jumble of possible associative ideas. The metaphor of the texture is apparent. In reading a painting, clear-cut and obvious meanings are impossible. "Thus, a reading can never turn the painting into a panorama of meanings, a synopsis of significations. The reading is not static, but dynamic, an open system of forms recomposing constantly and continuously; another way of clarifying the definition of the painting as ineffable." (ibid, 37)

So far, the semiological approach has concerned signifying unities of first-order articulations. Could one find in painting elements which will correspond with phonemes, thus with distinct signs without any meaning themselves? Marin admits that a negative answer to this question would necessarily force exploration of the limitations of a pictorial semiology. However, the exploration should be focused on meaningful structures with elementary signifying units, rather than on the elements themselves devoid of meaning. "The painting is not the assemblage, the combination of elements devoid of meaning, which, because of a certain degree of complexity by a mysterious act, will acquire this meaning. The signifying elements revealed by the analysis have immediate meaning because they cannot be comprehended but in their signifying articulation." (ibid, 39)

In the third part of Etudes sémiologiques, Marin provides a number of possible readings of paintings. His introduction to a number of concrete examples can be understood as a homage to the eye. He points out the enigmatic relationship between painting and spectator. According to Marin, the act of perception does not acquire meaning until its verbalization. If not, the gaze continues to wander. "However, in this journey between eye and painting, the nature of the words have changed: apparent, immediate language mumbling on the other side of silent contemplation in order to constitute it, to ground it in a certain meaning inseparably connected to it (otherwise thought would drift and the gaze wander on the surface, diffused in such a way that it is no discourse): that is what returns as discourse, what refers to itself, speaks for itself on the moment it speaks behind (or in) the painted appearances perceived by the eye." (ibid, 39)

The figures (colors, forms, lines) are not meaningless. They are, so to speak, expressive without a mimetic reason. They create language. "Thus, the painting and its figures are already linguistic, but they await the word in the gaze in order to reveal themselves as such." (ibid, 86)

In Marin's view, the visual text responds to other laws than those of linguistic grammar and syntax. Another vocabulary comes to the surface. In an original way, each artist articulates his personal use of language. He concentrates on a personal language which will express each painting in a process of possible combinations enabling each work to regulate itself. It is not simple to decipher these rules. In particular, when the actual pictorial rules are at stake rather than the non-mimetic, thus, painting as an autonomous order of meaning. Marin points out that reading a painting does not depend on a mysterious innate gift related to a certain gaze. It is a consequence of an often difficult and complex process of learning of codes which enable - according to a certain hierarchical mutual relationship - simulation of the creative construction of the painter consciously as well as unconsciously.

However, it might be better to concentrate on the concrete materiality of the artwork itself. In that way, the code connected with authorship is on the same level as a second series of codes related to ideologies, time-related representations, classes, social groups, a culture which reveals itself as an integrated entity in the painting. According to Marin, this integrating act of the process of creation will induce semantic main axes, which can be understood as real universals of the pictorial meaning. The description and understanding of these semantic main axes will be the scientific task of pictorial semiology.

5.3. Eco

5.3.1. The open artwork

In the introduction of his book The Open Artwork, Umberto Eco defends his view that the study of the work of art should not be restricted to the observation of the object. The ways of consumption should not be excluded because, in creating a work, the artist cultivates a type of consumption, often various consumptive possibilities, "... he (the creator) designs various possibilities of consumption which he keeps present in his mind." (Eco 1965, 11)

Eco wants to emphasize that the artist cannot deny that he works for a receiver of a message which he constructed himself by means of his object. Although the receiver will interpret this message and reveal its ambiguities, the artist will still feel responsible for this chain of communication. Each work to be created - the "poetic" - is a design for communication. It is a design about an object and its effect. "Thus, every investigation into poetics should keep the two aspects in mind; particularly when the poetics of an open artwork are involved, which are the design of a message provided with a wide range of interpretative possibilities." (ibid, 11)

Thus, The Open Artwork departs from the assumption that an artwork is a fundamentally ambiguous message, a multiplicity of signifieds which coexist in one single signifier. In Eco's view, that is the characteristic of each work of art. In contemporary art, the ambiguity is often an explicit purpose of a work.

Eco refers to the pictorial signs of the Informals as an example of "open" art, because of the fields of interpretative possibilities, configurations of stimuli in a fundamental indefiniteness. At the same time, these works offer a series of continuously changing readings, and moreover, they are structured as elements of groups which may have various mutual relationships.

The "open artwork" implies a certain world view. The artist gives the visual answer to the world view science propagates. This is not an implicit conceptual message to be discovered in the forms of art, but rather a structural metaphor. The "open" art as epistemological metaphor has a function of showing a new view of the world. Art provides a vehicle to imagine the world and interpret it in our sensibility. The "open" artwork reveals the discontinuity of the phenomena and the impossibility to acquire a definite common image of the world. "The discontinuity of the phenomena questions the possibility of a unified and definitive worldview; art offers us a possibility of representation of this world, the world in which we live and, thus, the possibility to accept it and to integrate it in our sensitivity. The 'open' art work intends to give an image of the discontinuity in complete lucidity: it does not say anything about it, it is this discontinuity. It offers itself as an intermediary between the abstract categories of science and the living ground of our sensitivity; it is as a transcendental plan of sorts, enabling us to understand new aspects of the world." (ibid, 124)

Eco warns against the danger of a boundless openness of the artwork as a consequence of an exaggerated interest of the spectators in the game of their private imagination. The artwork should not assume the role of a drug, which incites phantasms. The "open" artwork should remain a field of possibilities rather than all possibilities leading to nothing. "Like the reader who escapes the control of the artwork, at a certain moment the artwork seems to escape all control, even the author's and the 'sponte sua' seems to begin to speak as an electronic brain gone mad. What remains then is no longer a field of possibilities, but the vague, the original, the indefinite free of obligations, the all or nothing." (ibid, 127)

With this objection, Eco comes upon a second problem presented in the "open" artwork. How should one determine what the possible readings are to prevent communication from resulting in a chaos without any correspondence between the creator's will and the spectator's response? Eco refers to the distinction information theory draws between "meaning" and "information". The meaning of a message - for example a pictorial configuration as a certain number of formal relationships, rather than a bearer of semantic references - is a function of order, conventions, and a consequence of the "redundancy" of the structure. Therefore, it will be rather probable. Conversely, "information" is connected with improbability, which provides the possibility of informing. Thus, the more a structure is improbable, ambiguous, unexpected or disordered, the more the information will increase. Certain forms of communication demand "meaning", for example road signs. The artistic communication and the aesthetic effect search for "information" as an inexhaustible wealth of meanings. The value of art lies in the new order of its elements, thus, in increased information. Where "classical" art ultimately still attempts to confirm the structures which are accepted by the common sensibility it directs itself to, contemporary art wants to break with the probability of the common language. "Conversely, contemporary art, excluding all other values, apparently aims to break up the probability which regulates common language by questioning its premises on the very moment it uses it and by trying to transform them." (ibid, 128)

Although the artwork can provide more information than merely aesthetic, only aesthetic information is based on the wealth of the given form constituting the multiple aspect of artistic communication. However, what will remain is the question of how to determine to which extent the will of innovative-information can be reconciled with the communicative possibilities between creator and spectator. In this context, Eco points out how important it is that the eye receives direction in order to be able to achieve ordering. The wealth of communicative possibilities will fluctuate around the delicate turning-point of "openness", which reconciles a minimal order with a maximal disorder. This should produce a field of possibilities. "Also here the possibility of even richer communication is present, as it is open in a subtle balance, in a minimum of order which is compatible with a maximum of chaos. This subtle balance draws the line between the field where all possibilities are unclear and the field of possibilities." (ibid, 133)

This comprises the bottleneck of painting open to the wealth of ambiguities, the fertility of the informal and the challenge of being indefinite. It offers the spectator an extremely free adventure, which still should be a communicative one. "The communication of the maximum noise with the hallmark of an intention which gives it a signal value." (ibid, 134)

Without this identifying sign, the spectator can receive any message which nature or coincidence will provide without recognizing it as an author's artefact. According to Eco, the determination of this turning point, of this threshold does not belong to the domain of aesthetics. In each painting, it is an aspect of critical reflection to determine to which extent the various interpretative possibilities - that is, "openness" - organized in an intentional way are included in a field that gives choice to the direction of reading. Not until then does the message have a communicative value. If not, one lapses into in an absurd dialogue between a signal giving only noise and a receiver which is only solipsistic. "An artwork is open as long as it continues to be an artwork. Outside of it, the openness identifies itself with noise." (ibid, 136)

We believe that the limitation of the interpretative multiplicity of the artwork will find its point of reference in the limitation of the artist's intent. Of

course, these two domains do not coincide. Interpretations are possible independent of the authors' intent. Not all intentions will ultimately become visible.
However, no matter how indeterminable it is, one can still speak of a delineation
which in itself is capable of opening up new horizons. An interpretation which
will open up new horizons presupposes that its horizon is known. The openness
of an artwork completely loses its power if it becomes unlimited. The openness
of an artwork is not an interpretative caprice. If an artwork can mean everything,
it does not mean anything because it lost its authenticity as a work of art. This
might be the purpose of an artwork, but it is not a general characteristic of art.
Openness assumes "faithful" readers possessed by a desire for information, no
matter how manifold, which might be present in the work.

5.3.2. *Semiotics as a supplement to philosophical aesthetics.*

"I wrote four books on aesthetics before I became fascinated by semiotics, but
also after that I continued my research on art. Aesthetics is no narrow discipline
which can only be approached psychologically or metaphysically: it is a much
broader field. Because I feel attracted by what cannot be comprehended in
words immediately and I cannot bear that things remain ineffable, I employ
semiotics to approach certain problems and to clarify certain aspects. From the
perspective of semiotics, of course an aesthetic experience cannot be fathomed
but some phenomena can be explained. If I am involved in the problem of color,
as for the 'Mondrian lecture', I attack that initially by means of a categorization.
But it is a fact that at a certain point, our aesthetic experience of color will blow
up all those categories. Yet, it is language which has the possibility to evoke a
feeling of novel, unfamiliar colors as, for example, Joyce does." (Groot 1981,
236)

Eco's words show the value of the relationship between semiotics and
aesthetics. On the one hand, the two are contradictory, because the former has a
rather quantitative approach and the latter's impressions are rather qualitative.
On the other hand, a combination of the two is considered an improvement, in
the sense of supplementing each other's shortcomings.

In Eco's book <u>Apocallittici e integrati</u>, his attitude towards mass media
demonstrates the importance he attributes to semiotics. Eco contrasts two groups
of theorists. First there are apocalyptic defeatists. They observe in the mass
media a process of leveling out, an ideological manipulation leading to superfi-
ciality. Opposing them under the influence of McLuhan, are the "integrati", the
socially integrated, who observe a possible renewal of and increase in mass culture. However, according to Eco, the former's pessimism and the latter's opti-

mism are both evidence of great passivity. Both are directed towards the phenomenon as such, in other words, as object, as solid fact. The difference between both points of view is merely that the former withdraw themselves contemptuously from mass media and the latter confidently surrender to it. In Eco's view, semiotics will be able to breach this impasse. It does not study the message itself, but concentrates on the function of the message in the process of communication. Thus, the dialogue between transmitter and receiver becomes central.

Eco proposes using the word "code" rather than "language" because the word "language" connotes too many associations with speech. Eco wants to omit the linguistic model being applied to other systems of communication. Where communication takes place, there has to be a code. According to Eco, communication will only take place if the transmitter employs rules. Even where we do not see a code, there must be one in order to have communication. We have simply not found the code yet. That does not mean that no new phenomena or modifications can occur in the systems of communication. Eco claims that the purpose of semiotic analysis is to indicate where novel things happen and to demonstrate that we are bound to conventions, codes and ultimately to ideologies, whereas we thought we were free and acted freely.

Eco's approach belongs to what one generally calls a second phase of semiotics. (Sebeok 1975, 9-17) This phase beings with the insight that the sign is not an element between other elements in reality. On the contrary, a characteristic of all elements of the entire reality is under consideration. Thus, everything can be a sign. The sign character of the entire culture is studied.

In this context, Eco's article, "How culture conditions the colors we see", is very revealing. In this article, Eco assumes the position of a color-blind person. He does not base himself on the distinction which Itten introduced, between pigments as chromatic reality and our responsive perception as chromatic effect. Eco draws from old texts by Gellius among others to demonstrate how each culture and thus each language will define colors in a different way. Although the same pigments are under discussion, one finds very distinct manners of indicating the color effects in linguistic terms.

Gellius' Noctes Atticae, a study of various authors from Antiquity where one did not even discriminate between colors at times, demonstrates much confusion on this regard. Yet, its quotations are accepted as a good use of language. According to Eco, this idiosyncrasy cannot be explained psychologically nor aesthetically. In his view, this is something cultural which is interwoven with a linguistic system expressing visual experiences and perceptions. In order to solve Gellius' problem, one has to explore the semiotic structure of language. In categorizing colors and stating names of colors, one does not necessarily phrase an essential experience. Color terms do not express essential characteristics of perception. "When one utters a color term, one is not directly pointing to a state of the world (process of reference), but, on the contrary, connecting or correlating that term with a cultural unit or concept. The utterance of the term is determined, obviously, by a given sensation, but the transformation of the sensory stimuli into a percept is in some way determined by the semiotic relationship between the linguistic expression and the meaning or content culturally correlated to it." (Eco 1985, 160)

In order to solve the dilemma that color differences are based on natural elements but natural differences are shaped by culture, one has to verify the cultural meaning of color by empirically testing the distinction, rather than the other way around. The color terms in themselves do not have an exact chromatic content, since they have to be viewed in the entirety of semiotic systems influencing each other. Our color perception is determined by language, just as language is determined by how society will develop value systems, circumstances, and ideas.

The cultural determinism in perceiving colors Eco formulates implies an important task for art. Art provides the spectators the opportunity - forces them, so to speak - to perceive colors as indicated by the artist, which may differ strongly from the general classification of the relationship between colors and things. Because art attacks social codes and general categories, the possibility arises of creating a sophisticated social consciousness of our cultural manner to name the nature of things. Color in the arts will increase the possibility to perceive contents in a more differentiated way. "Thus the artistic activity, be it poetry of Vergil or the research on pigments by Mondrian, works against social codes and collective categorization, in order to produce a more refined social consciousness of our cultural way of defining contents." (ibid, 175)

Eco is reserved when he discusses the possibilities of a semiotics of painting. Although clearly semiotic in nature, there are still no satisfactory theoretical definitions to bridge the "empirical" limits. "There are 'empirical' limits beyond which stands a whole group of phenomena which unquestionable have a semiotic relevance even though the various semiotic approaches have not yet completely succeeded in giving them a satisfactory theoretical definition: such as paintings and many types of complex architectural and urban objects; these empirical boundaries are rather imprecise and are shifting step by step as new researches come into being." (Eco 1979, 6)

During his investigation, Eco becomes convinced that the initial approach, where a painting was analyzed in its smallest elements, is probably not the right track. Instead he combines methods of working with a demonstrated semiotic approach in their application. Eco has iconography and iconology in mind, which form very important chapters in semiotics. He rejects the attempt to interpret visual phenomena as linguistic utterances, because Eco becomes more and more convinced that they are perceptual phenomena. "After all, the way one approaches a painting from a semiotic perspective does not have any relationship with how language is used." (Groot 1981, 238) Within the semiotic approach to art, Eco attaches great value to the concept of "text". In his book A Theory of Semiotics, he devotes an important paragraph to this subject. (Eco 1979, 261-76) Eco considers the aesthetic text a type of composite laboratory model of all aspects of textual functions. The aesthetic application of the elements to arrive at a text can be viewed on various levels: 1) An aesthetic text implies a particular application of the expression; 2) This application of expression means reviewing the content; 3) Particularly in producing an idiosyncratic and highly original case of sign function, this double intervention is reflected to a certain extent in the codes the aesthetic sign function is based on and because of which a process of modification of codes is produced; 4) Even while focusing on codes, the entire intervention will provoke a new type of consciousness of the world; 5) As far as the aesthetic effect is discovered and perceived closely by the receiver - who makes a complex effort to interpret - the aesthetic transmitter should concentrate on the possible reactions of the receiver. Because of this, the aesthetic text will construct a network of various communicative acts, resulting in a highly original response.

The importance Eco attaches to the semiotic approach to aesthetic texts lies in how they can contribute to traditional philosophical aesthetics. This field has left many problems unsolved. Typically, it classifies the effects a spectator of a visual work may feel instead of defining what a poetic message is. It states "what" is sensed but not "how". "What differentiates the response of philosophical aesthetics from that of the layman is the sophisticated architecture of rhetorical devices which, by means of an imaginative interplay of metaphors, translate a sum of truisms." (ibid, 262)

5.3.3. *The communicative function*

Eco is rather explicit in defining the aesthetic function. He prefers the term "aesthetic" to "poetic" because he wants to expand this function to all forms of art. A message acquires an aesthetic function when it is ambiguous and self-focusing. Semiotically, one should understand "ambiguity" as the way to break the codifying rules. The disturbance of order demands attention and compels interpretation. Yet, not every breach of the norm is aesthetic. Therefore, Eco postulates that, in aesthetic texts, an ambiguity of expression should also bring about a corresponding ambiguity of content. Neither layer can be split. An increase in the degree of organization within a continuum of expression will inevitably cause a parallel increase in the continuum of content. The spectator should account for this double layering. "Looking at a work of art, the addressee is in fact forced to question the text under the pressure of a twofold impression: on the one hand he 'guesses' that there is a surplus of expression he cannot completely analyze (though maybe he could). On the other hand he vaguely senses a surplus of content. This second feeling is clearly aroused by the surplus of expression but it occurs even when this surplus of expression is not consciously grasped." (ibid, 269-70)

The ambiguity comes about because in both layers there are extreme redundancies, which increase informative possibilities. Due to this, one almost has to decide that an artwork does not communicate, because it communicates too much and, therefore, becomes incomprehensible. Yet, this is not the case. On the basis of "contextual solidarity" - when one modifies one element of the context, then all other elements will lose their original function - Eco concludes that there must be a systematic rule. This means that an artwork will have the same structural characteristics as language. There must be an underlying system of mutual correlations, and, thus, a semiotic plan that ingeniously gives the impression of non-semiosis. In that way, Eco arrives at the description of art as a texture of messages. "Thus art seems to be a way of interconnecting messages in order to produce a text in which: a) many messages, on different levels and planes of the discourse, are ambiguously organized; b) these ambiguities are not realized at random but follow a precise design; c) both the normal and the ambiguous devices within a given message exert a contextual pressure on both the normal and ambiguous devices within all the others; d) the way in which the norms of a given system are offended by one message is the same as that in which the norms of other systems are offended by the various messages that they permit." (ibid, 271)

The deviation from the norm originates from a general deviating matrix. The artwork acquires the status of a super-sign function. Not only does the deviating matrix represent a structural organization, but it also involves a reorganization of the codes themselves. Therefore, it introduces a proposal for a new codifying possibility. This new code, or idiolect, is a semiotic enclave which cannot be recognized by any member of the community. An aesthetic idiolect is the rule which dominates all deviations active on each plane of an artwork. A unique kind of diagram, rendering all deviations mutually functional. If critics know how to isolate the idiolect of a work, this still does not mean that they possess a formula to produce similar works. The idiolect of a work cannot help but produce completely identical works. However, if an idiolect of a corpus is at stake - particularly a period or a movement of works - this structural model is nothing more than a scheme that has to be reshaped again and again. The difference between this scheme and a certain work is similar to the scheme between a code and its possible messages.

The aesthetic idiolect cannot be decoded without any problems. The aesthetic text constantly transforms its denotations into new connotations, provided its layers are connected mutually in a semiotic way. Contents never exist in and of themselves but rather as a signifier for something else. Eco blames classical philosophy for expressing this effort of interpretation in terms of a pleasant feeling; particularly, as something that implies intuition. Eco emphasizes that art produces knowledge: "But common artistic experience also teaches us that art not only elicits feelings but also produces further knowledge." (ibid, 274)

Each text will threaten the codes, but reinforce them as well. The consumers will reveal the text's unexpected possibilities and, therefore, modify their attitude towards it. The conservation of the narrow dialectic relationship between message and code, feeding each other, makes the receivers aware of new semiotic possibilities and force them to reflect on existing ones. "By increasing one's knowledge of codes, the aesthetic message changes one's view of their history and thereby trains semiosis." (ibid, 274)

The aesthetic experience challenges the generally accepted organization of the content. It suggests that the semantic system can be organized differently. Because of this, the world will be viewed differently. "But to change semantic systems means to change the way in which culture 'sees' the world." (ibid, 274)

Eco admits that this epistemological emphasis on the function of the aesthetic text is rather metaphorical. In perceiving a painting, one often has the experience that things are not as they usually seem. Still that does not mean that concepts such as "truth" would be relevant in this context. The aesthetic text has to be analyzed semiotically in greater depth. In particular, the aesthetic texts can contribute immensely to that part of theory, textual production, which attempts to connect signs to the world. "If aesthetic texts can modify our concrete approach to states of the world then, they are of great importance to that branch of a theory of sign production that is concerned with the labor of connecting signs with the states of the world." (ibid, 275)

Eco attributes an enormous independence to the receiver who reads an artistic product. "Like a large labyrinthine garden, a work of art permits one to

217

take many different routes, whose number is increased by the criss-cross of its paths." (ibid, 275)

The understanding of an aesthetic text is based on two aspects. Firstly, there is a dialectic between acceptance and renouncement of the transmitter's code. Secondly, this understanding is based on the introduction and the rejection of the personal code. The aesthetic abduction consists of representing certain provisional codes to make the produced message understandable. The receiver does not know the rule of the transmitter. He attempts to deduce it from the incoherent facts of his aesthetic experience. Eco claims that with respect to the aesthetic sign as a communicative act, the receiver will never completely reveal the author's intention. "So that in the interpretative reading, a dialectic between fidelity and inventive freedom is established." (ibid, 276)

This remark is related to the view that the aesthetic text as a communicative act should be put first. In communicative considerations, one can hardly depart from a deliberate misunderstanding. Yet, a formalist attitude seems to be more productive: we propose not to give away the artwork in its material dimension rather than to try not to betray the author's intentions. The purposes of the author are not necessarily visible or even present in the artifact. Nothing will guarantee that the author does not betray himself in formulating desired purposes which he did not materialize. Art allows communication with objects which produce meaning. Communication need not necessarily occur with the creator of these objects. This remark does not detract from the importance of Eco's semiotic definition of an aesthetic text as a structured model for the unstructured process of communicative interaction. In that view, the artwork is situated within the combinatory possibilities of the given code and within a given artistic period. However, Eco's old idea of the open artwork is preserved within his more semiotic way of thought. "A responsible collaboration is demanded of the addressee. He must intervene to fill up semantic gaps, to reduce or to further complicate the multiple readings proposed, to choose his own preferred paths of interpretation, to consider several of them at once (even if they are mutually incompatible), to re-read the same text many times, each time testing out different and contradictory presuppositions." (ibid, 276)

In Eco's view, an aesthetic text is more important because it is an unpredictable source of "speech acts". The work of art needs the word of the interpreter. Or better said, the artwork exists because of the multiplicity of its simultaneous and successive interpretative comments: "The work of art is a text that is adapted by its concrete addressees so as to fulfil many different communicative purposes in diverse historical or psychological circumstances, without ever completely disregarding the underlying rule that has constituted it." (ibid, 310)

Eco has previously formulated the necessity of verbalizing the code, because of which the artwork must obtain its communicative function. (Eco 1972, 219-233) He bases his view on two contemporary art movements. Firstly, the art of the Informals, which he clearly prefers because of its "open" character. Secondly, New Figuration, which piques Eco's interest because of the references to mass culture codes. From these two perspectives, he poses the problem of the "poetic", which demands an explanation. According to Eco, the main characteristic of contemporary art exists in bringing about an individual code which the artwork implies. "Here (informal art) difficult problems arise: if the main characteristic of almost each artwork from contemporary art is to set up an individual code of the artwork, (which does not precede the work and is not its external reference, but is continuously present in the work), then this code can generally not be traced without external help and, therefore, not without an enunciation of poetics." (ibid, 232)

In abstract art based on forms, there is a possible reference to mathematical-geometric codes. However, they are loaded with cultural connotations. Thus, the autonomy of the code is secondary. This is not the case with so-called informal art, which is constituted by unnoticed rules the work creates. Yet, communication is only possible with a person familiar with these rules. Therefore, an abundance of preceding explanations by the artist persists. "The artwork aspires to autonomy with respect to prevailing conventions, in such a way that it states its own system of communication, but it only communicates partly as long as it is not supported by additional linguistic systems of communication (the enunciation of poetics), employed as a meta-language with respect to the linguistic code brought about by the artwork." (ibid 232-33)

Conversely, the New Figuration - a collective term of movements such as Pop-art, assemblage, Nouveau Réalisme - works again with the precise and conventional codes artists construct. They turn them into signs of another language and engender a new code which the interpreter has to discover. "The invention of an entirely new code, artwork after artwork (or rather series of works by the same author) continues to be one of the constant elements of contemporary art: but the institution of these new codes happens dialectically with respect to an existing system where we can recognize the codes." (ibid 233)

Reference to existing codes has expanded to recent movements in art, where frequent reference is made to codes of "styles" of the past or of an artist's period. It could almost be called a main characteristic of postmodernism and trans-avant-garde. However, language is still necessary in order to translate these manipulated codes.

5.4. Lévi-Strauss

More interesting than the historical "origin" or the religious function of art is Claude Lévi-Strauss' perspective, because of its philosophical bias and aesthetic implications. The idea of "structure" is productive in exploring the role of art for an individual within an exiting social order. Furthermore, Lévi-Strauss is the first anthropologist dealing with a comprehensive aesthetics.

5.4.1. Art as an actual form of "savage thought"

Lévi-Strauss admires Comte. Without any knowledge of totemism, Comte had a better understanding of the economy and range of a classificatory system in primitive society than do contemporary ethnologists. In Lévi-Strauss view, however, this is not connected with a certain period in history. To him, "savage thought" is not the thought of savages nor of a primitive or archaic society. "But rather mind in its untamed state as distinct from mind cultivated or domesticated for the purpose of yielding a return. This latter has appeared at certain points of the globe and at certain moments in history, and it is natural that Comte, lacking ethnographic data (and that ethnographic sense which can be acquired only by the collection and handling of data of this type) should have apprehended the former in its retrospective form, as a mode of mental activity anterior in time to the latter. We are better able to understand today that it is possible for the two to coexist and interpenetrate in the same way." (Levi-Strauss 1966, 219)

Lévi-Strauss makes a comparison with nature where, besides having wilderness, some areas are cultivated for agriculture or cattle raising. Because of their expansion, the latter areas threaten the former with extinction. Although savage thought is threatened as well, there are domains where it continues to be protected, such as in the domain of art. Lévi-Strauss claims that contemporary art has the status of a nature preserve. Indeed, the world of contemporary art exists alongside daily life in a society where citizens generally do not participate in the world of art. One can only speak of a number of specialists and a small number of interested people. Our hypothesis is: as long as contemporary art is locked away in the institution of a nature preserve, contemporary human beings will exhibit an incoherence in their outlook on life. This is especially true for the category who consider themselves "progressive".

An example of the status of a nature preserve could be that the artists are not obliged to answer to the community where they live. After all, they do not fulfil an immediate social function. Artistic freedom is guaranteed. Contrary to savage thought, domesticated thought is controlled in order to yield results. Thus, art must not produce any output.

Lévi-Strauss attributes a scientific value to aesthetic perception. He prefers any form of classification to chaos. Even on the level of aesthetic perception, classification can be useful. It is interesting to proceed in thought and act in such a way that a similarity will arise between what satisfies the aesthetic feeling and what comprises objective reality. The aesthetic properties (form, color, smell) give the spectator the right to state that these visible characteristics are a sign of particular but hidden properties. The search for a constitutive structure is already present in a primary form. Rather than staying indifferent to each coherence, it is useful to compose a possible incoherent classification on an aesthetic basis, because this will activate sensory attention. Lévi-Strauss attaches much importance to the "science of the concrete", based on a "logic of sensory perception". A conquest of the world as perceived by the senses becomes possible in terms of sensory perception. As regards the relationship to the exact sciences, Lévi-Strauss' main thought concerns parallelism. These two perspectives of reality are not in line. So-called primitive thought is not precursory - in the sense of less-developed - to exact thought. It is a conjunctive way of thought, but of earlier origin. "This science of the concrete was necessarily restricted by its essence to results other than those destined to be achieved by the exact natural sciences but it was no less scientific and its results no less genuine. They were secured ten thousands years earlier and still remain at the basis of our own civilization." (ibid,16) Thus, there are two different ways of scientific thought. They depend on two strategic levels where nature can be conquered by scientific knowledge.

Presently, art is still an aspect of this one strategy. A consequence is that art does not refer to things as adornment, decoration, beautiful prints or satisfaction of romantic sentimentality. On the contrary, art is connected with an outlook on life and a means of "conquering nature" through indicating its separate characteristics. Even if, in some cases, this indication proves equal to a magical approach - and thus might have little interest in an exact scientific approach - it is still of importance within the construction of an outlook on life and a system of values.

The need for order is at the basis of what Lévi-Strauss calls primitive thought; however, only as far as it is the basis of all thought. To depart from what is common in all thought will ease the access to forms of thought which seem alien to us. Visual art seems just such an alien form of thought. Organization often occurs in avant-garde art, for example, in some forms of object art which turn the organization of waste matter into artistic activity.

Remarkably, Lévi-Strauss points out that organization - besides being considered a general aspect of art - demonstrates at the same time an immediate relationship with the religious domain. Not being "useful" is a common property of both ritual and art, or is a ritual characteristic of art. One of the principles of the avant-garde as iconoclastic visualization is to destroy the established formal order. That almost never happens without reorganization which continues to be a characteristic of artistic creation and aesthetic perception. No matter how disorganized, for example, Arman's representations are, they still result from an accurate destructive reorganization.

5.4.2. *Art between science and myth*

A second phase which reveals art as a form of mythical or savage thought is the introduction of the techniques of the "bricoleur" (amateur, putterer) and the engineer. The application of the term "bricoleur" to people who call themselves "artists" will not please them. The relationship is complicated, because art cannot be listed in the domain of the engineer nor in the domain of the "bricoleur".

Lévi-Strauss claims that mythical thought is a kind of intellectual "bricolage" ("puttering"). Typical of this kind of thought is that, in order to express itself, it employs means with a heterogeneous construction which, no matter how extensive, is at the same time constrained. Lévi-Strauss points out the mythical nature of "bricolage" itself. For example, he has in mind what he calls "naive" art, designated more broadly as kitsch, without connecting any value judgement or evaluation to this term.

In Lévi-Strauss' characterization of mythical "bricolage", a parallel with art can be found. In spite of immense relevatory experiments, the means of visual art seem minimal. Artists can enlarge a circle, make an ellipse out of it or a labyrinthine rope, but the means continue to be minimal. Partly because they have to remain within the domain of art, partly because the enlargement of means is always accompanied by a return to earlier applications. In a bare-bones form this is paint and constitutive material. Minimal art knew how to make the most of this limitation.

To a certain extent, photography transgresses the boundaries of the artistic means of painting, drawing and graphic art. Obviously, it should not dissolve visual art, unless perhaps on the level of a somewhat utilitarian function of reproduction and documentation. In its relationship to visual art, photography has obtained a double role. It has become a resource for visual art, and in addition an autonomous branch of visual art with a full artistic stature. (Swinnen 1992) As long as the means of visual art are variations of, for example, qualities of paint, one can hardly speak of the heterogeneity of the composition, as one does in "bricolage". However, for some artistic media it is possible as, for example, in assemblage art.

In Lévi-Strauss' two kinds of scientific knowledge, the problem of situating art becomes even more obvious when studying his comparison in depth. "The 'bricoleur' is adept at performing a large number of diverse tasks; but, unlike the engineer, he does not subordinate each of them to the availability of raw materials and tools conceived and procured for the purpose of the project. His universe of instruments is closed and the rules of his game are always to make do with 'whatever is at hand', that is to say with a set of tools and materials which is always finite and is also heterogeneous because what it contains bears no relation to the current project, or indeed to any particular project, but is the contingent result of all the occasions there have been to renew or to enrich the stock or to maintain it with the remains of previous constructions or deconstructions." (Levi-Strauss 1966, 17) Thus, the "bricoleur" collects things because they can always be used for something. In this context, the means are determined by their utility as an instrument.

The difference between the "bricoleur" and the engineer becomes more obvious in the difference between sign and concept. The sign can be defined as a connection between an image and a concept. "Signs resemble images in being concrete entities but they resemble concepts in their powers of reference. Neither concepts nor signs relate exclusively to themselves; either may be substituted for something else. Concepts, however, have an unlimited capacity in this respect, while signs have not." (ibid, 18) Their difference and correspondence becomes clear in the example of the "bricoleur". The engineer works with concepts, because he is searching for a solution to exceed the limitations imposed on him by civilization. The "bricoleur" works with signs, because he does not go "beyond" the limitations. In fact, at least one of the ways the sign is opposed to the concept amounts to "that whereas concepts aim to be wholly transparent with respect to reality, signs allow and even require the interposing and incorporation of a certain amount of human culture into reality." (ibid, 20) The "bricoleur" only collects information which has been passed on whereas the engineer searches for new information. "Concepts thus appear like operators opening-up the set being worked with and signification, like the operator of its reorganization, which neither extends nor renews it and limits itself to obtaining the group of its transformations." (ibid, 20)

Although Lévi-Strauss does not discuss art much, the relationship between the "bricoleur" and the engineer can be applied to artists. Obviously, art as a system of signs is in favor of the "bricoleur", with the exception of conceptual art, where the artists pretend to be engineers. Assemblage art is a clear example of art with a "bricolage" character, where artists enter into a dialogue

with the instruments and materials available to them. From a collection of incoherent objects, they search for what each object could mean as an answer to a
problem they pose themselves. By means of internal organization of parts, they
arrive at a whole. Either the form of the material or the nature of the material are
important. However, these possibilities always remain limited because of each
piece's particular past and what has been previously determined in the piece, in
other words, the use it was originally designed for. Thus, the elements are limited from the beginning, because the "bricoleur" (assemblage artist) is directed
towards a collection of remains from human products. Conversely, the engineer
exploring the world is similar to the conceptual artist who questions the foundation of the art world.

　　Mythical thought can be considered an intellectual form of "bricolage".
Science is based on the distinction between coincidence (occurrence) and necessity (structure). "Bricolage" is characterized by the practical realm, whereas
mythical thought embodies structured entities. However, mythical thought does
not do so through other structured entities, but through rests and remains of
occurrences: particularly the waste of old colloquial language, petrified witness-
es to the history of individual and society. Thus, mythical thought develops
structures from the remains of occurrences. Conversely, science creates its
means and results in the form of occurrences from the structures it continually
modifies, such as hypotheses and theories. In Lévi-Strauss' view, both phases are
equally valid, rather than two separate stages in the evolution of knowledge.
"Mythical thought for its part is imprisoned in the events and experiences which
it never tires of ordering and re-ordering in its search to find them a meaning.
But it also acts as a liberator by its protest against the idea that anything can be
meaningless with which science at first resigned itself to a compromise." (ibid,
22)

　　The same could be said about artistic thought. Lévi-Strauss' central idea
on art's place in culture seems immensely important. In refraining from placing
it outside of knowledge (or pre-knowledge) and not-knowledge, art gains an
important stature as an orientation toward life. In that way, "aesthetic education"
will disappear as a category of supplementary education, and become the category of complementary education, in addition to the sciences. By assigning savage, mythical thought an equal place next to scientific thought, the subordination
of the former will disappear, and theoretically, it could even become preferred.
Art becomes even more important, because Lévi-Strauss situates it between both
realms, rather than in one of them. Accordingly, art obtains another synthetic
dimension.

　　For Lévi-Strauss, the artist is almost a scholar and at the same time a "bricoleur". After all, through manual work the artist produces a physical object, which is an object of knowledge as well. Lévi-Strauss distinguishes between both as "the scientist creating events (changing the world) by means of structures and the 'bricoleur' creating structures by means of events." (ibid, 22)

Thus, in the sciences, the priority of the relationship between structure and event is inversely proportional to that in "bricolage". In this respect, art has a middle-of-the-road position. In order to demonstrate this, Lévi-Strauss questions the causes of the aesthetic emotion. An initial answer is that art always provides a reduced representation, either by a decrease of scale or by a reduction in properties. The aesthetic power connected with this reduction results from the inversion of the process of knowledge. The real object can hardly be known in its totality, except by dividing its whole into parts. In a reduction - a sort of reduced model - the knowledge of the whole precedes the knowledge of the parts. "And even if this is an illusion, the points of the procedure is to create or sustain the illusion, which gratifies the intelligence and gives rise to a sense of pleasure which can already be called aesthetic on these grounds alone." (ibid, 24) In the quantitative reduction, the object seems qualitatively simplified, resulting in our increased domination of the object or, to a certain extent, the thing itself.

This is a very valuable property of the aesthetic domain. The entire history of modern painting can be considered an attempt to grasp "reality", which plays a major role in artistic observations including the illusion of understanding. In the twentieth century, this quantitative reduction constantly oscillated between two poles which could be called minimal art and hyperrealism. These terms were previously introduced as a way of representation rather than as historical movements. Painting will be able to continue to move between these two poles - "nothingness" and "totality" - according to a changing need for expression. It will succeed due to the desire to effectively realize totality by refusing it (nothingness, white-painted canvas) or by delicately suggesting it (pseudo-totality). Obviously, the realization of perfection (totality) will signify the end of art, because the image of art and the real object will coincide. This movement can occur within art history (movements, trends) as well as within the oeuvre of one artist in his search to understand reality (objects). Because of the reduced nature of the representations, these movements are by definition infinite, within a system which puts that freedom of expression first.

Lévi-Strauss assigns an active role to the spectator. Another aspect of the reduced model is that it is not just a passive reflection of the object. The manual production of the object enables a real experience of the object, and it becomes possible to understand how it is created. In "bricolage" as in painting, the problem can be resolved in various ways. "Merely by contemplating it he is, as it were, put in possession of other possible forms of the same work; and in a confused way, he feels himself to be their creator himself because the latter abandoned them in excluding them from his creation." (ibid, 24) The inner power of the reduced model implies that revealing the dimensions of sensory perception is compensated by adding rational dimensions.

A second aspect of the aesthetic emotion results from the unity arising between structure and event. Obviously, Lévi-Strauss does not consider the middle position of art between science and (intellectual) "bricolage" a subordinate one. The oscillating position of the artist is no undervaluation, but a possibility of arriving at "a nicely balanced synthesis of one or more artificial and natural structures and one or more natural and social events." (ibid, 25)

Indeed, even if the reduced model implies further knowledge of morphology, the image cannot be cut back to a diagram or a scheme. After all, the reduced model as image is the synthesis between the immanent properties of the object and the properties resulting from a spatial and temporary context. Lévi-Strauss states, "the painter is always a mid-way between design and anecdote, and his genius consists in uniting internal and external knowledge, a 'being' and a 'becoming', in producing with his brush an object which does not exist as such and which he is nevertheless able to create on his canvas." (ibid, 25)

Although the last part of the above-mentioned statement calls to mind Magritte's painting Ceci n'est pas une pipe, it can hardly be considered a reference to Surrealism. It is, rather, a clear formulation of two other poles in the history of modern painting alongside - but independent of - the minimal and maximal reductions discussed above, for example, Expressionism and Impressionism. The historical order is purposely represented incorrectly because these terms are used in the sense of manners of expression. Expressionism emphasizes "the scheme", the knowledge of "inwardness" or of "being". Conversely, Impressionism stresses the "anecdote", the knowledge of "outwardness", of "becoming". Lévi-Strauss' formulations prove that both are manners of expression which are inseparably interrelated. The shifts of emphasis can experience an infinite evolution within the two opposite poles, each comprising a part of the other pole, no matter how minimal.

Lévi-Strauss views the participating function of the spectator from the perspective of being human. According to him, each spectator is an artist permitting aesthetic emotion. In other words, the spectator will unite structure and event through the work of art.

5.4.3. *The function of modern art versus the function of primitive art*

The book Entretiens avec Lévi-Strauss (1959) by Georges Charbonnier is an interesting source of obtaining further insight into Lévi-Strauss' art theory. Lévi-Strauss points out that the distinction between the art of so-called primitive societies and art of modern times lies in individualizing the artistic product, as well as in its more figurative and representative nature. "The recent explorations of African sculpture show that the sculptor is an artist, that the artist is known, sometimes far and wide, and that the personal style of each author of masks or sculpture are recognized by the native public. Thus in contemporary art, the issue should be a growing individualization of the audience rather than the creator. No longer does the group as a whole expect that the artist produce certain objects created according to prescribed canons, but the amateurs (...) or a group of amateurs." (Charbonnier 1961, 38)

The primitive artist cannot or will not reproduce his model in an integral way. Thus, he feels obliged to signify it. Rather than representation, art appears a system of signs. Thus, both differences are related: after all, language presupposes a group "language (...) is a group phenomenon, it is constitutive to the group, it exists due to the group, since language does not modify, does not convert from choice." (ibid, 72-73)

To the extent that an element of individualization will occur in the artistic product, the semantic function of the work should disappear necessarily in favor of a greater correspondence with the model one tries to imitate rather than to signify. In Lévi-Strauss' view, this urge to represent is a sort of magic-inspired desire. It is based on the illusion that one cannot only communicate with reality, but also appropriate it by means of the representation. Lévi-Strauss calls this "the monopolization vis-à-vis the object" (ibid, 76), the means to appropriate an external beauty or wealth. According to Lévi-Strauss, one of the greater originalities of art in our civilization lies in this ambition to capture the object, instead of the owner or even the spectator.

Lévi-Strauss claims that the absence of academism - painting in the tradition of great masters - is a third distinction in primitive art. In primitive art, this problem does not present itself because the continuity of the tradition is guaranteed.

The question arises as to whether these three differences - no relationship to an entire community, concentration on representation and relationship to traditional schools - through which primitive art distinguishes itself, hold true for contemporary art as well. Impressionism, which can be considered the first manifesting modern movement, rejects the third distinction of a relationship to a traditional school. "In fact, he (the Impressionist painter) tries to escape the perception of the object through the school; he wants the object he has in mind, which inspires him, not to be the object as represented by old masters, but the real object, the object in its natural form." (ibid, 85-86)

However, this object has to be represented; it is still an object to be appropriated. Thus, Impressionism offers a superficial resistance; it is interested in the superficial rather than the fundamental. Yet, Impressionism cannot be considered merely formally. There is a modification of the subjects as well; they have an eye for the modest landscape of the suburbs, for nature where there is intervention. In this respect, Impressionism functions as a guide to civilization. "But of course, because this nature of the highest quality which one was free to represent in the seventeenth, eighteenth and still in the beginning of the nineteenth century is on the point of yielding the progress of industrial civilization, the bridges, railways, urban development, and because one has to teach people to be content with the little that remained of, for them, desperately lost nature, and because it is all that has been left for them; in Impressionism there is that didactic role, that function of guidance of civilization." (ibid, 88) Impressionism is the first movement to reflect on the disintegration of an overall picture based on a natural order. Afterwards, in various movements, art arises as a sign of the disintegration of a founded order.

Cubism attacks the second distinction, of concentration on representation in discovering the semantic truth of art. The essential aspect of art can be signified rather than merely represented. "Thus, it concerns a more profound revolution than Impressionism, although it starts by employing its results. Cubism goes beyond the object, to meaning." (ibid, 89) Cubism has a certain correspondence with primitive art, not accidentally, since Cubism was inspired immensely by primitive art. Cubists knew what the "primitives" could teach. Yet, the first distinction of a relationship to an entire community is not canceled out: the function of Cubism in society is not of the same communal nature.

In this respect, Lévi-Strauss wonders about the abundance of styles of painting from the same artist. It seems as if one academism is substituted with a different kind. "The academism of pre-Impressionist painting was - to use the language of the linguists - an academism of the signified: the objects themselves, the human face, flowers, a vase, one tried to represent were perceived through a convention and a tradition; while nonetheless, in that multitude of ways of painting we see in a certain period, at a certain moment, the academism of the signified disappears, however, in favor of a new academism which I would call the academism of the signifier." (ibid, 91)

Thus, the issue is an academism of language (langage). For example, in Picasso, Lévi-Strauss finds a "consumption" of all the sign systems ever used by humankind since it employed artistic expression. However, it is impossible for a true language to arise from this. After all, this concerns an individual production of art, which does not direct itself in a stable way towards the group. It is this aspect of Picasso's work that art criticism considers his greatest merit. However, one could refute this, because the total synthesis of human systems of signs could be the basis of a relative, i.e. Western, "universal" system of signs, a kind of artistic Esperanto. Be that as it may, in Lévi-Strauss' view, the artist does nothing but imitate existing languages. He gives an illusory transfiguration because only the outer appearance of the sign remains. The message is gone. What remains is a sort of cheap language game, a mere formal function of the sign. From a sociological perspective, these sign systems no longer function as communication within a group.

It is tempting to consider abstract art - as a synthesis of both previous types of art - the removal of the remaining difference between primitive and modern art, in particular as regards the aspect of community. However, Lévi-Strauss does not want to accept that. After all, abstract artists do not concentrate on multiplication of sign systems, but on analyzing their own system in various ways. As such, the individual system becomes exhausted completely and loses its possibility of signification. Lévi-Strauss states, in Marxist terms, that the two latter differences (concentration on representation and relationship to traditional schools) - which have been superseded - belong to the domain of the superstructures. The communal function of the artwork is a result of the infrastructures. However, as a consequence of an aesthetic creative dynamism, there is no pure formal evolution. Art finds itself in a hopeless situation. It does not have an impact on sociological reality, that is, no access to the entire community. In that sense, art is useless. Scientific knowledge has stripped the conscious aesthetic perception of objects of much which had been added in the non-scientific society. In our contemporary societies, the aesthetic perception has been purged of many things, causing it to have less social function.

In general, one could state that contemporary art does not reach the community because it does not intend to. Contemporary art is still in the stage of individualism. The avant-garde is no longer avant-garde for theoretical specialists, but it still is avant-garde for the community. There are forms of art which indeed appeal to the entire community because of where it appears (subway) or because it is applied art (design). But that is not the issue. The fact is that a large community is excluded or excludes itself from contemporary art. However, it does not help to act biased and regret this or to label the artists a-social and the audience Philistines. A number of observations can be made on this score.

Firstly, one could predict somewhat prophetically that that community will revive. At that moment, the concept of avant-garde will be an extinct situation for the entire community due to time and the related concept of tradition. Lévi-Strauss points out the difference between the concept of time in a primitive and in contemporary society. The former does not possess an essential evolution. The latter glorifies the principle of progress. Art has become non- and anti-social because of its rapid metamorphosis. The same is true for philosophy and morality. One could say that Western civilization is still based basically - as far as philosophy is concerned - on a nineteenth-century bourgeois-Christian moral-ity, albeit in a somewhat moderated form. These and other phenomena all suffer from a similar lack of influence on the community. The modified image of soci-ety comes about namely in a technological way, but the human aspect has not yet followed. Technological futurologists point out that large revolutions in tech-nology are behind us. We can only expect further development of existing inven-tions. We live in a period of time where new generations have overcome, by and large, their tribute to their nineteenth-century ancestors living before the techno-logical revolution. This generation is completely familiar with the novel-techno-logical world and its possibilities. Therefore, there is no reason to suppose that the forms, resulting from what was once called avant-garde, could not belong to the cultural world of the entire community. The recent evolution of art has point-ed in that direction. The so-called trans-avant-garde has transcended the achieve-ments of the novel forms of avant-garde. One will see a similar form of design evolve internationally - also in non-Western countries - within two or three years. This indicates a certain universalism, at least on the part of the creators. Naturally, Lévi-Strauss could not foresee this in his conversations with Charbonnier in 1959. In the context of universalism, he probably would have talked about a new academism.

However, futurological reflections are not the issue. We only want to pose the art philosophical question, "What does contemporary art mean for contem-porary human beings and what could it mean?" In the domain of art criticism, one assumes that contemporary art will become easier to understand. An increase in an interested audience could indicate this. However, the degree of the quality of understanding not increased similarly. It is true that a number of avant-garde principles - such as abstraction, conceptualism and minimalism - have become accessible to a general public. However, contemporary art has become more difficult because it is in a phase of meta-reflection. One does not have to comprehend much in order to observe that Duchamp's ready-mades are an obvious protest against established bourgeois painting. One can indeed understand - once one has abandoned the idea of art as a representation of reality - how one will end up in the abstraction of the white square on the white canvas. But what happens when artists move on and question the entire history of art?

The concept of progress is not the issue; ideas such as in-depth study, deconstruction, and negation are. The artistic act will become less and less obvious. Rather than art for the community, there is a need for more specialists in order to explain art qualitatively - more differentiated - as well as quantitatively. That implies that the work of each artist should be studied thoroughly: what do that pipe, that mussel shell, that almost white plane, that fountain mean as a quotation in works of subsequent artists? A long time ago, the discussion of grammar shifted to a discussion of literature. The art public increases, but the degree of comprehensibility decreases. The concept of mannerism comes to mind: exaggeration appeals, but the complexity that accompanies it is neglected. Lévi-Strauss speaks of a "academism of the signifier" since the signified disappeared long ago. Charbonnier discusses the marginality of the function of abstract art, which Lévi-Strauss merely considers a system of signs without an object. Science reduces the domain of the artist, who reacts desperately in order to be able to "exist". This inspires him to create his forms: "The point is not to feel legitimized; not to feel that there is a place; that there is something to say, that there is something to be seen; but proceeding from all these impossibilities he is still busy creating forms." (ibid, 102)

There is still an object, but no longer a collective one. Lévi-Strauss claims that this increases the contradiction between contemporary art and abstract art. "we merely have a system of signs, however 'outside language', since this system of signs proves to be the creation of an individual who, as a matter of fact, often succeeds in modifying it." (ibid, 104) Indeed, this art is only a system of signs. It refers mainly to the absence of a communicative language for a group that does not accept socially standardized language, because it implicitly imposes its own standard and demands obedience. Furthermore, this language can no longer serve to formulate non-standard contents or new standards. In that sense, art seems indeed a "non-linguistic system of signs". It changes constantly, because the sole meaning which has not been expressed adequately so far is that of being non-linguistic to the outsiders. Therefore, part of contemporary art has meaning for what one could call the "tribe" of outsiders.

In a certain way, Lévi-Strauss indicates a possible function of art as means of signification. The reason why primitive society does not make true copies - in contrast, for example, to Greek art of the fifth century or art of the quatrocento - cannot merely be explained on the basis of the material. "If one cannot provide a 'facsimile' of the model, then one is either satisfied with signifying it or one chooses to do so." (ibid, 100) Why one chooses signification over true representation may be a consequence of "too many" objects. Primitive communities have a very broad supernatural universe, which is why it cannot be represented by definition. If one would substitute this supernatural with "non-ratio-nal" or "other rational" or "non-established order", contemporary art will have "too many" objects as well. This domain can only become meaningful by means of art, which is precisely the function of a great deal of contemporary art.

5.4.4. *Art as a system of signs between language and object*

According to Lévi-Strauss, the structural correspondence with the object is an important characteristic of art, in contrast to speech, where a correspondence between words and the objects referred to is absent. "To the extent that the art-work is a sign of the object rather than a literal reproduction, it manifests some-thing which is not immediately given to the perception of the object and this is its structure, because the particular characteristic of the language of art is that there is always a profound homology between the structure of the signified and the structure of the signifier." (ibid, 108)

Thus, the artwork reveals knowledge of the structure of the object, which cannot be immediately perceived. Such a structural homology is very particular in the "ready-made". It is an implement which becomes artwork because it is sit-uated consciously in a new environment as for example in Duchamp's <u>Bottle Rack</u>. Because of the new context, the relationship between signified and signifi-er explodes. A semantic division is created. This results in a fusion because new structural characteristics become obvious which had not been noticed previous-ly. A different signifier fuses with a different signified, making the ready-made art.

Charbonnier's question whether everything will then become art seems senseless. "Who will prevent me from objectifying any object? Who will prevent me from considering any object as a 'ready-made'?" (ibid, 113) Duchamp's act was exemplary. It does not make sense to remove all implements from their con-text and exhibit them. Duchamp's objects can be considered symbols of the artis-tic value of daily reality. By this act he directs the eye towards the aesthetic, non-utilitarian function of the banal object. Hyper-realism will resume this after-wards, not in the form of the ready-made but as a very close approach to day-to-day reality. The aesthetic interest in the daily object proves that it is not the case that any object in any way possesses similar hidden possibilities as the fountain or the bottle rack. In Lévi-Strauss' view, it is not the object itself that is a work of art, but the object's certain organization, order, and relationships. "Similar to the words of a language, they have in themselves a very vague, almost empty meaning; they only acquire meaning in a context; ... in the 'ready mades', ... the 'sentences' made with objects have a meaning rather than the object, no matter what one may do or say." (ibid, 115) Thus, the theory of the context becomes indispensable.

According to Lévi-Strauss, art is a language but not just any language. Art as a signifying system, or as an entity of signifying systems always remains a mediation between language and object. The artist strives for an absolute imitation of nature, but does not succeed. If he did, there would be a reproduction of nature rather than the creation of a cultural product. The creation of art is connected with the "manual" aspect, with the fact that the artist will never completely be able to control his materials. Perhaps this is ".. the common denominator of all aesthetic manifestations." (ibid, 130)

Lévi-Strauss strongly emphasizes the realist view of the artist. Many artists have refused to evolve any further after having attained the technical limit in a certain direction. This both affirms and denies Lévi-Strauss' statement. Contemporary artists are sometimes afraid of this perfection because it is ultimately too simple. If the artist retraces his steps, this could be explained as a return by art to nature or non-art. Yet, at the same time, the artist feels attraction to and aversion for this turning point. In order not to lapse into art as classical realism - as Lévi-Strauss is inclined to do - the "inability to completely control the materials" should be extended to "a fight with the materials". Each artist should fight in such a way to powerfully express a certain aspect of a certain view.

According to Lévi-Strauss, an artwork should not lose all relation to the object which inspired it. In that case, it would no longer be an artwork but a linguistic object. Lévi-Strauss refers to Saussure, who considers language a system of signs without a material relationship to what it signifies. Since art should not be a complete imitation of the object - if it were to maintain its sign nature - it must continue to mediate between language and object. Lévi-Strauss claims that the common use in art criticism of the word "language" stems from a confusion between "language" and "message". Mistakenly, one is often afraid of the mystical connotation of the latter. After all, that word is also used by communication professionals, albeit in a different sense than Lévi-Strauss' view on art as language. "But the use of the term 'language' does not seem dangerous to me, since we just stated that all art is language, but often wrongly used and employed to discover a language or a message where there is really none. If all art is language, that is certainly not the case on the level of conscious thought; I mean that all means the artist can dispose of constitute just as many signs, and that the function of an artwork is to signify an object, to establish a meaningful relationship with an object." (ibid, 132-33)

Contrary to speech - which consists of a system of arbitrary signs without noticeable relationship to the objects they choose to signify - in art there is a constantly recognizable relationship between the sign and the object. Obviously, Lévi-Strauss does not know how to deal with abstract art. It brings his distinction between language and art into difficulties. Abstract art could be a system of signs which adopts an arbitrary position towards the object. "But is the language one pretends to impose on us a language which refers to the aesthetic emotion, or is it rather a system of signs as any other system of signs, say, such as the railroad code of signals?" (ibid, 138)

Lévi-Strauss persists in disregarding abstract art. Charbonnier attempts to defend it by stating that abstract art tries to release itself from its object, but not from nature. The object invites description. In painting abstractly, one more quickly achieves a complete synthesis. Lévi-Strauss does not want to deny the attractiveness of abstract painting, but rather its significant character. He claims that none of the abstract painters has ever formulated a system or a code. All abstract painters seem to have their own codes which change outside any semantic rule in the course of painting. Elements are connected based on the painter's preference. A meaning can arise arbitrarily similar to how one recognizes a natural object.

According to Lévi-Strauss, the danger for art is twofold. One, that it might become a pseudo-language rather than a language: "a caricature of language, a simulacrum, an infantile game on the theme of language which does not arrive at meaning." (ibid, 149) Two, that it might become completely a language of the same type as speech, though with the exception of the material used. In that context, "signification" will be possible but accompanied with the loss of true aesthetic emotion. Lévi-Strauss claims that "(the aesthetic emotion) is how we react when a meaningless object is promoted to the level of functional meaning; (...) the particular of the aesthetic transposition, let us call it the aesthetic promotion, is the transference on the level of the signifier of something which did not exist in its original state in the same way or of the same quality." (ibid, 150)

Lévi-Strauss claims that the question of the future of painting has two answers: there will either be a process of disintegration, resulting in the disappearance of painting, or a new beginning, "which will prepare this kind of Middle Ages we find ourselves in presently - without wanting to give this word a pejorative turn - but because I feel there is in the explorations and speculations of abstract painters something which reminds one of a certain form of medieval thought: this striving for gnosis, in other words a knowledge transcending sciences, this striving for a language that would be a para-language." (ibid, 162)

A "para-language", a coexisting language, or rather a system of signs parallelling language seems more precise than "language" or "pseudo-language". We believe that there is no reason to equate painting with articulated language. Not only because the aésthetic element would then be lost, but also since this would be superfluous and awkward from the perspective of articulated language. The reduction of painting to a pseudo-language - in particular an infantile game on the theme of language - is a linguistic denial of the intrinsic pictorial and visual qualities of the medium of painting. However, painting is indeed a para-language, a signifier searching for meaning supplementary to speech; meaning which at the very least is able to refer to itself. Abstract art explores the way of being of the signifier itself on its own level. This auto-reflexive exploration is indeed the richness of painting. One could call this affluence: the ability to search for the value of the element without repercussions to the whole. The element is self-sufficient.

The prefix "para" expresses at the same time something partial. Partial should be understood as minor domains flanking the major field (language), which cannot be separated from it and which are only connected with certain elements of a whole. We believe that an important characteristic of the para-language of painting is to only reveal a part, but as profoundly as possible. The ambition of speech is to summarize things in words, whereas it is the ambition of painting to understand certain things or even parts of certain things. Everybody who uses articulated language has a way of expressing their world through language. All painters express a fragment of their world. Sometimes an object, sometimes part of an object.

Lévi-Strauss' contempt for abstract art means a denial of the value of the fragment at the expense of the whole to be classified. Why would the phenomenon of "color" per se not be interesting as an object of painting? The same is true for form, line, plane, volume and nature of the material used. Surprisingly, Lévi-Strauss compares his work as an ethnologist with that of a botanist who searches for classifications in nature. What else is abstract art but a microscopic approach to objects? Or a reduction to basic form, often mathematical, so that the scientist will not wander around aimlessly. Thus, linguistics is not as close to a signifying painting as semiology is. Color dictionaries and grammars still do not exist.

In Lévi-Strauss' view, a paint stroke does not acquire meaning until a second code apart from the paint stroke itself is involved. In other words, there should be a relationship with the object. The materials the abstract painter employs are elements devoid of intrinsic meaning at the moment they lose their connection with reality. The comparison with language - phonemes in particular do not have meaning themselves but serve to distinguish meanings - could be valid for painting but only "in a painting which would have a remote relationship with the object, where the stroke of paint, for example, would serve to contrast the form and the background, the size and the color, the shadow and the light etc. ..., but not in a system where the stroke of paint would exhaust the possibilities of the system, where no second code would exist to transcend the stroke of paint itself, where the painter would only have the right to formulate his rules on one single level." (ibid, 156)

We do not believe in this parallel structure. The nature of the paint stroke is polymorphic and multicolored. Contrary to the uniformity of visual systems, the main purpose of painting is to multiply and distort existing signs.

Lévi-Strauss' statement that a painting does not acquire meaning until there is a connection with the object seems valid. That is, provided the "object" is not represented too narrowly as an existent object but in a broader sense as an aspect of reality. If this is not the case, then there is a risk of an empty construction which does not refer to anything, not even to itself: the purely decorative. Lévi-Strauss states in this context that abstract art "can seduce me, but I will remain the victim of its decorative aspect. In my view, what lacks is the essential attribute of an artwork that consists of introducing a reality of semantic nature." (ibid, 157) Lévi-Strauss seems to be on the wrong track. Firstly, because a large part of abstract art does refer to an object. Even a monochrome could do so. Naturally, if, in the work, a connection can be demonstrated with an object, one could claim that it is no longer abstract art. But that is begging the question. Lévi-Strauss mistakenly uses the name of a movement - with its large variety - rather than discussing the concrete works of artists.

Secondly, there is a large area of figurative art which does not refer to any reality, in the sense of trying to signify it. However, Lévi-Strauss views art either as a representation or as a means of evoking pleasant emotions. He is not aware that the formal characteristic of contemporary art lies in being purely itself, without representing anything else. It has attempted to understand and signify certain realities by means of an in-depth exploration into the "how", into the formal characteristics of the signifier. In that sense one could say that a large part of contemporary art is abstract. We believe that this is where the aesthetic approach is situated. Rather than in pleasant emotions or in recognizing the representation, it must be perceived in the way it has been shaped.

Yet, the risk of the decorative element of abstract art Lévi-Strauss pointed out still lurks. Abstract art is connected with the avant-garde and, thus, has a explorative function. As an explorer of new movements, abstract art has to pass on the acquired facts at a certain point. This does not influence the autonomy of abstract art. There is a way of protecting abstract art from its decorative aspect.

Therefore, one should not consider the future of painting a linear evolution, but a dynamic process where the abstract and the figurative enrich each other dialectically. Lévi-Strauss envisages a possible future for painting as a new beginning after the contemporary situation which he considers a kind of Dark Ages. But in the oeuvre of an individual painter, development can occur as well. Periods of exploring form by means of abstract art alternate with figurative application of new achievements. This so-called medieval concern about abstract art is often of a mystical nature. Not surprisingly, Lévi-Strauss has claimed that in the explorations and contemplations of abstract painters, there are similarities with certain methods of medieval thought: the urge for gnosis, for a knowledge transcending science, for a language which must be a para-language. Perhaps art history has experienced this new beginning with the trans-avant-garde. "The point is to know whether the development of pictorial art, for several centuries, is a construction of painting or rather a progressive destruction, and whether or not we are experiencing the last stage of this destruction." ibid, 157)

Both Charbonnier as well as Lévi-Strauss criticize abstract art; it does not engender any religious or social questions, it does not disturb but reassures, it is evasive. According to Lévi-Strauss, art has yet another task. "It is not the task of art in society (...) to simply offer the consumer (so to speak) sensory satisfaction. Art is also a guide, a means of education, and I would almost say a means to learn to know the surrounding reality." (ibid, 164) Lévi-Strauss claims that only two modern movements qualify for this educative function of art. Impressionism is not only a revolution of pictorial technique and a way of perception, but also a revolution of the object of painting itself. In this movement, one focuses on the simple landscape rather than the previous grand landscapes. Thus, it indicates the transformation of the world. Cubism teaches us to live with the products of industry. But why doesn't Lévi-Strauss continue along the same line? Some abstract works teach us to live with industrial waste. One could write an art history of the twentieth century departing from Lévi-Strauss' statements on Impressionism and Cubism. In all respects, abstract art has brought about a revolution in perception. The disappearance of recognizable representation still troubles the general public. Abstract art can refer to chaos as the disintegration of establishment. In that sense, abstract art is an anti-ideological iconoclasm or the impossibility of continuing to represent a figure.

Remarkably, Lévi-Strauss does not draw any conclusion from the following valid statement: "A painterly 'order' exists, a kind of closed universe, and it seems to me that the contemporary artist reacts against yesterday's painters rather than the contemporary world." (ibid, 173) In the context of this "painterly order", abstract painting occurs as a necessary evolution. Scientists of all disciplines should start from this point instead of from personal presumptions based on incomprehension.

5.5. Barthes

5.5.1. Art as a structuralist activity

Roland Barthes claims that structuralism is not a school or a movement, but an activity, an organized succession of mental operations. This activity can situate itself within science as well as within art. It consists of a reconstruction of an "object" clarifying the functional rules of this object. Thus, the reconstructed structure is a simulacrum, an artificial image, which intends to reveal what remains invisible or incomprehensible in the natural object. Comprehension is the new component arising in the two moments of structuralist activity: the dissection of the natural object and the construction of the artificial image. In other words, a world comes into being similar to the first one, intending to make the former comprehensible. Therefore, between science and art there is no "technical difference", "This is the reason one can say that structuralism is mainly an imitative activity, and herein the fact is found that there is indeed no technical difference between, on the one hand, learned structuralism and, on the other, literature in particular, art in general: both are part of a mimesis not founded on the analogy of substances (as in so-called realistic art), but on the analogy of functions (which Lévi-Strauss calls homology)." (Barthes 1964, 215)

Barthes does not see a difference when scholars such as Troubetskoy, Dumézil, Propp and Lévi-Strauss or artists such as Mondrian, Boulez and Butor, construct a certain object - called "composition" - by revealing certain units and combinations according to certain rules. The original object can be derived from social reality or from the reality of imagination. According to Barthes, art is determined by what human beings add when they construct the object, " ... it is not the nature of the copied object which determines art (a persistent prejudice of each realism, however), but what human beings add by reconstructing it: the technique itself is the essence of each creation." (ibid, 216)

"Technique" should not be understood as the deduced meaning used in colloquial language for art in the sense of expertise or proficiency. This would only serve to cloud the discussion of the '60s on art education. At that time, the question was posed whether technique or vision should be taught, where "technique" was understood as visible perfection of imitation. Barthes employs "technique" in the non-deductive sense of "how" something comes about, the way an artwork is created. "It is to the extent wherein the purposes of structuralist activities are inseparably connected with a certain technique that structuralism exists in a distinguishable way with respect to other ways of analysis or creation: one composes the object again in order to reveal functions and this is, if one could say so, the road the work takes; this is the reason why one should speak of activity rather than of structuralist work." (ibid, 216)

In Barthes' view, the structuralist activity - including art - comprises two typical operations: segmenting and ordering. By segmenting the original object - which produces a simulacrum - one tries to find mobile fragments which bring about a certain meaning because of the difference in mutual position. The fragment itself - for example a geometric color plane in Mondrian's work - does not have any meaning. Yet, the smallest variation in configuration involves a modification of the whole. The components only mean something because of their margins or the division between the other components within the whole. Conversely, they only mean something because of the margins which distinguish them from other possible components, with which they form a so-called paradigmatic category: a supply of objects demonstrating relationship as well as difference.

Because of segmention, the components are known. By ordering the components, combinatory rules are discovered or determined. Although the syntax of art is very varied, each work with a structural plan is subject to fixed rules. In this context, stability, that is, the regular return of units and combinations of units, which produce meaning, is highly important. Following linguistics, Barthes considers this stability a determination of the term "form". "... the linguists call these combinatory rules forms and it would be of great importance to preserve this strict use of an obsolete word: it is said that the form admits the relationship of the unities not to be seen as a pure consequence of chance: the work of art is what human beings draw from chance." (ibid, 217)

A statement such as "The artwork is what tears human beings away from coincidence" seems like oratory language. It is stunningly true but still disputable. Examples of things which tear human beings away from coincidence can easily be given, but they do not have to be works of art. More in accordance with Barthes is relating his statement to Aristotle, who interprets the term "technè" as distinct from "tychè". (Barthes 1982, 202) In Barthes' view, technique is the essence of all creation. Both statements reveal what Barthes means: the artwork is a path to cultivation of the unexplored coincidence. Ordering - one of the structuralist's activities - provides a foundation for non-figurative art. In that case, thought should not necessarily be directed towards the analogy of copies and models. One should have an eye for the regularity which combines the unities. However, to those who do not see a single form, these works seem to have occurred by coincidence and to be therefore useless.

According to Barthes, the importance of structuralism lies in how the simulacra reflect the world, or better how they transform it. First, the functional manifests itself in the simulacrum. However, human beings are not considered bearers of a host of meanings, but producers of meanings. "And because, in his view, this production of sense is more important than sense itself, because function is extensive to the works, it is that structuralism turns itself into activity and refers the execution of the work and the work itself to a similar identity ..." (Barthes 1964, 219).

The artist and the researcher alike follow a reverse path to meaning. In Barthes' view, their function is divination (mantéia). Like the prophets in Antiquity, they "state" where meaning is situated but they do not name it. Structuralism has an eye for form within a modifying history. Therefore, the aesthetic comes strongly to the fore and the world is "stated" time and again in a new way. It is art's task to translate the old worn-out languages.

5.5.2. Art as a struggle against stereotypes

In The Pleasure of the Text, Barthes explains the importance of "novel" as cultural principle and, therefore, in art. He does not mention the term "art". However, art appears to be a synonymous to "novel". "Novel" is a series of terms which all relate to the concept of "stereotype": repetition, the language of power, the ruminating linguistic machines of official institutions such as education, the sports world, advertising, mass events, tear-jerkers etc. Although Barthes uses "linguistic" language, his view can be applied to visual language as well. The stereotype is an instrument of ideology. Conversely, the novel is part of the field of pleasure. The novel does not coincide with fashion, but is considered a criterion for all criticism. "The Novel is not a manner, it is a value, a foundation of all criticism: our evaluation of the world does not, as in Nietzsche, - and certainly not directly - depend on the opposite of the noble and vile but on the opposite between the Old and the Novel." (Barthes 1973, 65)

Barthes explains as well why art, as a non-stereotype, is a value which produces pleasure. He claims that art is an exception. Art is never a rule abusing another autonomous organism by imposing on it and falsifying it. Art is its own rule. "The opposite (the axe of value) is not necessarily prevalent between consecrated and named contraries (materialism and idealism, reformism and revolution etc.); but it is everywhere and always between the exception and the rule. The rule is the abuse, the exception, the pleasure." (ibid, 67) Ideological examples (materialism, idealism etc.) could be substituted with "isms" from art history, which would then be epigrammatic rather than exceptional.

Barthes' criticism of repetition is detached from formal repetition, such as for example the ritual, but directed towards that form of mass culture which repeats contents and reproduces ideological schemes. This mass culture modifies superficial norms, outward appearances, which continue to have the same meaning. Therefore, "fashion" is not identical to "novel". Conversely, in art, a new form has a novel meaning. Thus, the novel as value constitutes all criticism: in the first place, the criticism of the novel value of the form itself, but also social criticism. In Barthes' view, semiology should protect art, as the novel form producing novel meaning, against non-art, as the stereotype modifying forms while preserving meaning. He represents stereotypes as natural products with an innate meaning, although they are produced by society. This is what Barthes calls a myth: the representation of a historical event as a natural occurrence. (Barthes 1957) It is the social-critical function of semiology to reveal this myth. "Well, in my opinion, semiology departed from a purely passionate movement: to me (around 1954) it seems that a science of signs could activate social criticism and that Sartre, Brecht and Saussure could have joined each other in this project; in fact, the point was to understand (or to describe) how a society produces stereotypes, that is, supplements of artificiality which it then consumes as innate meanings, in other words supplements of nature." (Barthes 1978, 14)

Related to Barthes' aversion to the stereotype is his refusal of the arrogance of triumphing discourses, such as those of the sciences, the military and particularly what he calls the "doxa" or public opinion. "The Doxa (a word that will return) is the public Opinion, the spirit of Majority, the petit bourgeois Consensus, the Voice of the Natural, the Violence of the Prejudice. One could call each manner of speaking which is adjusted to appearance and the opinion of practice doxology (Leibniz's word)." (Barthes 1975, 51)

Against the doxa, he sets the para-doxa, the conflicting opinion, including art, that fights ideology. But para-doxa can become doxa. The fight continues. Barthes refers to aesthetics as a possible solution. He quotes Brecht, who does not criticize ideology directly but via aesthetic links. Contra-ideology disguises itself as a fiction, albeit not a realistic one. Barthes considers the production of rules for indirect and transitional discourse a possible role for aesthetics in our society, as a new form of ideological criticism. "Perhaps the role of aesthetics in our society is to formulate rules of an indirect and transitive discourse (it can transform language, but hides its domination and good faith)." (ibid, 108)

Along the same line, Barthes formulates the role the intellectual should play in a bourgeois consciousness. He attributes a role to the intellectual which may be valid for the artist as well, least of all because there is no reason not to consider this group intellectual. Their task is to contribute to the process of decomposition of bourgeois consciousness. "Let us accept that the historical task of the intellectual (or of the writer) is presently to maintain and to emphasize the decomposition of the bourgeois consciousness." (ibid, 67)

The term "decomposition" should not be equated with "destruction". Barthes means the former as: disentangling while acting as if one remains within that consciousness. He claims that, in Western civilization, one needs bourgeois consciousness at this time. The destruction of bourgeois consciousness presupposes a leap forward. But according to what linguistic use? To leave that consciousness untouched means that one lapses into a dogmatism. Barthes prefers decomposition. "While in decomposing, I agree to accompany this decomposition, to decompose gradually myself: I skid, get caught and am dragged along." (ibid, 68)

Barthes rightly claims that art as an intellectual activity needs Western bourgeoisie to prevent it from becoming non-art; non-art in the sense of a dogmatic refusal of artistic means and an ideological preference to leave these artistic means unused. Barthes posits two perspectives. First, that decomposition should remain internal. Secondly, that the decomposer will ultimately decompose himself as a consequence of becoming a non-dogmatic outsider.

We believe that the problem of the decomposition within the bourgeois consciousness has consequences for the relationship of artwork to spectator. The "odd" thing about an artwork is that it is an attempt to decompose bourgeois consciousness. In this context, "odd" can be described as what does not satisfy bourgeois consciousness. The bourgeois citizen views the artist as odd, but the artist makes a fool of the citizen, and thus of everybody. He does this with art that aims at the decomposition of that bourgeois consciousness. This is the reason the bourgeois disgusts contemporary art. Once the issue is the decomposition of one's consciousness, rather than beauty and decoration, a different problem is posed. In this context, one could question the belief that the bourgeois is open to decomposing his bourgeois consciousness and thus part of himself.

One could state that the "decomposition of the bourgeois consciousness" is one of the major issues in modern art. In order to demonstrate this, the history of modern art should be rewritten. Much modern art seems incomprehensible unless observed as attempts to decompose bourgeois consciousness from within. Remarkably, function and motive coincide, which is not the case when the issue is destruction as an external attack. This demonstrates that Barthes prefers decomposition, "... in order to destroy bourgeois consciousness one should stay away from it, and this externalization is only possible in a revolutionary situation: in China, class consciousness is presently in the process of destroying itself, rather than decomposing; ..." (Barthes 1975, 68)

Modern art is not in such a revolutionary situation. Therefore, Barthes is able to compare the phenomenon of deconstruction with a sweet metaphor, "... to make it decline, break down, collapse, on the spot, like one would do with a bag of sugar by drenching it with water." (ibid, 67)

5.5.3. *The painting as a sum of possible readings by various types of audiences*

The aspects of Barthes' view mentioned so far are particularly based on language but seem valid for visual art as well. Indeed, visual art should protect the image against the doxa, stereotype, ideology and other influences of prevailing power. Think of the position of the image in publicity, political propaganda or kitsch. Barthes does not draw a sharp line between linguistic and visual language as producers of meaning. In various places, he quotes painting as an example of text.

In the book L'obvie et l'obtus, Barthes writes concretely about a number of painters. In an article where he approvingly discusses Schefer's book (Schefer 1969), he poses the question of whether painting is a language? Although it is almost a cliché to represent painting as a language, one still does not succeed in formulating a vocabulary and a general grammar for it. Neither does one succeed in distinguishing between the signifiers, the signifieds and the system of rules of substitution and connection. According to Barthes, semiology does not really get a grip on art. The question of whether painting is a language should not be posed. What is important is to question the relationship between the painting and the language one is forced to appeal to in order to read the painting and describe it. This is not only of importance for the professional critic. The painting is the sum of its possible readings. The painting is nothing but its multiple description, "The painting only exists through the story I tell about it, no matter who writes it or even through the sum and the organization of the readings one can make of it: a painting is only its particular multiple description." (Barthes 1982, 175)

Corresponding to Barthes' dynamic view on art as a producer of meanings, he views the analysis of painting as infinite. The image is not an expression of a code. It is the variation of an act of codification. The structure of the system of the painting is to structure itself. Thus, Barthes rejects a theologizing semiology which intends to put only one model against the heterogeneity of the various artworks. The painting should become a text in the making, because of which the difference between them will be reduced.

As a result of his text on Twombly's work, Barthes introduces the double problem of representation and meaning. Abstract art is a phenomenon in the history of painting all artists have to deal with. Language does not leave art alone. Contrary to professionals in the field, Barthes does not consider it naive to wonder what a work represents. Human beings always search for sense. Even if they create non-sense, they ultimately produce the sense of non-sense. Barthes is able to justify the recurrent problem of meaning because it is this question that blocks the path to the universality of painting. "If so many people (as a consequence of cultural differences) have the impression before a canvas "not to understand anything", then this is because they want a meaning and the canvas does not offer them one (they think)." (ibid, 140)

"To discover sense" is indeed a cultural problem and the concept of universality is an unattainable purpose. Ironically, Barthes points out that the desire for meaning is expressed in how the spectator bonds with the title of a work. In general, in museums these titles can be found at eye level. In classical painting, the title reflects what is represented, a form of analogy. In modern art, this practice is discouraged by the title "Untitled", which confuses the spectator. If there are titles, they refer to the constitutive world rather than to what is or is not represented. In contemporary art, what is represented is not unanimous: the entire culture is the subject of the canvas, expressed through a series of previous paintings. Thus, one could speak of intertextuality between the canvas and previous paintings. In classical painting, the subject of the canvas is "what happens". It is not easy to determine the subject of a modern canvas, and of sometimes even the subject. Barthes points out that, "... the 'subject' of the canvas is also the one who observes it: you, I." (ibid, 175)

Barthes attaches great importance to the role of the spectator. He even claims that aesthetics as a discipline could be the science which does not study the work in itself, but how the spectator or the reader reads the work, a sort of typology of discourses. Barthes divides the spectators into five categories of "subjects": 1) The cultural subject, who is eloquent and can narrate elaborately; 2) The professional subject, who knows the history of painting and can talk about the artist's place in it; 3) The subject of pleasure, who enjoys the canvas; he does not know how to express himself, is virtually speechless, and is only able to say that the canvas is beautiful. Language does not allow one to express why one enjoys something beautiful. Thus, pleasure can only be intuited between the lines by means of distorted and overrational discourses; 4) The subject of memory. A certain element continues to act at an unconscious level. It invokes memory after the work is at a distance; 5) The subject of production, who wants to reproduce a work out of a desire to create a work.

Summarizing, Barthes proposes considering aesthetics the study of the inner monologues of the spectators. This proposal implies an additional aesthetisizing dimension, when, in an article on pop-art, he claims that, "No matter which it is, from poetics to the comic strip or erotic stories, art exists from the moment a look has a Signifier as an object." (ibid, 187)

In his article on Réquichot, Barthes goes even further in placing the fate of the painting in the beholder's eye. An aspect of the aesthetic, related to the ability to abstract, is that one can observe various paintings in one painting. Ultimately, there are as many works as levels of perception. Time and again, one can create a new work by defining, by observing partially, by enlarging, and by focusing on detail. In that way, one is released from the historical context. "Like writing is in writing through the palimpsest, in the painting (regardless of whether that is the right word) are various paintings: not only (with Réquichot) because canvases are rewritten or replaced as partial objects in new entities, but because there are as many artworks as levels of perception: isolate, observe, enlarge and approach a detail and you create a new artwork, you traverse ages, schools and styles, out of very old works you create very new ones." (ibid, 203)

Barthes permits himself a freedom of gaze an art historian will probably disagree with. A historian cannot afford this: one's gaze should be related to a historical context. As a man of pleasure, Barthes wishes to breach all visual boundaries. He wants to penetrate the image thoroughly. The gaze of pleasure wants to see what is not allowed to be seen and, thus, is delimited by prohibition rather than by factual perception.

Barthes claims that if art's mere purpose were to improve perception, it would be nothing but a pseudo-science. By producing something else present in the object, an entire epistemology is undermined. This unlimited perception will release the spectators of the current hierarchy of perception, designation and association. There is no reason to favor the first observation: perception should be multiplicitous from the beginning.

5.6. *Foucault*

Michel Foucault did not write an "Aesthetics". Yet, in his oeuvre, art often is treated as argumentation in his philosophical theory. A number of texts explicitly deal with art. Moreover, Foucault attaches importance to the gaze and perception. At the end of his life, Foucault often emphasizes the idea of a lifestyle. In his final two works, he departs from the diagnosis that, in the modern world, it has become impossible to found a morality. One can no longer conform to nature or reason, nor can one relate to an origin in an authentic way. However, art is excluded from this. In viewing a style of life, "style" should not be understood as a path of distinction. It should rather be considered in the sense of the ancient Greek, for whom the artist is primarily an artisan and an artwork a piece of work. "One could have some high hopes for this diagnosis: the I, which considers itself a work to be completed, could maintain a morality which neither supports tradition nor reason; as artist of and for itself it could enjoy an autonomy which modernity could not ignore." (Veyne 1987, 71) Foucault's affinity with ancient morality proves to be an aesthetization of the person.

5.6.1. *Art as the heterotopic enclave between fundamental codes of a culture and its scientific theories*

Foucault often refers to art as a metaphor to confirm his theories. His famous work, Les mots et les choses, originates from a literary text where Borges quotes a Chinese encyclopedia on the classification of the animal kingdom. It turns the scientific world upside down by placing unusual classifications next to each other such as "i) those who thrash around as madmen; j) numerous; k) those who are drawn with a fine camel-hair brush ..." Foucault maintains that the function of such a text is to evoke pleasure. After all, such a text shakes our thought process and undermines the schemes for orderly classification of the animal kingdom. Our thousand-year old understanding of the concepts of "the similar" and "the other" are shaken. It goes without saying that painting - at least Surrealism, but in fact all movements which go against habitual perception - can fulfil such a function as well.

Foucault's argument proves that he considers the function of art the creation of heteropies rather than utopias. Utopias comfort. They might be out of place on this earth, yet they reveal a wonderful, unblemished space. As a dream image, they do not assume a revolutionary shape but are very soothing. Conversely, heteropies are alarming. They undermine language in a hidden way because they prevent things from becoming designated, and wreck or confuse common names. Previously, they have ruined not only the syntax of sentence construction, but likewise the syntax that holds words and things together. And that is less obvious, "This is why utopias permit fables and discourse: they run with the very grain of language and are part of the fundamental dimension of the fabula; heteropias (such as there are those to be found so often in Borges) dissociate speech, stop words in their tracks, contest the very possibility of grammar as its source; they dissolve our myths and sterilize the lyricism of our sentences." (Foucault 1973, xviii)

Thus, art questions existing classifications. It proposes a particular order. Foucault situates art between two co-operating poles of thought. One are the fundamental codes of culture and the other scientific theories. The fundamental codes of culture are codes dominating language, schemes of perception, possibilities of exchange, techniques, values, and the hierarchy of cultural practices. These codes determine the empirical order they manifest themselves in for all human beings. The scientific theories or the interpretations of philosophers explain why there is generally a certain order, which law it obeys, which principle is accounted for, and why a certain order is chosen.

Between these two fields, Foucault sees a domain which is as fundamental, although it has a particularly mediative role. However, this domain is more vague and obscure, and less easy to analyze. Art thrives in this no man's land between empirical and scientific theory. In this enclave, culture frees itself unremarkably of empirical orders prescribed by its primary code. Because of this, both orders lose their original transparency; culture no longer is permeated passively by those orders. Then it discovers that those orders are neither the only nor the best possibility.

Foucault proves that art belongs to this enclave by departing form Borges' literary work. The leitmotif is precisely the naked experience of order and its ways of being. This enclave is a phase for words and perceptions and the movements which are supposed to express it. Therefore, it plays a critical role. "It is on the basis of this newly perceived order that the codes of language, perception, and practice are criticized and rendered partially invalid". (ibid, xxi) Thus, art can be called a different order, a heterotopic order. It "exists" between the empirical order and the theory on the existence of this empirical order, which have less right to exist.

In line with the implicitly formulated function of art, Foucault begins his first chapter with the analysis of Velasquez's painting Las Meninas. In this painting, Foucault sees the central hypothesis of the book presented in a particular way; the autonomy of the representation and the falsification which occurs as soon as a human being appears as subject and object of the representation.

According to Foucault, the epistème of the classical period is dominated by representation. In the concept of representation, one can distinguish two moments. As an act of imagination - often posed against perception - representation is a matter of thought. It can be distinguished from represented things (the objects) as they really are. Perception can be distinguished from representation, in as far as it is primarily directed towards things as they really are. If one does not trust perception in this respect - which, according to Foucault, is the case in the classical period - then perception will also be treated as representation. A representation always stands for something else. It expresses this in a certain way and derives the right to represent that other. These two moments can increase or neutralize each other. In his analysis of Velasquez's painting, Foucault opts for the negative position. He discusses the invisibility of what one observes related to the invisibility of the observer, the spectator. "It may be that, in this picture, as in all the representations of which it is, as it were, the manifest essence, the profound invisibility of the person seeing - despite all mirrors, reflections, imitations, and portraits. Around the scene are arranged all the signs and successive forms of representation; but the double relation of the representation to its model and its sovereign, to its author as well as to the person to whom it is being offered, this relation is necessarily interrupted." (ibid, 16)

Because representation always stands for something else without ever being able to be that something else, it is never the thing itself. But as a representation of that other, it will never be imaginary. In that sense, one could state that the subject is removed from the representation as well. It is a characteristic of each representation that in the content of representation, subject and object disappear as entities. "But there, in the midst of this dispersion which it is simultaneously grouping together and spreading out before us, indicated compellingly from every side, is an essential void: the necessary disappearance of that which is its foundation - of the person it resembles and the person in whose eyes it is only a resemblance. This very subject - which is the same - has been elided." (ibid,16)

5.6.2. Art as counter-discourse

There are more interesting views on art to be distilled from the course of Les mots et les choses. Although specific reference is made to literature, many considerations can be applied to art as well. The canvas certainly can be viewed as a discourse, but indeed, in what Foucault calls the modern era, as a specific form, "the counter-discourse". (ibid, 44) In this era, art acquires a different function. It frees itself of all values allowing access to various domains in the classical period: good taste, pleasure, the natural, the true. In its space, art gives rise to all that can guarantee the denial of that space: the scandalous, the ugly, the impossible. It breaks with all genres and only wants to reveal itself, brilliant in the shine of its own being. "It breaks with the whole definition of genres as forms adapted to an order of representations and becomes merely a manifestation of a language which has no other law than that of affirming - in opposition to all other forms of discourse - its own precipitous existence." (ibid, 300)

Art reaches beyond itself, as if the content of its discourse were the interpretation of its form. Only "the simple act of writing" is valid. The move to action painting is near.

The idea of modern art as "counter-discourse" becomes more distinct when connected to the experience of transgression. Foucault attaches much value to the concept of transgression, showing his appreciation of Bataille. In an article on Bataille, Foucault clarifies how one can understand this concept. "Sacrilege in a world which does not contribute any positive value to the sacred - is not that what one could more or less call 'transgression'?" (Foucault 1986, 56)

According to Foucault, transgression is not only the way to acquire a direct access to the content of the sacred, but also the way to restore it as an empty form. The restoration of this empty form seems a task for modern art. Not only is modern art as avant-garde an act, but also a transgression, referring to the margin. Foucault claims, that margin and transgression owe each other the proximity of their existence. A margin cannot exist if it is not capable of being transgressed. And the other way around: a transgression is useless, if it can only overstep an imaginary margin. In other words, a margin is set to be transgressed, which is certainly the case in modern art.

According to Foucault, each moral command is situated within thought. Apart from religious forms of morality, modern thought does not formulate any form of morality. Therefore, in modern thought, the ethical is situated in the transgression. "For modern thought, no morality is possible. Thought had already 'left' itself in its own being as early as the nineteenth century; it is no longer theoretical. As soon as it functions it offends or reconciles. Even before prescribing, suggesting a future, saying what must be done (...), thought is in itself an action - a perilous act." (ibid, 328) In Foucault's view, Sade, Nietzsche, Artaud and Bataille have revealed this. Art as "counter-discourse" as formulated and articulated by these authors substitutes for morality, that is, an experience as a transgression of the margin.

Foucault claims that modern culture breaks with the view of the Enlightenment. In this view, science is universal and autonomous and art a matter of objective judgement of taste. Morality consists of self-legitimation of universal laws by autonomous individuals. Together, these three domains are constituted in human nature. However, the image of modern culture Foucault gives in Les mots et les choses does not offer a place for "human nature". No longer is science autonomous or universal, and neither is morality possible. The task of the articulation of the margins of experience is in the power of avant-garde literature and art. All scientific, aesthetic and moral problems are reduced to linguistic problems, and languages have no ground outside themselves. "That literature in our day is fascinated by the being of language is neither the sign of an imminent end nor proof of a radicalization: it is a phenomenon whose necessity has its roots in a vast configuration in which the whole structure of our thought and our knowledge is traced." (ibid, 383)

Similar to the avant-garde, modern visual art is fascinated by the question of what it actually is. This is an argument for the spectator to constantly pose the question "What is art?", at least as far as contemporary art is concerned.

5.6.3. The mutual irreducibility of word and image

Foucault has directed his thought explicitly towards painting and the problem of the relationship between image and language within visual art. He bases himself on some of Magritte's "language paintings". In Foucault's view, the relationship between language and painting is an infinite one. Language is not determined by what one perceives, but by successive syntactic forms. This should not be considered a failure of language, but the mutual irreducibility of word and image. "Neither can be reduced to the other's term: it is in vain that we say what we see; what we see never resides in what we say. And it is in vain that we attempt to show, by the use of images, metaphors, or similes, what we are saying; the space where they achieve their splendor is not that deployed by our eyes but that defined by the sequential elements of syntax." (ibid, 9)

In his text on Magritte's painting Ceci n'est pas une pipe, Foucault tries to demonstrate that Magritte breaks with what he calls the two principles dominating Western art from the fifteenth till the twentieth century. The first principle, "affirms the separation between plastic representation (which implies resemblance) and linguistic reference (which excludes it)." (Foucault 1973, 39)

The two domains (language and image) never coincide. A subordination predominates. This is the case, for example, in a painting where the representation of a book can be observed or, conversely, in some texts where the image is merely an additional illustration, "as if it would merely take a short cut." The second principle "poses the equivalence between the fact of resemblance and the affirmation of a good representation." (ibid, 42) In other words, when an image resembles something, it is that something. An image of a pipe makes one expect: this is doubtless a pipe; thus, as self-evident as illustrated textbooks in primary education. Magritte's painting runs counter to these principles. In his work, Magritte demonstrates that image as well as language are external to things. Magritte mangles word and image in such a way that the image does not refer to the word nor the other way around. No longer does either of them represent something real. In the painting Ceci n'est pas une pipe, language as well as image ignore the representation. However, that does not mean that the representation disappears. "Magritte makes the old space of representation reign, but only superficially, since it is merely a polished stone bearing figures and words; underneath there is nothing." (ibid, 56-57)

In Les mots et les choses, Foucault considers representation the major characteristic of the epistemological field, the so-called epistème of the classical period, which could still be active. According to Foucault, Magritte demonstrates its emptiness.

Magritte also rejects the second principle, which claims that correspondence does not imply confirmation of the image. Foucault states that this occurs because Magritte employs resemblances without correspondences. The distinction is that the correspondence assumes an original and, therefore, is related to a hierarchy. Conversely, the resemblance is subordinated to repetition. Because of that, it is impossible to say what the original is. Thus, there is no inclination towards hierarchy either. In that way, it becomes independent and a game of infinite, minimal repetition results, without any affirmation, without any representation.

Magritte's work can foster an analysis of the phenomena of withdrawal of common perception. Moreover, the discussion between Magritte and Foucault is an example of fundamentally different perspectives and the repercussions on interpretation. Not surprisingly, the Foucault experts and the Magritte experts disagree on the analysis of Ceci n'est pas une pipe. "In circles of Foucault experts, the essay is praised as an example of philosophizing from the artist, from the artwork itself. However, Magritte experts and friends criticized the essay sometimes fiercely. Foucault interprets a great number of paintings and is sometimes very convinced while discussing images or details of images. According to the critics he forget that the paintings do not have anything to say, that they are extremely simple, sometimes even banal." (Kaulingfreks 1984, 166)

At stake are two different basic attitudes. Magritte's friends want to let the painting speak for itself and stay within the painting. For them, nothing can be added to the image. Conversely, Foucault's analysis does not depart from the painting. However, it is an interesting example of how a philosopher interprets art as illustrative material for his philosophy. There is no reason why a Magritte fan should prohibit such an interpretation. An artwork can be as fascinating as its spectator is.

5.6.4. The author is multiple

Foucault certainly is not interested in Magritte's "intentions", since he does not value the identity of the creators of images. In his view, the author is multiple. As sometinmes in Latin, "author" should be indicated grammatically by a multiple substantive noun. According to Foucault, the question "Who is the author?" can never be answered with a unity visible in the work. Thus, the spectator has no identity as one perceiving the work as a reflection of the identity of the creator. In line with his criticism on subject centrism, Foucault questions authorship as a unifying principle. In so doing, he does not deny the existence of the inventive individual, but the individual's undividedness and "originality". On the same subject, many different perspectives arise simultaneously, which cannot be reduced to each other or to one more profound point of view. Therefore, Foucault rejects the idea of "the author as principle of grouping of the discourse, as unity and origin of its significations, as focus of its coherence." (Foucault 1971, 28) Foucault claims that such an authorship only exists as fiction, in such a way that the oeuvre can also not be understood as unity. In another book, where these problems are extensively treated, Foucault states, "The oeuvre can neither be considered as immediate unity, nor as fixed unity, nor as homogeneous unity." (Foucault 1969, 36)

The "coincidence" of the discourse of the oeuvre is disputed by commentary or art criticism. Commentary wants to situate the coincidence. It wants to be part of the oeuvre. In addition to the text, it wants to say more as a completion of the text at the expense of the multiplicity of the text. According to Foucault, commentary directs the "coincidence" of the discourse in a certain direction at the expense of the openness of the work. Therefore, the novel is not the novel, in the sense of what has not yet happened. The novel reveals itself in an accompanying commentary, which is a repetition of the novel event. Thus, the discourse is controlled and defined by the "commentary" as well as by the "author". Foucault maintains that the coincidental aspect of the discourse is limited by the commentary on the basis of the game of identity, which has the form of "repetition" and of the "identical". The principle of the author limits that same coincidental aspect by means of the game of an identity which has the form of "individuality" and the "I".

This brings to mind Nietzsche. The relationship between Nietzsche, Foucault and other French philosophers is known. (Bolle 1981) In an article on Nietzsche, Foucault states: where the soul pretends to shape itself into unity, where the I invents for itself an identity or coherence, there the genealogist searches for the beginning. And more: he searches for numerous beginnings, which are left by the almost invisible color and the almost erased trace, where even the least developed historical eye cannot be mistaken. The analysis of the origin leads to the decomposition of the "I". But Foucault wonders why the genealogist Nietzsche rejects the origin (Ursprung). He poses that question because, in the origin, one wants to comprehend the exact essence of things, their purest possibility, their identity carefully directed inward. Conversely, the genealogist discovers that the essential and timeless secret does not underlie things. He discovers the secret that they are without essence, that their essences are built up from shapes alien to them. Therefore, in a Nietzschean sense, Foucault states: "In contrast to the historiography of historians, 'real' historiography is not based on any constant element: nothing in a human being - and neither his body - is firm enough to be able to understand other human beings and to recognize himself in them. No matter where one searches for a firm point in time to address oneself to history to comprehend it in its totality, all that is able to characterize it as a patient and constant movement should be destroyed systematically. What enables the comforting game of reçognition has to be cut up in pieces. In the field of history, knowing does not mean retrieving and certainly not 'discovering oneself'." (Foucault 1981, 26)

In particular, that last thought seems applicable to art as an art historical document; in art, recognition and discovering oneself are wrong tacks as well. In line with Nietzsche, Foucault rejects the metaphysical sense of interpretation as slowly revealing a meaning hidden in the origin. However, the "becoming" of human beings is a series of interpretations. Interpretation then means violently or cunningly mastering a system of rules - without any essential meaning - and introducing this system into another game and subjecting it to different rules. Or as Foucault endorses: "The death of interpretation is to believe that there are signs of something, that is, a hidden essence awaiting us at the end of our interpretative journeys. Conversely, the life of the interpretation is to believe that there are only interpretations. If modern critical knowledge is certainly a hermeneutics of profundity, one should not consider this an exploration of the underlying structures, but rather becoming conscious of all analytical implications which Nietzsche has seen so well: 'interpretation has (..) become an infinite task'." (Merquior 1986, 85)

6. POSTSCRIPT: THE POSTMODERNISM DEBATE

In the postmodernism debate, Jean Baudrillard first has the floor. He is an example of an author who sharply formulates the postmodern view on the function of contemporary art. Next, Lyotard and Habermas enter into a discussion. Lyotard is considered the major spokesperson of postmodernism. Conversely, Habermas views the assignment of Modernism as incomplete.

6.1. *Baudrillard*

6.1.1. *The artwork as signed object within a system of objects*

In Pour une critique de l'économie politique du signe, Baudrillard departs from art in order to analyze the political economy of signs. He treats the artwork as a sign - that is, as a signed object - and as an object whose value is determined by trade. In that way, he tries to complete Marxist views on political economy with the concept of "political sign economy".

Baudrillard points out that, besides being a painted surface, the painting is a signed object. The sign indicates the act of painting. By means of its signature, the painting enters the world of objects. Thus, the canvas becomes unique as a cultural object with an extraordinary differential value. It is a sign within a system: the oeuvre of the artist. "Hardly perceptibly but radically, the signature introduces the artwork in the different world of the object. And the canvas becomes unique - no longer as a work, but as an object - when it is provided with this stamp. Then it becomes a model where a visible sign confers an extraordinary differential value. But it is not a value of meaning - the actual meaning of a painting is not at stake here - it is a differential value, founded by the ambiguity of a sign that does not reveal the artwork; within a system of signs, the sign makes the artwork recognize and evaluate and, while it differentiates the artwork as model, the sign has integrated it in a series, which is the work of the artist." (Baudrillard 1972, 114)

Baudrillard indicates what this inclusion in a system of signs means for the artwork-spectator relationship. The sign does not make one perceive. It merely brings about recognition within the system of signs. Within this structure, the differential value within a world of objects is questioned rather than the value of the artwork's meaning. Baudrillard claims that the signed painting as a cultural object is not only read in its differential value, it is perceived that way as well. In the "aesthetic emotion", critical reading and perception directed towards the systems of signs are confused. In Baudrillard's view, this ambiguity is not only related to painting; it defines the "consumption" of all cultural goods.

According to Baudrillard, the modified meaning of what one calls modern art enables the introduction of art into a system of objects. Traditionally, the meaning of art lies in the reflection of the phenomena, a reflection of an order which guarantees an outstanding beauty. Baudrillard claims that the characteristic of the modern artwork is that its meaning is included in the act of inventing those phenomena. Then the value lies in the singularity of the artist's gesture. The creating subject postulates his "being different" again and again as a "continuation of absence". Thus, order is substituted with a series: an oeuvre as a succession of irreversible inventive moments of creation. "We are in time rather than in space, in difference rather than in resemblance, in series rather than in order." (ibid, 116)

Baudrillard maintains that modern art is only "contemporary" if it is produced in a series of "acts". In other words, contemporaneous, in its own movement, rather than related to the world. According to Baudrillard, this does not mean that modern art is not contemporary. On the contrary, it is contemporary in an indirect, critical way, because the world shows a similar ambiguity. Rather than being critical realism or a form of involvement, the main function of modern art is to save that gestural moment, that intervention of the subject, by means of viewing the act of painting as a breach. "And this is where the truth of modern art lies: if it testifies to our time, then it does not do so through direct allusion nor through its pure gesture which ignores a systematized world, but by testifying to the systematics of this complete world through the inverted systematics, homology of its empty gesture, a pure gesture which marks an absence." (ibid, 122)

In Baudrillard's perspective, viewing art as a sign is very different from searching for the so-called "actual" meaning of the artwork. By considering the artwork an object within a system of objects, it acquires a completely different function. Now the painting is no longer viewed as aesthetic object, the aesthetic qualities are no longer criteria. Baudrillard considers the painting as a sign, where the collectors of art distinguish themselves either as members of their own group, or as a means to refer to a group with a higher social status. In that sense, art is an example of application within the principle of analysis of the social logic of consumption, as Baudrillard poses in his book La société de consommation. Ses mythes, ses structures. (1970)

Art as an object with a social-economic sign value engenders the question of how to understand art in a different perspective. Certainly when this aspect is related to the participation of the general public. In his book A l'ombre des majorités silencieuses ou la fin du social (1982) Baudrillard points out the intangibility of the masses. He states that the masses - in fact everybody - are not the objects of repression or manipulation and, thus, it is impossible to free them. They are the despair of politics because they are only present, inert, as a pure object. The masses set their silence against each political impulse desiring to have them speak. Time and again one tries to seduce the masses into reaction. However, the masses can be seduced into doing anything which will just lead to nothing.

6.1.2. *The artwork as a fatal strategy to meaningful thought*

One cannot blame Baudrillard for playing a starry-eyed idealist. In his view, each form of critical radicalism has become useless. All negativity has been resolved in a world which almost seems to be a completed realization. There is nothing left but to develop "fatal strategies" against the enigmatic zero in things and discourses, since only "fatal strategies" will be able to escape the compelling logic of objects. How? By blackmailing and challenging reality, against the principle of reality which for the most part constitutes objects. By postulating the futility and worthlessness of reality. By following axioms and rules different from those to which objects respond.

An example of such a fatal strategy is art which, in confrontation with the challenge of consumer society, becomes more valuable than normal goods. Art should not expect any good from critical denial because this will only be its ridiculous and powerless mirror. This situation can be compared with dialectic thought, which has become a mirror of capitalism because of critical denial. Art should surpass the formal abstraction of goods glorified as fetishes. By cultivating the exchange value, it can distance itself even more from the usage value. In other words, art should exaggerate its uselessness as a reaction against the destruction of the old objective ideals such as beauty, authenticity, and functionality. "The only radical and modern solution is to accentuate in goods what is novel, original, unexpected, and brilliant, namely the formal indifference for purpose and value, the priority of total circulation. That is what the artwork should intend: shock, alienation, surprise, commotion, fluidity and even destruction, transience and unreality; it should appropriate all these characteristics of value." (Baudrillard 1985, 184-185)

The artwork as a new triumphing fetish: in that sense it should work at deconstructing its traditional aura, its authority and illusionary power. Only then may it shine in the pure obscenity of goods. The artwork should destroy itself as a familiar object and become distortedly alien. Remarkably enough, Baudrillard derives the "only truly aesthetic and metaphysic, ironic and cheerful response" to the challenge of goods from Baudelaire, who considers it a characteristic of the modern.

Nevertheless, Baudrillard is the outstanding postmodern author. However, the question is whether he would agree with this statement. After all, the concept of "postmodernism" brings about a unifying principle within the diversity of cultures, whereas Baudrillard's thought turns against such a unifying signification. In his book Oublier Foucault (1977) Baudrillard states that the "power" in Foucault's work is nothing but an instrument to analyze reality. His criticism is that a principle such as "power" does not suffice, because it is based on a principle within the "meaningful thought" Foucault wants to denounce. According to Baudrillard, in this way Foucault demonstrates trust of a certain order, contrary to his view of reality as an entity of coincidence, dissemination, contingency and futility. Conversely, Baudrillard views society as a system of signs, an enclosed totality of mere formal differences. No longer does Baudrillard speak of the modification of meanings, but of their disappearance. Not surprisingly, one of his articles is published in a volume on "Postmodern Culture". (Foster 1983) In this article, Baudrillard discusses the "ecstasy of communication". He claims that we live in the omnipresence of communication, in an immense hyperreality of information. It arises via the media and it dissolves each originally existing division between intimacy and publicity. In such a "society of spectacle", nothing but messages circulate as empty codes in a system of meaningless exchange.

Perhaps some forms of visual art can function as an oasis of communication, as a resort for the ecstasy of communication.

6.2. *Habermas*

In the discussion on modernism versus postmodernism, Jürgen Habermas, an adherent of critical theory, plays an important role. His view on postmodernism clarifies the thought of young French philosophers. Habermas calls them "young conservatives" as they are said to reject "truth" and "reason". He claims that the "modern" is still a project to be completed. Rationality should not be removed. At least one standard should be maintained as an explanation of the dissolution of all rational standards. Or, as Rorty - appointed American arbitrator in this discussion -states: "If we have no such standard, one which escapes a 'totalizing self-referential critique', then distinctions between the naked and the masked, or between theory and ideology, lose their force. If we do not have these distinctions, then we have to give up the enlightenment notion of 'rational criticism of existing institutions', for 'rational drop outs'." (Rorty 1985, 162)

In line with Horkheimer and Adorno, two of his predecessors, Habermas considers criticism a negation within critical theory. Lyotard undermines the foundation of such "theory" by representing it as one of the many meta-narratives of philosophy. Lyotard will be treated after Habermas' view on the function of art and his defense of the "modern", which will clarify the concept of the "postmodern".

6.2.1. *Aesthetic and therapeutic criticism*

Habermas distinguishes between two forms of criticism: the therapeutic and the aesthetic. The former implies that individuals with a "false" consciousness change by means of self-reflection, with the assistance of a competent therapist, in such a way that they become more true to themselves and others. Especially cases of self-deception are treated. Aesthetic criticism is directed towards the interpretation of needs. Habermas claims that, in line with art criticism which "opens the eyes" in order to be able to perceive through arguments the beauty of a work of art, aesthetic criticism provides the linguistic means to indicate what really interests us. Although arguments play an important role in therapeutic as well as in aesthetic criticism, both are characterized by an asymmetric relationship between those involved. Furthermore, in aesthetic criticism, certain standards play a role, which, according to Habermas, do not have a universal character, but are culturally specific. "Cultural values are not universally valid; they are, as the name implies, limited by the horizon of the social world of a certain culture. Values can only become plausible in the context of a specific form of life." (Habermas 1981b, 71)

Habermas points out that, besides therapeutic experiences, aesthetic ones can contribute to the discussion of identity. By placing oneself in the position of the characters of novels or plays and by simulating their acts, the reader or spectator can experiment with certain representations of identity and related interpretations of needs. Thus, he can discover how it "feels" to end up in certain situations, to enter into certain relationships or to break them off. The gained experiences can be introduced into discussions and public debates on the advantages or disadvantages of certain representations of identity and related interpretations of needs.

Standards of value can be helpful in judging the authenticity of expressions. According to Habermas, they cannot be justified in a discourse, because standards cannot claim universality. However, they can be thematized argumentatively following the model of aesthetic criticism. The reasons produced serve to make the authenticity of an artwork obvious to such an extent that the spectator is able to experience this authenticity. In that way, authenticity is motivated rationally to accept the evaluative standard in question. Thus, art may evoke the experience of an "example" to be followed; however, not in the sense of the ethical normative "good" example. "In a prototypical case, they have the form of aesthetic criticism. Because of this, the form of argumentation varies, especially where the correspondence to value standards has been made an expression of our evaluative language. This occurs in the discussions of literature, art and music criticism, however, in an indirect way. In this context, reasons have the particular function to reveal a work or an exhibition, in such a way that they can be observed as an authentic expression of an exemplary experience, or as the embodiment of a claim to authenticity." (ibid, 41)

6.2.2. Art's becoming autonomous and its consequences for communication

In his book <u>Strukturwandel der Öffentlichkeit</u>, Habermas develops a theory of art and culture based on an analysis of social structures and political functions, where communicative relationships between producers and public are central. In the bourgeois public domain during the Enlightenment, the boundary between layperson and professional was transgressed. The art critic is not only an educator; as a representative of the public, he can also act as a spokesperson. "In the institutions of art criticism, including literature, theater and music criticism, the lay opinion of the mature public or the public considering themselves as such organizes itself. The new profession corresponding to this receives in contemporary jargon the name of art judge. He accepts a particular dialectic task: he understands himself as representative of the public and at the same time as its educator. The art judges can consider themselves the vox populi - in their fight with artists this is their central topos - since they are not aware of any authority besides argumentation and feel one with all who have themselves convinced through argumentation. At the same time, they can address the public itself when they as experts refer to "dogma" or "trend" and the lack of judgment of the uneducated." (Habermas 1962, 59-60)

　　　In the second half of his book, Habermas sketches the decline of the bourgeois public domain in the background of this ideal model. This decline starts with the transition from competitive capitalism to monopolistic capitalism. The modern mass media rob the public of its possibility of participation and argumentation. Under the influence of this development, the literary public deteriorates. The general public is divided into a minority of art connoisseurs and masses of cultural consumers. In other words, there is a division between art - which becomes "autonomous" - and cultural industry. Habermas considers culture becoming autonomous as a process where the communicative relationships between producer and receiver - relationships characterized by parity and equality during the Enlightenment - become more and more disturbed. "Through such connections, the separation of an 'intelligence' from the bourgeois educational class could be explained; these have namely, in spite of their ideologically preserved self- consciousness, entirely maintained their indeed hardly praiseworthy leading role, also within the new audience of the consumers of culture. (...) This close relationship of artists and writers with their audience has loosened somewhat since Naturalism. At the same time, the 'uninvolved' audience loses its critical power over the producers. Modern art lives from now on under a veil of propaganda: the publicized recognition of artists and work is only coincidentally connected with their recognition in a large public." (ibid, 209)

In his book Theorie des kommunikativen Handelns, Habermas develops another view on art. He no longer considers the process of becoming autonomous a disastrous development which art is simply subjected to under the specific circumstances of late capitalism. Habermas views this process as a necessary development embodied in an evolutionary progress. In this book, Habermas stresses the productive activities of the artist and the critic rather than the communicative relationships of the spectator. This is clearly demonstrated in the changing role of the art critic. Contrary to his previously stated role, the critic now functions as a sympathizing co-worker, a congenial co-producer. Because of his interpretation, the art critic contributes to shaping the artwork. His function can be compared with that of an actor or musician, who bring a theater piece or music to life by expressing it. In that way, the critic guides the audience and opens their eyes to the quality of an artwork. The correct attitude of the audience is not critical but contemplative and emphatic. At that moment, the audience completely loses their grasp of the artist. The critic is no longer mediator, but belongs to the actual process of the production of art. Habermas characterizes this production using the ancient concept of genius, "The gifted artist is able to authentically express all experiences which he has in a concentrated contact with a decentralized subjectivity, freed of the obligation of knowledge and action." (Habermas 1981a, 456)

Habermas gives a clear image of the consequences of art becoming autonomous for the general public. Because of what he calls the "colonization of the world of life", the daily communicative practice becomes permeated by cognitive-instrumental organizations of action, including all one-sided reaction accompanying it. This development leads to loss of meaning. Certainly if one includes the deterioration of the production of meaning in the world of life caused by the emancipation of science, morality and art as regards the daily communicative practice. Because of the rationalization of religious world views, these three domains have ceased to differentiate as regards each other. They have continued to develop each according to a particular internal logic. Therefore, in science, morality and art, internally directed educative processes have arisen which are monopolized by independent subcultures of experts. Not surprisingly, the fragmentation by professionalization of the various cultural domains leads to a deterioration of cultural tradition. The aesthetic and other experts are not able to integrate their domain into the entire scope of the world of life. "In the corresponding cultural systems of action, the scientific discourses, the moral and legal-theoretical investigations, as well as art production and art criticism, become institutionalized as the task of experts. The professionalized treatment of the cultural tradition under a continually abstract aspect of validity reveals the autonomy of the cognitive-instrumental, the moral-practical and the aesthetic-expressive realm of sciences. - From now on there is also an internal history of sciences, of moral and legal theory, of art - certainly not linear developments, but still learning processes. As a consequence of this professionalization, the distance between experts - cultures and the general public will increase. What culture obtains through specialist treatment and reflection does not end up in everyday practice just like that. With the cultural rationalization, the space of life devaluated in its traditional substance threatens rather to become impoverished." (Habermas 1981b, 481-82)

6.2.3. The project of the modern

Habermas' attempt to rescue "the project of the modern" follows naturally from the paradigm of his theory on the communicative act, in particular the necessity to hold on to a communicative rationality. In his Adorno lecture, Habermas points out the growing distance between the culture of experts and the culture of the general public. He departs from Surrealism's failed attempt to renounce art. In Habermas' view, this attempt arises because modern art cannot keep its promise of happiness. All the more, because since Baudelaire, modern art has been the critical reflection of irreconcilability with the social world. According to Habermas, one becomes more aware of this as art removes itself further from life and withdraws into pristine final autonomy. Habermas is very harsh in judging the Surrealist attempt to denounce art. He calls it a "Nonsense Experiment", accentuating rather than affecting the structures of art and proposes the following: "The radical attempt to cancel art ironically pushes those categories to the fore with which classic aesthetics used to define its domain of objects; obviously, these categories have themselves changed in the process." (Habermas 1981a, 458)

However, Habermas takes the statements of the Surrealists too literally. Perhaps one can stamp their explicit purposes as "nonsensical experiments". However, this is not the case for their material products. After all, their break with a certain type of art itself realizes a breakthrough. Their deviating forms and non-conformism opens new paths which are certainly not nonsensical: the effect of an experiment gains an autonomy unrelated to the purposes of the experimenter. Habermas believes that the Surrealist revolt is a false attempt to abolish art. First, because destruction does not equal liberation. Secondly, one cannot withstand cultural deterioration by violently severing access to one cultural domain, in this case art. Theoretical knowledge and morality should be involved as well. He considers this false abolition of art by the Surrealists to be a deviation of the project of the modern. According to Habermas, this should not be a reason to view the project as lost. He maintains he is able to posit a solution to the aporia of the cultural modern on the basis of the reception of art. In Habermas' view, there have always been two opposing tendencies: art criticism as a productive supplement to the artwork, and art criticism as a compromise to the general public's need for interpretation. At the rise of the avant-garde movement, these tendencies started to polarize to a greater extent, "Bourgeois art directed both expectations to its recipients: on the one hand the layman should be educated by the expert, on the other hand he was allowed to behave as a connoisseur relating aesthetic experiences to personal problems in life." (ibid, 460)

Habermas regrets that the second form of art criticism, relating the aesthetic experiences to the individual problems of life, has lost its radicality. However, in his view, this is part of the completion of the project of the modern. Artistic production is doomed to decrease semantically, not only in its specific process but also as a mere object of experts wishing to categorize it under an abstract valid aspect. According to Habermas, that exclusive concentration on one dimension will explode when, in an individual history of life, the aesthetic experience is overruled and, thus, incorporated in a form of life. "The reception by the layman, or rather the daily expert, obtains another direction than the professional critic focusing on the inner development of art." (ibid, 461)

In praising the importance of the relationship between art and personal problems of life, Habermas emphasizes theme and content as the source of the layperson's recognition of the experience of life, at the expense of problems of form, which is the domain of the expert. However, there is no direct access to the work of art without the trained eye. The artwork is not a sounding board for personal experiences and anecdotes. Without discovering the path through the labyrinth of forms, there is no confrontation with the experience of life.

Habermas wants to believe theoretically in the "project of the modern", but has little hope. This project has to be realized on all levels. Partial realization means failure and, thus, an incomplete project. Habermas did not counter the impression that there is a fundamental difference between modernists and post-modernists. The modernists cannot think without the illusion of a Utopian project that has to be completed. Conversely, the postmodernists spare themselves such an illusion.

6.3. Lyotard

6.3.1. The heteromorphic world view of postmodernism

No doubt, Jean-Francois Lyotard is the spokesman of a philosophy departing from a disillusioned - and as such desperate - world view and the modern project, which wonders whether a world view is conceivable at all. In the discussion between "modernists" and "postmodernists", he is Habermas' opponent. Lyotard has labelled the concept of "postmodernism". "Simplifying to the extreme, I define postmodern as incredulity toward meta-narratives. This incredulity is undoubtedly a product of progress in the sciences: but that progress in turn presupposes it. To the obsolescence of the meta-narrative apparatus of legitimation corresponds, most notably, the crisis of metaphysical philosophy and of the university institution which in the past relied on it. The narrative function is losing its functors, its great hero, its great dangers, its great voyages, its great goal. It is being dispersed in clouds of narrative language elements - narrative, but also denotative, prescriptive, descriptive, and so on. Conveyed within each cloud are pragmatic valencies specific to its kind. Each of us lives at the intersection of many of these. However, we do not necessarily establish stable language combinations, and the properties of the ones we do establish are not necessarily communicable." (Lyotard 1984, xxiv) In the book Postmodernism explained to children, - absolutely no children's book - Lyotard elaborates on the concept of meta-narratives. Like myths, they aim at legitimatizing institutions, social and political practices, legislation, ethics and modes of thought. However, different from myths, they do not search for this legitimation in an improving, original act, but in a future to be realized, in an idea to become effective. This idea - for example freedom, Enlightenment, socialism - has an legitimatizing value because of its universality. It gives direction to all human realities. An example of such a meta narrative is the "Incomplete Project of the Modern", which Habermas still favors. In Lyotard's view, this project is not incomplete, but destroyed. Auschwitz is a symbol of that destruction. But Auschwitz is also the victory of the capitalist techno-sciences over other candidates for the universal finiteness of human history. These two examples, anti-fascism and anti-capitalism, demonstrate that one can hardly label Lyotard a neo-conservative.

In his thesis The Postmodern Condition, Lyotard elaborates on the destruction of the credibility of "Meta- Narratives" which promise the emancipation of humanity. He doubts we can continue to categorize events as a universal history of humanity. After all, there is no community, no "we". Lyotard analyzes the social context on the basis of Wittgenstein's concept of "language game". He rejects the modern analysis of community as a functional entity or as a dialectic duality. From a postmodern perspective, the social realm is atomized in smooth networks of language games. The "self" is incorporated into a complex and mobile fabric of relationships. It is situated along junctures of communicative circuits where it continues to have some influence on passing messages. Against the monopolizing tendencies of the "Grand Narratives", Lyotard pleads for a heteromorphy of language games, for a plurality of the numerous little narratives which tell about daily life. Lyotard does not stress so much the quest for a universal consensus on the rules of those language games as a merely local and temporary agreement. That agreement is related to the present conversation partners who cannot be treated unequally in their speaking, listening and acting. "Rules are not denotative but prescriptive utterances, which we are better of calling metaprescriptive utterances to avoid confusion (they prescribe what the moves of language games must be in order to be admissible). The function of the differential or imaginative or paralogical activity of the current pragmatics of science is to point out these metaprescriptives (science's 'presuppositions') and to petition the players to accept different ones. The only legitimation that can make this kind of request admissible is that it will generate ideas, in other words, new statements." (Lyotard 1984, 65)

The condemnation of the terror of the "Grand Narratives" demonstrates the right of heteromorphy. This heteromorphy is constituted by a social context. The context should be understood as an indefinite number of games with rules dependent on the players. The players are not independent of the obligation imposed on them by the institutions, but they are able to influence the rules of the game. Thus, Lyotard does differ from Habermas. Habermas aims to direct the elaboration of the legitimation towards a universal consensus by what he calls "discourse", in other words, the dialogue of argument. This assumes that all speakers are able to agree on rules or meta-instructions which are universally valid for all language games. However, this presupposes that the purpose of the dialogue is consensus. According to Lyotard, the language games are clearly heteromorphic and dependent on heterogeneous pragmatic rules. Consensus is a condition of discussion rather than its purpose. In Lyotard's view, that purpose is paralogism, thus the search for dissent.

Lyotard also criticizes Adorno. His criticism of the Frankfurt School can be understood as a break with his own thought before 1968, where he developed a view on society strongly related to the critical theory of Frankfurt. After May '68, Lyotard stops believing in any truth. His theme becomes nihilism rather than revolution. Against the class struggle, he poses a permanent post-bourgeois cultural revolution. "If Marxism is not true, it is not because it is false, but because nothing is true." (Descombes 1979, 211)According to Lyotard, Adorno assigns art an eschatological function. However, art neither redeems, nor reconciles. It is art's power to stay within nihilism and to accept and manifest this.

In his book <u>Economie Libidinale</u> (1974), Lyotard expresses the despair resulting from a crisis after May '68 which he shares with so many. This crisis is connected with the ultimate finality of the attempt to moralize politics. In an interview, he formulates his disbelief in its rationalist foundation, "Definitely, there is no rationalism, not even in Jürgen Habermas' sense, which could escape this terrible moment of nihilism or complete skepticism." (Reijen 1987, 104)

6.3.2. The painting demonstrating to the eye what perception is

Lyotard's Aesthetics from the book <u>Discours, Figure</u>, is a defense of the value of the eye as a sense, and thus, of the sensory. "This book is a defense of the eye, its localization. It has darkness as a prey. The twilight which after Plato's word threw a grey veil over sensibility, which has thematized it incessantly as a lesser being ... this twilight is the interest of this book." (Lyotard 1971, 11)

Lyotard stands up for aesthetics as the domain of the eye and the will. He sets this against the spoken word connected to the ethical. The power of the spoken and the written word lies in writing its history and passing it on as true, although initially the eye and visual perception might have been more important. In the evolution of humanity, sensory perception assumes precedence over rationality. The more the sensory domain decreases and becomes inefficient, the more the power of rationality is able to increase. In that sense, Lyotard's book as a defense of the eye seems important. He makes his glorification of perception more explicit, "What is savage is art as silence." (ibid, 13)

In his introduction, Lyotard considers the concept of silence the idiosyncrasy of art as compared to the spoken word. The silence of the artwork is the denial of the spoken word. At the same time, it is the spatial confirmation of what is unknown, in contrast to the word, which easily acquires meaning and loses it again. The figure exceeds the spoken word, since it has not been signified yet and, thus, anything is possible. The figure transcends the symbol. It manifests itself spatially in such a way that the linguistic space cannot incorporate it without being undermined. Because of its expressivity and desire, art is always the other. Art desires to be free figuration. In line with Hegel, Lyotard states that the symbol should be "seen" in order to provoke thought. Once the object is signified by language, that is, incorporated within a discourse, thought, which orders everything, becomes active. However, the word always fails to incorporate figuration completely. This very difference is the beauty of figuration.

However, the silence of beauty, the silence before the word, the surpassing of the discourse is impossible. Each discourse has its opposite, its objects which it discusses and which are its horizon and boundary. However, at the same time the discourse is the condition of the object, since it must discuss and express objects. The silence results from this disunion included in the word and completed in how the artwork expresses itself.

In an enigmatic way, Lyotard is referring to reading an artwork. He discusses the moment of searching for the difference, for the authenticity of the figure and the discourse in their being opposites. Ultimately, the artwork will always remain silent since it anticipates the eye. It expects gazes which are not dazzled immediately by the mediating word. It rejects words which are faster than the eye. But the eye does not participate in the discourse. Therefore, there is no naturalness between the eye and the word.

Lyotard breaks with the trend of theorizing on "reading" a work of art, such as has become fashionable among semiotics. In their view, everything can be read since everything can be considered part of a structure comparable to a linguistic structure. However, then the discourse is analyzed rather than the object, which is a shift in problem. The question "How can one transform that which can be seen into words?" persists. Lyotard continues to emphasize the power of the eye.

This power is nothing but the energy which activates a text transforming the work into an artwork. The energy needed is external sensuousness and pleasure and goes against the rational discourse. "To turn consciousness into a discourse is to omit the energetic. It is making oneself an accomplice to the entire Western ratio, which kills art altogether with the dream. One does not break at all with metaphysics by introducing language everywhere, one realizes it; one brings about the repression of the sensible and the pleasurable." (ibid, 14)

Thus, the perception of art belongs to the domain of sensuousness and at the same time the unconscious. Both are repressed by Western rationalism. There is a relationship between dream and artistic reality. Both cannot be read without being repressed. "One cannot read the painting, as today's semiologists maintain; Klee said that one can graze it, it permits observation, it offers itself to the eye as an exemplary thing, as a natural state, in Klee's opinion, because it makes one observe what can be observed. Or, it makes one observe that observation is a dance." (ibid, 14-15)

In line with Klee, Lyotard claims that a painting has to be exhausted with the eye. Thus, the painting is not read. After all, reading demands a movement of the eye which differs from perceiving a painting. In reading, one starts at a certain point and traverses known signs whether or not understood and finally ends up at a certain point. If one does not understand one can go back to the text. In perceiving a painting, as a flat surface with colors organized in a certain way, something else happens. Now perception does not necessarily have to follow a horizontal line. Moreover, the used signs are not known as in alphabetical signs. Therefore, each work is an exemplary thing. The linear left-right movement is substituted by being at a standstill at certain planes or spots which are "exhausted". One has to jump from one spot to the other according to an inherent rhythm. Perception is synonymous with "dancing". Pictorial signs do not have the automatic recognition of the alphabetical script or other standard signs. Therefore, one has to perceive actively in order to let the painting reveal what perception is. In Lyotard's view, to observe a painting is to follow the path it points out. It means taking advantage of the traces - no matter how indirect - the painter applied compellingly. A painting is a movement brought to life by the eye and fixed within a frame.

Yet, Lyotard does not discredit the discourse completely. The discourse is not only meaning and rationality, it is at the same time expression and affection which, immediately poses the problem of the truth of the discourse. By introducing an outward instance apart from the linguistic structure, the speaker risks that he knows what he is saying, resulting in sophism or even "terrorism". After all, if a discourse neglects meaning, the word can advance any signifier. If the meaning of what one says is not taken seriously, communication collapses. One no longer even "knows" what the words mean to say. Lyotard's statement is characteristic of the contemporary verbosity on art. However, the crisis of truth is entered upon as well. "Nobody can speak of truth today, each personification is ridiculous, all that is "official" does not tear us away from alternative thought or ignorance but immerses us again in clericalism, which relies upon it." (ibid, 17)

Yet, Lyotard makes an attempt. Freud's statement that, "Utopia is that truth never appears where one expects it." (ibid, 17) inspires two thoughts. First, truth manifests itself as a deviation of meaning and knowing. This deviation is a deconstruction of the order of the discourse. Opposite to this is expression as presence of sense. However, expression is not always truth. According to Lyotard, one should learn how to distinguish between expression which confuses the gaze, and expression, which urges the gaze in such a way that the invisible becomes visible. The latter is the artist's task, a floating regard, a fundamental indifference with respect to the established. The first expression is produced by the action of the dream. It wants to misguide. The second expression will materialize. However, they function in an identical way.

Nonetheless, Lyotard develops a second thought from Freud's statement. If truth does not appear where one expects it and no discourse can reveal it in a complete meaning, then truth does not present itself as a unifying theory but as fragments which can be connected in different ways. Lyotard rejects the concept of unity. He thinks it absurd to believe that one can comprehend diversity in a unifying discourse. In his view, it is time for philosophers to abandon the attempt to produce a unifying theory as the final word. One should even stop indicating it as a unifying instance. "We can only touch the thing itself metaphorically, but this laterality has not to do with existence, as Merleau-Ponty believed, which is too close to the unity of the subject, which he acknowledges at the end; it has to do with unconscious or expression which, in a similar movement, offers and preserves all content. This laterality is difference or depth." (ibid, 19)

Sense is present as absence of meaning. The meaning tries to dominate the sense of the work by discussing it. One can bring about meaning no matter what one will say. But, "Sense is only the deconstruction of signification." (ibid, 19)

We believe that this always happens in a painting. The meaning of a work - in particular what an artist tries to reveal in a specific way - arises by means of the destruction of an existing meaning, as these exist in dictionaries or in non-artistic language. The mere information in a meaning does not make sense, as most meanings are known and few artists have introduced new meanings. Moreover, colloquial or scientific language seems the best means of communicating meanings. According to Lyotard, the sense of a meaning defined within a context is its deconstruction. By deconstructing an existent, prevailing meaning and reconstructing it in a different way, the work of a painter acquires meaning. After all, he reveals meaning in a new figure. In a painting, the figurative comes into being by means of the pictorial. This does not mean that the image has to be figurative in the sense of immediately recognizable, but that the image shows a reformed meaning which acquires sense because of the process of reforming itself. This figuration is not abstract in the sense of a decorative game with elements, as for example Vasarely demonstrates. However, it can be a form where the meaning has to be recovered after deconstruction. This recovered meaning is never fixed or rigid, but has to be recovered again and again by the spectator. If not, the work of art is not art but an emblem, and its discourse is not an interpretation but a slogan. The act of exploring perception in order to see how meaning has become a puzzle without a key is the fundamental aesthetic experience.

6.3.3. *The philosopher and the artist as comrades against the establishment*

On the basis of his book <u>Discours, figure</u>, one can speak of Lyotard's aesthetics, which is very rare in contemporary philosophy. Lyotard also devoted numerous texts to oeuvres of favorite artists and his exhibition <u>Les Immatériaux</u> (1985) is certainly highly remarkable for a philosopher. Lyotard searches for what philosophy and painting have in common and, in his view, that is representation. Although he has renounced his "Grand Narratives", Lyotard still considers it a common task for philosophy and painting to represent the absolute. He is convinced that one cannot represent the absolute. Still he believes that one can represent that it is absolute. In Lyotard's view, this is the task of both philosophy and art. After all, he calls artists his fellows in an experiment. Together they combat the establishment. To Lyotard, the "postmodern" is, in that sense, not a conservative reaction to the progressiveness of the modern. On the contrary, it is its condition. "The establishment, if only yesterday's, should be considered suspect. Which space does Cézanne mock? The impressionist one. What do Picasso and Braque? Object to Cézanne. What prejudice does Duchamp break in 1912? The prejudice that a painting should be created, albeit Cubist. And Buren doubts the other prejudice, he believes to have emerged unscathed from Duchamp's work: the place where the work should be exhibited. A remarkable catalyst, the 'generations' stumbling over each other. A work can only become modern when it is first postmodern." (Lyotard 1987, 20-21)

    Lyotard has labelled the concept of postmodern. He does not understand postmodernism as a historical period which will conclude the modern, but as a reference to a way of thought as explained in his book <u>The Postmodern Condition</u>. A concept has the description one contributes to it. Lyotard's basic thought is that postmodernism offers a multitude of views on reality against the terror of unifying thought.

6.4. *Postmodernism as a multitude of views on reality*

This contemporary discussion deserves our attention, because the question of "What is art?" should be situated within existing movements of cultural philosophy. In postmodernism, the relationship between ethics and aesthetics comes to the fore very clearly. An aesthetic attitude is understood as the willingness to have thought, feeling and acting be influenced by art or other aspects of form. The basis for this is the important function of art as emphasized in Kaulingfreks' Magritte study. "Art is a particular way of becoming conscious of reality and it expresses and communicates this becoming conscious. Particularly in our century, one has accounted for this function of art very clearly; also in the world of art itself." (Kaulingfreks 1984, 9)

The question we want to pose is related to the problem of freedom of thought. The pressure from the norm of the authoritative tradition has been replaced by an equally high pressure from the new established norm of the avant-garde. In other words, the terms "old" and "new", "traditional" and "modern" are as authoritative. The struggle between old and new is still a struggle for power rather than for freedom.

Of course one can substitute the entire problem with a history of terms, intending to historicize the discussion into a timeless matter. In that way, one relates "postmodernism" to the famous quarrels of the seventeenth century. Around 1870, the English parlor painter Chapman used the word postmodernism in his writings in order to distinguish himself from the Impressionists, who were classified as modern. In 1947, the term appears in Toynbee's works to indicate the last present phase of Western cultures, which started in 1875. The term "modern" is even more telling in its use. Lalande claims that "since the tenth century, it has been a frequently used term, in philosophical or religious polemics; and virtually always with an allusion, either praising (openness and freedom of spirit, knowledge of innovative discoveries or the latest formulated ideas, absence of laziness and routine); or pejorative (imprudence, concern with fashion, love if change because of change, inclined to lose oneself, without judgement and without understanding the past as an impression of the moment)." (Lalande 1980, 640)

Thus, the term modern is ambiguous in its connotations. Nor is it novel. According to Jauss, who has researched its previous history, at the end of the fifth century the word "modern" was used for the first time to define the new official Christian present against the heathen Roman past. With changing content, in Europe "modernity" has again and again expressed the consciousness of an era which refers back to Antiquity to understand itself as a result of something old to become something new. In postmodern architecture, one still refers to style elements of art from Antiquity. (Jencks 1986)

Eco points out the danger of overusing the term postmodernism: "Unfortunately 'post-modern' is a term that can be applied to everything. I have the impression that it is used indiscriminately. On the other hand, it seems as if one attempts to let it slide back in time: first it seemed to be used for certain writers or artists who worked the last twenty years, after that it gradually returned to the beginning of the century, then even further back, and this still goes on, shortly the category of postmodernism will end up with Homer." (Eco 1984, 81-2)

Eco ironizes the trendy abuse of the concept. Yet, he points out how the concept can be made understandable and applicable: "Still I do not believe that postmodernism is a tendency which can be described chronologically; it is a mental movement or rather a 'Kunstwollen', a way of acting. We could say that each era has its own postmodernism, like every era will have its Mannerism (so that I even wonder whether postmodernism isn't the modern name for Mannerism as meta-historical category)." (ibid, 82)

We could agree with Eco in general. However, two restrictions are required. First, Eco should express his meta-historical objections more concretely, and more determinedly about the movement which runs from the past to the anti-past in order to return to the past, where that anti-past belongs as well. Secondly, we do not believe that Mannerism coincides with what is called postmodernism. Its disintegration could be a result, a consequence of its abundance.

Thus, Mannerism could be considered a fourth stage before the inevitable break. It is difficult to reflect on one's own era and it is dangerous to speculate on the one to follow. Yet, we view postmodernism as different from a common new movement and a next move of Modernism. In Modernism, the aggression of the novel norm is very disturbing. Even if the novel norm maintains it is not normative, implied commands and prohibitions are still involved. No matter how strongly the avant-garde shifts boundaries, it cannot neutralize them. The basis of this shift in boundaries is mainly self-justification and defined out of not-being the other. Truth as foundation always appears to be a Barthesian myth and an alleged truth.

In our century, "Modernism" consists of the assumption of power of the concept of "novel" as a criterion within the values of art criticism. One could refer to a monopoly of the "novel" as a norm or to the myth of the novel. In contemporary art, "novel" seems to be a major quality inversely proportional to the antique market, where being antique is equated with quality in a natural way. The antithesis good-bad is substituted for by novel-old. Barthes calls this "novel" a basic value of all criticism. Modernism is a narrative of the novel as truth. The avant-garde seems the impetus within this movement, the principle of action where the traditional forms are destroyed by definition. On this tabula rasa, Modernism has built its belief in novel aesthetic values: limitation to the conceptual, minimal specification, pure emptiness, mere nothingness, the world reduced to the mythic anecdote etc. This destructive tendency has been necessary in twentieth- century art. It is the definition of art itself. However, "the tradition of rebelling against tradition" (Boomgaard 1985, 63) leads to the exhaustion of possibilities. The ongoing echo of destruction of the tradition of form - this is the discourse of Modernism - is doomed to become the sound of the drum of a failed revolution. Even if one calls it - in line with Habermas - the "incomplete project". Modernism appears to be a myth as expressed in the nihilistic saying "nihil novi sub sole". "Nothing novel" means that the novel does not have a foundation to make itself absolute as the mere truth. Out of this consciousness postmodernism arises. From the insight that a certain form does not reflect in an absolute way a certain content, postmodernism defends a multitude of "styles" which are identical and simultaneous. Against an art which is manifest for itself and which shifts boundaries to the existent - in particular the novel avant-garde - an art comes into being which playfully makes novel achievements prosper and applies new possibilities in a specific synthesis. The latter is a more operational definition of the concept of "trans-avant-garde" as introduced by Oliva. He views the concept of "trans-avant-garde" as another metamorphosis of avant-garde itself. (Oliva 1980)

The confusing use of terms needs some clarification. The relationship between Modernism and the avant-garde of the twentieth century implies that the avant-garde is an instrument of Modernism. Thus, the avant-garde is more limited, less extensive, even less complex than Modernism. The achievements of the avant-garde connote the concept of modern. The same is true for the relationship between postmodernism and trans-avant-garde. Here the problem of the relationship between the propositions "trans" and "post" arises. Both express "beyond", however, not identically. Still, the relationship continues to be a valid one. Since the avant-garde is in a trans-situation, Modernism attains its post-situation. "Trans" means that one refers to the avant-garde; it is not an anti-avant-garde. The proposition "trans" refers to the past and the future. As past, the trans-avant-garde goes beyond the beginning of the avant-garde. As future, it transcends the avant-garde by arriving at mutual syntheses between the avant-gardes. The latter may happen as reference to a distant past (quotation), but farther reaching, something which is novel without a claim of truth. The logical result of the slogan "anything goes" is that the non-avant-garde has a reason to exist, which means an "amicable" break with the avant-garde. However, the proposition causes a more drastic break with respect to Modernism. Here the proposition "post" is beyond any doubt. Characteristic is that the proposition "neo" is not used in either case to suggest a resurrection. Thus, a break is obvious. In the concept of "post-modernism" the element "post" does not have a pejorative connotation, in contrast to certain movements in art like post-expressionism. However, this is to the disadvantage of the concept of "Modernism", which has the pejorative element transplanted. Nonetheless, there is a difference in nuance. Because of a slight modification in the principle of movement - in other words the transcendence of the avant-garde - a fundamental categorical difference arises: postmodernism is a category farther. The "simplicity" of the avant-garde in its constant search for a new principle, a unifying theory, has been broken by the multitude of the trans-avant-garde and its search for multiform syntheses. Because of this, Modernism has failed. The unifying view which constitutes it appears to be a lie: a view on reality rather than reality itself.

The term avant-garde (Poggioli 1982, Perniola 1972, Bürger 1974) goes back to the twelfth century. Nevertheless, not until the previous century is it used in an artistic context as an extension of a social meaning. In the nineteenth century, art is entirely understood as a form of a social avant-garde attitude. Not until 1910 does one speak of avant-garde art as a counterpart of other movements. Around that time there are various avant-gardes: Futurism, Cubism, Suprematism, Dadaism, Surrealism etc. They oppose various bourgeois academic expressions. After 1945, almost every new movement is considered avant-garde. The avant-garde becomes more a problem than a movement. Some consider it the eminent principle of innovation of the cultural revolution. For others it no longer even exists. Between these two extreme perspectives, there is a view that the post- or trans movements have a monopoly on innovation.

What remains is the constant urge for innovation. The negation of the tradition is the necessary condition of the so desired originality. This is all based on the principle of multiformity: there is no right form. Indeed, this principle of multiformity is the basis of the avant-garde, but no movement is faithful to it. After all, each movement is inclined to make its new insight absolute and render it a new law as a definition of art itself. Conversely, the trans-avant-garde cultivates this principle of multiformity and is less ascetic and looser than the avant-garde.

In Oliva's (Oliva 1980) view, at this point in time the trans-avant-garde is the only avant-garde possible. In the avant-garde, he rejects the idea of progress in art. It is a form of historic optimism to think that the development of art will be an evolution along a continuous line. The art Oliva calls "trans-avant-garde"

shows - in his view - a continuous desire for change. In contrast to the demateri-
alization of the work of conceptual art, it chooses a rehabilitation of manual
ability. This is accompanied by pleasure in production, because of which the tradition of painting belongs to art once again. The value of the trans-avant-garde
art is eclecticism; it is not a movement but an attitude. It tries to reconcile two
levels of culture: higher culture, which is the domain of the avant-garde, and
lower culture, which is a product of imagination and mass civilization. The
trans-avant-garde considers the pictorial language a means to change, a transition from one work to the other, from one style to the other, a nomad of visual
images. In this nomadic attitude, there is no definitive perspective. Oliva's theory
seems to be related to the immediate interpretation of a number of Italian
painters. In that context, the consequence of each theory - wanting to be concretely applicable and still generally valid - is that at some points it legitimizes a
number of accidental expressions of art.

Unlike Oliva, we consider the concept of trans-avant-garde less related to
a certain movement. In the avant-garde's urge to innovate, the act itself - breaking boundaries and revealing new horizons - is generally more important than
its result. The trans-avant-garde attracts a large number of artists who can vary
as regards style and expression. They do not necessarily have a relationship,
besides their attitude concerning the avant-garde. They are the new undeveloped
domain which is released because of the avant-garde's shift in boundaries. In
their specific way, they explore new views and thus, arrive at more profound
results than the avant-garde itself. This is similar to the distinction the linguist
Saussure introduces between language and speech. The linguistic system is an
entity of conventions, followed by individuals of a linguistic community.
Therefore, a linguistic system is a social institution independent of the individual who cannot create nor correct this linguistic system. Certain avant-garde art
can be viewed as such a system of signs. Once such a system becomes history, it
can be viewed as a social institution. The trans-avant-garde can be considered as
a use of language (speech) by artists applying the linguistic system of the avant-
garde. Thus, for example, assemblage art can be viewed as an application of
Duchamp's system. In that way, each "ism" can be considered such a system.
The users are the "neo-, post- or trans-isms" who freely use the system. In this
context, epigonism could come to mind. However, epigonism is a duplicate of
the system rather than an individual application. In applying the system, one can
criticize it or use various ones. Contemporary art wants to cut across institution-
alization time and again. This is how this sign system differs completely from
non-artistic verbal language. In that sense, there are system modifiers who could
be called avant-garde, and individual users of the systems who could be called

trans-avant-garde. In this perspective, the trans-avant-garde cannot be linked with the historical movement of the last decade. In general, the modification of the system is more appreciated than the application of the system. However, postmodernism rejects the intrinsic value of system modification, which is one of the characteristics of Modernism.

In the 1980s, the trans-avant-garde made use of pictorial sign systems. An explanation for this is that a certain existing art form - in this case conceptual art - has to generate its antithesis - in this case pictorial painting. From a theoretical perspective, this could have happened differently. In the meantime, there is a conceptual trans-avant-garde in the sense of realizing concepts in an almost manual way. Lyotard is in favor of the "conceptuals". In an interview concerning his exhibition <u>Les Immatériaux</u>, he states: "for a hundred years, the avant-garde has carried through thought and invention to such an extent that it is completed unthought that anybody will decently take a paintbrush and put something on the canvas. I know it still happens that way, that it even comes back, but I think it is a disaster and I don't believe it will last very long. All that neo-expression-ism and that so-called postmodern architecture! They do not have any inventive-ness. As if I would only speak in old quotations. Who would be interested in that? What is interesting at the moment, are artists who work with computers, video and so on. That will produce something impressive. That is not a reflec-tion on "what do I want to show" or "what effect do I want to achieve" but it is a reflection on the material (materiaux), on the method. This reflection of the artist in advance is fully comparable with that of the philosopher." (Wester 1985, 11)

We agree with the view on art this philosopher expresses, but they are not the words of an art critic and, therefore, too one-sided. There is no reason to search for a truth in art which will exclude another truth. The fragmented truths do not have to fit together like a puzzle. The concept of art is confusing in its generality. "Art is art" is not a valid tautology. The discussion of whether art is a product of thought or of the senses is completely superfluous. Each form of art has a right to exist but no form must necessarily continue to exist.

Postmodernism is a plea for the multitude or pluralist, thus more tolerant, view of reality. This is contrary to the aggressive "singular" retaken positions of the avant-garde. The trans-avant-garde is less authoritative than the avant-garde. It does not define itself as a necessarily aggressive reaction to the strong imperi-um of the established "old guard". Therefore, the trans-avant-garde defines itself less negative as a reaction to the existent achievements and makes a less arrogant impression. Against the presumption of the avant-garde that it knows better it sets the "not-knowing" or the "yes but". Its weapon is irony, which puts tradition as well as anti-tradition into perspective. Thus, the trans-avant-garde continues to be critical but within another category. As a consequence of the erosion of the term "avant-garde", the change of category was necessary in order to remain critical.

In order to remain modern, Modernism requires the proposition "post". In order to remain before the "garde" as a guardian of the establishment, the avant-garde demands transcendence; on the condition that the application of the multitude of new principles as a foundation of the "modern" is more important than posing the firm principles of innovation itself.

SOURCES

K. Abraham, *Oeuvres complètes, tome I: 1907-1914, Rêve et mythe* (Paris, Payot, 1965).

T.W. Adorno, *Prismen, Kulturkritik und Gesellschaft* (Frankfurt am Main, Suhrkamp, 1955).

M.C. Aelbrecht & J.H. Barnett & M. Griff, eds. *The sociology of art and literature* (London, Duckworth, 1970).

V.C. Aldrich, *Philosophy of art* (London, Prentice-Hall, 1963).

J. Aler, ed. *De functie van de kunst in onze tijd* (Den Haag, Servire, 1962).

J. Aler, ed. *Actes du cinquième congrès international d'esthétique*, Amsterdam 1964 (La Haye-Paris, Mouton, 1968).

L. Althusser, *Pour Marx* (Paris, Maspero, 1971).

L. Althusser, *Drie opstellen over kunst en ideologie* (Nijmegen, SUN, 1980).

R. Arnheim, *Art and visual perception, A psychology of the creative eye*, New version (Berkeley- Los Angeles- London, University of California Press, 1954).

R. Arnheim, *The Gestalt theory of expression*, Psychological Review 56 (1949), pp. 156-171.

R. Arnheim, *Toward a psychology of art*, Collected essays (Berkeley- Los Angeles, University of California Press, 1966).

R. Arnheim, *Visual thinking* (Berkeley- Los Angeles- London, University of California Press, 1969).

R. Arnheim, *New essays on the psychology of art* (Berkeley- Los Angeles-London, 1986).

H. Arvon, *L'esthétique marxiste* (Paris, Presses Universitaires de France, 1970).

R. Barthes, *Essais critiques* (Paris, Editions du Seuil, 1964).

R. Barthes, *Le Plaisir du texte* (Paris, Editions du Seuil, 1973).

R. Barthes, *Roland Barthes par Roland Barthes* (Paris, Editions du Seuil, 1975).

R. Barthes, *Leçon, Leçon inaugurale de la chaire de sémiologie littéraire du Collège de France, prononcée le 7 janvier 1977* (Paris, Editions du Seuil, 1978).

R. Barthes, *Le grain de la voix, Entretiens 1962-1980* (Paris, Editions du Seuil, 1981).

R. Barthes, *L'obvie et l'obtus, Essais critique III* (Paris, Editions du Seuil, 1982).

R. Barthes, *Mythologies* (Paris, Editions du Seuil, 1970).

R. Bastide, *Art et société* (Paris, Payot, 1972).

J. Baudrillard, *Le système des objets* (Paris, Gallimard, 1968).

J. Baudrillard, *La société de consommation, Ses mythes, ses structures* (Paris, Gallimard, 1970).

J. Baudrillard, *Pour une critique de l'économie politique du signe* (Paris, Gallimard, 1972).

J. Baudrillard, *A l'ombre des majorités silencieuses ou la fin du social* (Paris, Denoël-Gonthier, 1982).

J. Baudrillard, *Les stratégies fatales* (Paris, Grasset & Fasquelle, 1983).

M.C. Beardsley, *The aesthetic point of view, Selected Essays,* (Ithaca & London, Cornell University Press, 1982).

M.C. Beardsley, *Aesthetics from classical Greece to the present: A short history* (New York, University of Alabama Press, 1985).

W. Benjamin, *De auteur als producent* (Nijmegen, SUN, 1971).

W. Benjamin, *Der Begriff der Kunstkritik in der deutschen Romantik* (Frankfurt am Main, Suhrkamp, 1973).

W. Benjamin, *Das Kunstwerk im Zeitalter seiner technischen Reproduzierbarkeit: drei Studiën zur Kunstsoziologie* (Frankfurt am Main, Suhrkamp, 1973).

W. Benjamin, *Illuminations* (London, 1973).

J. Berger, *Art and revolution* (London, Writers and Readers, 1969).

J. Berger, *Ways of seeing* (Harmondsworth, Penguin, 1972).

D.E. Berlyne, *Conflict, arousal, and curiosity* (New York, Mc Craw-Hill, 1960).

R.J. Bernstein, ed. *Habermas and modernity* (Cambridge/ Massachusetts, MIT Press, 1985).

E. Bloch, *Das Prinzip Hoffnung* (Frankfurt am Main, Suhrkamp, 1959).

M. Blonsky, ed. *On signs* (Oxford, Basil Blackwell, 1985).

H. Bloom et al., *Deconstruction and criticism* (New York, Seaburry Press, 1979).

K.R. Boff e.a., eds. *Handbook of human perception and preformance* (New York, John Wiley & Sons, 1986).

E. Bolle, *Macht en verlangen, Nietzsche en het denken van Foucault, Deleuze en Guattari* (Nijmegen, SUN, 1981).

J. Boomgaard & S. Lopez, *Van het postmodernisme* (Amsterdam, SUA, 1985).

D.J. Bos, ed. *Michel Foucault in gesprek, Sex, macht en vriendschap* (Amsterdam, De Woelrat, 1985).

P. Bourdieu & A. Darbel, *L'amour de l'art: les musées d'art européens et leur public* (Paris, Editions de minuit, 1966).

P. Bourdieu, *La distinction, Critique sociale du jugement* (Paris, Editions de Minuit, 1979).

J. Bouveresse, *Wittgenstein: la rime et la raison, Science, éthique et esthétique* (Paris, Editions de Minuit, 1973).

J.M. Broekman e.a., *Structuralisme, Voor en tegen* (Bilthoven, Ambo, 1974).

C.P. Bru, *Les éléments picturaux* (Leuven, Vander, 1975).

M. Bucquoye, ed. *Interieur '86, catalogus 10de Biënnale* (Kortrijk, Interieur, 1986).

P. Bürger, *Theorie der Avantgarde* (Frankfurt am Main, Suhrkamp, 1974).

J. Burnham, *The structure of art* (New York, Braziller, 1973).

G. Charbonnier, *Entretiens avec Lévi-Strauss* (Paris, Union Générale d'Editions, 1961).

A. Comagnon, ed. *Prétexte: Roland Barthes, Colloque de Cerisy-La-Salle 1977* (Paris, Union Générale d'Editions, 1978).

H. Damisch, *Théorie du nuage, Pour une histoire de la peinture* (Paris, Editions du Seuil, 1972).

A.C. Danto, *The transfiguration of the commonplace, A philosophy of art* (Cambridge/Massachusetts - London/England, Harvard University Press, 1981).

S. de Beauvoir, *La force de l'âge, Tome I & II* (Paris, Gallimard, 1960).

Th. de Boer e.a., *Fenomenologie en kritiek* (Assen, Van Gorcum, 1981).

Th. de Boer e.a., *Hermeneutiek, Filosofische grondslagen van mens- en cultuurwetenschappen* (Meppel, Boom, 1988).

F. & M. Deconinck, *Voelbare grafische kunst, catalogus rondreizende tentoonstelling, 4 dln, met vertaling in braille* (Brussel, Feeling v.z.w., 1989).

G. Deleuze, *Foucault* (Paris, Editions de Minuit, 1986).

W.A. De Pater, *Taalanalytische perspectieven op godsdienst en kunst* (Antwerpen, Nederlandse Boekhandeling, 1970).

J. Derrida, *De la grammatologie* (Paris, Editions de Minuit, 1967).

J. Derrida, *Marges de la philosophie* (Paris, Editions de Minuit, 1972).

J. Derrida, *Of Grammatology* (Baltimore, 1974).

J. Derrida, *La vérité en peinture* (Paris, Flammarion, 1978).

J. Derrida, *L' écriture et la différence* (Paris, Editions du Seuil, 1979).

J. Derrida, *Sporen, De stijlen van Nietzsche* (Amsterdam, Het Wereldvenster Weesp, 1985) met inleiding van G. Groot.

J. Derrida, *The truth of painting* (Chicago, 1987).

V. Descombes, *Le même et l'autre, Quarante-cinq ans de philosophie française, 1933-1978* (Paris, Edition de Minuit, 1979).

H. Dethier, *Art et idéologie dans le réalisme socialiste, Lier en Boog 5.2.* (1987), pp. 66-85.

H. Dethier e.a., ed. *Provocatie en inspiratie, Provocation et inspiration, Liber amicorum Leopold Flam, 2 dln.* (Antwerpen, Ontwikkeling, 1973).

J. M. M. De Valk, *Encyclopedie van de sociologie* (Amsterdam-Brussel, 1977).

G. Dickie, *Art and the aesthetics* (Ithaca & London, Cornell University Press, 1974).

H.L. Dreyfus & P. Rabinow, *Michel Foucault, Beyond structuralism and hermeneutics* (Chicago, University of Chicago Press, 1983).

M. Dufrenne, *Esthétique et philosophie* (Paris, Klincksieck, 1967).

M. Dufrenne, *Phénoménologie de l'expérience esthétique, tome I L'objet esthétique, tome II La perception esthétique* (Paris, Presses Universitaires de France, 1967).

M. Dufrenne, *Art et politique* (Paris, Union Générale d'Editions, 1974).

M. Dufrenne e.a., *Vers une esthétique sans entrave* (Paris, U.G.E., 1975).

D. Dutton, ed. *The forger's art, Forgery and the philosophy of art* (Berkeley-Los Angeles-London, University of California Press, 1983).

J. Duvignaud, *Sociologie de l'art* (Paris, Presses Universitaires de France, 1967).

J. Duvignaud, *La sociologie* (Paris, Denoël-Gonthier, 1972).

U. Eco, *Apocallittici e integrati* (Milano, Bompiani, 1964).

U. Eco, *L'oeuvre Ouverte* (Paris, 1965)

U. Eco, *A theory of semiotics* (Bloomington, Indiana University Press, 1979).

U. Eco, *La structure absente* (Paris, Mercure de France, 1984).

U. Eco, *Naschrift bij de naam van de roos* (Amsterdam, Bert Bakker, 1984).

U. Eco, *How culture conditions the colours we see*, in M. Blonsky, ed., *On signs* (Oxford, 1985), pp. 157-75.

A. Ehrenzweig, *L'ordre caché de l'art* (Paris, 1974).

A. Ehrenzweig, *The psychoanalysis of artistic vision and hearing, An introduction to a theory of unconscious perception* (London, Sheldon Press, 1953).

A. Ehrenzweig, *The hidden order of art, A study in the psychology of artistic imagination* (London, Paladin, 1970).

W. Elton, ed. *Aesthetics and language* (Oxford, Basil Blackwell, 1954).

F. Erwald, *Les dieux dans la cuisine, Vingt ans de philosophie en France* (Paris, Aubier, 1978).

J.B. Fages, *Comprendre le structuralisme* (Toulouse, Privat, 1968).

L. Feenstra e.a., ed. *Waarnemen* (Meppel-Amsterdam, Boom, 1989).

J. Fekete, ed. *Life after postmodernism, Essays on value and culture* (New York, St. Martin's Press, 1987).

L. Flam, *Gestalten van de Westerse subjectiviteit* (Amsterdam-Antwerpen, Wereldbibliotheek, 1965).

L. Flam, *De kunstenaar* (Brussel, VUB, 1981).

A. Flew, ed. *Logic and language, First series* (Oxford, Basil Blackwell, 1951).

E. Fisher, *Von der Notwendigkeit der Kunst* (Dresden, Verlag der Kunst, 1959). Eng. ed.: *The necessity of art, A marxist approach* (Harmondsworth, Penguin, 1986).

D. Formaggio, *L'art* (Paris,1981).

M. Foucault, *Les mots et les choses, Une archéologie des sciences humaines*

(Paris, Gallimard, 1966).

M. Foucault, *L'archéologie du savoir* (Paris, Gallimard, 1969).

M. Foucault, *L'ordre du discours* (Paris, Gallimard, 1971).

M. Foucault, *The order of things* (New York, 1973).

M. Foucault, *Ceci n'est pas une pipe, Deux lettres et quatre dessins de René Magritte* (Montpellier, Scholies Fata Morgana, 1973).

M. Foucault & G. Deleuze, *Nietzsche als genealoog en als nomade* (Nijmegen, SUN, 1981).

M. Foucault, *De verbeelding van de bibliotheek, Essays over literatuur* (Nijmegen, SUN, 1986).

H. Foster, ed. *The anti-aesthetic, Essays on postmodern culture* (Port Townsend-Washington, Bay Press, 1983).

P. Francastel, *La réalité figurative: éléments structurels de sociologie de l'art* (Paris, Denoël-Gonthier, 1965).

R. Francès, *Psychologie de l'art et de l'esthétique* (Paris, Presses Universitaires de France, 1968).

S. Freud, *Psychologische Schriften, Studienausgabe, Band IV* (Frankfurt am Main, Fischer Taschembuch Verlag, 1982).

S. Freud, *Bildende Kunst und Literatur, Band X* (Frankfurt am Main, Fischer Taschembuch Verlag, 1982).

P. Fuller, *Seeing Berger, A revaluation of ways of seeing* (London, Writers and Readers, 1982).

S. Gablik, *Progress in art* (London, Thames en Hudson, 1976).

H.G. Gadamer, *Wahrheit und Methode* (Tübingen, Mohr, 1960).

H.G. Gadamer, *Kleine Schriften II Interpretationen & IV, Variationen* (Tübingen, Mohr, 1967 & 1977).

H.G. Gadamer, *Truth and Method* (London, 1975).

H.G. Gadamer, *Die Aktualität des Schönen, Kunst als Spiel, Symbol und Fest* (Stuttgart, Reclam, 1983).

H. Gaus, *The function of fiction* (Gent-Leuven-Antwerpen-Brussel, Story-Scientia, 1979).

T.F. Geraets, ed. *Rationality today, La rationalité aujourd'hui* (Ottawa, Editions de l'université, 1979).

E.H. Gombrich, *Freuds Aesthetics*, Encounter 1966, pp.30-40.

E.H. Gombrich, *Meditations on a hobby horse* (London, Phaidon Press, 1978).

E.H. Gombrich, *Ideals and idols, Essays on values in history and in art* (Oxford, Phaidon Press, 1979).

E.H. Gombrich, *Art and illusion, A study in the psychology of pictoral representation* (Oxford, Phaidon Press, 1980).

N. Goodman, *Languages of art, An approach to a theory of symbols* (Indianapolis, Hacket Publishing Company, 1976).

N. Goodman, *The way the world is, Review of Metaphysics 14* (1960), pp. 48-56.

N. Goodman, *Ways of worldmaking* (Indianapolis-Cambridge, Hacket Publishing Company, 1981).

A. Graafland, ed. *De bevrijding van de moderne beweging* (Nijmegen, SUN, 1988).

A.J. Greimas, ed. *Sign, language, culture* (Den Haag-Parijs, 1970).

P. Groot & M. Brouwer, *Gesprek met Umberto Eco: 'Steeled in the school of the old Aquinas'*, Museumjournaal 26/5 (1981), pp. 236-41.

J. Habermas, *Strukturwandel der Offentlichkeit, Untersuchungen zu einer Kategorie der bürgerlichen Gesellschaft* (Neuwied-Berlin, Herman Luchterhand Verlag, 1962).

J. Habermas, *Kleine Politischen Schriften, I-IV* (Frankfurt am Main, Suhrkamp Verlag, 1981).

J. Habermas, *Theorie des kommunikativen Handelns, I & II* (Frankfurt am Main, Suhrkamp Verlag, 1981).

J. Habermas, *Der philosophische Diskurs der Moderne, Zwölf Vorlesungen* (Frankfurt am Main, Suhrkamp Verlag, 1985).

N. Hadjinicolaou, *Histoire de l'art et lutte des classes* (Paris, Maspero, 1973. Dutch ed.: *Kunstgeschiedenis en ideologie*, Nijmegen, SUN, 1977).

R. Haller, ed. *Aesthetics, Proceedings of the 8th international Wittgenstein symposium, Part 1* (Vienna, Hölder-Pichler-Tempsky, 1984).

C. Harrison & F. Orton, eds. *Modernism, criticism, realism* (London, Harper & Row, 1984).

A. Hauser, *The social history of art* (London, Routledge & Kegan Paul Ltd., 1951).

A. Hauser, *Soziologie der Kunst* (München, Beck, 1974). Eng. ed.: *The sociology of art* (Chicago-London, University of Chicago Press 1982).

M. Heidegger, *Sein und Zeit* (Tübingen, Neomarius, 1949).

M. Heidegger, *Holzwege* (Frankfurt am Main, Klostermann, 1950).

M. Heidegger, *Der Ursprung des Kunstwerkes* (Stuttgart, Reclam, 1978).

M. Heidegger, *Basic Writings* (London, 1978).

M. Heidegger, *Being and Time* (Oxford, 1980).

H.E. Hilderson, *Kunstschildersmateriaal* (Gent, Story-Scientia, 1978).

E.D. Hirsch, *Validity in interpretation* (New Haven-London, Yale University Press, 1971).

D.C. Hoy, Foucault, *A critical reader* (Oxford, Basil Blackwell, 1986).

W. Hudson & W. van Reijen, eds. *Modernen versus postmodernen* (Utrecht, HES, 1986).

S. IJsseling, *Filosofie en psychoanalyse, Enige opmerkingen over het denken van M.Heidegger en J. Lacan*, Tijdschrift voor Filosofie 2 (1969), pp. 261-289.

S. IJsseling, *Retoriek en filosofie, Wat gebeurt er wanneer er gesproken wordt?* (Leuven, Acco, 1982).

S. IJsseling, ed. *Jacques Derrida, Een inleiding in zijn denken* (Baarn, Ambo, 1986).

W. Iser, *Die Appellstruktur der Texte* (Konstanz, Universittsverlag, 1970).

J. Itten, *Kunst der Farbe* (Ravensburg, Otto Maier Verlag, 1961).

R. Jakobson, *Essais de linguistique générale* (Paris, Editions de Minuit, 1963).

A. Janik & S. Toulmin, *Wittgenstein's Vienna* (New York, Weidenfeld and Nicolson, 1973).

H.R. Jauss, *Toward an aesthetic of reception* (Minneapolis, University of Minnesota Press, 1982).

M. Jay, *The dialectical imagination* (Boston, Little-Brown and Company, 1973).

C. Jencks, *What is post-modernism?* (London, 1986).

P. Johnson, *Marxist aesthetics* (London-Boston-Melbourn-Henley, Routledge & Kegan Paul, 1984).

M. Kagan, *Vorlesungen zur marxistisch-leninistischen Aesthetik* (Berlin, Dietz Verlag, 1974).

M. Karskens, *Waarheid als macht, Een onderzoek naar de filosofische ontwikkeling van Michel Foucault*, 2 vol. (Nijmegen, Stichting Te Elfder Ure, 1986).

R. Kaulingfreks, *Meneer iedereen, Over het denken van René Magritte* (Nijmegen, SUN, 1984).

B. Kempers, *Kunst, macht en mecenaat, Het beroep van schilder in sociale verhoudingen 1250-1600* (Amsterdam, Arbeiderspers, 1987).

M. Klein, *Contributions to Psycho-Analysis* (London, Hogart Press, 1950).

R. Klibansky, ed. *La philosophie contemporaine: chroniques IV* (Firenze, La . Nuova Italia Editricie, 1971).

J.J. Kockelmans, *Heidegger on art and art works* (Dordrecht, Nijhoff, 1985).

M. Korthals, *Kritiek van de maatschappijkritische rede, De structuur van de maatschappijkritiek van de Frankfurter Schule* (Muiderberg, Coutinho, 1986).

H. Kreitler & S. Kreitler, *Psychology of the arts* (Durham N.C., Duke University Press, 1972).

E. Kris, *Psychoanalytic explorations in art* (New York, International University Press, 1971).

J. Kristeva, *Recherches pour une sémanalyse* (Paris,Editions du Seuil, 1969).

A. Kroker & D. Cook, *The Postmodern scene, Excremental Culture and Hyper-Aesthetics* (New York, St. Martin's Press, 1986).

R. Kuhns, *Psychoanalytic theory of art, A philosophy of art on developmental principles* (New York, Columbia University Press, 1983).

H. Kunneman, *De waarheidstrechter, Een communicatie-theoretisch perspectief op wetenschap en samenleving* (Meppel-Amsterdam, Boom, 1986).

J. Lacan, *The four fundamental concepts of psychoanalysis* (London, 1979).

D. Laing, *The marxist theory of art* (Sussex, Harvester Press, 1978).

A. Lalande, *Vocabulaire technique et critique de la philosophie* (Paris, 1980).

H. Lefebvre, *Contribution a l'esthétique* (Paris, Editions Sociales, 1953).

T. Lemaire, *Over de waarde van culturen* (Baarn, Ambo, 1976).

C. Lévi-Strauss, *Race et histoire* (Paris, Gonthier, 1961).

C. Lévi-Strauss, *La Pensée Sauvage* (Paris, Plon, 1962).

C. Lévi-Strauss, *The savage mind* (Chicago, 1966).

C. Lévi-Strauss & D. Eribon, *De près et de loin* (Paris, Editions Odile Jakob, 1988).

J.-F. Lyotard, *Discours, figure* (Paris, Klincksieck, 1971).

J.-F. Lyotard, *Economie libidinale* (Paris, Editions de Minuit, 1974).

J.-F. Lyotard & J. Monory, *Récits tremblants* (Paris, Editions Galilée, 1977).

J.-F. Lyotard, *Les transformateurs Duchamp* (Paris, Editions Galilée, 1977).

J.-F. Lyotard, *La condition postmoderne, Rapport sur le savoir* (Paris, Editions de Minuit, 1979).

J.-F. Lyotard, *Des dispositifs pulsionnels* (Paris, Union Générale d'Editions, 1980).

J.-F. Lyotard, *The postmodern condition* (Minnesota, 1984).

J.-F. Lyotard, *Le postmoderne expliqué aux enfants* (Paris, Editions Galilée, 1986).

K. Mannheim, *Wissenssoziologie* (Berlin, Luchterhand Verlag, 1964).

H. Marcuse, *Soviet Marxism, A critical analysis* (New York, Routledge and Kegan Paul, 1969).

H. Marcuse, *One dimensional man, Studies in the ideology of advanced industrial society* (Boston, Beacon Press, 1964).

H. Marcuse, *Eros and civilization, A philosophical inquiry to Freud* (Boston, Beacon Press, 1955).

H. Marcuse, *Konterrevolution und Revolte* (Frankfurt am Main, Suhrkamp, 1973).

H. Marcuse, *The aesthetic dimension, Toward a critique of Marxist aesthetics* (London, Macmillan Press Ltd., 1979).

J. Margolis, *Philosophy looks at the arts, Contemporary readings in aesthetics*

(New York, Scribner, 1962).

L. Marin, *Etudes sémiologiques, Ecritures, peintures* (Paris, Klincksieck, 1971).

W. Meewis, *Iconologie van de action painting, Theorie en werk van een aantal action painters in het ruimer verband van het abstract expressionisme,* Verhandelingen van de Koninklijke Academie voor Wetenschappen, Letteren en Schone Kunsten van België, Klasse der Schone Kunsten, Jaargang 45, 37 (Brussel, 1983).

M. Merleau-Ponty, *L'Oeil et l'esprit* (Paris, Gallimard, 1964).

M. Merleau-Ponty, *Sens et non-sens* (Paris, Nagel, 1966).

M. Merleau-Ponty, *Phénoménologie de la perception* (Paris, Gallimard, 1976).

J.G. Merquior, *L'esthétique de Lévi-Strauss* (Paris, Presses Universitaires de France, 1977).

J.G. Merquior, *Foucault ou le nihilisme de la chaire* (Paris, Presses Universitaires de France, 1986).

R. Merton, *Social theorie and social structure* (New York, Free Press, 1968).

A. Moles, *Psychologie du kitsch, L'art du bonheur* (Paris, Denol-Gonthier, 1971).

A. Moles, *Théorie de l'information et réception esthétique* (Paris, Flammarion, 1973).

A. Mooij, *Van psychoanalyse naar antropologie, Wijsgerig perspectief op maatschappij en wetenschap 6,* (1975), pp. 360-77.

A. Mooij, *Taal en verlangen, Lacans theorie van de psychoanalyse* (Meppel, Boom, 1979).

S. Morawski, *Inquiries into the fundamentals of Aesthetics* (Cambridge/Massachusetts - London, MIT Press, 1974).

J. Mukarovsky, *Structure, sign, and function, Selected essays by Jan Mukarovsky.* Translated by J. Burbank & P. Steiner (New Haven-London, Yale University Press, 1978).

C. Neutjens, *Methoden als listen* (Leuven-Amersfoort, Acco, 1984).

C. Norris, *Deconstruction: theory and practice* (London-New York, Methuen, 1984).

G. Nuchelmans, *Overzicht van de analytische wijsbegeerte* (Utrecht-Antwerpen, Spectrum, 1969).

C. Offermans, *Macht als trauma* (Amsterdam, De Bezige Bij, 1982).

A.B. Oliva, *The Italian trans-avantgarde, La transavanguardia Italiano* (Milano, Bompiani, 1980).

A.B. Oliva, *The international trans-avantgarde, La transavanguardia internazionale* (Milano, Bompiani, 1982).

R.E. Palmer, *Hermeneutics: Interpretation theory in Schleiermacher, Dilthey,*

Heidegger·and Gadamer (Evanston, 1969).

H. Parret, *In het teken van het teken, Een confrontatie van het klassiek-wijs-gerige en het structurele teken,* Tijdschrift voor Filosofie, 2 (1969), pp. 232-60.

H. Parret, *Het 'pro en contra structuralisme en de literatuur'* in: J. Broekman, Structuralisme. Voor en tegen (Bilthoven, 1974).

H. Parret, *Het denken van de grens, Vier opstellen over Derrida's grammatologie* (Leuven, Acco, 1975).

M. Perniola, *L'aliénation artistique* (Paris, Union Générale d'Editions, 1977).

J.M. Peters, *Semiotiek van het beeld* (Leuven, Centrum voor Communicatiewetenschappen KUL, 1979).

J.M. Peters, *Van woord naar beeld* (Muiderberg, Coutinho, 1980).

A. Philippot-Reniers, *Zijn en ruimte* (Brussel, VUB, 1974).

R. Poggioli, *The theory of the avant-garde* (Cambridge/Massachusetts-London/England, Harvard University Press, 1982).

M. Rader, ed. *A modern book of aesthetics* (New York, Holt-Reinehart and Winston, 1960).

H. Read, *The philosophy of modern art* (London, Faber and Faber, 1952).

H. Read, *Art and society* (London, Faber and Faber, 1967).

B. Readings, *Introducing Lyotard, Art and Politics* (London-New York, Routledge, 1991).

F. Reijnders, *Kunst-geschiedenis, verschijnen en verdwijnen* (Amsterdam, SUA, 1984).

R. Rorty, *Habermas and Lyotard on Postmodernity*, in R.J. Bernstein ed., Habermas and modernity (Cambridge/Massachusetts, 1985), pp. 161-175. M.A. Rose, *Marx's lost aesthetics, Karl Marx & the visual arts* (Cambridge, Cambridge University Press, 1989).

W. Rubin, ed. *Primitivism in the 20th century art, Affinity to the tribal and the modern, vol. I & II* (New York, Museum of Modern Art, 1984).

J. Sadzik, *Esthétique de Martin Heidegger* (Paris, Editions Universitaires, 1963).

J.P. Sartre, *L'imaginaire, Psychologie phénoménologique de l'imaginaire* (Paris, Gallimard, 1940).

J.P. Sartre, *Situations, II & IV & IX* (Paris, Gallimard, 1948 & 1964 & 1972).

J.P. Sartre & M. Sicard, P*enser l'art, entretien,* in: Obliques, Sartre et les arts, 24-25 (1978), pp. 15-20.

M. Schapiro, *On some problems in the semiotics of visual art: field and vehicle in image signs,* in: A.J. Greimas, 'Signs, language, culture' (The Hague-Paris).

C. Schavenmaker & H. Willems, ed. *Over het schone en de kunst van de mens,* Symposion, teksten voor filosofie-onderwijs (Alphen aan den Rijn-Brussel, Samson, 1988).

J.L. Schefer, *Scénographie d'un tableau* (Paris, Editions du Seuil, 1969).

C.J.M. Schuyt, *Filosofie van de sociale wetenschappen* (Leiden, Martinus Nijhoff, 1986).

R. Scruton, *The aesthetic understanding* (London-New York, Methuen, 1983).

T.A. Sebeok, ed. *The tell-tale sign, A survey of semiotics* (Lisse, Peter De Ridder Press, 1975).

R. Sekuler & R. Blake, *Perception* (New York, Knopf, 1985).

J. Serri, *Roland Barthes, Le texte et l'image* (Paris, Ville de Paris, 1986).

R.A. Sharpe, *Contemporary aesthetics, A philosophical analysis* (Brighton, Harvester Press, 1983).

M. Sicard, *Esthétiques de Sartre*, Obliques, Sartre et les arts, 24-25 (1978), pp. 139-54.

L. Simmel, ed. *The reach of mind, Essays in memory of Kurt Goldstein* (New York, Springer, 1968).

Y. Simonis, *Claude Lévi-Strauss ou la <passion de l'inceste>, Introduction au structuralisme* (Paris, Flammarion, 1980).

M. Solomon, ed. *Marxism and art: essays classic and contemporary* (New York, Knopf, 1975).

J. Stolnitz, *Aesthetics and philosophy of art criticism, A critical introduction* (Boston, Riverside Press, 1960).

J.M. Swinnen, *De paradox van de fotografie* (Antwerpen, Hadewych, 1992).

W. Szafran, *Louis-Ferdinand Céline, Psycho-analytisch essay* (Brussel, VUB, 1974).

W. Szafran, *Psychoanalyse en onbehagen in de cultuur: Grenzen aan de remedies* (Gent, Psychoanalytische Perspectieven, 1987).

J. Vanbergen, *Voorstelling en betekenis, Theorie van de kunsthistorische interpretatie* (Leuven-Assen-Maastricht, Van Gorcum, 1986).

F. Vandamme & R. Vanden Brande, *Waarheid, taal & kunst* (Gent, Communication & Cognition, 1984).

A.A. Van den Braembussche, *Theorie van de maatschappijgeschiedenis* (Baarn, Ambo, 1985).

W.J. van der Dussen, *Filosofie van de geschiedenis* (Muidenberg, Coutinho, 1986).

H. Van Gorp & R. Ghesquiere & R.T. Segers, eds. *Receptieonderzoek, mogelijkheden en grenzen* (Leuven, Acco, 1981).

L.J.M.G. Van Haecht, *Inleiding tot de filosofie van de kunst* (Assen, Van Gorcum, 1978).

M. Van Nierop, *Martin Heideggers ontologie van het kunstwerk* (Amsterdam, Centrale Interfaculteit Universiteit van Amsterdam, 1977).

M. Van Nierop, *Denken in tweespalt - interpreteren in ambivalentie* (Delft, Eburon, 1989).

W. Van Reijen, *De onvoltooide rede, Modern en postmodern* (Kampen, Kok Agora, 1987).

D. Veerman & C. Van Bohemen, *Postmodernisme, Politiek zonder vuilnisvat* (Kampen, Kok Agora, 1988).

P. Veyne, *De latere Foucault en zijn moraal*, Krisis 27 (1987), pp. 64-73.

J.F. Vogelaar, ed. *Kunst als Kritiek, Tien teksten als voorbeelden van een materialistiese kunst-opvatting* (Amsterdam, Van Gennep, 1973).

F. Wahl, *Qu'est-ce que le structuralisme?*, 5, Philosophie (Paris, Editions du Seuil, 1973).

M. Wallis, *Studies in semiotics, Arts and signs* (Bloomington, Indiana University Publications, 1975).

R. Wellek & A. Warren, *Theory of literature* (Harmondsworth, Penguin, 1963).

R. Wester, *Een gesprek met J.F. Lyotard, de filosoof van het postmodernisme*, Vrij Nederland (June 22, 1985), pp.10-11.

E. Willems, *Arph, kunstfilosofische onderzoekingen* (Amsterdam, 1978).

L. Wittgenstein, *Lectures & conversations on aesthetics, psychology and religious belief*. Compiled from notes taken by Y. Smythies, R. Rhees and J. Taylor, ed. C. Barrett (Oxford, Basil Blackwell, 1966).

L. Wittgenstein, *Notebooks 1914-1916* (Oxford, Basil Blackwell, 1961, reprinted 1969).

L. Wittgenstein, *Tractatus Logico-Philosophicus* (London, Routledge and Paul Kegan, 1969).

L. Wittgenstein, *Philosophische Untersuchungen - Philosophical Investigations* (Oxford, Basil Blackwell, 1953).

R. Wollheim, *Art and its objects* (Harmondsworth, Penguin, 1978).

R. Wollheim, *On art and the mind* (Cambridge/Massachusetts-London/England, Harvard University Press, 1983).

P. Zima, *L'école de Francfort* (Paris, Editions Universitaires, 1974).

HIGHER INSTITUTE FOR FINE ARTS - FLANDERS

On October 7, 1885, King Leopold II added a Higher Institute to the Antwerp Academy of Fine Arts, founded in 1663. The education it offered was designed to 'meet art's highest aspirations'. Besides the lecture courses, the students were given the opportunity to work in their own studios, under the guidance of 'well-known, famous masters'.

Higher education has undergone a thorough evolution during the last couple of years. In the context of the restructuring of higher education, the FLANDERS HIGHER INSTITUTE FOR FINE ARTS, also, needed to make a choice that would be directed to the future. Hence, following the initiative of Luc Van den Bossche, Minister of Education, the government presented a new formula.

In order to safeguard the Institute's international artistic outreach, its pedagogic achievements and its role as a platform for art, a new, autonomous structure was worked out. The HIFA will now to be run by an advisory committee consisting of representatives from the world of education and art. The HIFA offers young artists from Belgium and other countries the possibility to work in their own studios for three years, guided by working artists, theorists and technicians. Emphasis will be placed on concentrating on the work, on reflection and on discussion. About 45 places are available. Each year, about 15 studios become available for new artists. In general, these students will have a higher education in art, or have a few years' experience as independent artists.

Based on a personal portfolio, a project description and an interview, a group of artists and theorists will make a selection from the approximately 100 applications that arrive every year from all over the world.

During the working period at the HIFA, candidate laureates can have studio visits both from theorists and artists to evaluate the evolution of their personal work, Moreover, lectures, group discussions, excursions and workshops will be organized for the benefit of the candidate laureates. They are encouraged to participate in these events as much as possible. These activities will be mostly directed at actual developments in the visual arts. The approach is programmatic; the candidates laureates' practical work will be combined with a debate about social, intellectual and historical implications of the production of art.

THE HIGHER INSTITUTE FOR FINE ARTS - FLANDERS is an international working community where young artists can further develop their personal training, both individually and collectively. Contacts are meant to enrich one's own insights. In this sense, the HIFA is an art laboratory where one can experiment visually as well as study one's own vision in depth.

At the start of the working year, each candidate laureate determines their own program, in consultation with the teachers, including a self-chosen theme, the techniques and materials they will be using.

After three years of training, the HIFA will grant the title of LAUREATE IN VISUAL ARTS FROM THE FLANDERS HIGHER INSTITUTE FOR FINE ARTS.

Admission forms can be required at
HIFA, Isabellalei 81, B-2018 Antwerp, Belgium.
tel. +32 3 281 46 19; fax. 32 3 281 50 26;
e-mail.hisk@innet.be